NUDES

A RotoVision Book
Published and distributed by RotoVision SA
Route Suisse 9
CH-1295 Mies
Switzerland

RotoVision SA
Sales & Editorial Office
Sheridan House, 114 Western Road
Hove BN3, 1DD, UK

Tel: +44 (0)1273 72 72 68
Fax: +44 (0)1273 72 72 69
E-mail: sales@rotovision.com
Web: www.rotovision.com

10 9 8 7 6 5 4 3 2 1

ISBN 2-940378-02-9
978-2-940378-02-9

Art Director *Tony Seddon*
Book Design *Lanaway*

Reprographics in Singapore by
ProVision Pte. Ltd.
Tel: +656 334 7720
Fax: +656 334 7721

Printed and bound in Singapore by Star Standard PTE Ltd.

NUDES

A UNIQUE COURSE IN A BOOK TAKING YOU FROM BEGINNER TO EXPERT

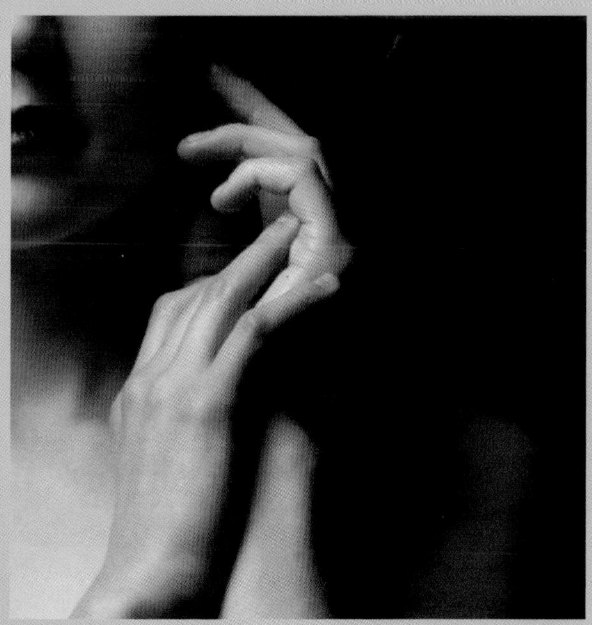

DUNCAN EVANS

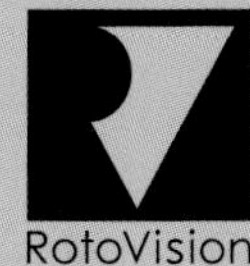

RotoVision

CONTENTS

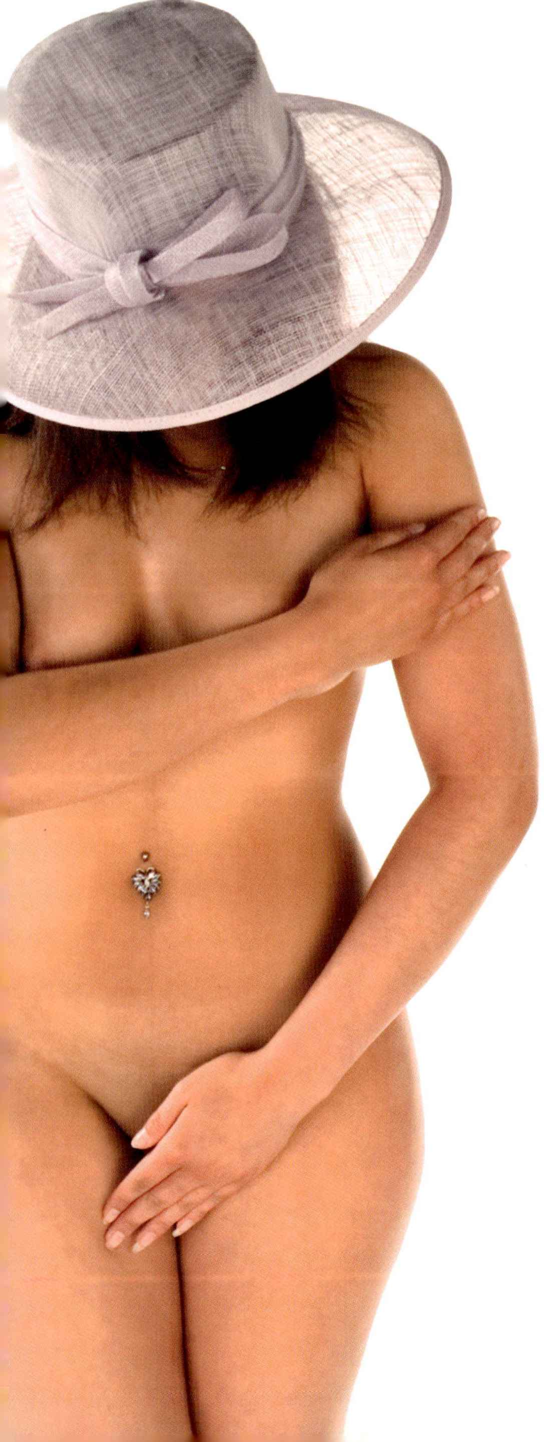

1 GETTING STARTED

The cameras, hardware, and accessories you need to shoot nudes, and where you can take models to photograph them.

2 WORKING WITH YOUR SUBJECT

How to work with a nude model to bring out the best in them, from directing to expressions and atmosphere.

3 PORTRAIT STYLES

The technical basics for nude portrait shoots. Learn about image lengths, then move on to eyes, angles, and abstracts.

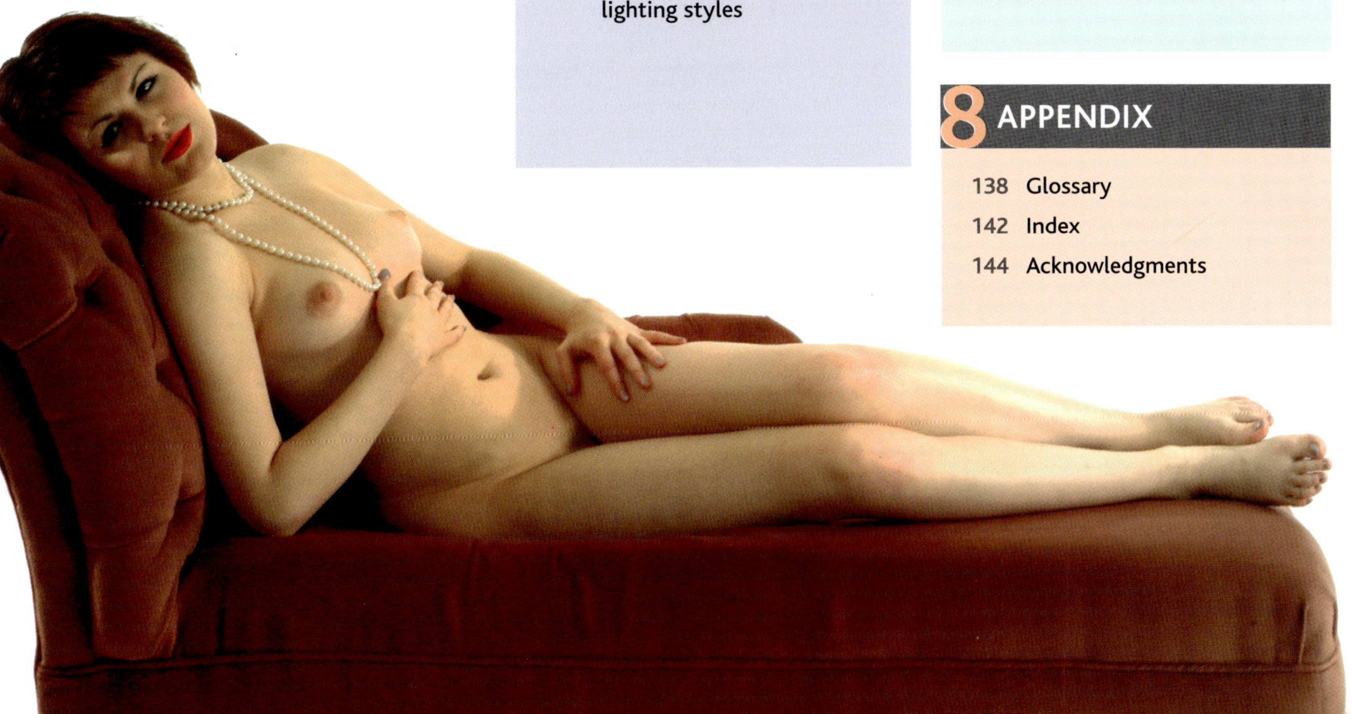

INTRODUCTION

In the creative fields of painting, sculpture, and, more recently, photography, the nude has long been recognized as a key way of depicting the human form artistically. It is one of the greatest challenges for a photographer to produce work that is stylish, artistic, and esthetically pleasing, while featuring only the human body. The photographer must master the technical challenge of producing images in the studio or on location, where interesting clothing is not available to disguise the mediocrity of the lighting. He or she must also confidently steer the relationship between the photographer and the subject. The person modeling for the camera must have confidence in the photographer's creative and technical abilities.

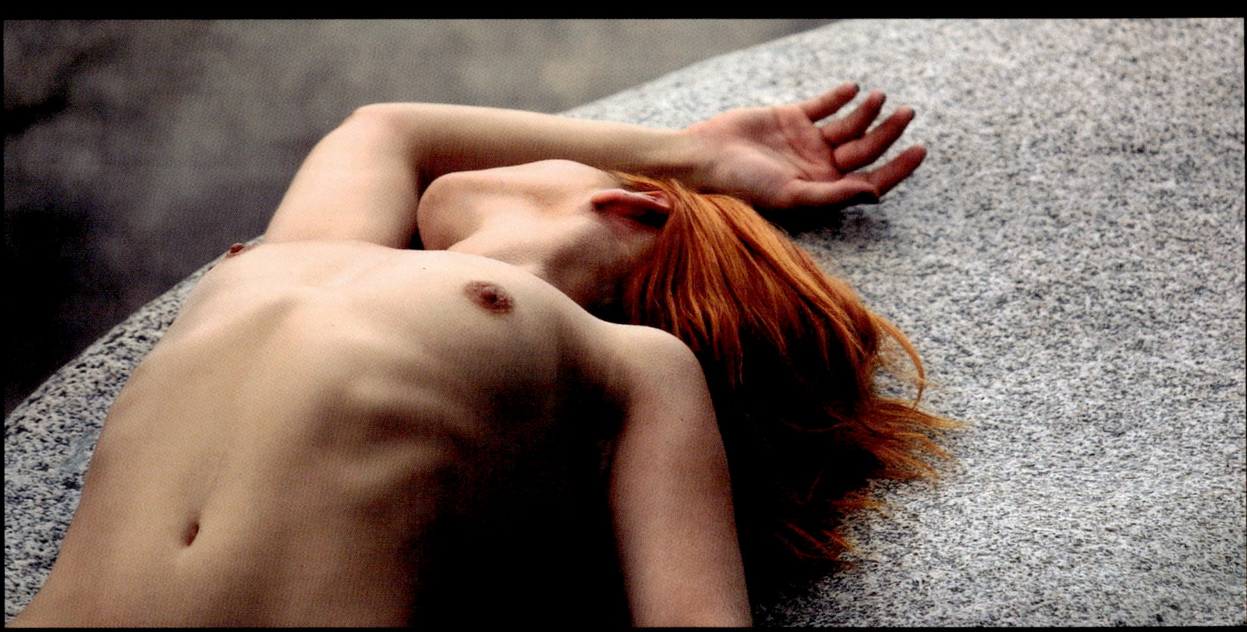

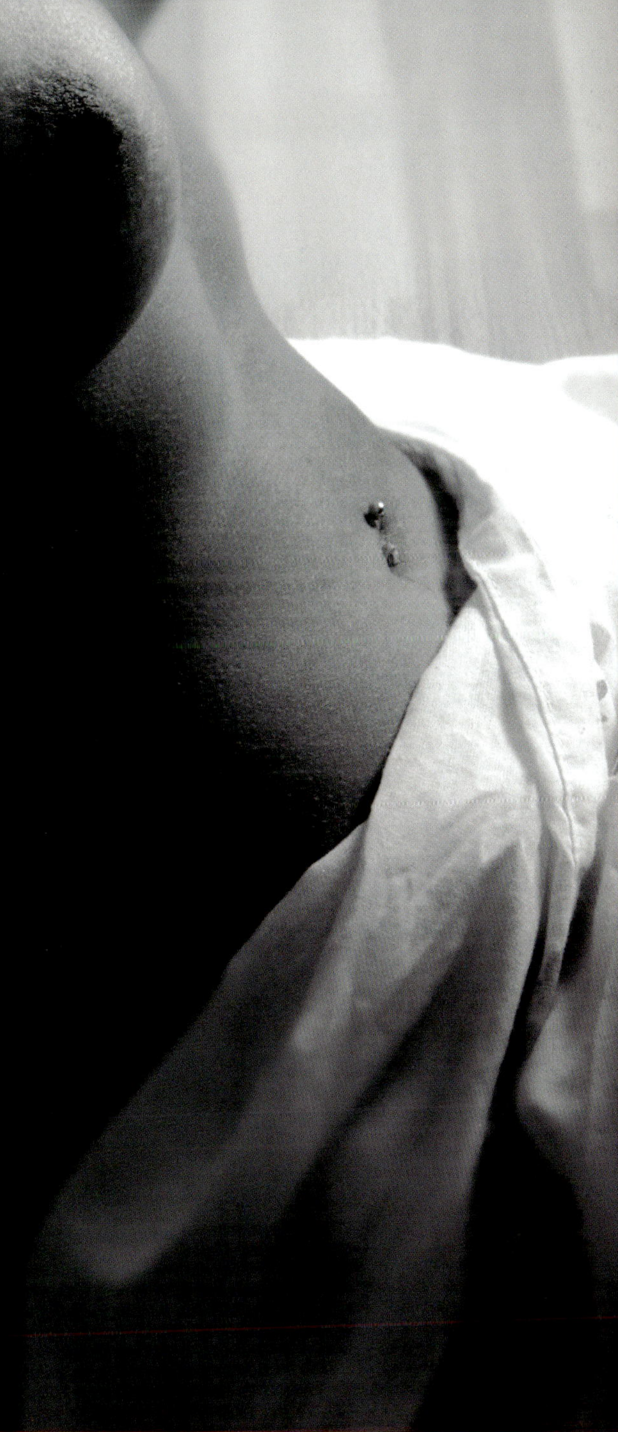

Even experienced nude models may be nervous when working with a new photographer for the first time.

Nude photography is a daunting, but inspiring, genre for the inexperienced photographer to tackle, and that's where this book comes in. Our aim is to explain the basics of posing, composition, and lighting, both in the studio and on location, with clear examples followed by workshop tutorials. In each chapter, we set you assignments to create a specific type of image to fulfill a brief. There are shots to show you what the intention is, and lighting diagrams so that you can follow our setup if your own inspiration fails. However, the challenge is there for you to create memorable imagery of your own.

We discuss working with your subject, portrait styles, location shoots, lighting and framing, image editing, and printing and publishing options. You will discover where you can find models, how to create atmosphere, and what expressions to look for. We look in-depth at shooting sequences of images, and focus on the technical considerations of image length and the effect it has on composition. We also cover subjects such as eye contact, abstract imagery, impersonal crops, using props, and how to photograph couples together.

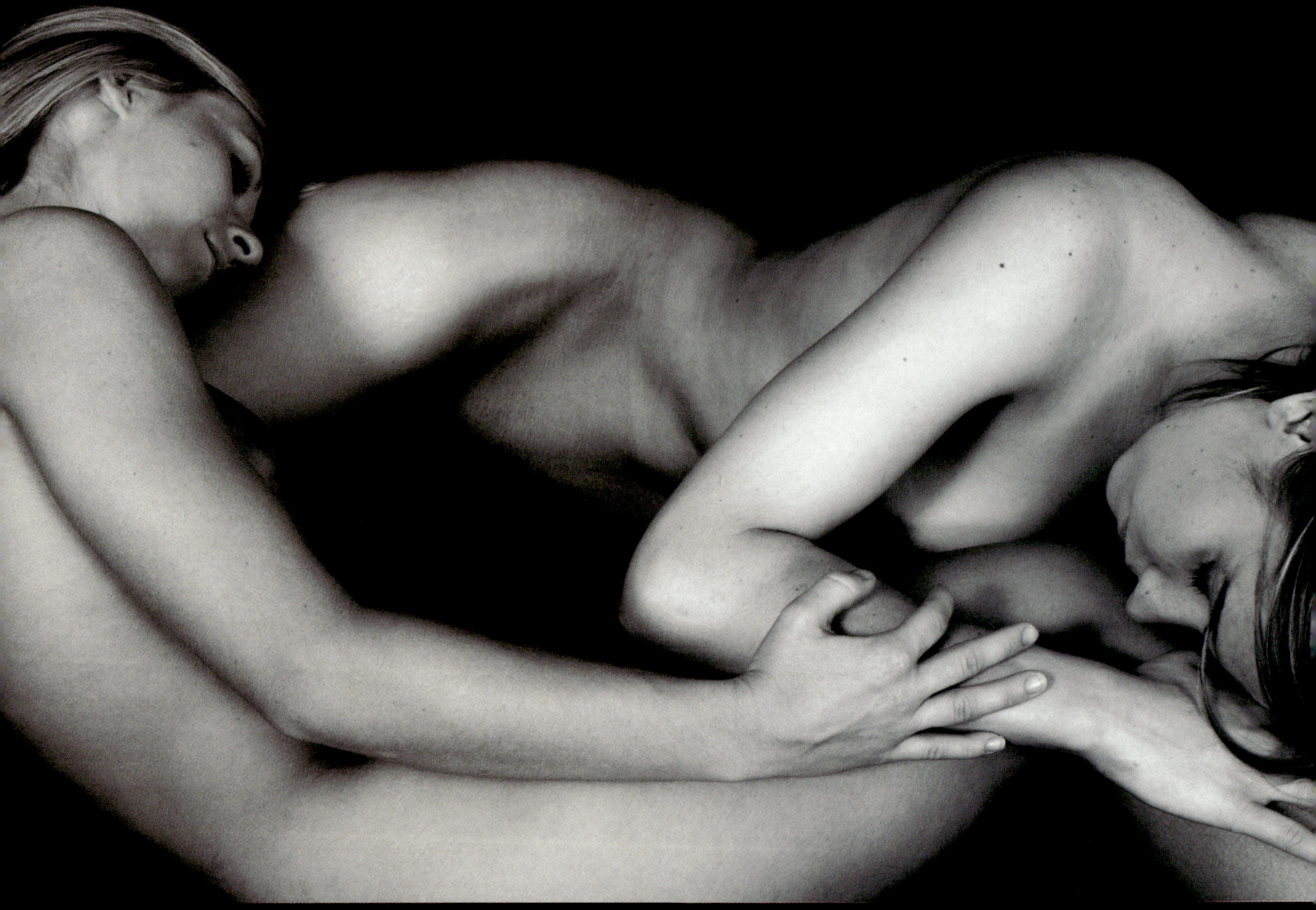

Location shooting adds a frisson to nude photography. Unlike studio work, you have a huge variety of backgrounds to work with. Inside or out, there is more to interact with, whether it's urban grime or scenic countryside. Ultimately though, your success with nude photography rests with lighting and composition. Being able to use light creatively, whether from studio equipment or natural sources, is what lifts photographs from the mundane to the magnificent. We cover all the studio options here: low key, high key, framing, and the creative use of color. The assignments will test your ingenuity and grasp of the technologies involved. Don't worry though, because suggested shots and lighting diagrams are given to help you, too.

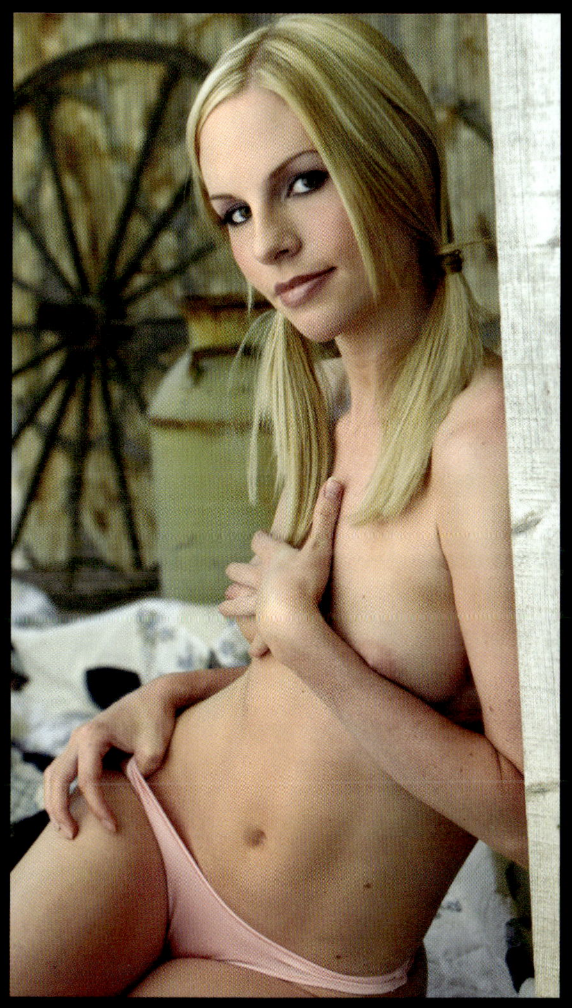

For whatever reason you decide to shoot artistic nudes, there are few topics as challenging and as rewarding in photography. *Digital Photography Workshop: Nudes* is your guide to successfully compose, light, and capture those winning shots.

Duncan Evans, LRPS

www.duncanevans.co.uk

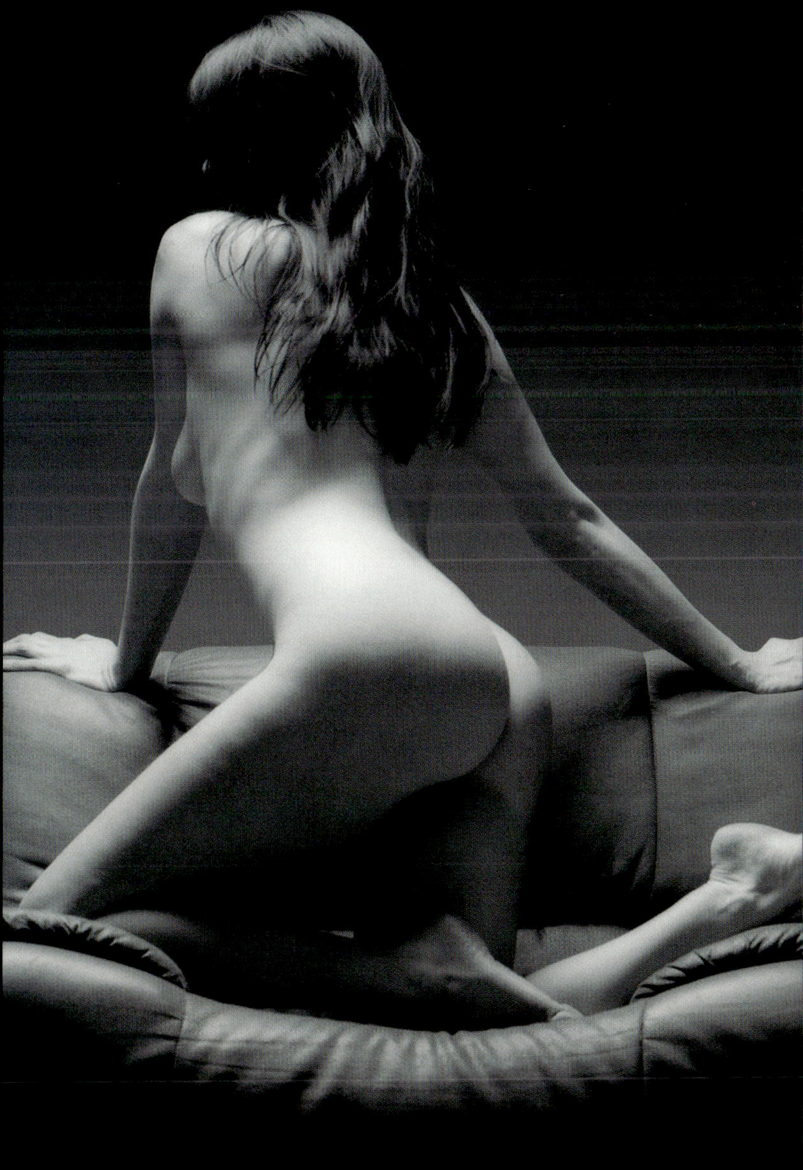

1 GETTING STARTED

While it is perfectly possible to shoot fine artistic nude pictures with only the simplest of cameras, it must be said that the more control and variety of lenses, as well as general equipment, you have at your disposal, the more sophisticated the artistic images you can create. In this opening chapter, we look at the hardware options available, as well as the problems (and how to solve them) with shooting on location.

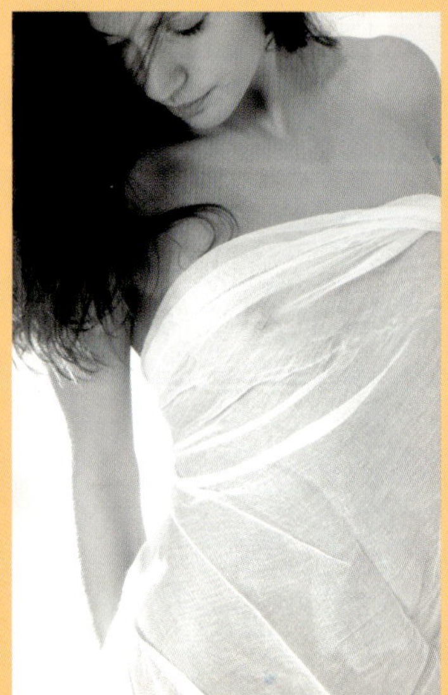

▲ Why shoot digitally? The advantages heavily outweigh the disadvantages in the digital versus film question.

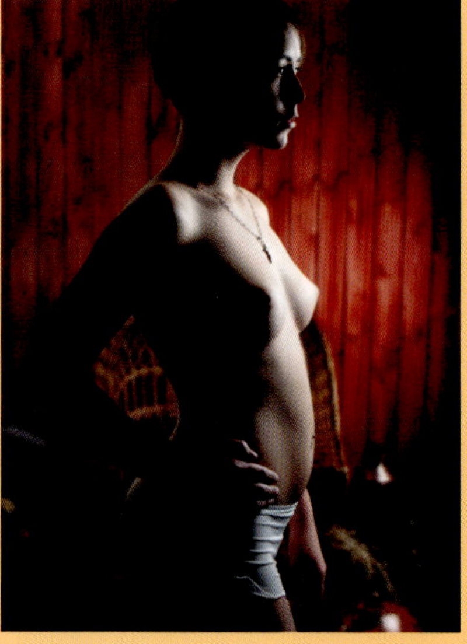

▲ Cameras and lenses. The range of equipment that is available, what you can do with it, and what you really need.

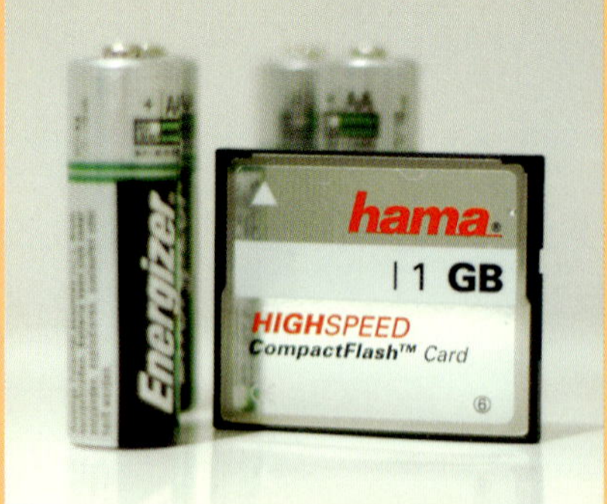

▲ Essential accessories. We discuss all the items and gadgets that you really can't afford to be without.

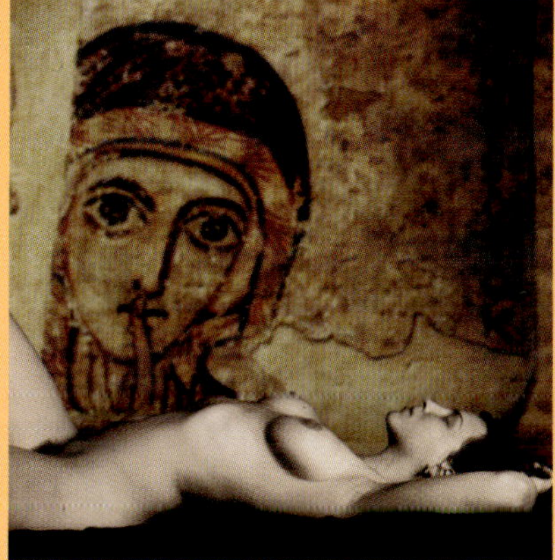

▲ Props and backgrounds. Add interest to your compositions and give your models something to interact with.

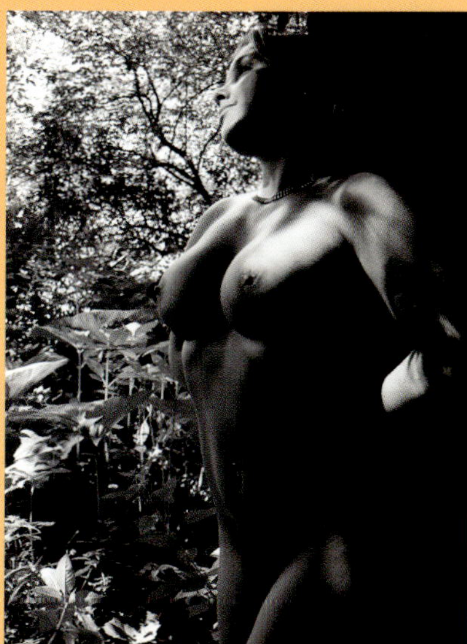

▲ Locations and the law. Shooting nudes in public places carries some risks. Balance the image you want against the potential trouble.

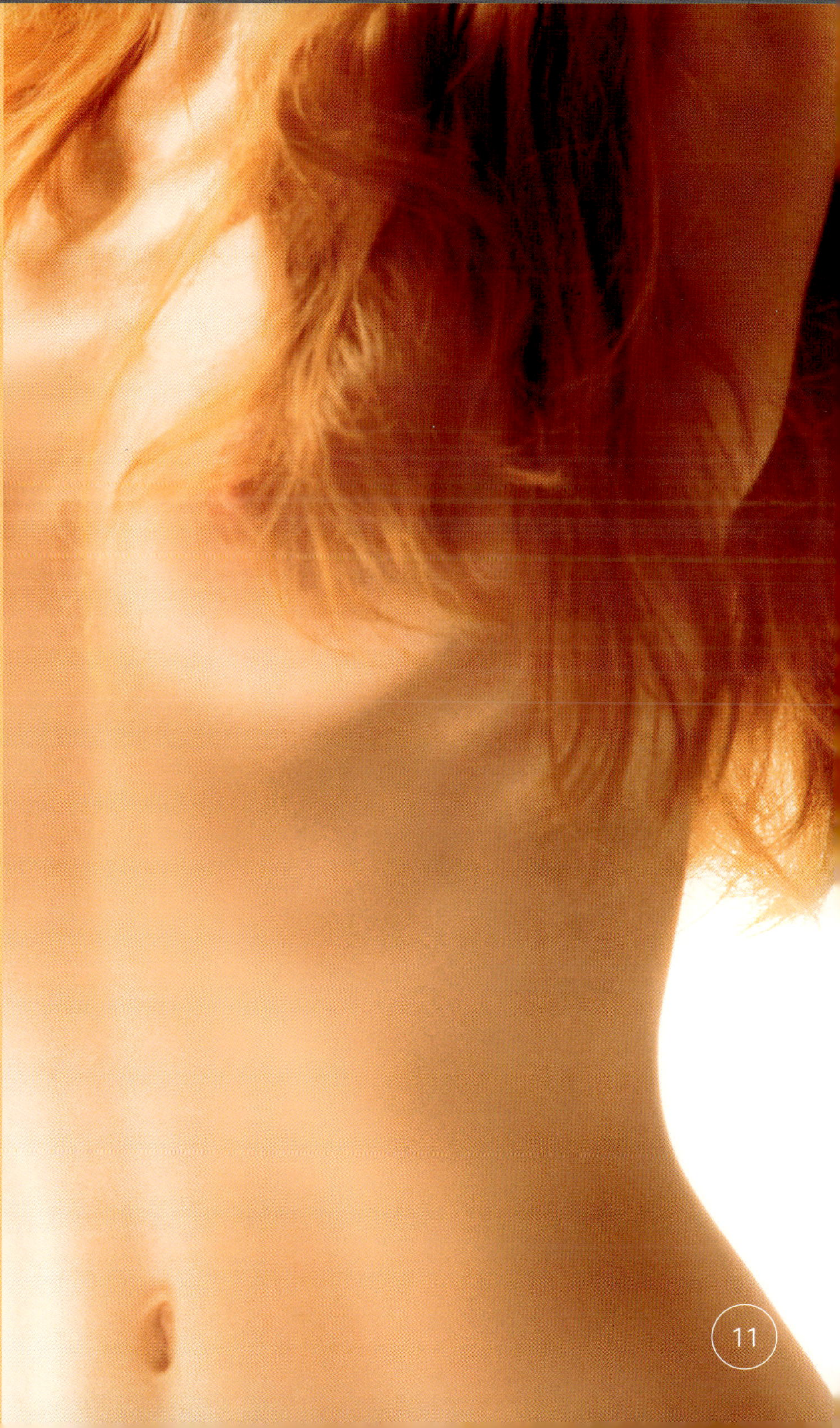

WHY SHOOT DIGITALLY?

There are a number of reasons, both technical and practical, why shooting nudes digitally is more advantageous than using film. Nude photography poses more challenges than straightforward portrait photography. The main issue is the potential awkwardness of the interaction between you and your naked subject. You will have to cope with their reaction to you and the environment they are in. The less experience either you or the model have with nude photography, the more likely it is that nerves, unease, and lack of confidence will come into play.

What has this to do with digital, you may ask? The fact that digital photography gives you instant feedback will help you to smooth over the initial awkwardness. When you shoot a good image, you will see immediately that it has worked well. You will be reassured that you are in control and getting things right, and you can show the model the image. She or he will be reassured that you both know what you are doing, and that you are collaborating on creating stylish, interesting images. Once the model is relaxed, engaged with the shoot and the concept behind it, the process becomes much easier.

HISTOGRAMS

Shooting nudes digitally also offers technical advantages. You can check images on the LCD screen to make sure that the general composition is working. In addition, most cameras come with a histogram function that allows you to check the spread of tones in an image. If all the levels are to the right on the histogram and you are not trying to shoot a high-key image (see pages 106–107), then the image is overexposed and the highlights may well have been lost. Underexposed images are not as bad as overexposed ones, but the more underexposed an image is, the more digital noise will appear when the image is brightened.

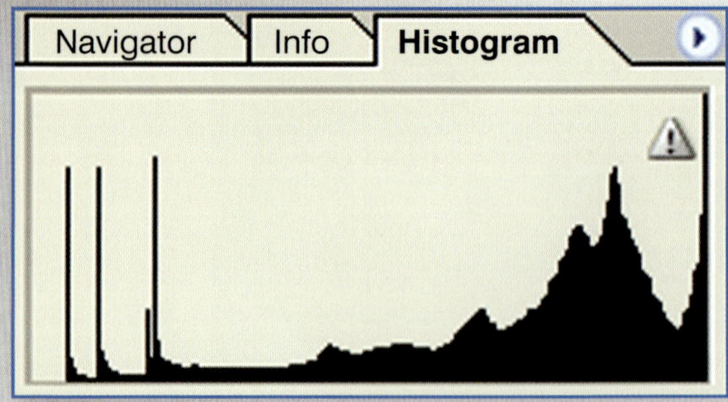

▲ The histogram of the image shown right shows the weight of the data in the light end of the spectrum, but note that the dark end has been retained so that the hair is dark enough.

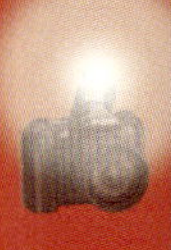

BRIGHT IDEA
Want to get some gritty, handheld shots in subdued, natural lighting, like using fast black and white film? Ramp the digital ISO up to ISO 800 or 1600 and convert the color image to monochrome on the computer.

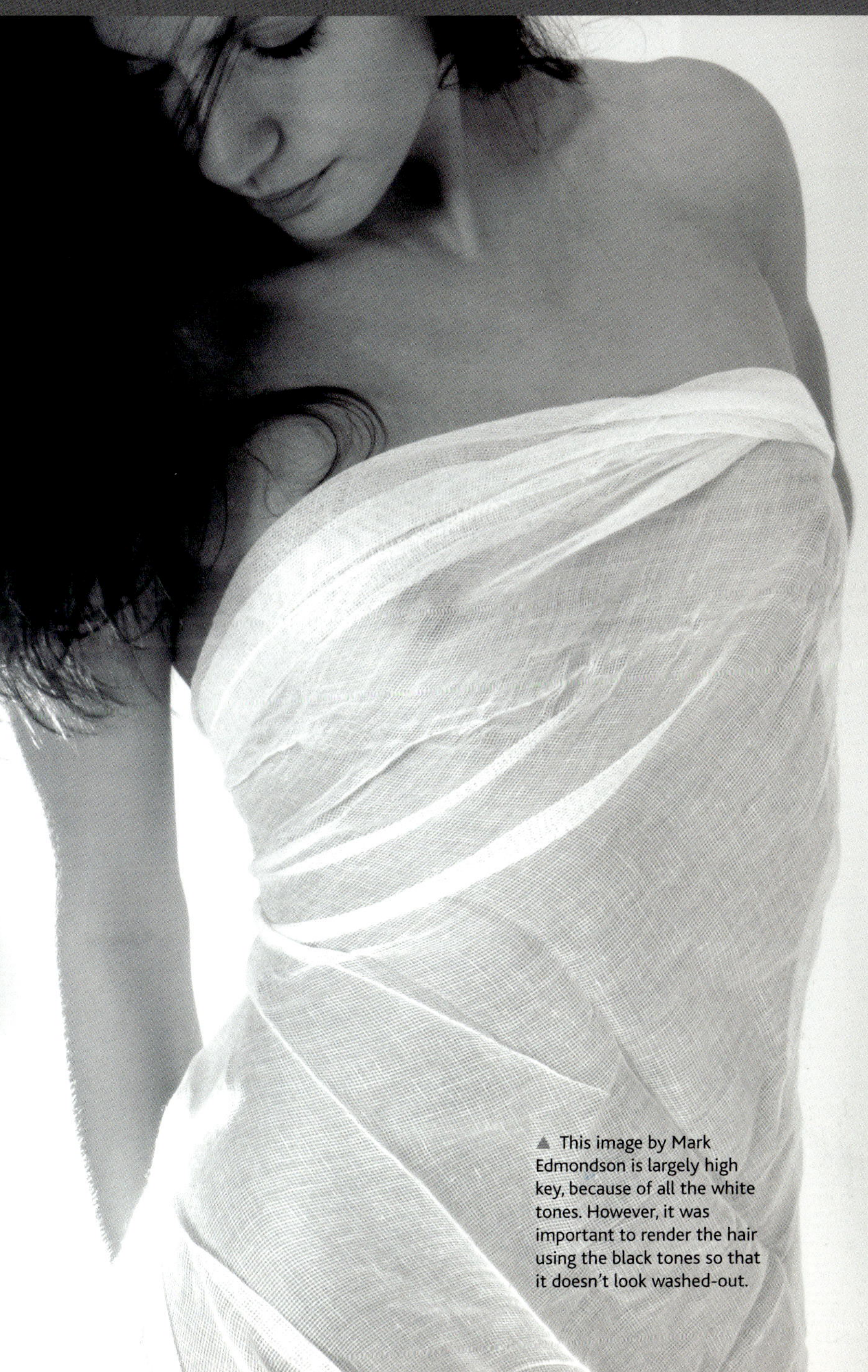

▲ This image by Mark Edmondson is largely high key, because of all the white tones. However, it was important to render the hair using the black tones so that it doesn't look washed-out.

FREEDOM TO SHOOT

If you put a memory card of 1 Gigabyte (Gb) or more in your camera, you will be able to shoot a lot of high-quality JPEG images of 6 Megapixels (Mp) or more before having to stop the flow of shooting. If you require top quality and shoot TIFFs rather than JPEGs, the card will fill up more quickly. However, once the card is full, you can simply insert a second card, place the first one in a card reader, and transfer the images to a computer while you carry on shooting. With much greater freedom to shoot, you can be more adventurous with your ideas.

DIGITAL ISO

One major advantage of digital is the ability to change the ISO rating for each shot. A faster ISO rating does not make the CCD/CMOS more sensitive, in the way that faster (and larger) film grain is more sensitive, but reduces the time taken before the elements on the chip send a charge to the processing unit, setting the tonal level for each pixel. This has the same effect as using faster film in that, as the ISO rating is doubled, the shutter speed is made faster (or, more accurately, the time the shutter is open is halved). This allows you to shoot using faster shutter speeds in lower light conditions than would otherwise be possible.

TOOLS AT A GLANCE
HISTOGRAM

CAMERAS AND LENSES

With a subject that is quite demanding, as nude photography is, you may be tempted to think that you need all manner of high-spec camera gear, lighting, and lenses. Be warned that having a mountain of gear will not make you a better photographer, or make you any more imaginative. It may, however, allow you to create more varied and more technically difficult images. That does not mean that if you don't have a lot of money at your disposal, or a willing benefactor, you should give up: you just have to work harder and be more creative with the equipment that you have.

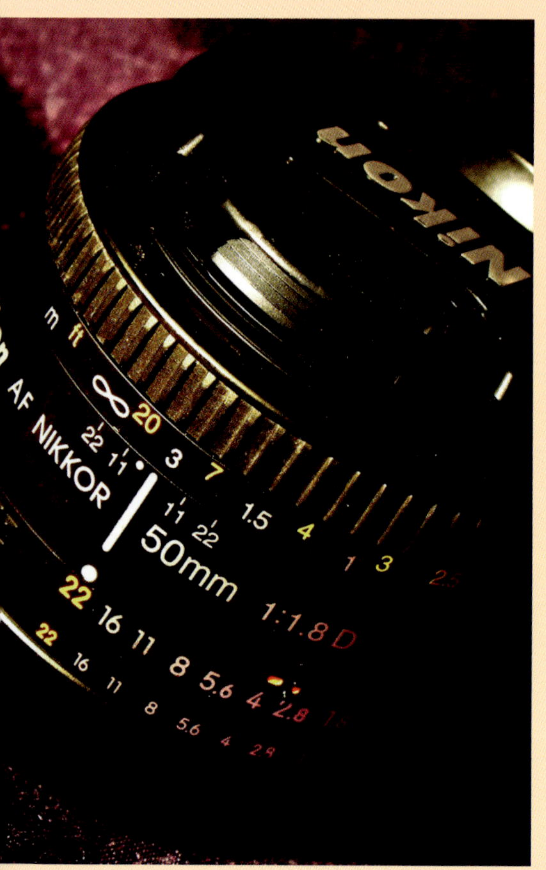

▲ The 50mm prime lens should be considered your standard lens for nude portraiture.

NATURAL LIGHT

Shooting under natural light, whether outside or indoors, means that you can use any camera, SLR or compact, as long as it offers enough pixels. For commercial reproduction, you will need a camera with a minimum resolution of 6Mp. Fortunately, prices have come down quite drastically, and technical specifications have improved, so you need only a modest outlay to obtain a compact camera with sufficient resolution. If you are starting off with modest equipment, ensure that it has full manual control so that the aperture, shutter speed, and ISO rating can all be set manually. Aperture controls the depth of field, while shutter speed allows you to create motion effects. The ISO allows you to continue shooting when light levels are low. The problem with compact cameras is that they have extended depth of field (the area of the image in sharp focus from the front of the scene to the back), so that it is very difficult to get the background out of focus. A digital compact using an aperture of f/2.8 typically has as much depth of field as f/8 on a single-lens reflex (SLR).

STUDIO USE

When you are shooting in a studio, in order to connect to the electronic studio flash equipment you will either need your camera to have a PC sync socket, or have an adapter that comes with one and slots into the hotshoe on top of the camera. There are some adapters for the prosumer compact cameras, ones that look like mini-SLRs and offer lots of features. However, with very low prices, the best option is to buy a budget digital SLR (D-SLR). The budget model might not come with a PC sync socket, but will certainly have an adapter available that allows connection to the lights.

An alternative to this is the infrared trigger adapter that slots into the hotshoe. Most studio lights have an infrared sensor so that they can detect when other lights are fired and will fire at the same time. The infrared camera trigger can be used to set them all off without the need for cables and wires.

BRIGHT IDEA
After the initial outlay of an SLR body, the next expense is buying lenses. You can find discounted, new lenses, and good condition second hand ones at camera shops and on Web sites like eBay.

TOP TIP

The closer you get to your subject, and the wider the lens, the greater the distortion in the image. Either avoid this distortion or maximize the effect for creative use.

LENSES

A compact camera comes with a built-in lens that moves through a set focal range. If this is all you can afford, it is important to buy one that has a good range—a 3x optical zoom is simply not good enough. The great advantage of the digital SLR is that you can buy lenses to suit the job in hand. However, this is also considerably more expensive.

There are two types of lenses: prime and zoom. A prime lens is set at one focal length only, whereas the zoom moves through a range. The advantage of the zoom is that it is more flexible and means you don't have to change lens. The advantage of the prime is that the quality is better and, crucially, it usually has a wider maximum aperture. This is important for throwing backgrounds out of focus. For nude photography, a wide-angle zoom lens (18–50mm) for confined areas, a 50mm prime lens for standard length work, and a telephoto zoom lens (70–20mm) for shooting from a distance should cover most of your needs.

▶ By using a wide-open lens, you can throw the background, and any potentially distracting elements, out of sharp focus.

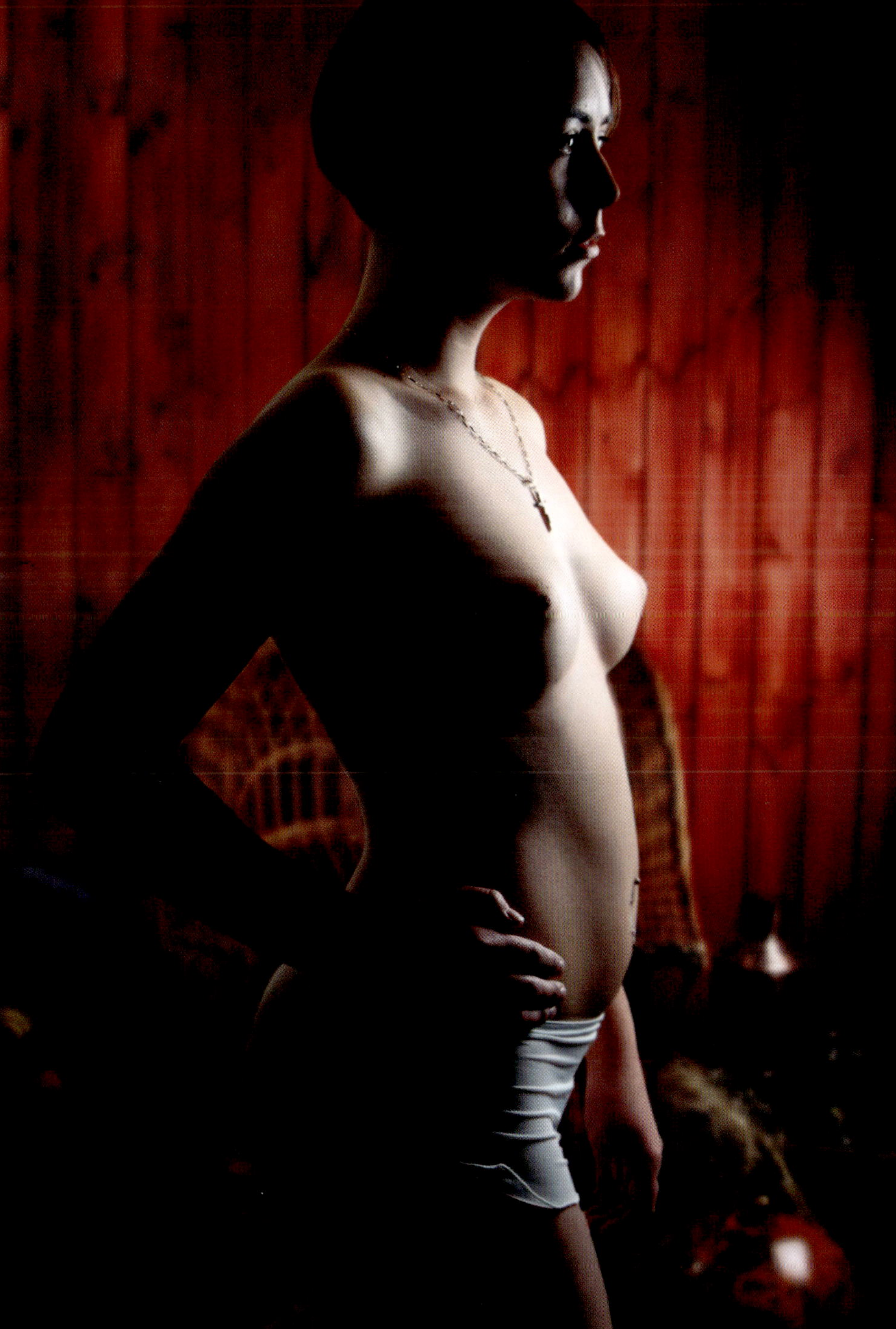

CAMERA TYPES

AUTOMATIC COMPACT

CONTROLLABLE COMPACT

PROSUMER COMPACT

BUDGET D-SLR

CONSUMER SLR

FULL-FRAME PRO SLR

ESSENTIAL ACCESSORIES

The traditional film photographer's kit bag needed to be filled with filters, different film stocks and speeds, as well as the regular lenses and camera body to take the shots with. Now, thanks to white balance control and variable ISO ratings, the digital photographer can dispense with a number of these items. However, these items have simply been replaced by other, usually electronic, items, particularly if you are traveling. Here's the lowdown on the items you need.

GIVE ME POWER

Power is everything in digital photography. Your camera is its own mini-lab, developing the pictures and storing them, as well as capturing and displaying them. This all consumes huge amounts of power. As a result, regular AA batteries are no good to you; use rechargeables instead, either Ni-Cad (Nickel Cadmium) or Ni-MH (Nickel Metal Hydride). Large, proprietary batteries in compact models tend to be Ni-Cad, whereas SLRs tend to use Ni-Mh AA-size batteries. Either way, when out shooting you will want to have one or even two sets of fully charged batteries for backup. This requirement also makes a battery charger a high-priority purchase.

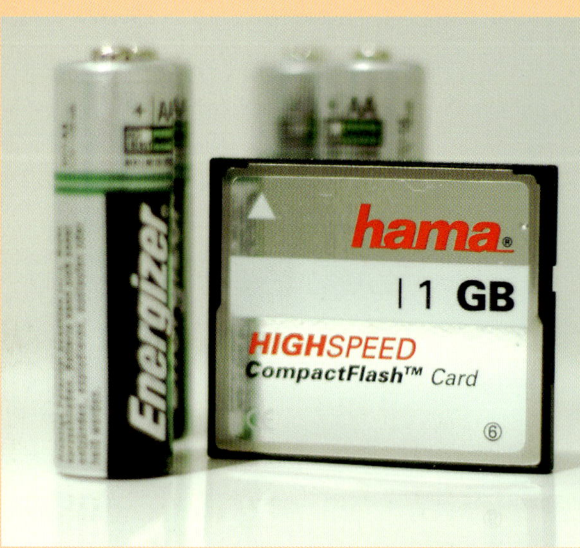

▲ Stock up on rechargeable batteries and high-capacity memory cards.

MEMORY CARDS AND STORAGE

Memory cards are what your pictures are stored on. So, the bigger the card capacity, the more pictures you can store without having to change the card. Consider a couple of 1Gb cards a sound investment. If on vacation or traveling, then you will need more cards. Otherwise, a portable hard drive storage device offering 80Gb or more for under $150 is a good idea.

FILTER IT OUT

Digital photography dispenses with the need for certain filters. White balance control, for example, means that you won't need a magenta filter to counter a green color cast. You can also change exposure and contrast on the computer. However, filters are still relevant to digital users; you may need fewer of them, but you will still need them.

The first filter to go in your kit bag is the polarizer. This is a circular lens that cuts out light at certain angles, so it is very useful when shooting reflective surfaces. It can be used to maximize, or virtually remove, surface reflections from water, glass, and steel. For water shots, a polarizer means that you can either remove reflections and see into the water, or maximize the reflection so that the clouds, or the subject standing in the water, are vividly reflected.

The polarizer also darkens sky color; this is most effective at 90 degrees to the sun. It does not have quite the same effect as it does with film, where the color becomes deeper and richer; in digital, it just makes the color darker. However, if the sky is a

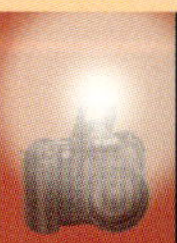

BRIGHT IDEA
Don't put all your eggs in one basket by buying a huge 4Gb memory card—if it fails, you lose everything that you have shot in that session.

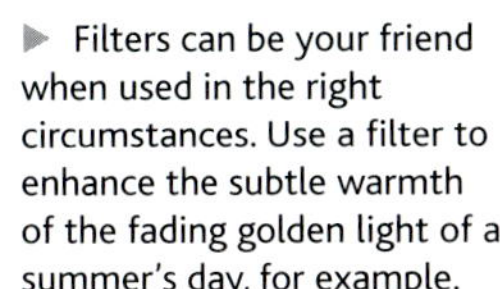

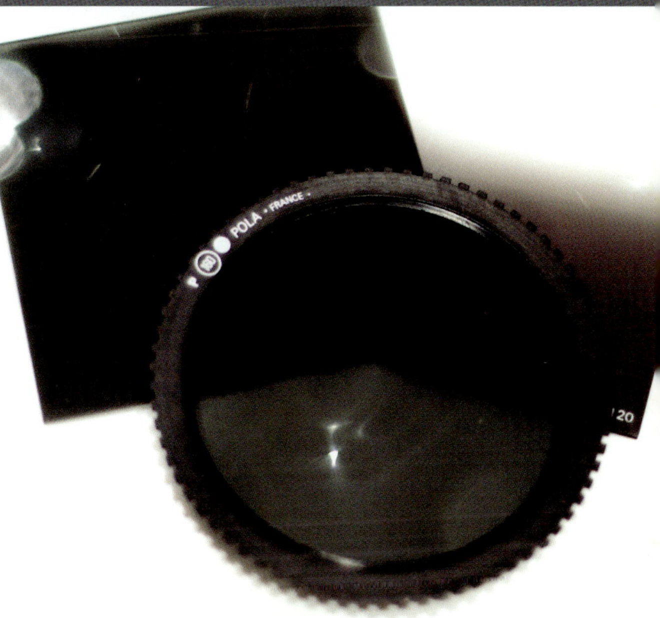

► Filters can be your friend when used in the right circumstances. Use a filter to enhance the subtle warmth of the fading golden light of a summer's day, for example.

washed-out cyan, it's worth using. The point to be aware of with a polarizer is that it reduces light coming into the camera, so the shutter speed will be one to two stops lower.

The graduated neutral density filter (the ND grad) is invaluable in landscape photography, although less so for outdoor nude photography. This is a square filter, gray at one end and transparent at the other, merging between the two in the middle. It is used to balance exposures where you have a very bright sky or a very reflective ground surface. If used with nudes, it would cut the subject in two if they were standing up, so it is only useful if the model is lying down below the level of the horizon and there is a very bright sky.

The cousin to ND grad is the ND. This is solid gray and comes in varying strengths. This is used to reduce light, either so that longer shutter speeds can be used for creative motion effects, such as with water, or to limit the light so that wider apertures can be used for depth-of-field effects. If you want to shoot an outdoor nude with a wide aperture to blur the background and it is sunny, the ND will help you.

Warming and cooling filters need to be used carefully. If you set the white balance of the camera to a higher color temperature than it actually is, then the picture will be warmer. Set it to a lower temperature than it actually is, and the result will be more blue—colder. However, this can take practice, and some cameras are more flexible than others. It can be easier to use a filter to do the same job, but beware: you must set the white balance manually if you are using either of these filters. Otherwise, the auto white balance (AWB) system will interpret the color from the filter as the actual conditions and will set itself to cancel that color out.

One other filter you should consider is the ultraviolet (UV) filter. This screws onto the end of your lens and negates UV light, which appears as haze, particularly on warm days. Another, entirely practical, reason for using it is that a UV filter is cheap, it has no other effect or detriment, so you can leave it attached to the lens at all times and it will protect it for you. A scratched UV filter is cheap to replace; a scratched lens is not.

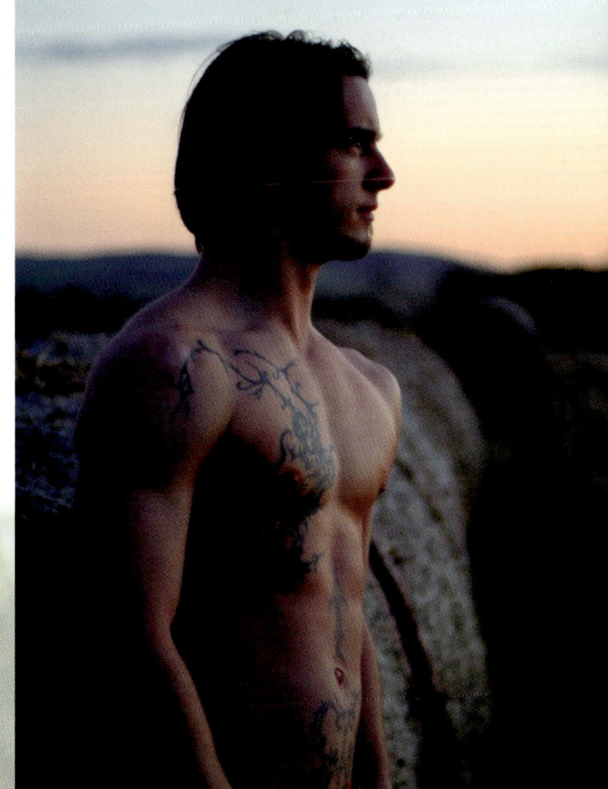

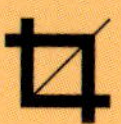

ESSENTIAL ACCESSORIES
RECHARGEABLE BATTERIES AND CHARGER
FILTERS
MEMORY CARDS
PORTABLE STORAGE

PROPS AND BACKGROUNDS

One way in which you can add variety, interest, and atmosphere to shoots in the studio, or even in your own home, is to use backgrounds. The imaginative use of background fabrics, backdrops, or illustrations can help to disguise the fact that a photograph was taken in humble surroundings. For studio work, you can use background fabrics to give a different color and texture to the image. When you are using simple fabric backgrounds, try to use a shallow aperture, or place your subject as far away from it as possible, so that it remains out of focus.

TOP TIP

When you use a fake background, the idea is to add atmosphere to a shot, not to really pretend that you are somewhere else. Ensure that the subject stands far enough away from it so that any lighting used does not cast a shadow on the background, as this will ruin the atmospheric effect.

Many classical painters and Victorian photographers loved to set up picturesque backgrounds in their studios and arrange props and furnishing in the foreground as sets for their subjects. This tradition has been taken up by many photographers wishing to add atmosphere to their images. For the digital photographer on a budget, the cost of picture-based background fabrics can be prohibitively high. There is a digital alternative, however, and that is to arrange all the foreground props and furnishing as usual, but shoot it against a white background. The background can then be added digitally, behind the model and the props.

Props themselves serve two purposes. The first is that they can be used to complement the background to achieve an overall stylistic effect. The second is that props give models something to do. This is important if you are working with a novice model, as they will usually be nervous on a nude shoot. Inexperienced models tend not to know what to do with their hands and the use of props can solve these problems. By handling the prop, the subject is given a focus for their attention. Try to avoid using kitsch props, unless you can use them in a clever or ironic way.

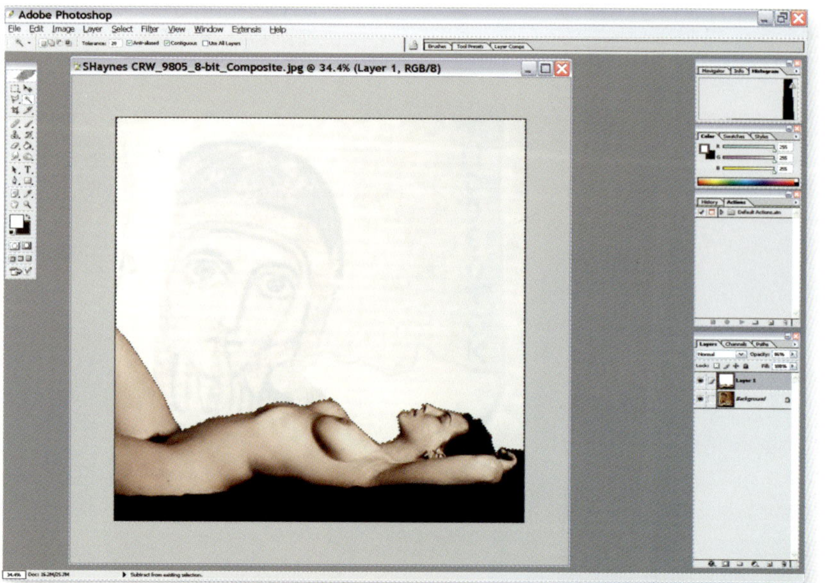

◄ Stephen Haynes of the USA shot this image in two stages, then together in Photoshop. The model was shot against a blank background in the studio. The other background was from a temple that Stephen visited while in the Mediterranean.

▶ The two pictures were added together as new layers. The Magic Wand was then used to select and delete the white studio background.

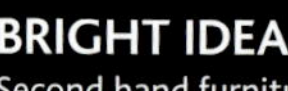

BRIGHT IDEA

Second hand furniture shops are ideal places to pick up low-cost items to create or decorate a set with, or to use as props in a photo shoot.

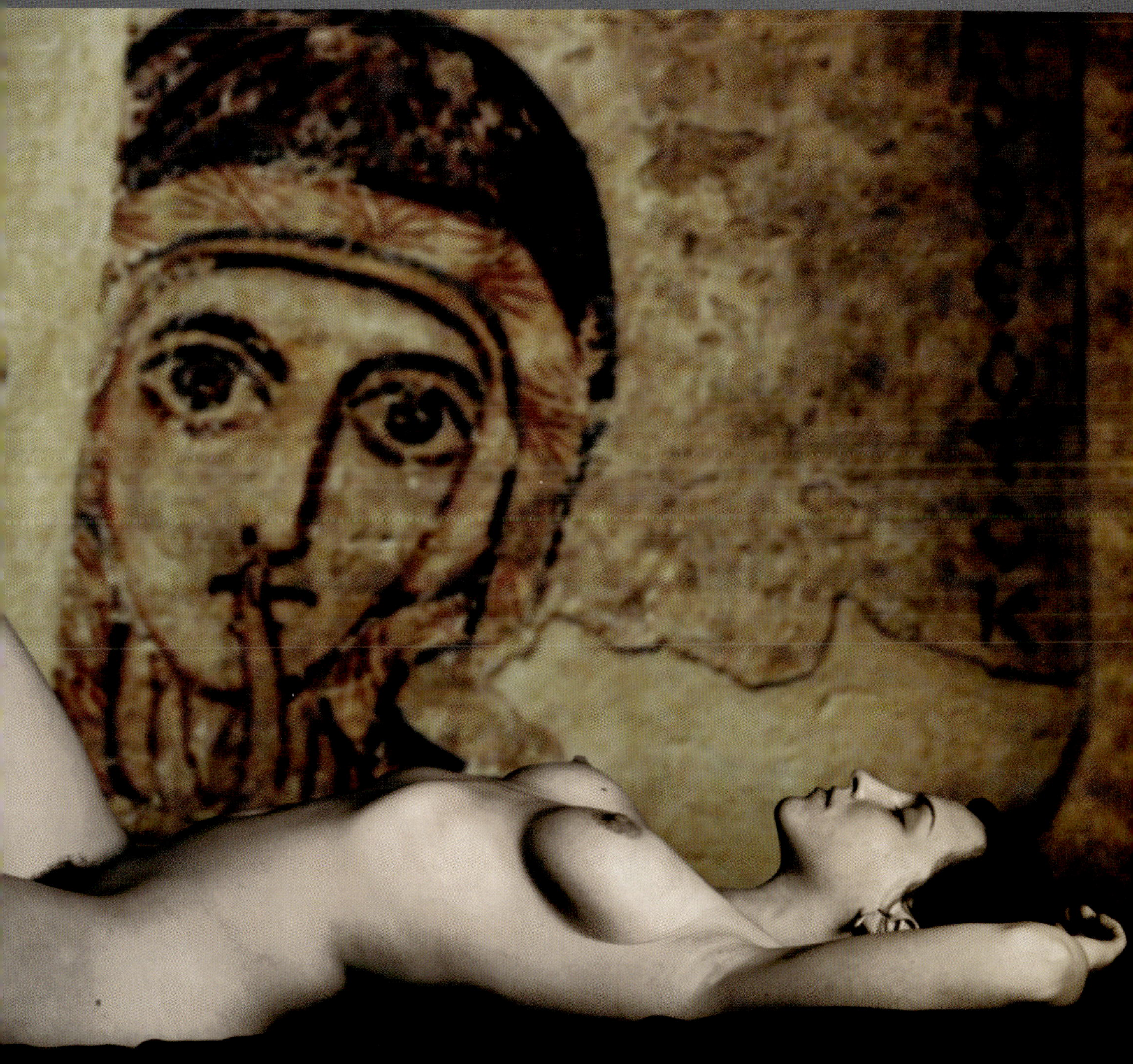

TOOLS AT A GLANCE
LAYERS
MAGIC WAND
ERASER

LOCATIONS AND THE LAW

There is little doubt that the easiest and most comfortable place to shoot nudes is in the confines of the studio. However, this also limits what sort of shots you can produce. Branching out into location work means that you can take your studio skills and apply them in rich and varied environments.

Finding suitable locations can be challenging. Generally, the more luxurious the setting, the harder or more expensive it is to obtain permission to shoot there.

Beaches are a place where people are used to seeing exposed flesh, so you shouldn't attract too much unwanted attention. The combination of sun, sea, and sand offers plentiful photographic opportunities. For other outdoor locations, the more scarcely populated the place, the better chance you have of shooting without interruption or interference. Ruined buildings, whether rural or industrial, offer fantastic contrasts with the smooth skin tones of your model. Rural locations, from buildings to fields, woods, and streams may also fuel your creativity. Work hard with composition and lighting to lift your shots out of the ordinary.

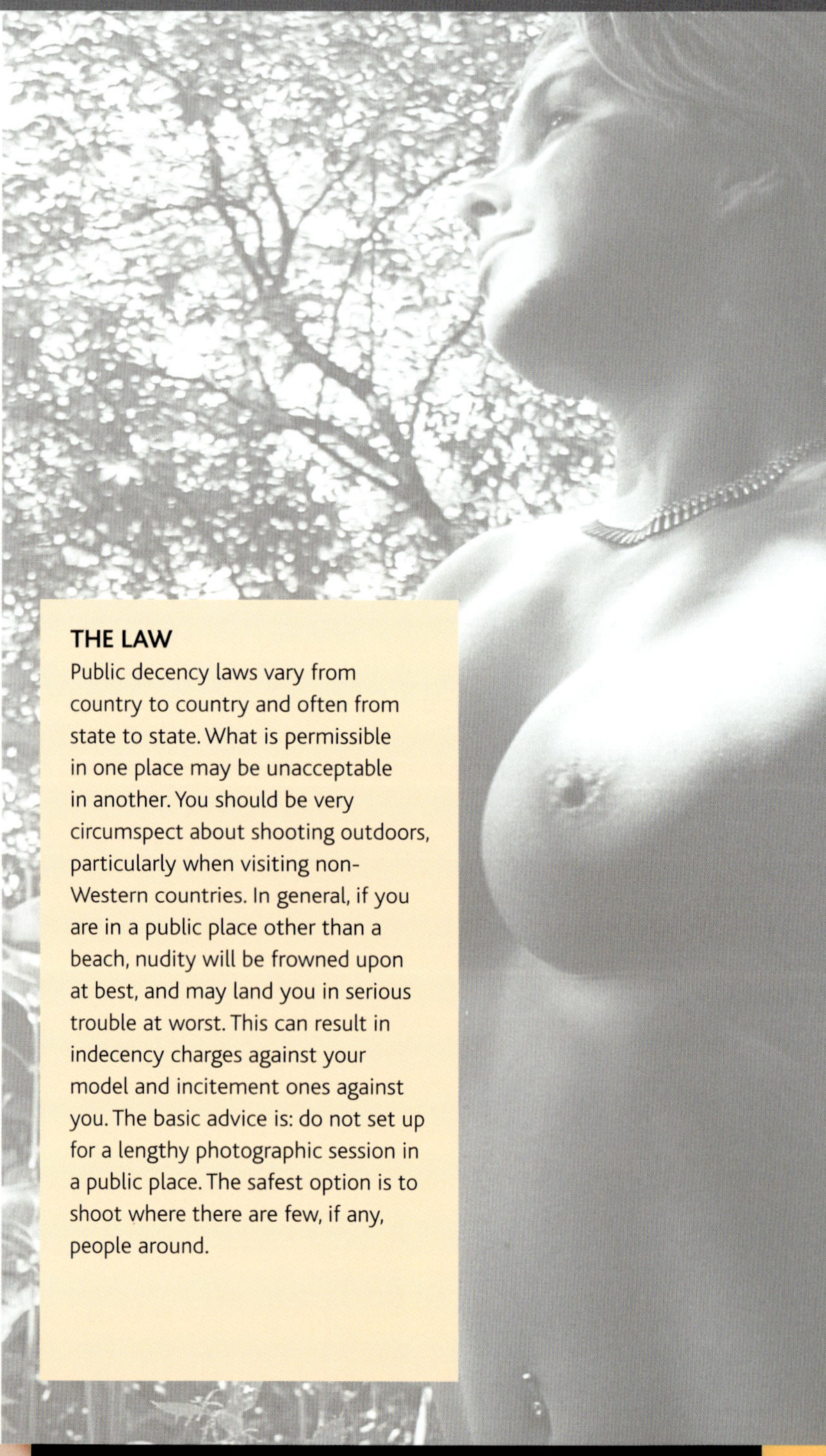

THE LAW

Public decency laws vary from country to country and often from state to state. What is permissible in one place may be unacceptable in another. You should be very circumspect about shooting outdoors, particularly when visiting non-Western countries. In general, if you are in a public place other than a beach, nudity will be frowned upon at best, and may land you in serious trouble at worst. This can result in indecency charges against your model and incitement ones against you. The basic advice is: do not set up for a lengthy photographic session in a public place. The safest option is to shoot where there are few, if any, people around.

BRIGHT IDEA
Having someone to help on a nude location shoot is highly recommended. The other person can be used to mind baggage and to perform basic crowd control to keep people out of the shot and from loitering.

PHOTO EDITING

▶ Mark Edmondson shot this image in a local wood using a Canon consumer digital SLR.

▼ The shadows were darkened using the Curves function. Two other control points held the midtones and highlights in place.

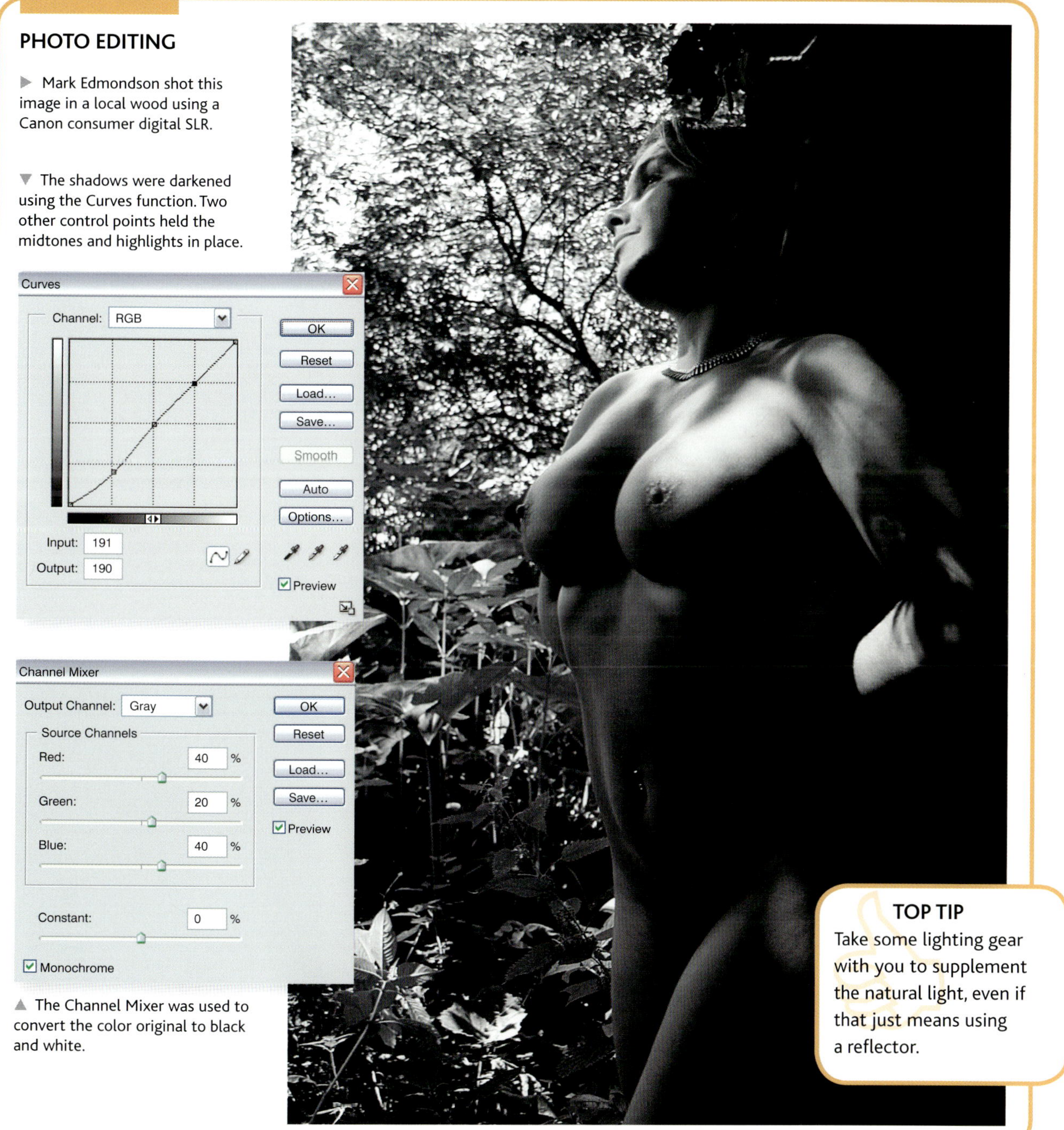

▲ The Channel Mixer was used to convert the color original to black and white.

TOP TIP
Take some lighting gear with you to supplement the natural light, even if that just means using a reflector.

2 WORKING WITH YOUR SUBJECT

Novice photographers tend to find working with a nude model more challenging than shooting regular portraits. It's more of a challenge for a novice model, too. Being able to create a good working relationship and knowing how to find subjects, pose models, and bring out the best in them requires a good deal of skill and empathy. Experience is invaluable, but you only get that by shooting. The more practice you get, the easier it will be to direct your model and create the right creative atmosphere.

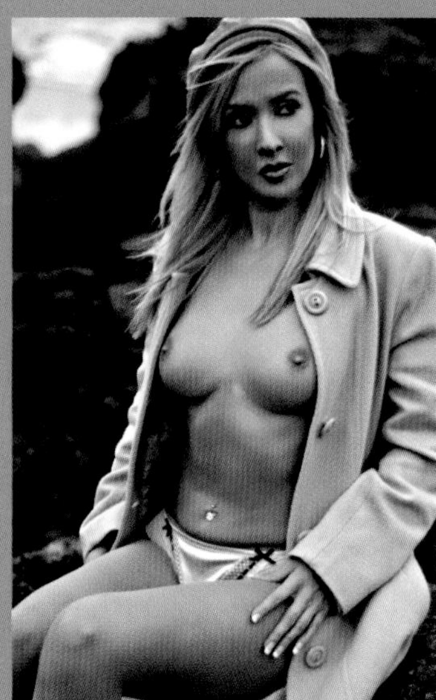

▲ Finding subjects to shoot. Finding models who are prepared to be photographed nude is quite a straightforward process.

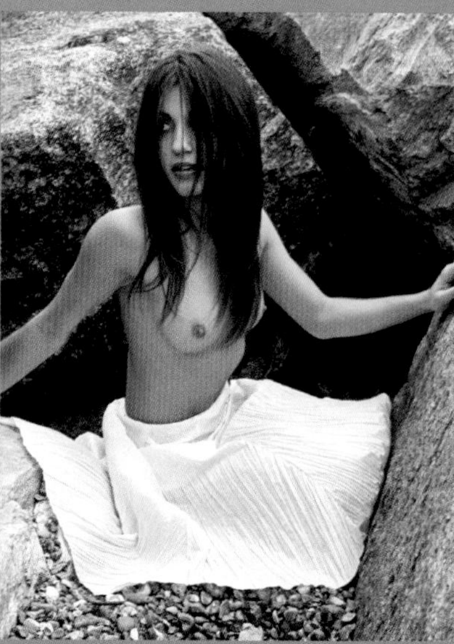

▲ Directing your subject. This is one of the great challenges, and it is made much harder if you are working with an inexperienced model.

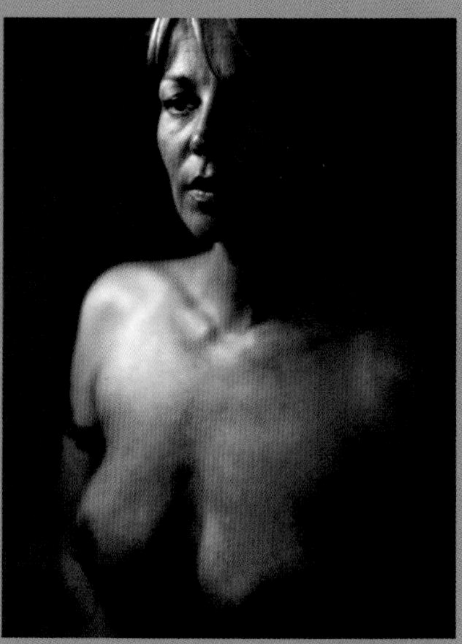

▲ Expressions and atmosphere. The look on your subject's face and the atmosphere you create must be sympathetic.

▼ Shooting a sequence. The advantage of rapid firing can be more naturalistic results, providing you have the composition already worked out.

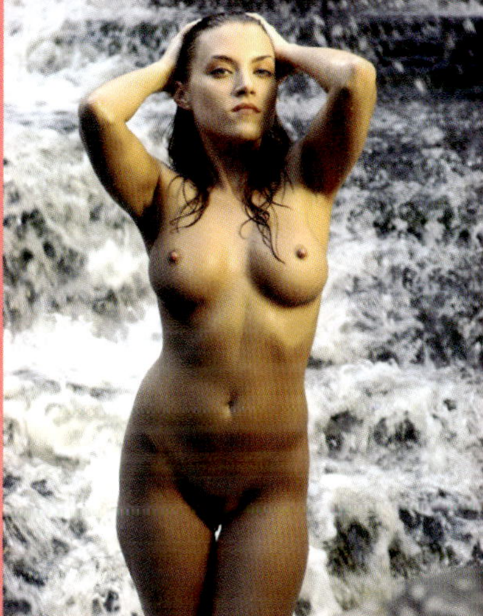

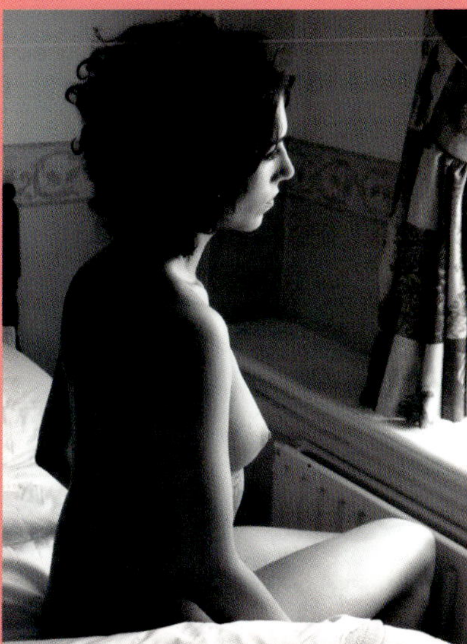

▲ Working around the subject. Don't move the model and lights—move yourself and see what using a different angle can reveal.

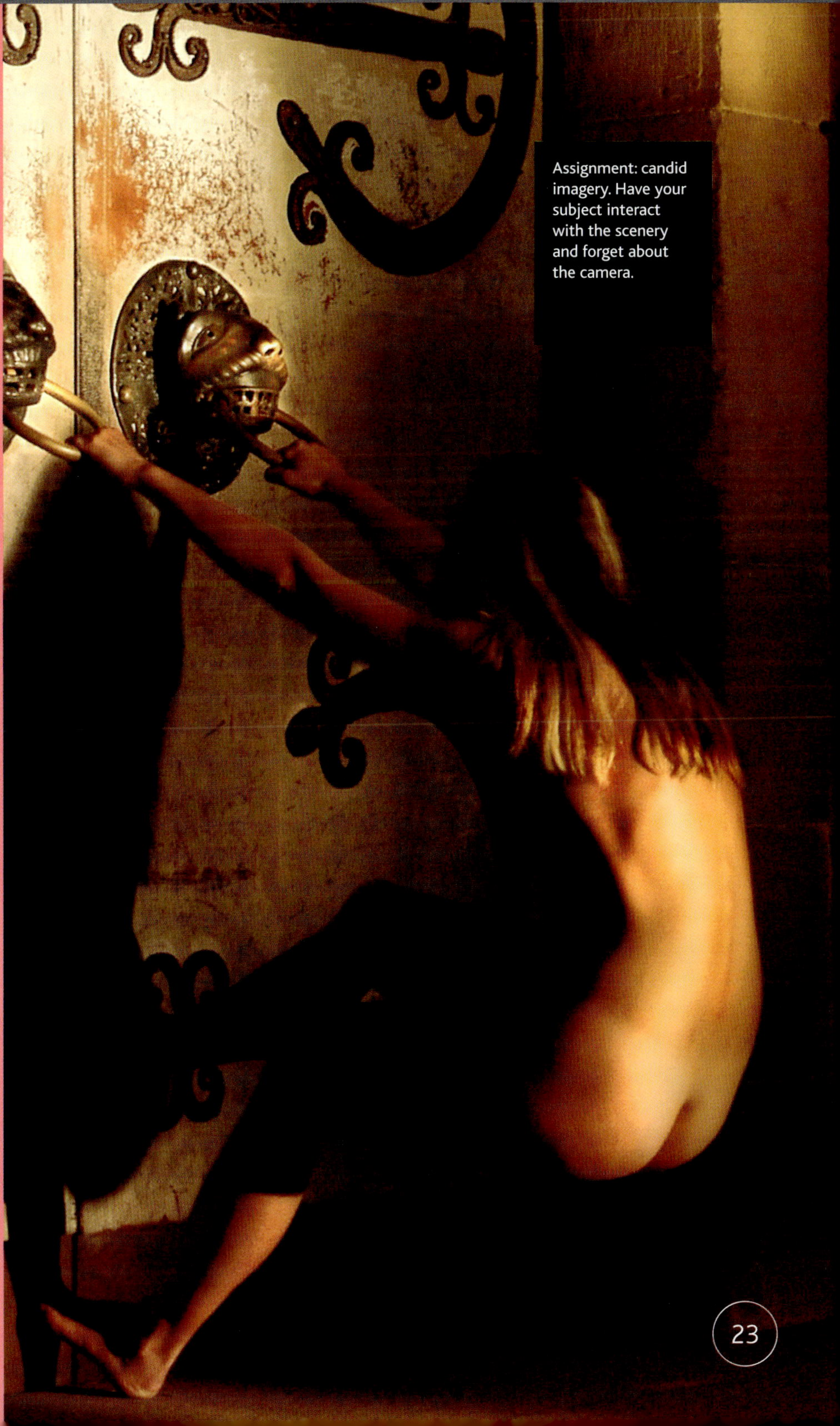

Assignment: candid imagery. Have your subject interact with the scenery and forget about the camera.

FINDING SUBJECTS TO SHOOT

With straightforward portraiture, you will always be able to find people who are willing to pose for you. If you have the nerve, you might even try approaching strangers to ask them to pose for you. The same cannot be said of nude photography, so be prepared for the fact that it is more challenging to find suitable models for your creative nude work. However, the good news is that digital technology can facilitate your search for subjects, as well as enhancing your photography. An indirect consequence of the spread of digital technology is the vast increase in photographer–model contact Web sites.

The rise of digital photography has drawn in people who would never previously have become involved in this creative field. It has also promoted the dissemination, sharing, and presentation of photos as never before.

As a result of these developments, it has never been easier to find models for artistic nude photography: your potential subjects are all online. Web sites such as www.onemodelplace.com and www.net-model.com (there are many others too) offer worldwide model, photographer, and stylist databases. You can search the databases for models in your area and get in touch with the ones who seem suitable to see if they are available on the dates you want to shoot. All models will advertise the level of nudity they are prepared to work with, so there will be no embarrassing misunderstandings. The Web sites also have messageboards where you can advertise your particular shoot, what it's for, and how much you are prepared to pay, and then see if any potential models respond. Any further discussion can take place by e-mail, usually ending with a booking and an exchange of cellphone numbers.

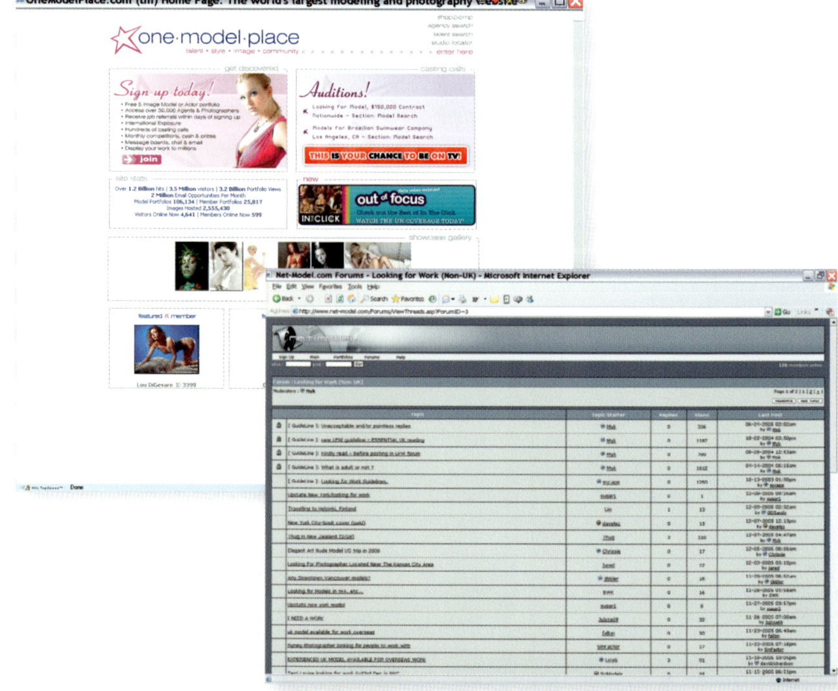

▶ When you want to find models for your photo shoots, simply search one of the many online databases that publish models' and photographers' contact details. Models will state clearly on these websites whether or not they are prepared to pose nude. They should also state what their rates of pay are.

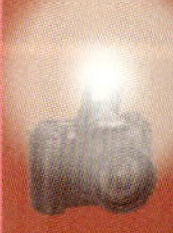

BRIGHT IDEA
Want to shoot something special and out of the ordinary? Post your concept up on a messageboard as a joint artistic endeavor, with no fee for either party.

RATES OF PAY

Roughly speaking, the going rate for a model found through a Web site is $65–$85 per hour, with a minimum booking of two hours. If the location is more than 10 miles away, you may be expected to contribute toward the model's travel costs as well. However, that is not to say that you have to pay those rates. Some models may agree to "TFP" (Time for Prints), complemented by "TFCD"—Time for a CD of high-res pictures. Some models prefer prints, some prefer a CD. It is rarer to find a model who will model nude for prints or a CD, but there are some around. Be warned that they may be rather inexperienced and have little idea about posing. If you are on a budget, you can offer part-pay and part-TFCD, or simply post the lower pay level on your noticeboard advert. You may receive fewer responses, but there will still be some models who will reply to an advert offering $40 per hour.

TOP TIP

If you intend to use your photos in any commercial environment, or profit from them, then you will need to obtain a model-release form. This is an agreement that assigns all copyright in the photos shot in a session to you, the photographer. Some models may ask for an extra 10% on top of the agreed fee, so ensure that it is made clear right from the start.

PHOTO EDITING

▶ Megan Rose is a published model who commands good rates of pay. However, as I was willing to provide a CD of images for promotional use, she agreed to a fee almost half that of normal.

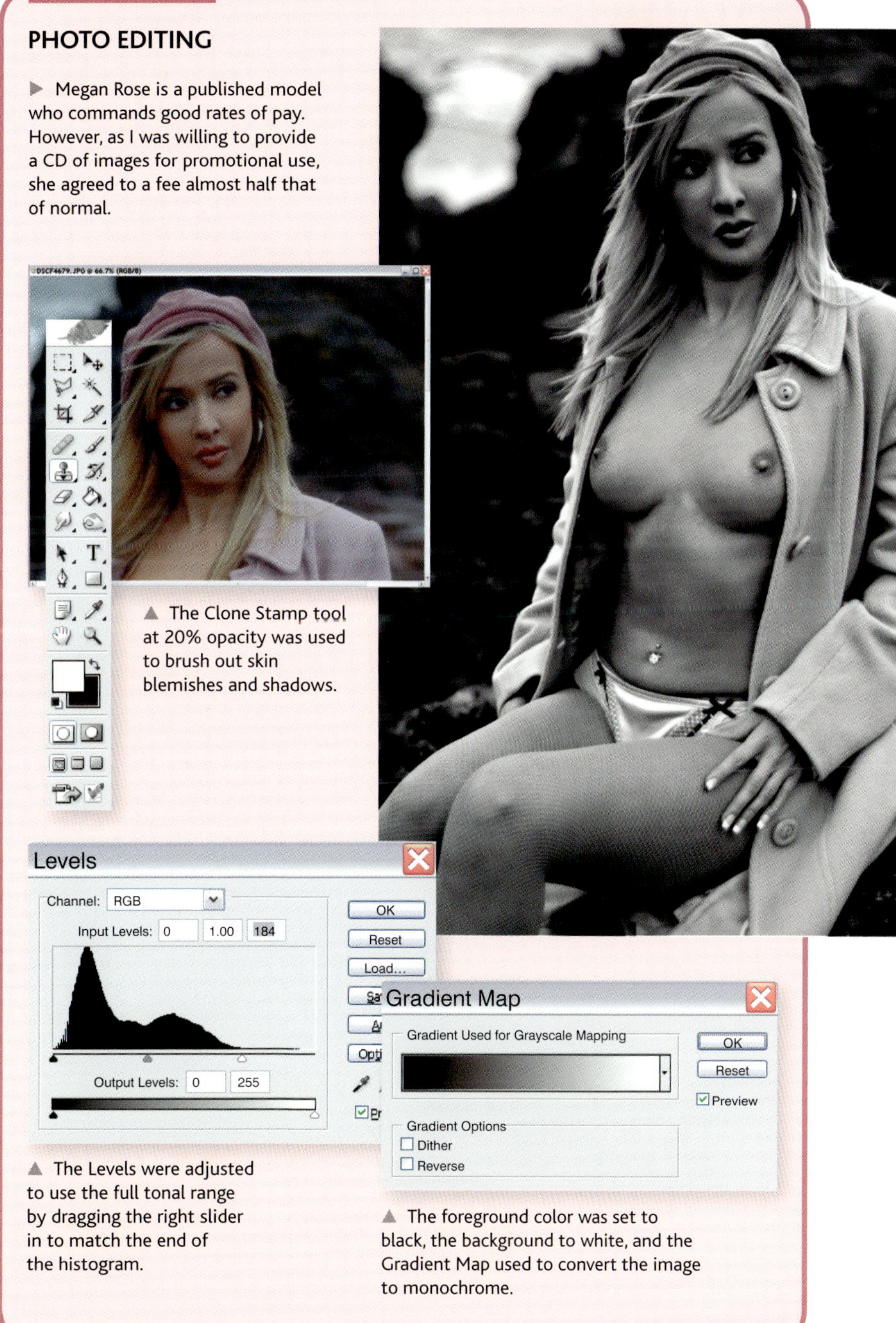

▲ The Clone Stamp tool at 20% opacity was used to brush out skin blemishes and shadows.

▲ The Levels were adjusted to use the full tonal range by dragging the right slider in to match the end of the histogram.

▲ The foreground color was set to black, the background to white, and the Gradient Map used to convert the image to monochrome.

TOOLS AT A GLANCE
CLONE STAMP
IMAGE > ADJUSTMENTS > LEVELS
IMAGE > ADJUSTMENTS > GRADIENT MAP

DIRECTING YOUR SUBJECT

Directing, or posing, the model, in nude photography is more important than in portraits. In a portrait session the idea is to have the subject express themselves to reveal their character, unless it's an advertising shoot where you are dictating the look and feel. With nudes, people don't generally wander around without any clothes on, so whether you are looking to express part of their individuality, or create a specific mood and theme, your model will need to be carefully guided.

SETTING IT UP

The setup for the main picture opposite was quite simple. The model sat down on pebbles between some large water-break rocks on the seashore. The sun was high overhead, slightly behind, so that there was plenty of light coming down between them. The photographer used a 28mm lens and was around 6 feet (1.8m) away, using an aperture of f/8 on a high ISO setting of 400 as this was intended to be monochrome.

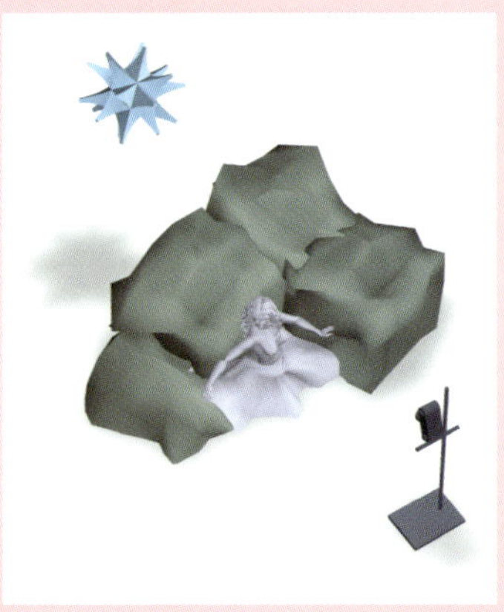

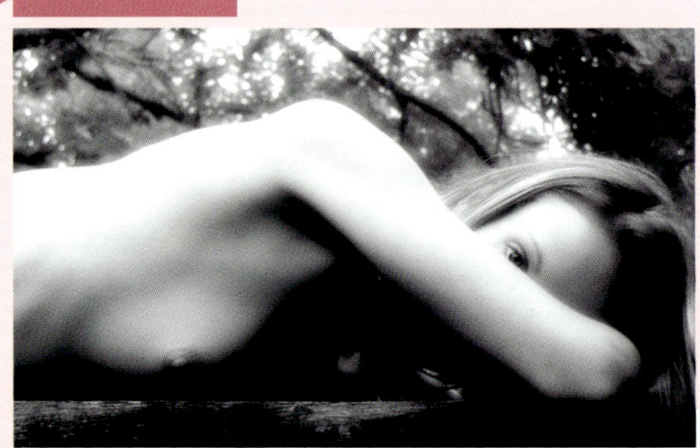

01 Revealing and hiding are the key elements to this picture by Mark Varley. The position of the model's arm reveals one breast and hides most of her face, but one eye is visible, looking back at the camera. If your subject is shy, then this type of pose can be a good way to start.

02 The model in this studio shot by Mark Edmondson is anything but shy. Her legs are positioned aggressively, but take note of her arms; they offer dynamic, yet complementary angles. In pictures that you want to look more active, use your model's arms to create shapes.

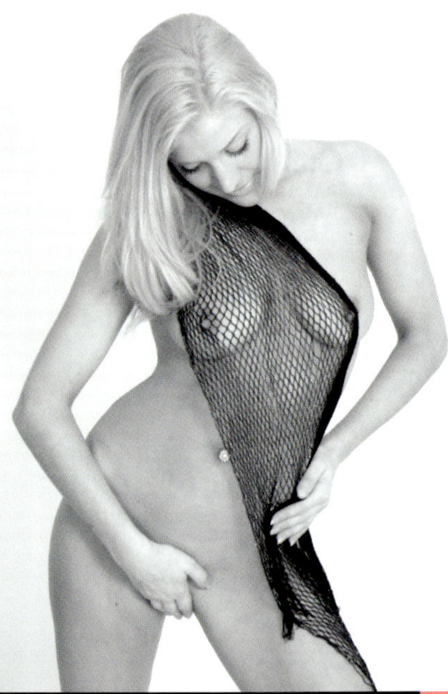

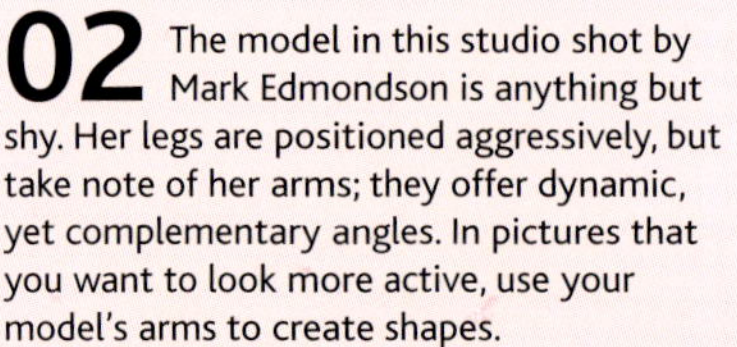

BRIGHT IDEA
Music is a great device for helping your subject relax, as long as it is something pleasant and light. The more relaxed the subject, the more natural the poses will be.

TOP TIP

If you find that your subject seems lacking in inspiration, get him or her to rapidly run through a series of poses. Explain that it doesn't matter if the pose doesn't work. If your subject does not have so much time to think, she or he will adopt more natural positions.

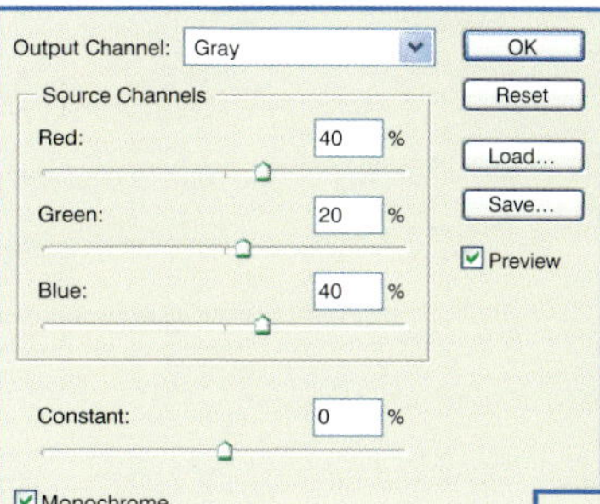

◀ The final image (below) was shot in color but destined for conversion to monochrome using the Channel Mixer.

▼ The Brightness/Contrast control was used to tweak both elements to give the photo slightly more impact. A black border was then added with the Canvas Size option.

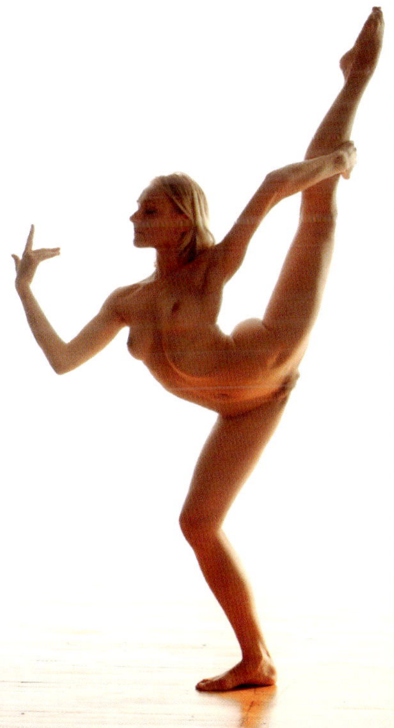

03 The subject of this photo is a trained ballet dancer and therefore can create and hold poses that show off her physical ability. Athletes, gymnasts, and dancers are more flexible than many models, so make use of that in the studio.

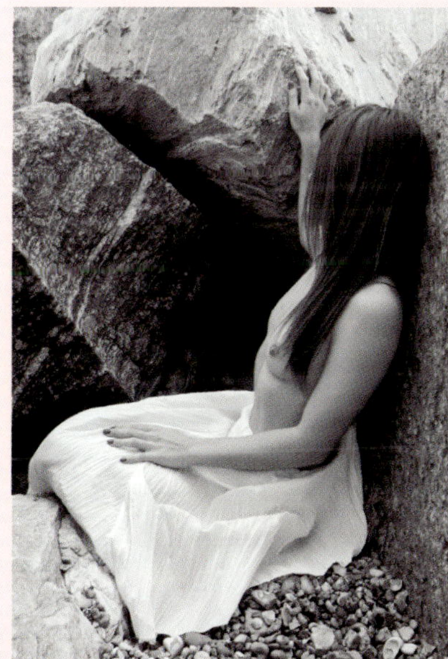

04 The next two pictures are from the same session. In this rather unsuccessful shot, the model simply sits in the gap between the rocks. You can't see her face, which might add some intrigue, but the pose offers little of interest.

05 This is a much better picture: we can see the model's face, although she is not looking at the camera, and the pose is more dynamic. There might even be a narrative to this picture: is she hiding from someone, or playing a game?

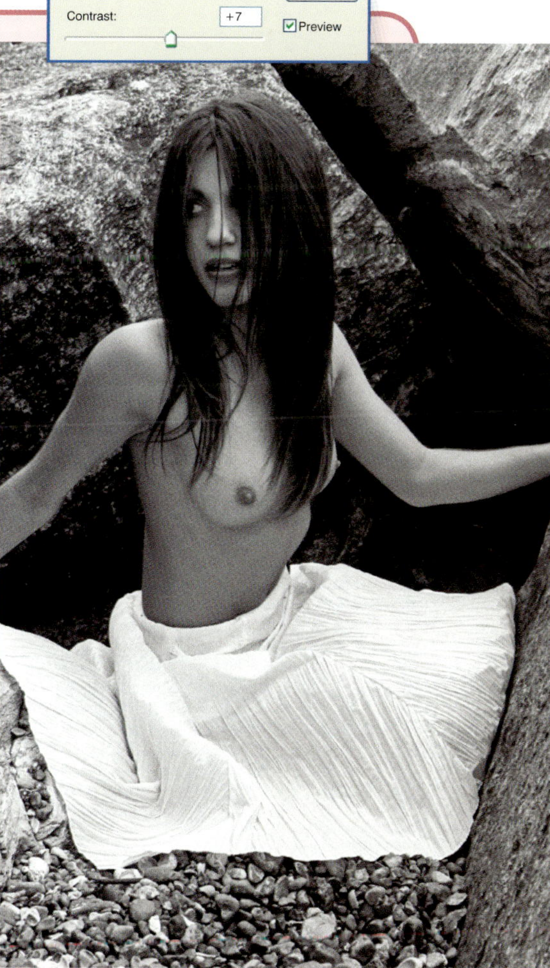

TOOLS AT A GLANCE
IMAGE > ADJUSTMENTS > CHANNEL MIXER
IMAGE > ADJUSTMENTS > BRIGHTNESS/CONTRAST
IMAGE > CANVAS SIZE

EXPRESSIONS AND ATMOSPHERE

When you are working with creative nude photography, the expressions of the model and the atmosphere of the shot play a much bigger role in the success or failure of an image than in, say, fashion photography. Here, there are no clothes to hide behind, though carefully integrating the model with the environment is often a very good substitute. So look instead, particularly in the studio, to elicit interesting expressions and creating subtle or powerful atmosphere. Atmosphere can often be affected with lighting styles, which we discuss later (see Chapter 5). Concentrate on conveying expressions that match the kind of scene you are creating, and you will produce much more convincing and powerful images.

SETTING IT UP (STEP 4, OPPOSITE)

The only light source was from a window, so the aperture on the 50mm lens was thrown wide open to f/1.8. This gave a shutter speed of 1/60 sec—fast enough for a handheld shot. The model was angled to the light so that it falls across her from one side and makes her face the focus of the image. The depth of field was extremely limited because of the wide aperture, thereby throwing the lower torso and the background out of focus.

TOP TIP

When photographing a model where there is lots of shadow and splashes of light, use center-weighted metering and meter off the light patches on the subject's skin. This will ensure detail is not lost, while retaining most of the shadows.

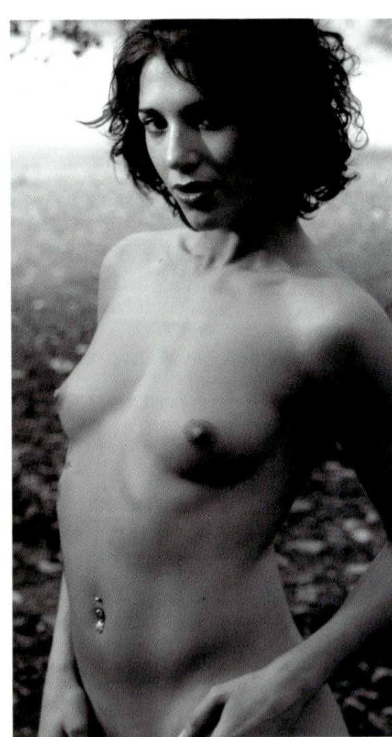

01 Although many artistic nude images feature the model looking moody or serious, there's nothing wrong with having your model smile—this can be equally effective.

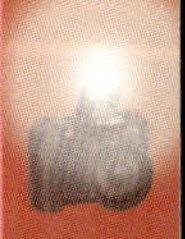

BRIGHT IDEA
If you want someone to look sad, get them to look downward, to either side of the camera. It automatically gives them a more reflective look.

02 You can convey a defiant look, or one with some attitude, without it being confrontational. This model is strutting a pose and playing with her hair, but any sense of confrontation is avoided by her not looking at the camera.

03 This shot is atmospheric, thanks to the subdued lighting. It was taken in the ruins of an old priory—hence the ornate window in the background. The light outside was flooding in, and the model was placed in a patch of light coming from a window out of camera view. The cross and the fabric add to the faux-religious feel of the image, which has been further developed by using the Diffuse Glow filter in Photoshop.

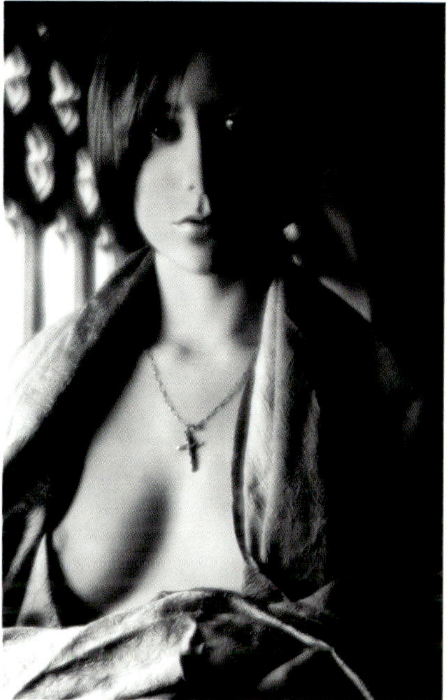

04 This shot features an older model, so she has lots of character in her face. She was positioned so that there would be light and shadow across her torso and a splash of light illuminating her face. Contrast adjustments have enhanced the shadows and creases, so that the model now looks thoughtful, vulnerable, and almost world-weary.

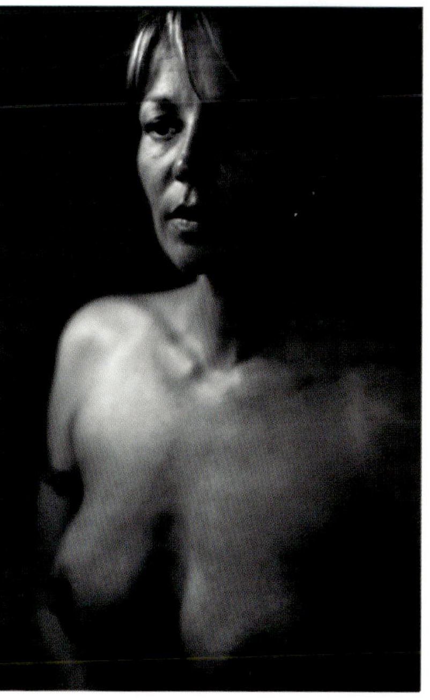

TOOLS AT A GLANCE
IMAGE > ADJUSTMENTS > GRADIENT MAP
IMAGE > ADJUSTMENTS > CURVES
IMAGE > FILTER > DISTORT > DIFFUSE GLOW
IMAGE > FILTER > TEXTURE > GRAIN

SHOOTING A SEQUENCE

There are a number of reasons why you might want to shoot a sequence of images. If you take a shot and think you have captured exactly what you wanted, then you could be missing out on a better shot, or, at the least, a variety of shots. It is always a good idea to take variations of a shot that you have set up. Not only can the extras throw up a good shot, but it also gives you more to use yourself. And with digital, the extra shots don't cost you anything. Another good reason for shooting a sequence is that you might be photographing an activity where only a number of images showing different actions adequately conveys the situation. Whatever your reasons, it makes sense to take those extra shots.

SETTING IT UP

In this sequence, the model was splashing about at the bottom of a waterfall. The camera position was about 20 feet (6m) away on a rock ledge above her. Supplemental light came from a portable tungsten lamp off to the right, which gives the model that warm look despite the cold water. The lens was a 28–200mm zoom so that some closeup shots could be taken. A fast shutter speed was used to freeze the movement of the water.

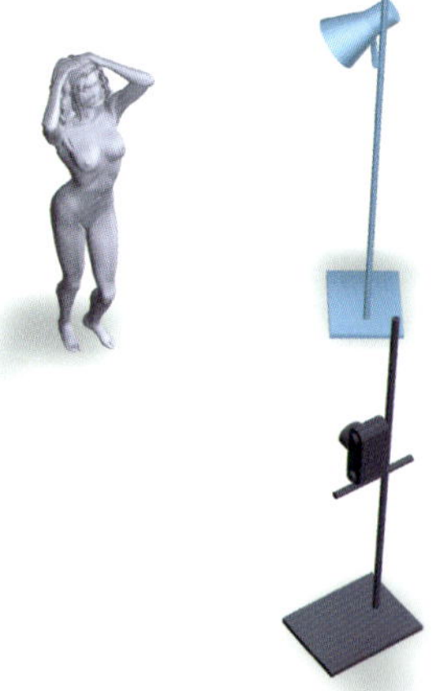

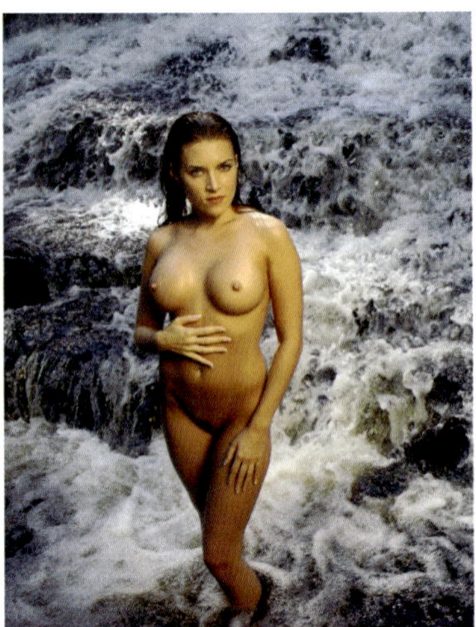

01 In this first shot, the zoom is set at the wide angle, showing the subject within the environment and the waterfall in the distance.

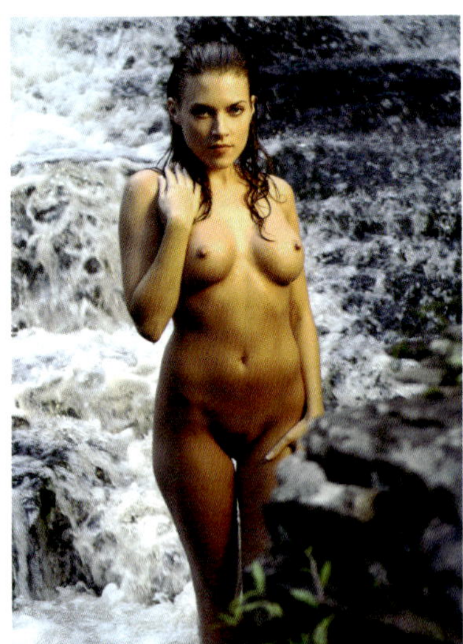

02 Now the view has zoomed in, the composition is tighter. The camera position has moved though, introducing the edge of the rock plateau, almost as if the model is now hiding from the camera.

TOP TIP
To isolate a subject that you are shooting a sequence of, use a long telephoto lens, such as a 200mm, and shoot from about 50 feet (15.2m) away. This will give you more candid-style images.

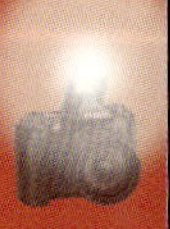

BRIGHT IDEA
Check the environment that you are working in. In this example, it was safer for the photographer to move around the subject rather than to have the model move around in the fast-flowing water.

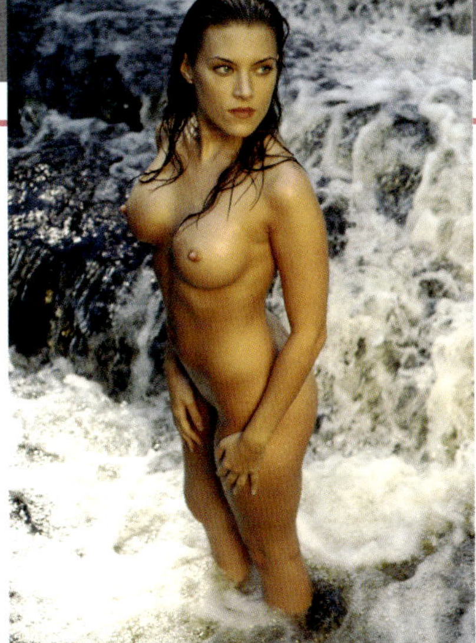

PHOTO EDITING

▼ Finally, the shooting position has changed so that it isn't so far above the model. The shooting length is three-quarters, giving a tight composition yet still including the background. The light from the side casts a pleasing yellow glow across the model's torso and she adopts a sultry look.

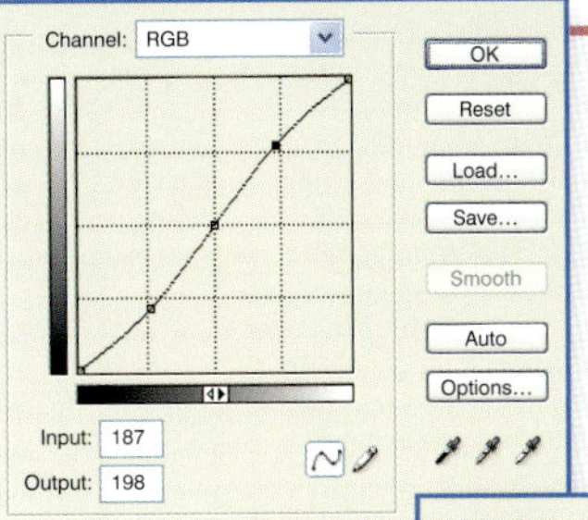

◀ Curves was used to darken the lower tones a little and add brightness to the highlights.

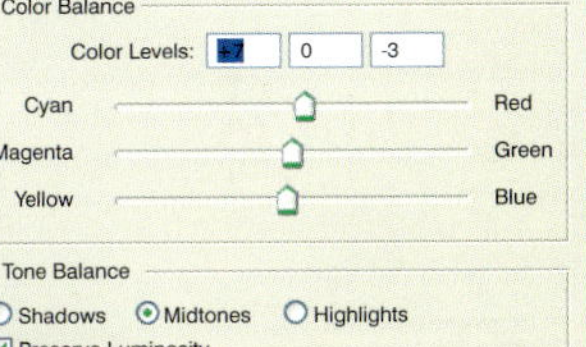

03 Moving to get a clear shot, the model is ideally positioned within the frame and seems unaware of the camera. However, by keeping moving and changing the focal length, there are more looks and aspects yet to be revealed.

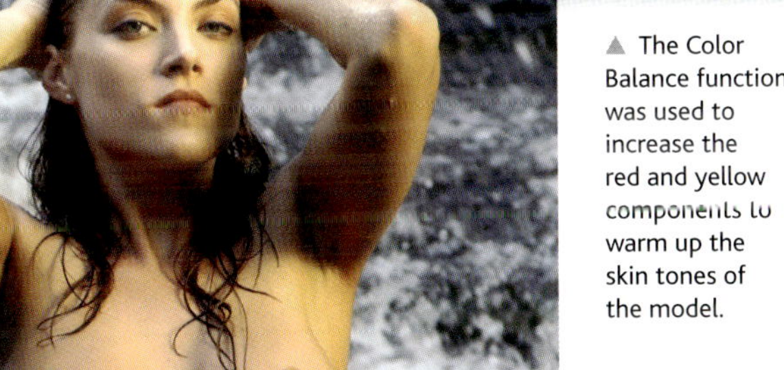

▲ The Color Balance function was used to increase the red and yellow components to warm up the skin tones of the model.

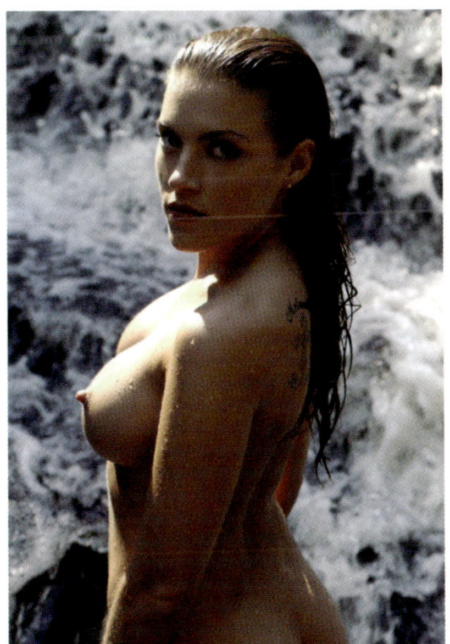

04 This shot is at the end of the telephoto, giving a closeup with the model staring right back into the camera, resulting in a more direct and challenging picture.

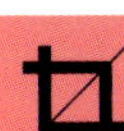

TOOLS AT A GLANCE
IMAGE > ADJUSTMENTS > CURVES
IMAGE > ADJUSTMENTS > COLOR BALANCE

WORKING AROUND THE SUBJECT

One way to introduce variety into a sequence of shots is to work your way around the subject, shooting from varying distances and angles. This approach works best on location, rather than in the studio, where the background occupies only one area and the lights are set up. On location you can walk around the subject, looking for interesting angles and lighting effects, and also move the subject themselves, so that their immediate environment changes.

SETTING IT UP

This shoot in a hotel room was done with a Fuji digital SLR and a 28–70mm short telephoto lens. The light from the window was quite bright. The aperture was set to the widest available. On a telephoto zoom like this, that was f/3.5–f/4.5, giving shutter speeds of around 1/60; this is fast enough if you can hold the camera quite still.

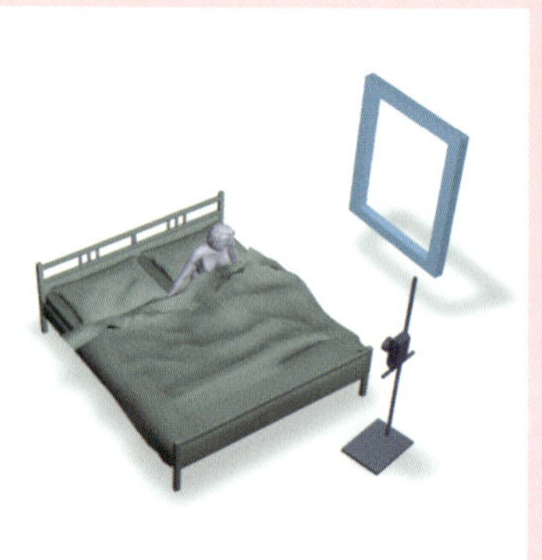

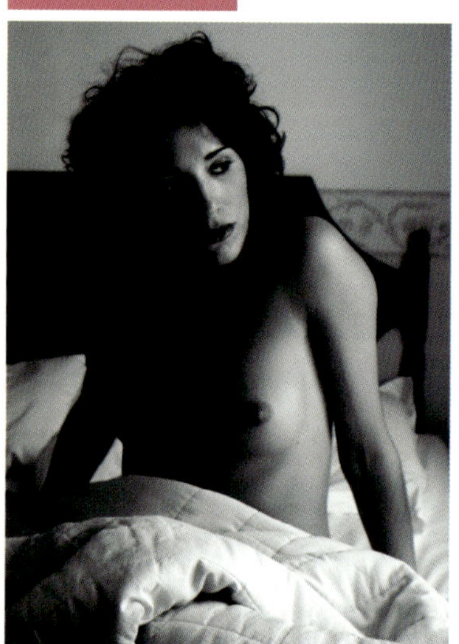

01 The exercise started with the model sitting up in bed, looking away from the camera into the light. The light illuminates one half of her body and leaves the rest in shadow.

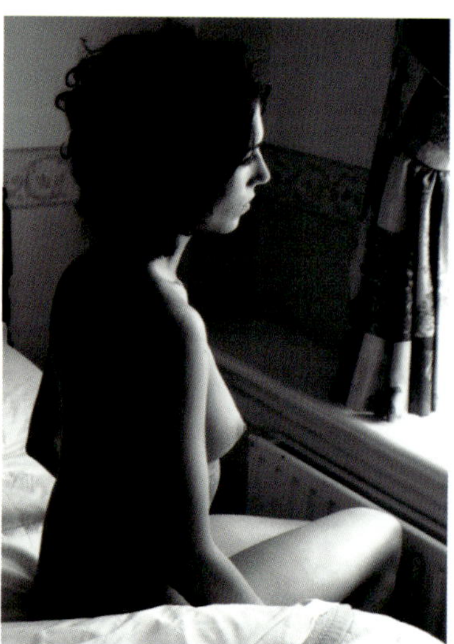

02 Now, with the model sitting up, there is contrast between the front of her torso, flooded with light and only slightly visible, and her back, which is in shadow.

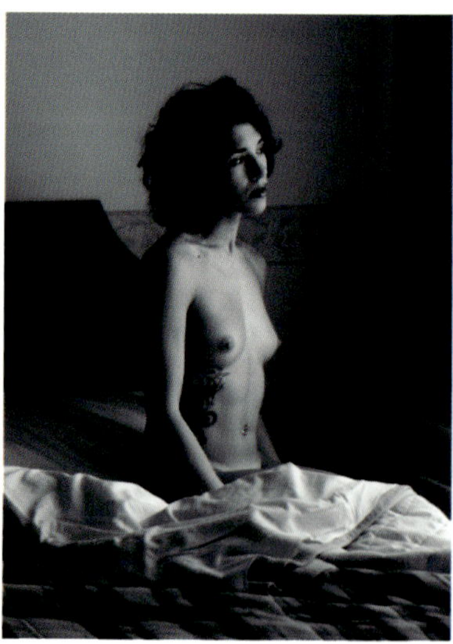

03 Don't be afraid to drop back and try different focal lengths, showing more of the environment. Although this image doesn't need any more space above the model's head, as it is, she is framed very nicely by the bed and walls.

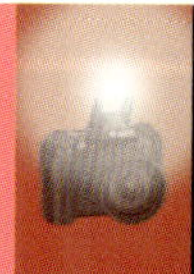

BRIGHT IDEA

As you will be changing focal lengths, getting in close and then dropping back, it is better to use a short telephoto lens rather than a prime lens. This gives you flexibility when working in a confined area.

PHOTO EDITING

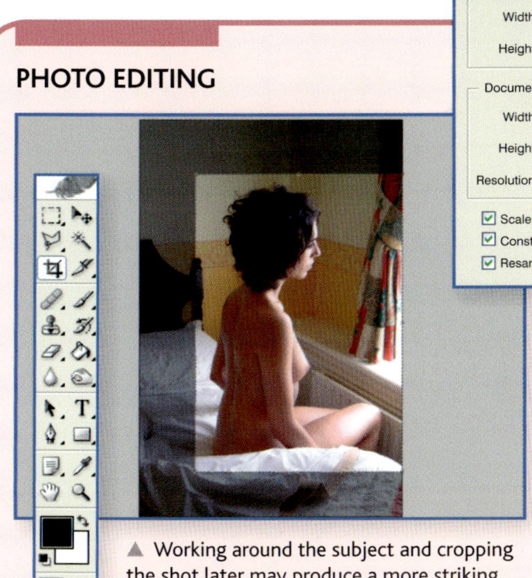

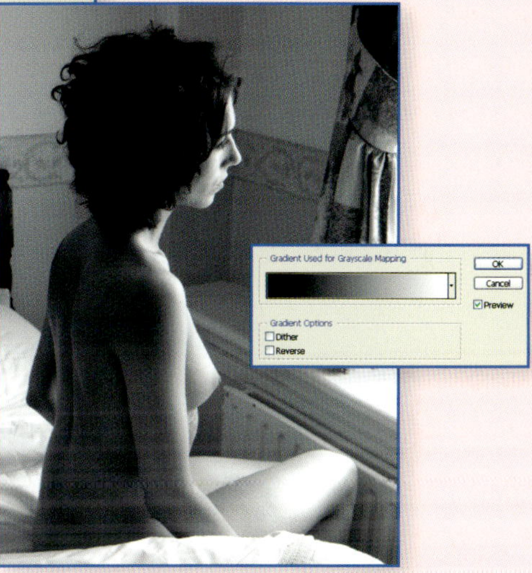

▲ After cropping, some interpolation may be required to bring the file size up to a higher resolution for printing.

▲ Working around the subject and cropping the shot later may produce a more striking image. The original shot has the model sitting in the middle. After cropping, she is moved to the left and looks out to the right.

▲ The Gradient Map is an excellent, and very quick, method of generating a black and white image from a color one. It results in a completely even spread of tones throughout.

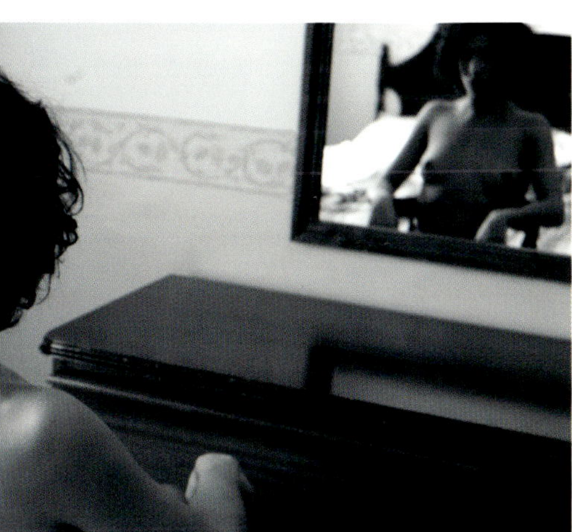

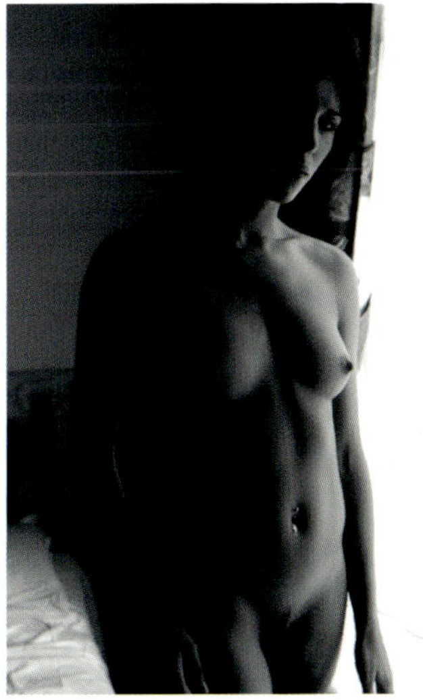

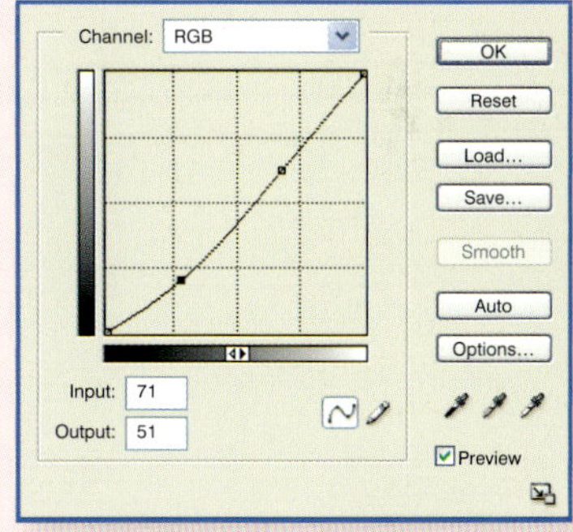

04 Here the model sits in a chair; the point of focus is on her back, while in the mirror we can see her front, though now out of focus. In such cases, you need to work the angles so that you don't shoot your own reflection in the mirror.

05 Here, the model turns sideways on to the light, creating patterns of light and shadow across her front. Her tilted head conveys an inquisitive mood, while the large amount of shadow adds mystery.

▲ The resulting monochrome image was very balanced, but Curves was used to darken the shadows and midtones to make it more moody.

TOOLS AT A GLANCE
IMAGE > ADJUSTMENTS > CROP
IMAGE > IMAGE SIZE
IMAGE > ADJUSTMENTS > GRADIENT MAP
IMAGE > ADJUSTMENTS > CURVES

ASSIGNMENT: CANDID IMAGERY

The concept of candid imagery in artistic nude photography throws up some interesting questions. By definition, candid photography is a genre in which the subject is unaware that they are being photographed going about their daily business. In terms of nude photography, if this is applied strictly, then the photographer has strayed into the dubious territory of voyeurism, not to mention questions of legality and invasion of privacy. So, what we are really talking about here is the style of candid photography. Your challenge is to produce a series of pictures showing the subject interacting with the environment, but not acknowledging the photographer at all. There should be no obvious poses and no eye contact with the camera.

SETTING IT UP

For this scene, shot by Björn Oldsen, the model was shot with light being filtered from windows above and to the right. The lens was a 50mm and the shots were taken from between 6 feet and 20 feet (1.8–6m) away. An aperture of f/5.6 was used to get some depth of field and let in enough light to shoot in these subdued conditions.

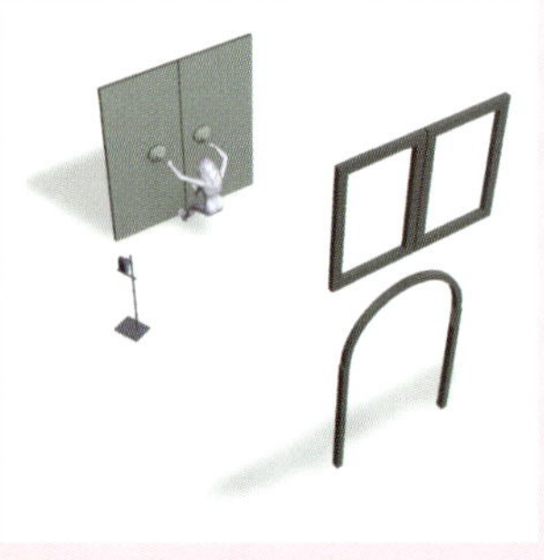

TOP TIP

As the model should interact with the background to some degree, you don't want it completely out of focus, so avoid using a wide-open aperture.

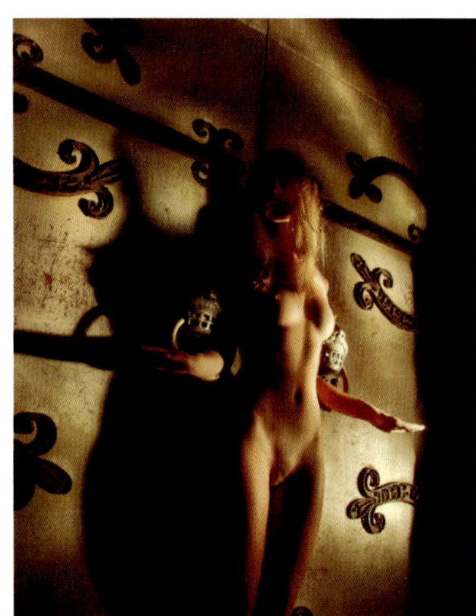

01 The model starts by posing against the doors. This is really what we have in mind for this series. There shouldn't be any obvious interaction with the photographer.

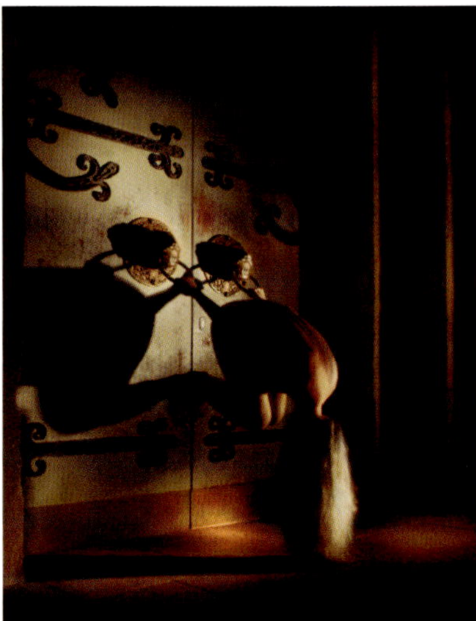

02 There's an ambiguity here that accentuates the picture. Is the model performing acrobatics, or trying very hard to open the doors? Either way, it fits the terms of this challenge.

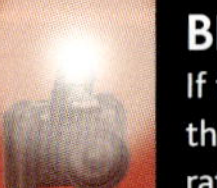

BRIGHT IDEA
If the subject is finding it difficult to turn off to the fact that the photographer is there, give them something to do, perhaps with a prop, so that they can focus their attention on that rather than the presence of the camera.

PHOTO EDITING

▶ This is the best shot for this assignment. The model interacts with the location, posing the question of whether she is trying to open the doors to escape, or stop them from being opened from the other side. A door at the end of the hall has been opened slightly to let a narrow beam of light shine on her and the floor.

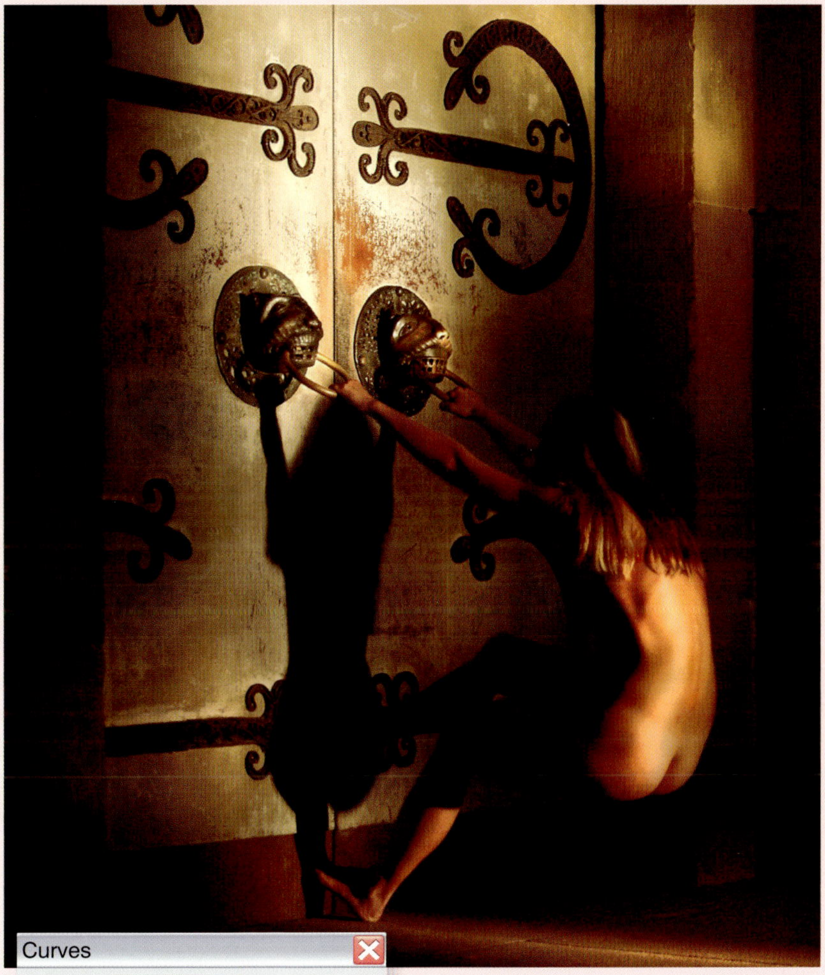

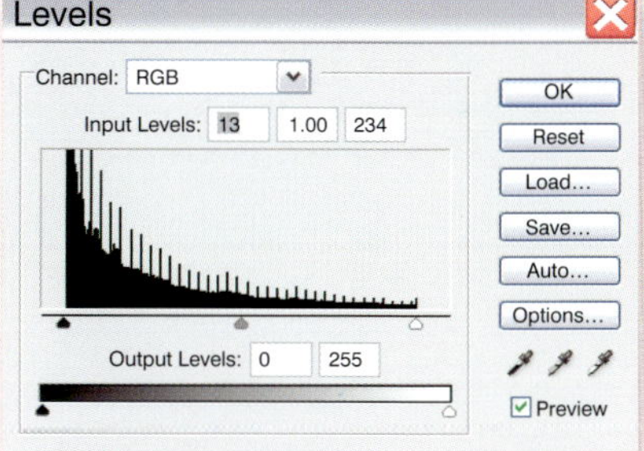

▲ The Levels were adjusted so that the full tonal range was used in the shot. It was slightly flat originally.

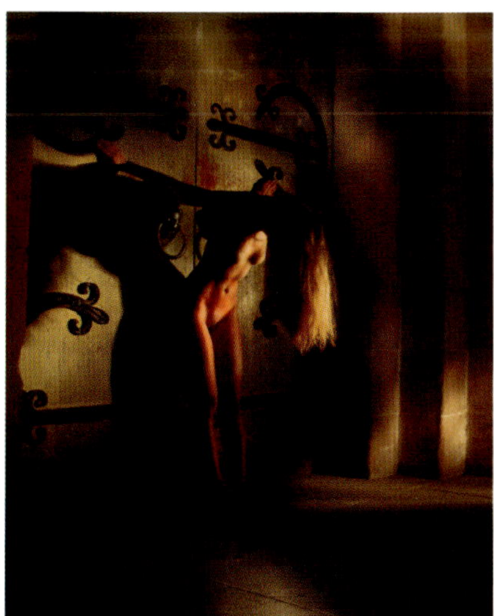

03 In purely artistic terms, this is the most pleasing shot. The model hangs her head while her arms are outstretched, in a pseudo-religious pose.

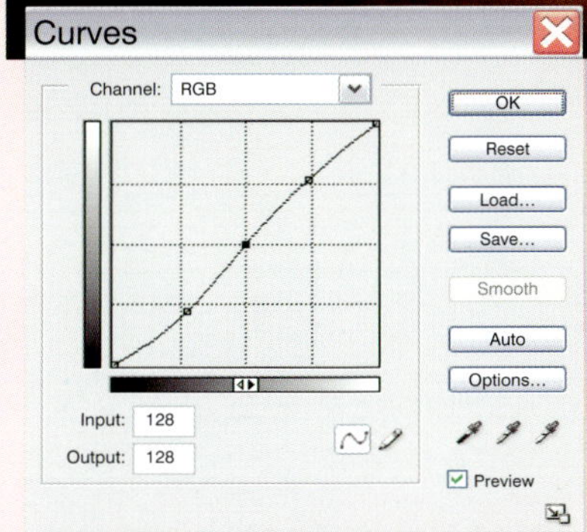

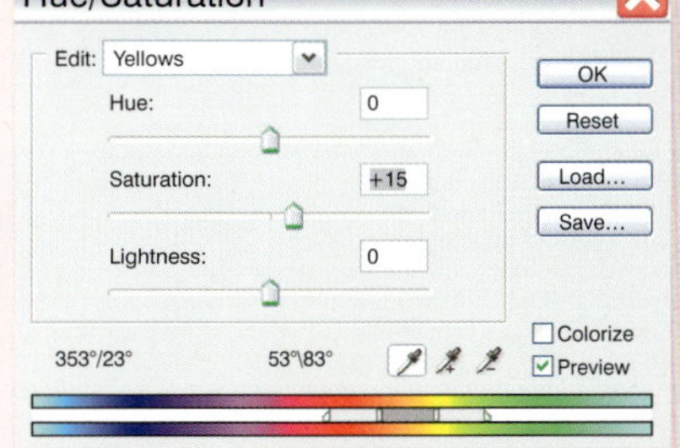

▲ An S-shape Curves function was used to darken the shadows to make the picture more mysterious, and to lighten the highlights.

▲ Finally, the Hue/Saturation tool was used, picking up on the yellows, to increase the saturation and make the image warmer.

TOOLS AT A GLANCE
IMAGE > ADJUSTMENTS > LEVELS
IMAGE > ADJUSTMENTS > CURVES
IMAGE > ADJUSTMENTS > HUE/SATURATION

3 PORTRAIT STYLES

Discover how varying the length of a shot can affect the mood and intention of the picture. Think about the impact of eye contact and use wide angles and unusual shooting positions. Use props, and think about when to focus in on individual elements for abstracts. Once you know the rules, you can break them.

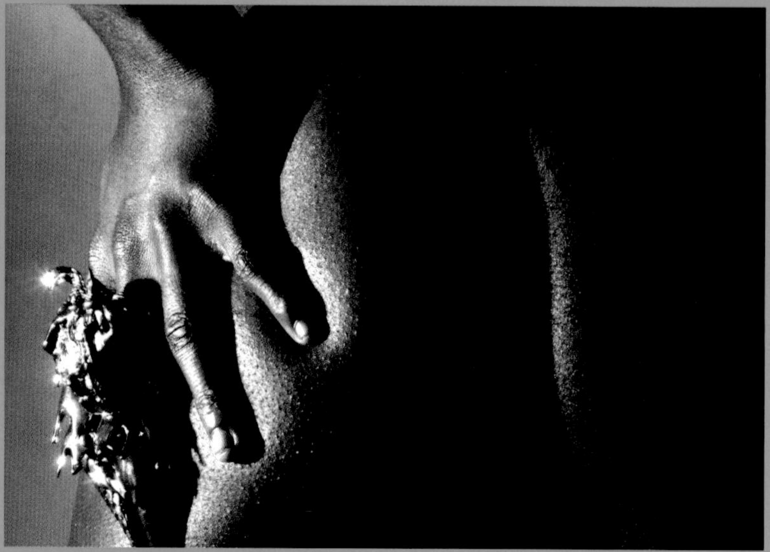

▲ Image length. Experiment with different image lengths to create variety and expression in your nude shots.

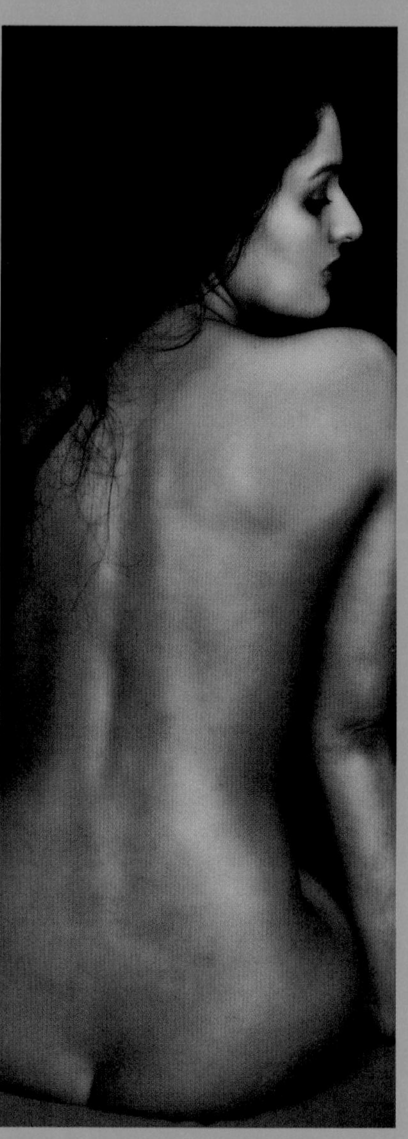

▲ Reverse view. Shoot from behind to reveal shape and hair detail.

▼ Assignment: image lengths. Produce a series of pictures using a number of different image lengths.

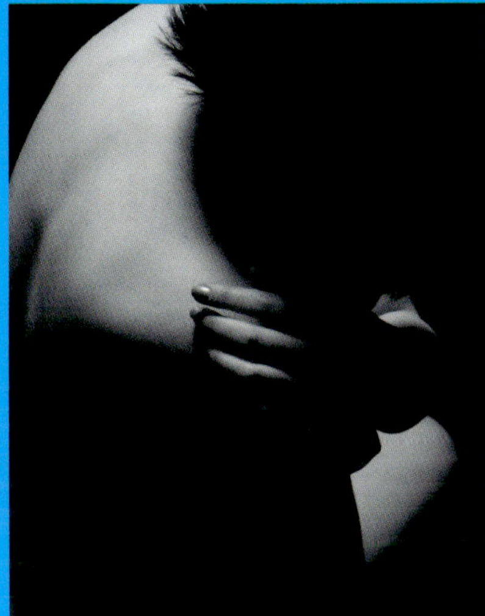

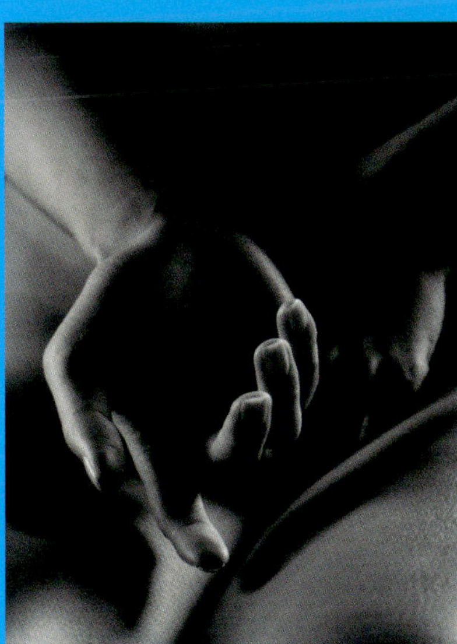

▲ Assignment: body part abstracts. Your challenge is to explore the landscape of the body

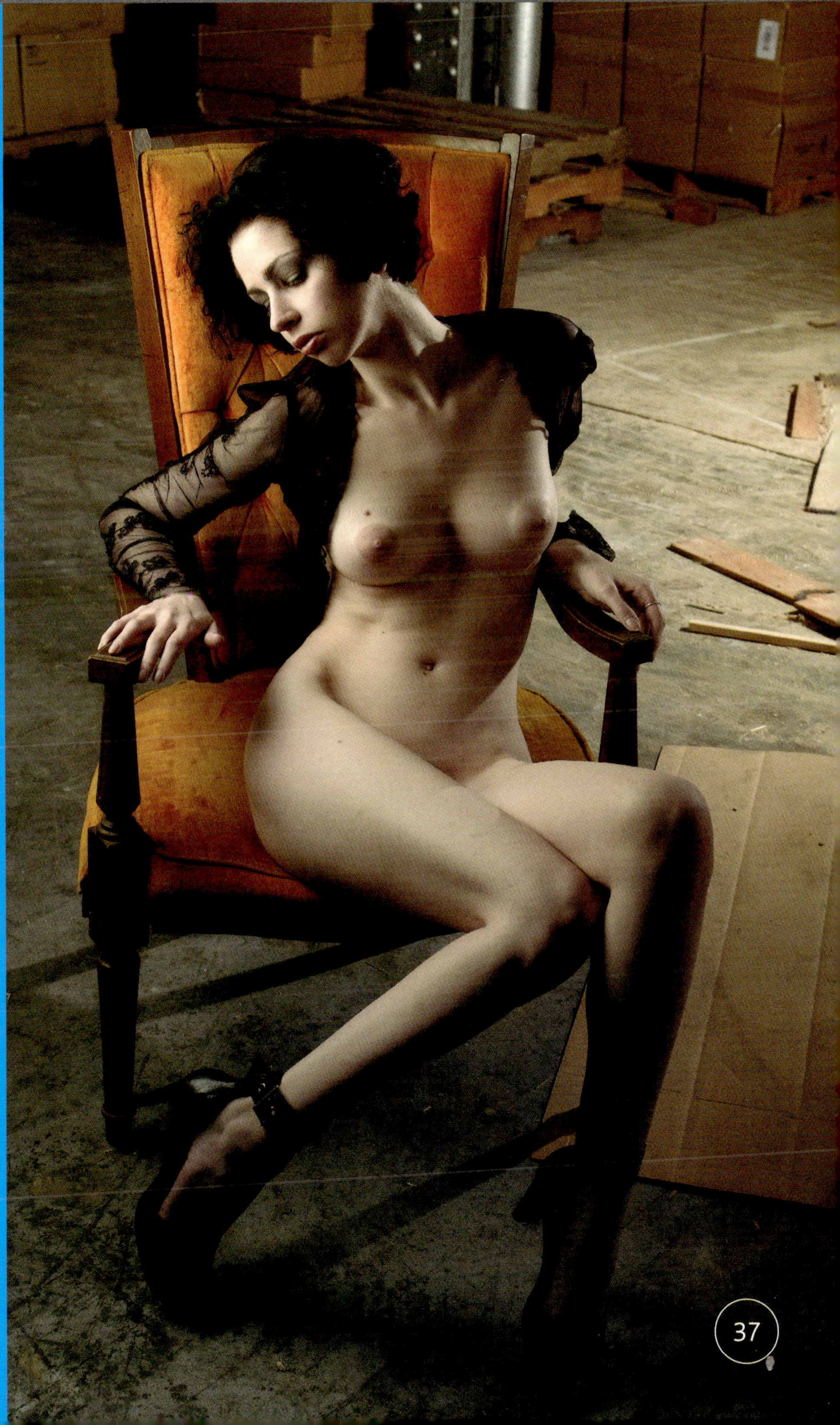

IMAGE LENGTHS

In regular portraits, the length of the image dictates how busy the subject has to be and how creative the shot must be to retain interest. Nudes operate on similar principles, but then you need to throw half of the rule book out of the window. If you start off with the basics, however, you can then progress to bending the rules and knowing when to ignore them completely.

SETTING IT UP

This is the setup for the three-quarter length shot on the opposite page. The subject faces the camera, with her head hidden and her hands carefully placed. The key light with a softbox set to f/11 is wide to the left, while a large fill light at f/9.5 is set to the right. Two bare flash units are aimed at the background at a higher power setting of f/16 to whiten it out. The lens length is around 50mm with the subject standing 6 to 10 feet (1.8–3m) away. The camera is set to f/11 to coordinate with the key light and 1/125 sec to synchronize with the lights.

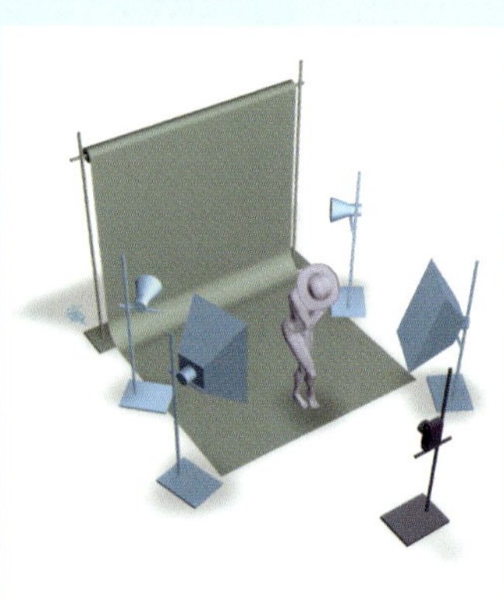

CROPPING FOR SUCCESS

Nudes work can be transformed by your choice of crop. Get angles and dynamic movement into the frame by accenctuating diagonals and the subject's relationship with the frame; alternatively, go for a radical crop and focus in on details, textures, and body forms.

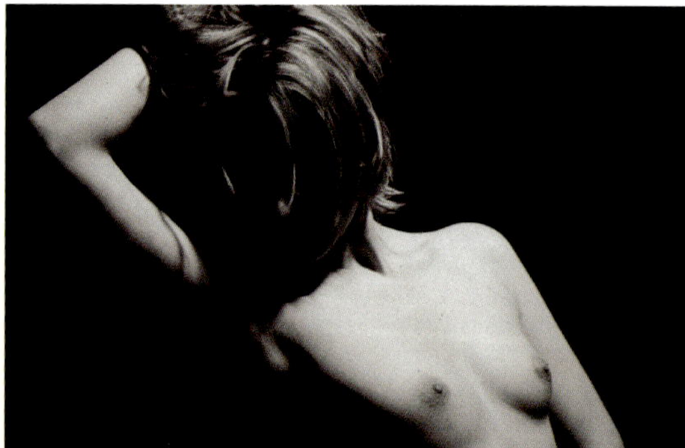

◀ Simon Young's shot uses a harsh light on the torso, then hides the face in the model's hair and the shadows by turning it away, adding mystery to the image.

▶ In nude photography, you can crop closely into any area. In this shot, Mark Edmondson has zoomed right into the buttocks of the model, who is wearing a very ornate ring, and fired the flash across both the buttocks and the eye-catching jewelry.

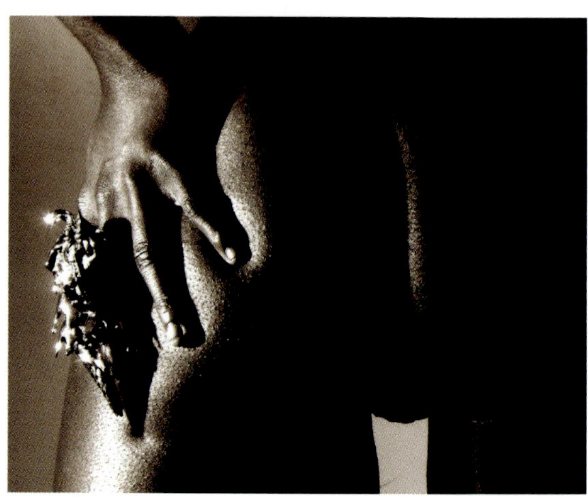

BRIGHT IDEA
If you have a shot set up for a particular length, shoot it, then change the length and look to see what you need to do to make the new length interesting enough to photograph—whether it's a change of lights or pose.

FULL-LENGTH

The typical full-length shot either requires participation with the scenery, with the pose both believable and stylish, or it should be minimalist, concentrating solely on form. In full-length shots, hands and feet come into play, and ensuring that these look natural should be a priority.

Full-length shots don't always require the subject to be standing up, or even at a regular angle. Here, Robert King has created a dynamic image by having the model stretched across the shot.

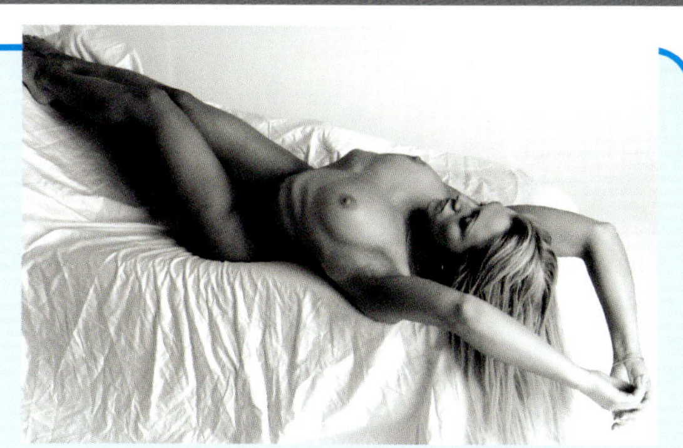

THREE-QUARTERS

This is the easiest length to shoot in portraits as you don't have to worry about the feet, and the background is less involved than with a full-length shot. To some extent this is true of nudes, but as a lot of nudes are shot in the studio, there is often little background anyway. That places the onus on the photographer to create interest through pose and lighting.

▶ This is the shot that the setup refers to. It's a classic three-quarter-length shot, with fairly standard lighting, ensuring that the background is completely white. To generate interest, photographer Simon Pole has hidden the model's head behind a hat and arranged her arms modestly across her body.

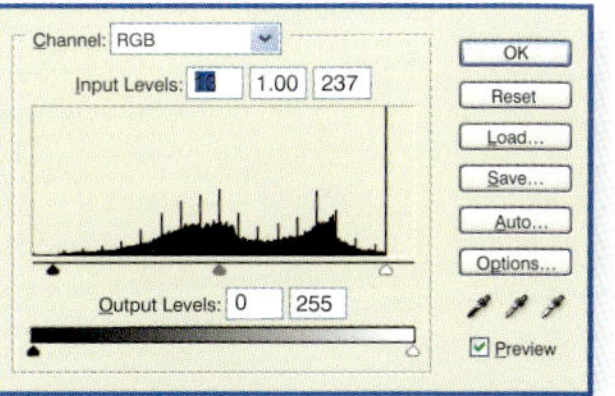

▲ The Levels command was used to ensure the white elements were completely white by moving in the carat on the right.

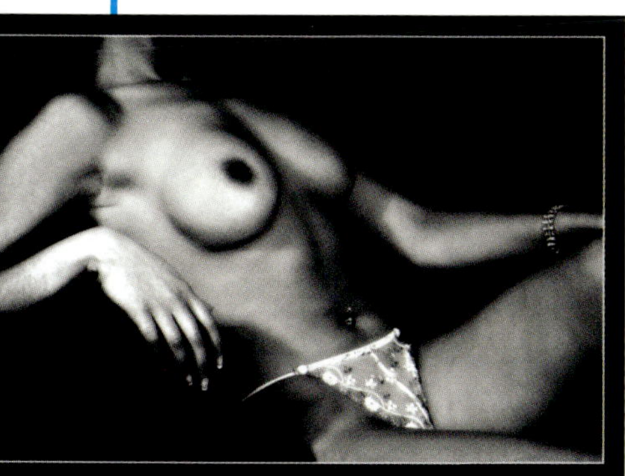

▲ This three-quarters shot shows the model lounging in a chair. The subject's head has been deliberately excluded to concentrate on her form and features rather than her individual personality.

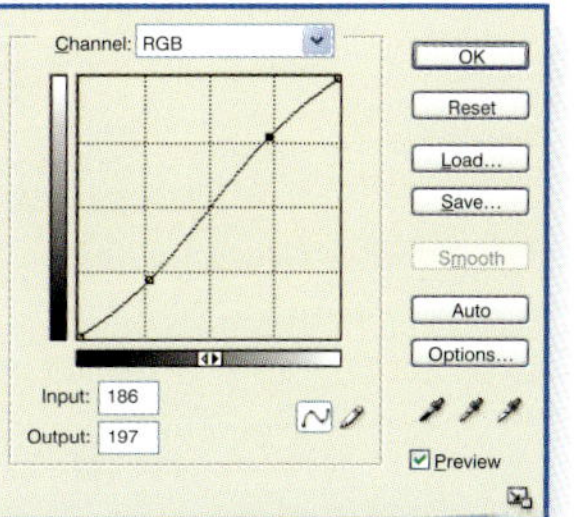

◀ Curves was then used to add a little more contrast to the image.

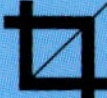

TOOLS AT A GLANCE
IMAGE > ADJUSTMENTS > LEVELS
IMAGE > ADJUSTMENTS > CURVES
IMAGE > ADJUSTMENTS > CHANNEL MIXER

ASSIGNMENT: IMAGE LENGTHS

This assignment concerns image lengths. Having supplied images on spec to an image bank, they have asked you for a set of different lengths of the same model using the same lighting. You need to provide a variety of poses and lengths, so that prospective buyers are faced with a wide choice, based around a single lighting and subject concept. You must set up the lights and define an area within which the model can move, and produce a series of full-length, head-and-shoulders, and three-quarter shots.

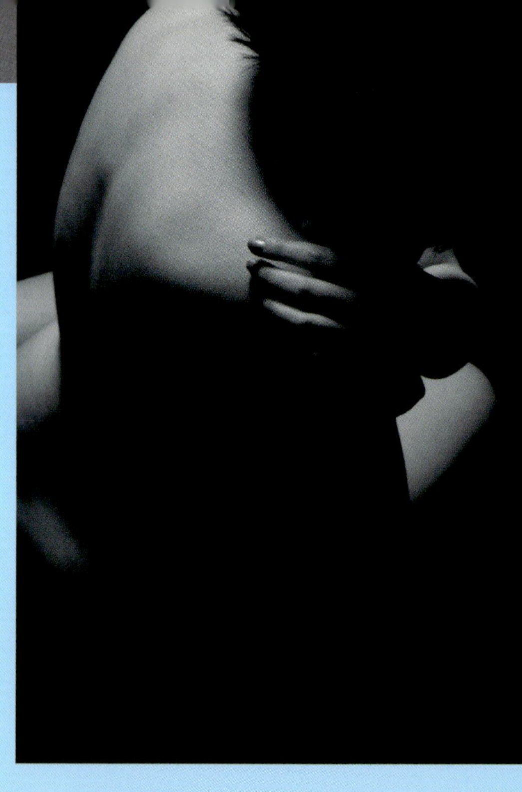

SETTING IT UP

The lighting for this setup is deceptively simple. It consists of a flash unit with a small softbox suspended on a boom arm about 5 feet (1.5m) above the model. The light comes directly downward. Meter it when the model is standing up, as that is where it will be brightest (when she sits on the floor, the light will be spread out and will not be as strong). Set up the background to be black and ensure that the light and the model are far enough away from it so that no light spills over. Use a 50mm portrait lens. Alter your position from 6 feet (1.8m) for the head-and-shoulders shots to 15 feet (4.5m) for the full-length ones.

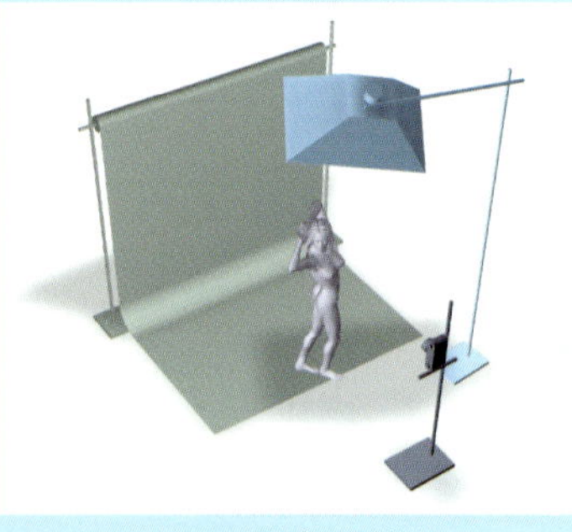

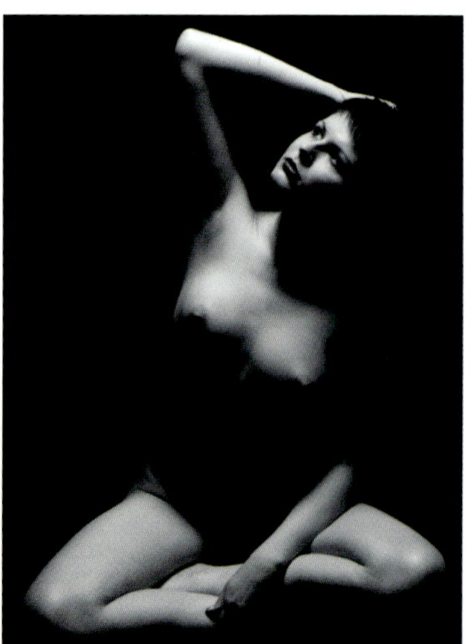

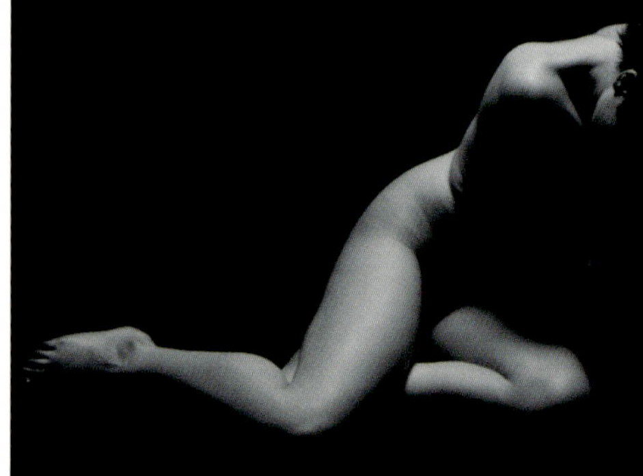

01 This is full-length in that it shows all of the model, but by her sitting cross-legged, the height is reduced. The model has an open, questioning look as she stares into the bright light.

02 As befits the fact that the light is more diffuse at ground level, the pose here is more subtle and atmospheric. Despite the fact that you cannot see the model's face, this is a full-length shot.

BRIGHT IDEA
Light spreads and the intensity falls off the further away from the source it is. Try to make the photos where the model is on the ground look more moody as the light will be weaker. Alternatively, open up the aperture on ground-level shots to make them brighter.

PHOTO EDITING

◄ Just because we want a head-and-shoulders shot doesn't mean you have to be predictable. The key elements here are the model's head and shoulders, her fingers, and the fact that her head is hanging down. This is a very low-key image that concentrates on atmosphere.

► ▼ Then the Curves command was used to make the shadows darker, particularly the area on the floor that was too light.

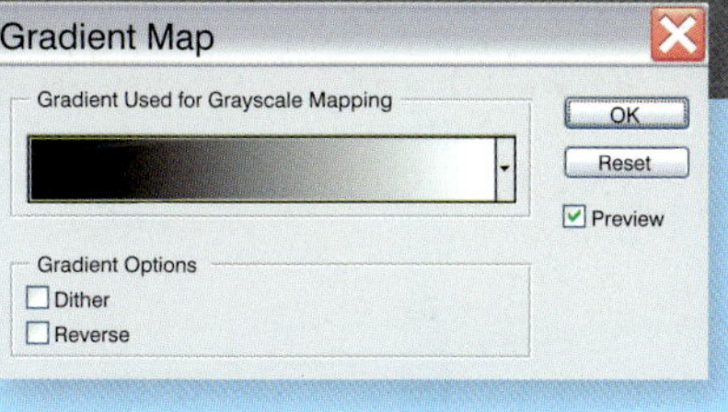

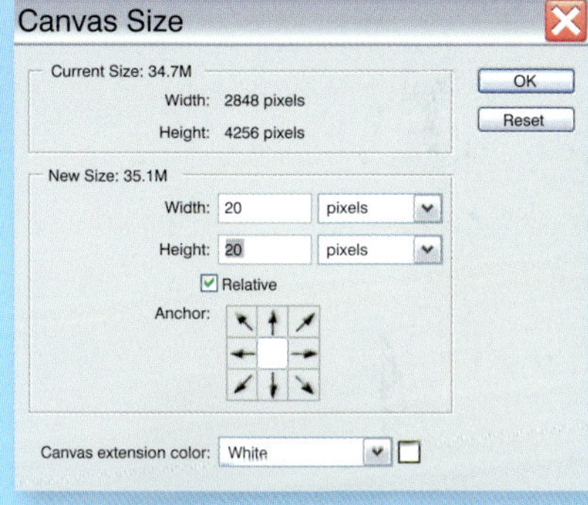

▲ The Gradient Map with a black–white gradient was used to convert the picture to monochrome.

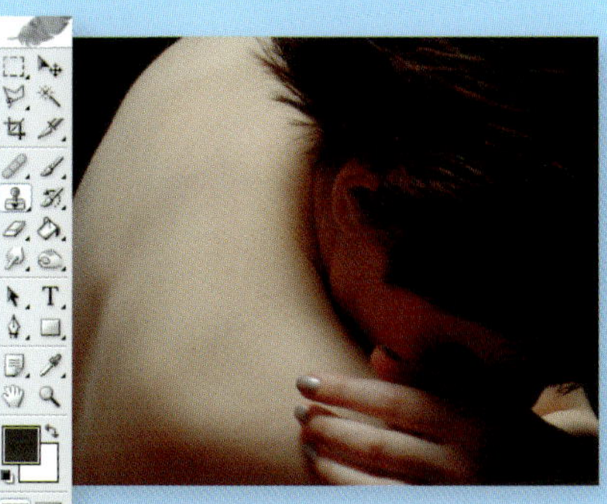

▲ Firstly, the Clone Stamp tool set to the lighten blend mode at 100% opacity was used to remove minor spots and skin blemishes.

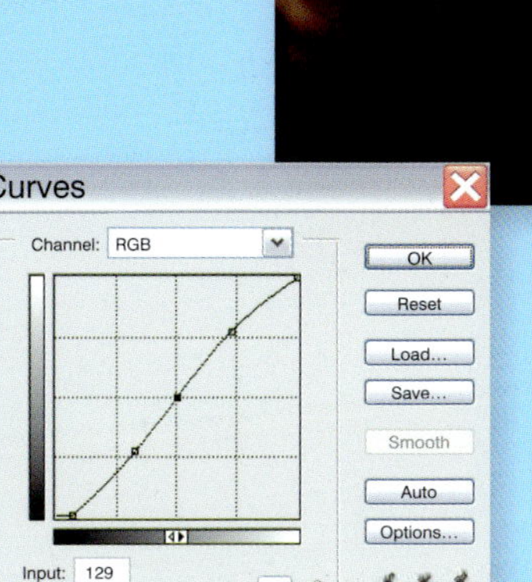

▲ Finally, the Canvas Size option was used to add a pencil-thin white border, then a slightly thicker black border.

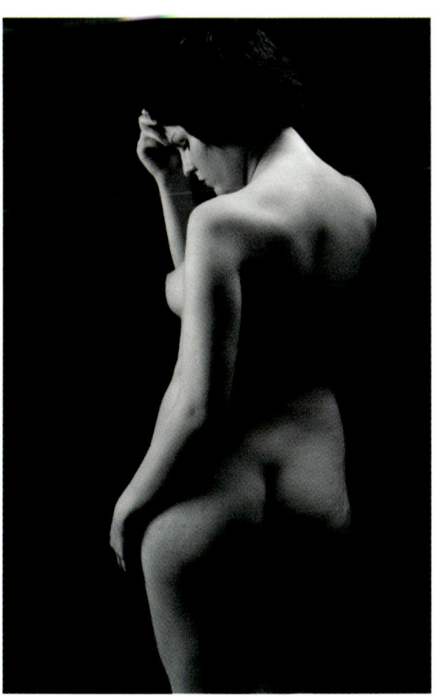

03 This is the classic three-quarter-length shot, with the torso angled because the legs are flat to the camera. The highlights are all around the shoulders, leading arm, and the just-visible breast.

> ### TOP TIP
> To obtain different image lengths it is tempting to use a short telephoto or wide-angle zoom, but you'll end up with distortion as soon as you get close to the subject. Let your legs do the work instead.

04 This is slightly shorter than the three-quarter-length shot. Because the light at the top of the picture is brighter, the model makes a much more dynamic pose with her arms and torso.

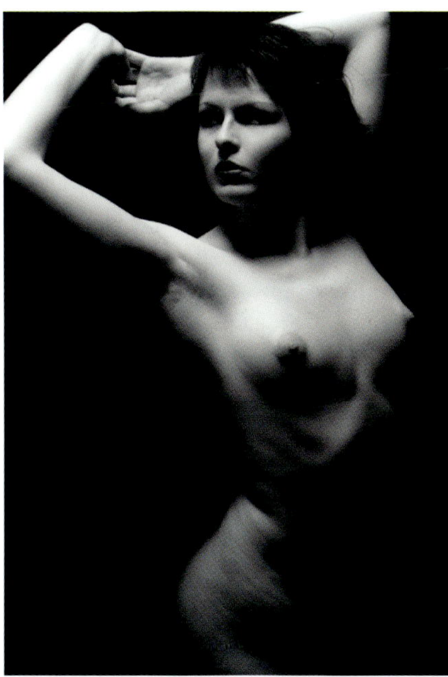

TOOLS AT A GLANCE
CLONE STAMP
IMAGE > ADJUSTMENTS > CURVES
IMAGE > ADJUSTMENTS > GRADIENT MAP
IMAGE > CANVAS SIZE

REVERSE VIEW

When shooting from behind a nude subject, there is an element of mystery, as they are turned away from the camera. Photographically, the back, legs, and buttocks are the key areas, but don't forget that the model's head, if turned to one side, can be incorporated too. The challenge is to show less, but be more creative.

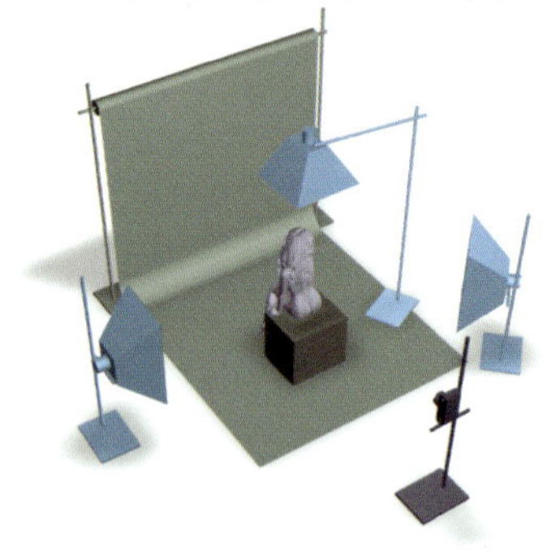

SETTING IT UP

For the main picture opposite, the lens was a 50mm. The photographer stood about 10 feet (3m) away, with the model sitting on a couch facing a fabric backdrop, but with her head turned in the direction of the key light. This light was to the right at camera height, set to f/8. A fill light was on the left, providing additional illumination, but at a much reduced power of f/4. A hair light over the top of the model, also set to f/4, added faint highlights.

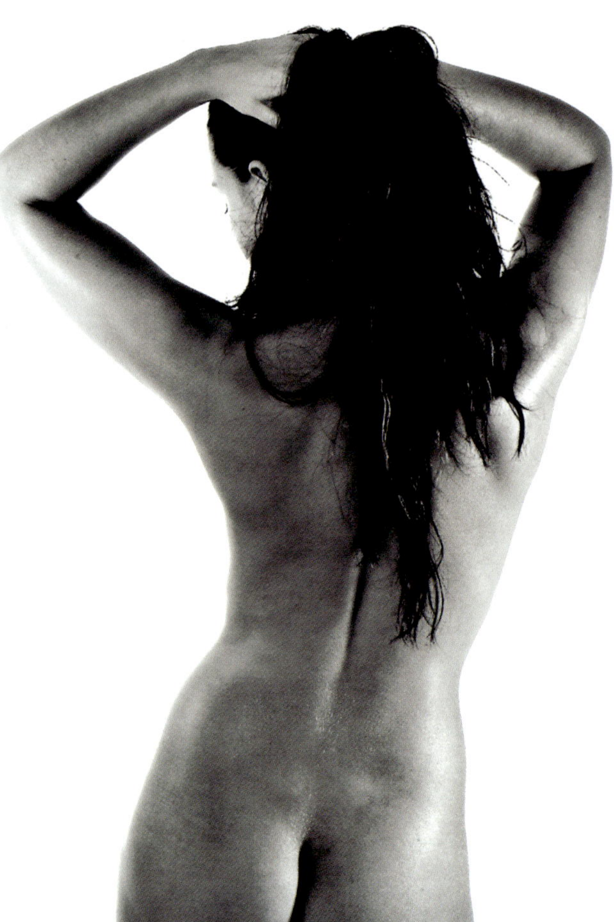

01 This is a straightforward shot, with the model flat to the camera, facing a white wall that is overlit. The model's back is lit by the key light, and while she is making a shape with her arms and hair, consider this a starting point then move on.

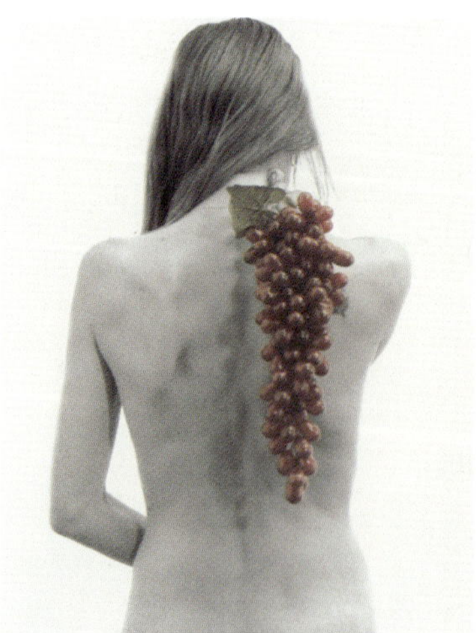

02 This high-key shot is by Mark Varley. The model's head is dropping down, giving a more subdued aspect. Over the shoulder, contrasting with the spine, is a bunch of grapes. To mark them out further, they have had their color retained, while the rest of the image has been converted to monochrome.

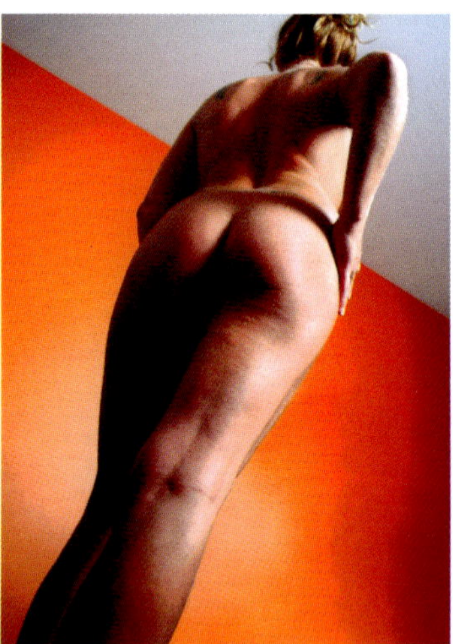

03 Just because you are shooting from behind doesn't mean you can't play around with angles and lenses. This uses a wide-angle lens and is shot from the floor, looking up. It makes the legs appear very long and sets the figure against the two-tone color background.

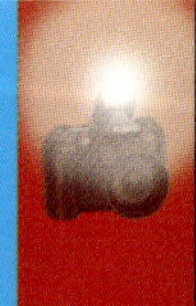

BRIGHT IDEA
If you are stuck for studio lighting, use your flashgun but point it at a wall, ceiling, or reflector to bounce light onto the subject and make for much smoother dark–light transitions.

PHOTO EDITING

▼ Here the model is sitting on a couch, with her head turned toward the camera to provide a connection with the viewer. The lighting setup is explained in the setup box; the concept was to give a more classical feel to the shot, with highlights and shadows against a dark background.

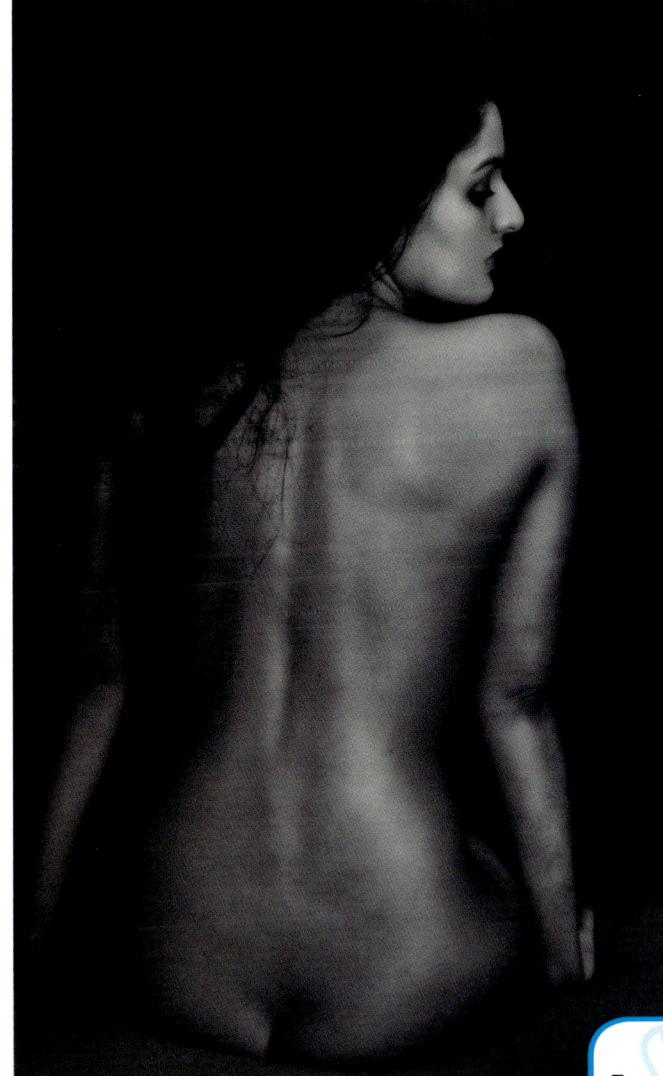

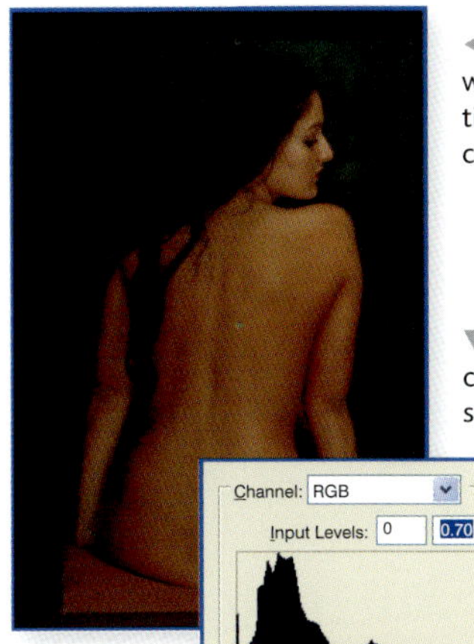

◄ Firstly the image was cropped to tighten up the composition.

▼ Then the Levels command was used to spread the tones out.

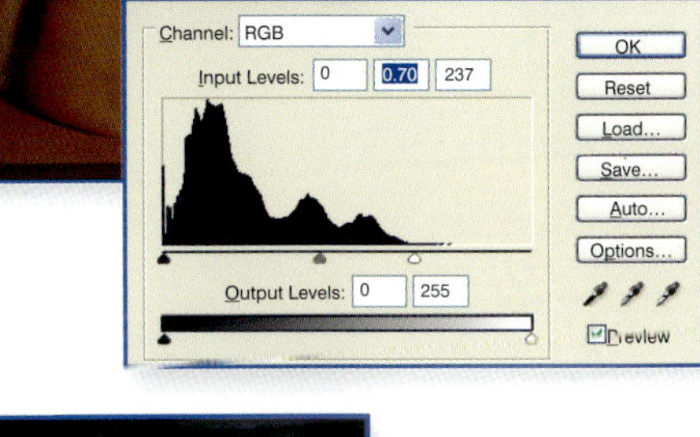

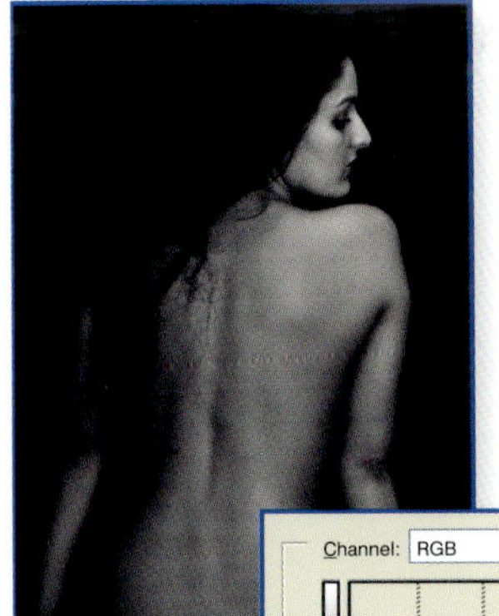

◄ The image was converted to monochrome with the Gradient Map and a black–white gradient.

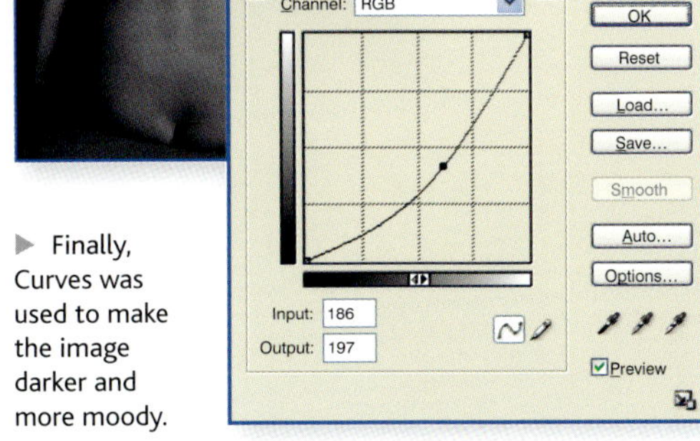

▶ Finally, Curves was used to make the image darker and more moody.

TOP TIP

To create a moody look, you need to use a narrow enough aperture to prevent any ambient light being recorded. Set your flash power high to achieve this.

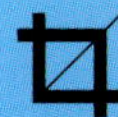

TOOLS AT A GLANCE
CROP
IMAGE > ADJUSTMENTS > LEVELS
IMAGE > ADJUSTMENTS > GRADIENT MAP
IMAGE > ADJUSTMENTS > CURVES

MAKING EYE CONTACT

While many nude pictures are mysterious, aloof, and abstract, you can also engage the viewer by making eye contact with the subject. Concentrate on the eye contact working effectively in combination with the expression and the pose, so that together they portray an overall meaning. Connecting with the viewer can make for very powerful images, and also lend it a degree of intimacy that is otherwise not present. You are inviting the viewer to relate to the person and situation, not just to admire the composition of the shot.

SETTING IT UP

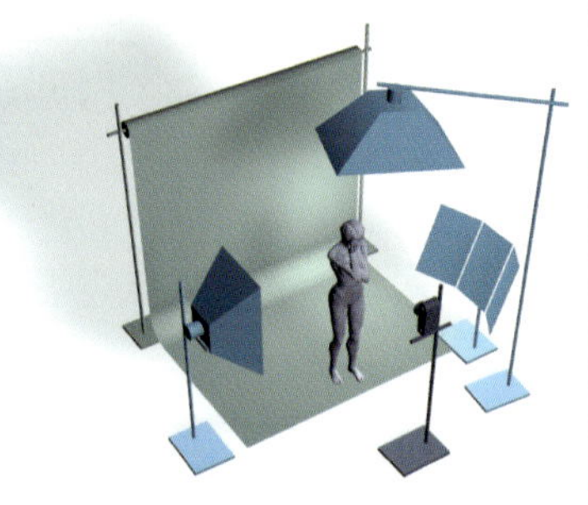

Although this was a closeup shot, it involved two lights and a reflector. There was a main light to the left, fitted with a softbox. That was set to f/11 power. There was also a smaller light, providing a narrower spread of light, over the top, slightly to the right of the model. This put light onto the model's hair and exposed breast but not her face. To the right of the model was a reflector with three panes, bouncing a little light back up into the shadow areas and, crucially, back at her face, which would have been too dark otherwise. The camera was fitted with a 50mm lens, which on this digital SLR gave an effective focal length of 75mm, positioned just 6 feet (1.8m) away.

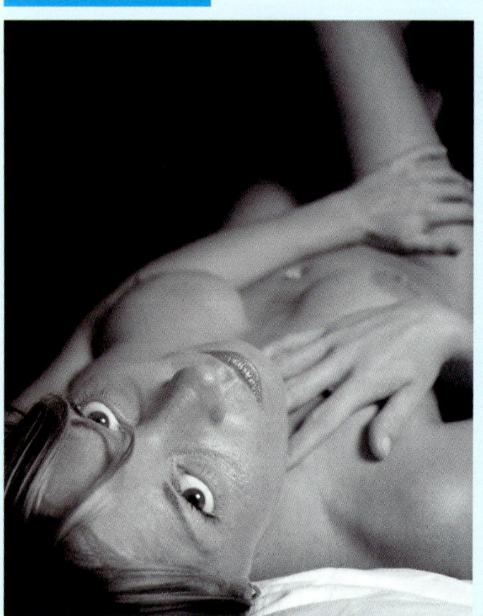

01 The unusual angle, using a wide-open aperture and focusing on the eyes to throw the rest of the picture out of focus, gives this image a sense of vulnerability.

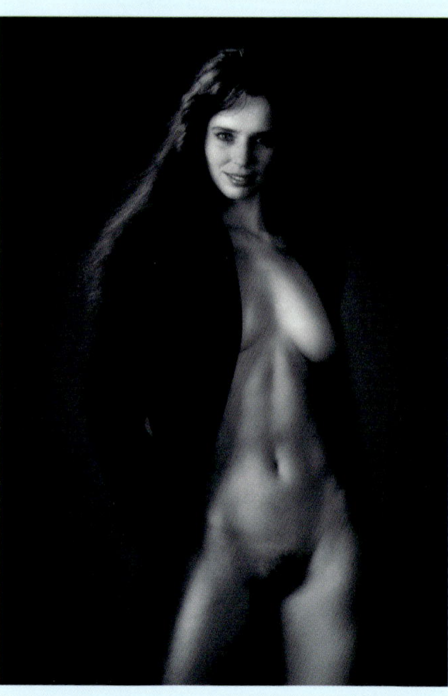

TOP TIP

Focus on the eyes and use a wide aperture to throw the rest of the picture out of focus. This connects the viewer directly to the subject.

02 In this shot from Björn Oldsen, the subject is posing stylishly, in a dynamic fashion. With the smile, the eye contact makes this a happy and positive picture.

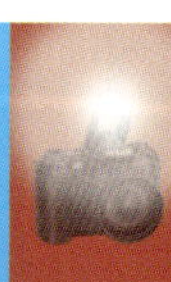

BRIGHT IDEA

Shoot the same image with a range of facial expressions and your subject looking at the camera. Then ask him or her to look away and shoot the same expressions. Compare the two sets to see how different the same picture can look.

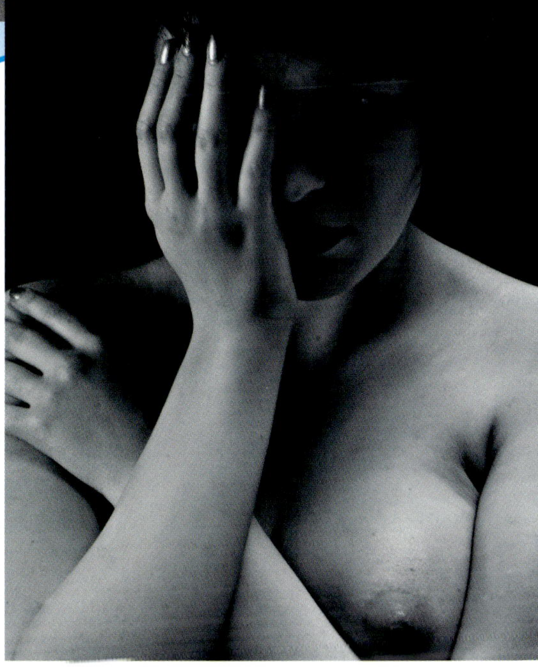

PHOTO EDITING

◀ This image has been composed so that the key light to the left illuminates the model's hand and arm. The overhead light puts light into the hair and reveals the breast to the right. A reflector bounces light back up to the dark side of the model's face to show that she is playing games with the camera.

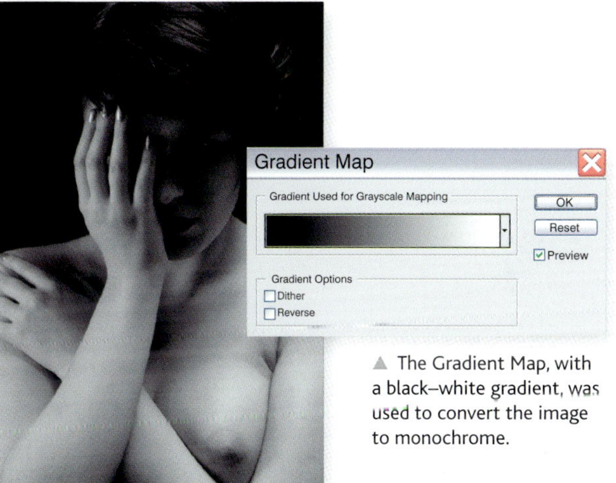

▲ The Gradient Map, with a black–white gradient, was used to convert the image to monochrome.

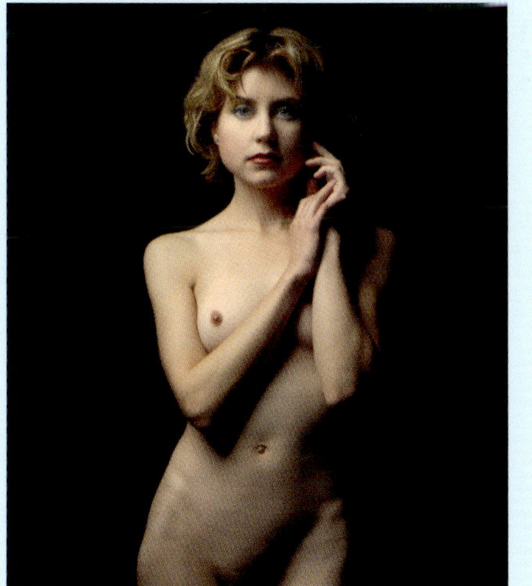

03 The use of side lighting here creates a very subtle-looking picture. The direct gaze of the model hints at melancholy and that she has a story to tell. It makes the picture look like the subject wants to say something, but cannot or will not.

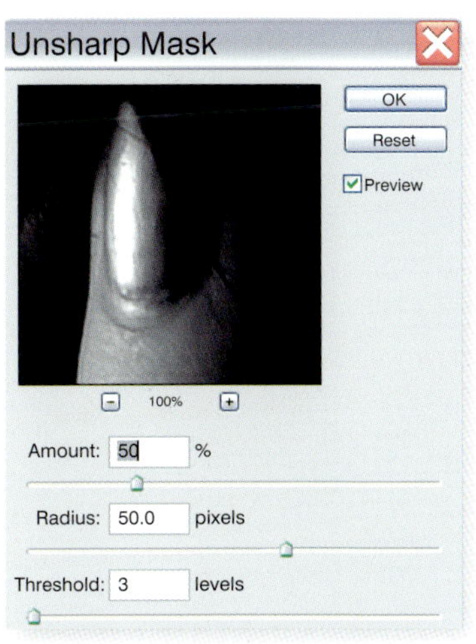

▲ Then the Unsharp Mask filter was used with settings of amount: 50 and radius: 50. Rather than sharpening the image to any degree, this adds a lot of contrast along the lines and borders.

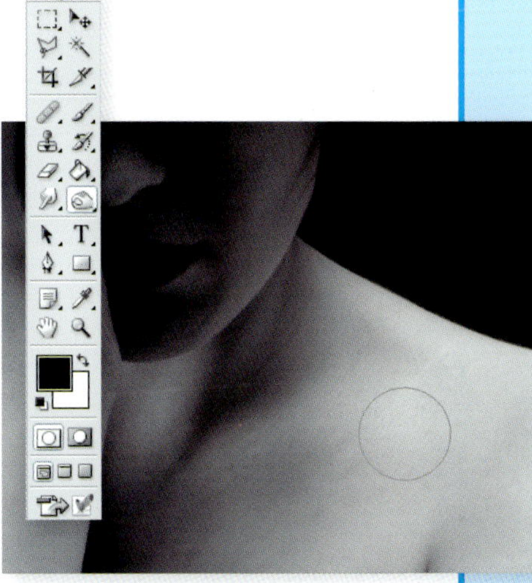

▲ The Burn tool was used to make the darker areas even more dark, and to make the skin textures look more pronounced.

TOOLS AT A GLANCE
CLONE STAMP
IMAGE > ADJUSTMENTS > GRADIENT MAP
FILTER > SHARPEN > UNSHARP MASK
BURN

WIDE ANGLES

There are three reasons why you might use a wide-angle lens. First, if the area is confined so that moving back is impossible, a wide-angle lens allows the width of the scene to be captured. Second, it can be used to include both foreground and background objects in the same shot with the same kind of weighting. Third, it can be used close up to distort the subject's features.

SETTING IT UP

This setup is for the image on the opposite page. There is a key light to the left set at f/11 and a fill light overhead, hanging on a boom, set to f/8. It is important to have enough depth of field in the shot. The 18mm wide-angle lens (27mm equivalent on a digital SLR) was focused on the edge of the chair and panned up to include the subject. You have to juggle getting close enough to the chair and getting in the way of the lights. The camera was set to f/11 at 1/125 sec.

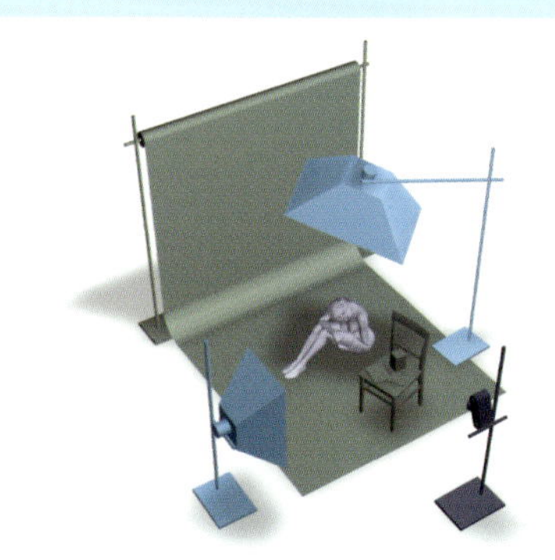

01 Brian Martin's photo shows how you can get quite close to the subject with a wide-angle lens, filling the width of the image, without causing undue distortion, if the subject is flat to the plane of the camera.

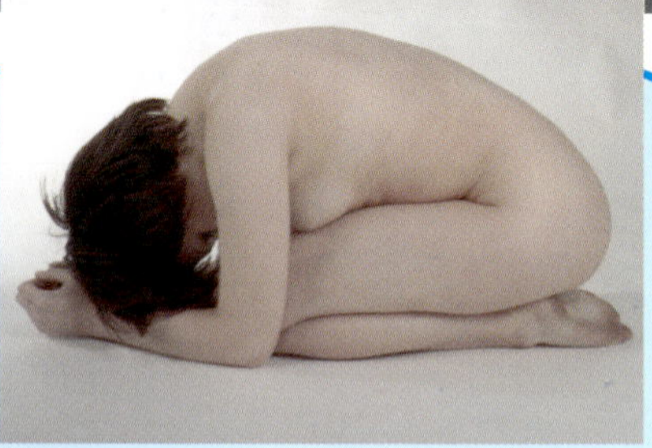

TOP TIP

A wide-angle lens has more depth of field at the same aperture than a telephoto. Use it when you need detail throughout a scene.

02 Here, a wide-angle lens has been used so that more of the background scenery is in the picture. The model's legs seem much longer in comparison to the rest of her figure, but because the camera position has been elevated, the effect is quite subtle.

03 This Stephen Haynes study shows that you can combine some of these ideas by exaggerating the limbs of the model that are near the camera, yet also fill the rest of the composition with space.

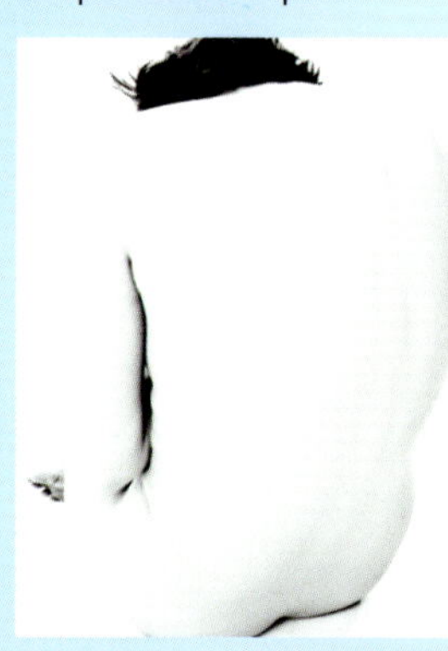

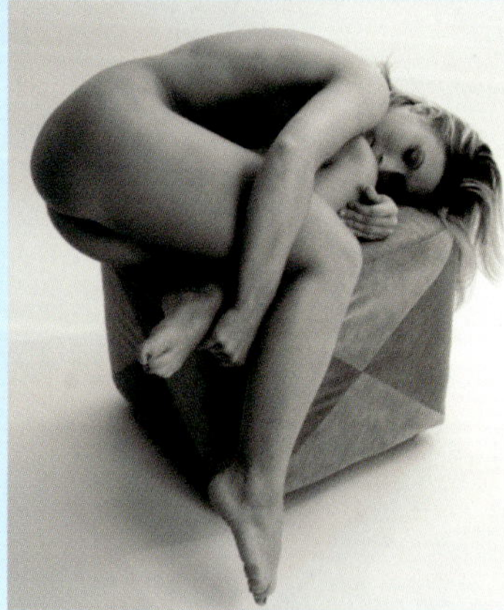

04 By sitting the camera right up against the subject, this being taken at floor level, the wide-angle lens distorts to creative effect. The bowed head becomes little more than a tuft of hair on the enlarged back.

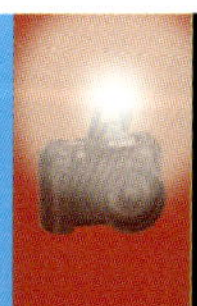

BRIGHT IDEA

With a wide angle, try using a very wide aperture and situate the subject very far away. Focus on something in the foreground and the person in the background will be rendered as an interesting, blurry figure.

PHOTO EDITING

▼ The concept of this picture was to use props to suggest a wartime story. A wide-angle lens was required to get both the chair and props in view along with the model, with them all being in reasonably sharp focus. The camera was right above the chair, but, with an aperture of f/11, the model is also in focus.

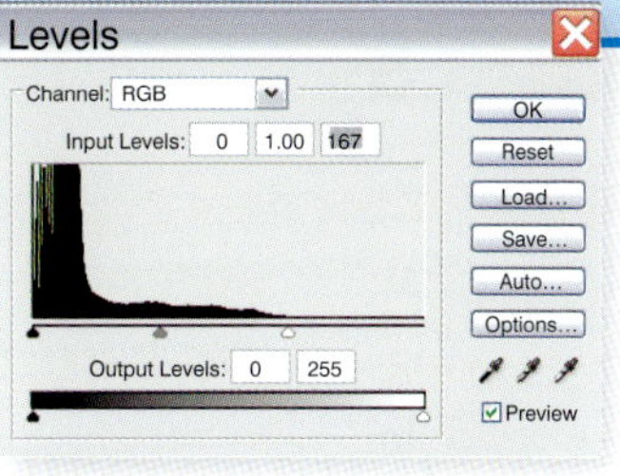

◀ The Levels were adjusted to use the full range of tones.

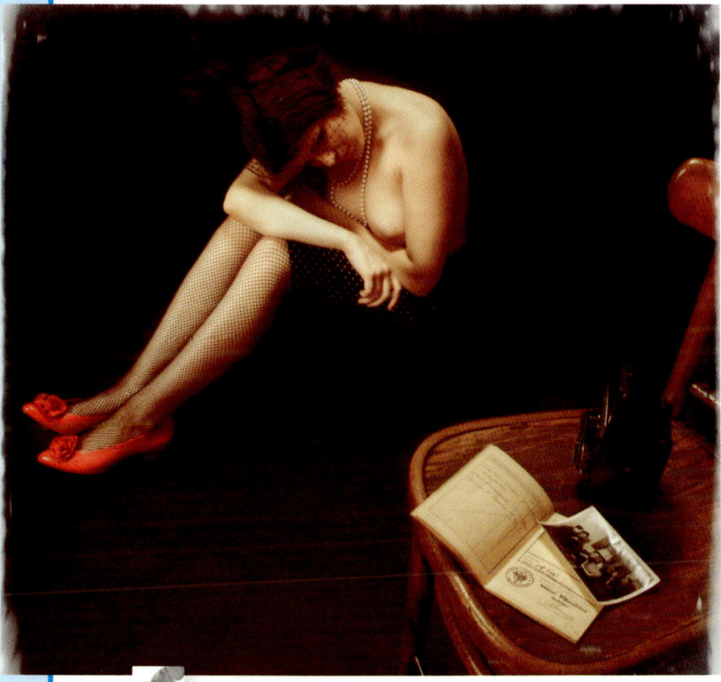

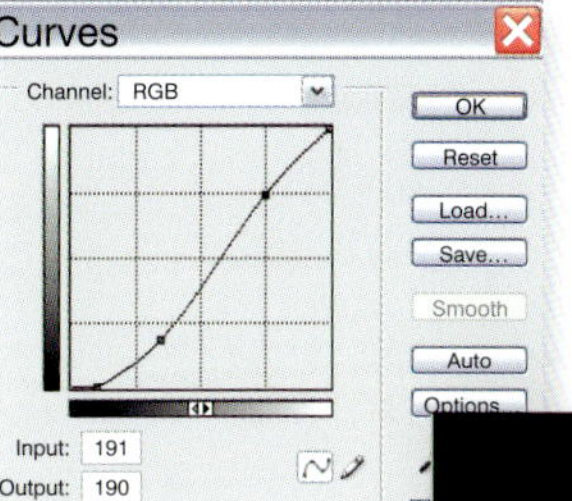

▲ There was too much light on the floor of the scene, so a Curves Adjustment Layer was used to darken it. The Layer Mask was painted on to ensure other areas such as the camera on the chair didn't become too dark.

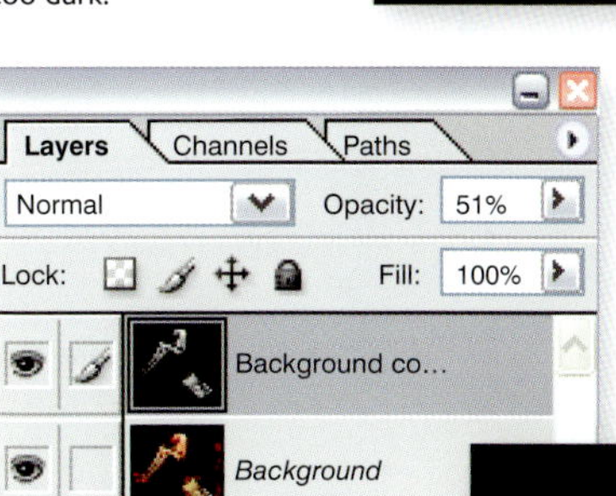

◀ There's too much wasted space above the model, so the Crop tool was used to trim it down and produce a square-format image.

▲ The layers were flattened and then a duplicate layer was created. This was converted to monochrome with the Gradient Map. A sepia tone was added to this layer with variations and then the layer opacity was reduced to 50%. Finally, an edging effect was added.

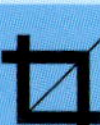

TOOLS AT A GLANCE
CROP
IMAGE > ADJUSTMENTS > LEVELS
CURVES ADJUSTMENT LAYER
DUPLICATE LAYER
IMAGE > ADJUSTMENTS > GRADIENT MAP
IMAGE > ADJUSTMENTS > VARIATIONS
EDGE FILTER

THE IMPERSONAL FORM

One of the strengths of shooting nudes is that you can remove what would be essential in a portrait—the face, head, or features—and concentrate on the figure, form, and lighting. Without the face, direct contact with the viewer is taken away, so there is no automatic assumption about the subject. Instead, the photographer must develop the shape and show lines and character in the image.

SETTING IT UP

You can use a fixed lens of 50mm, which on a digital SLR gives a field of view of 75mm, so taking you right into the figure. Or you can use a short telephoto lens, which gives greater flexibility. With the prime lens you need to move around more, or crop the image later. In the "Tree" image there are two background lights aimed at a white backdrop, one key light to the left of the camera, and a fill light, set to almost the same power, to the right.

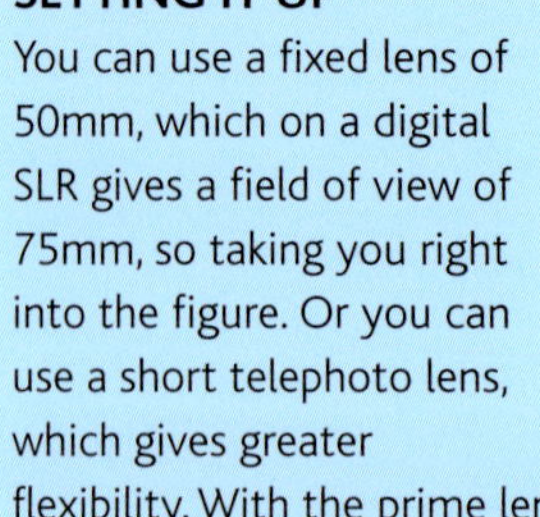

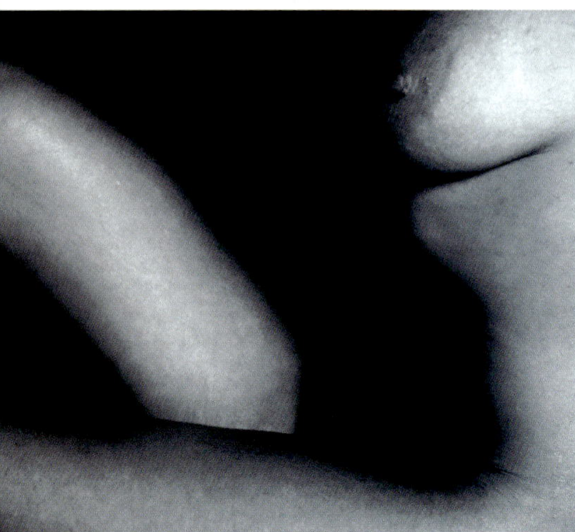

01 This is a basic version of an impersonal shot, showing angled legs against an upright torso. The image was shot against a black background so that no other details would show.

02 This image by Mark Varley shows a development of this concept by placing the model on her side, with lighting from above. The figure is more three-dimensional as she recedes into the distance.

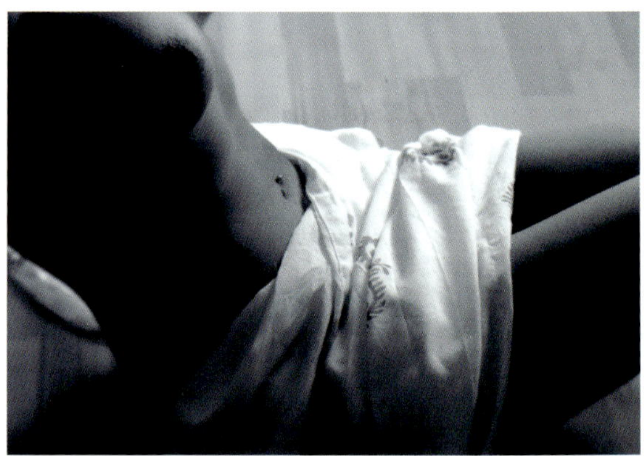

03 Here the key light is on the other side of the model, so the shadows are nearest the camera. The camera points downward, while the model's legs make slightly different angles leading out of the picture.

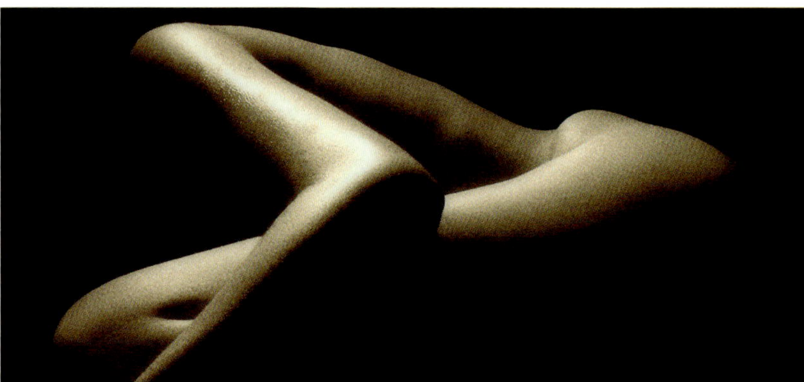

> ### TOP TIP
> To obtain this type of shot, set up the lights then zoom in close. Take a shot then move your model into a different pose while looking through the viewfinder so that you see an impersonal view.

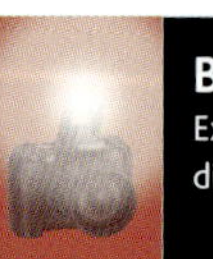

BRIGHT IDEA
Experiment with a shot that does show the head and shoulders by cropping it to see the difference it makes. After cropping, you will need to use interpolation to restore the file size.

PHOTO EDITING

▶ This image was titled "The Tree," as it is a closeup shot showing the model's torso bending up to her hair, which, there being a lot of it, hangs across the top of the image. The lighting for this involved four lights, despite it being such a closeup shot—see the lighting diagram.

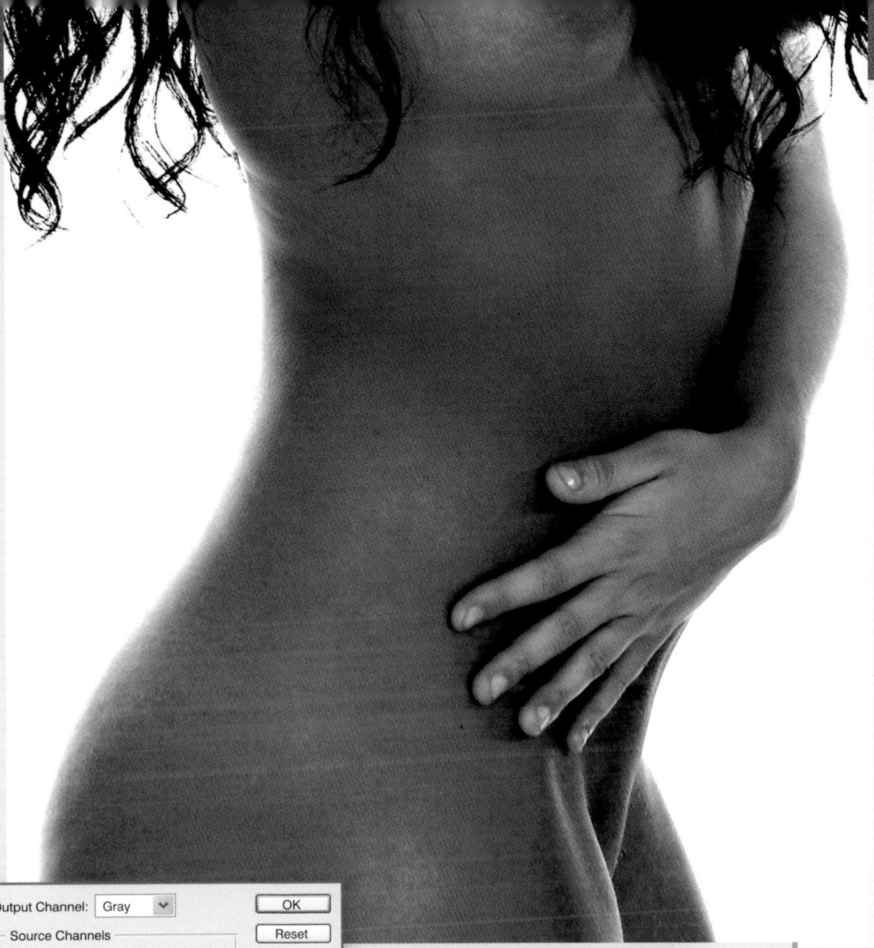

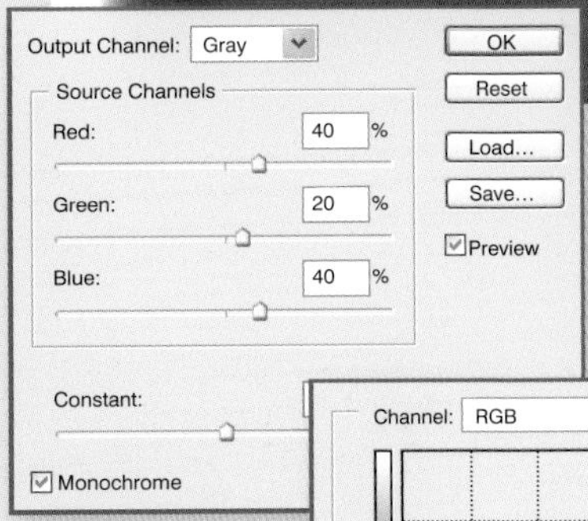

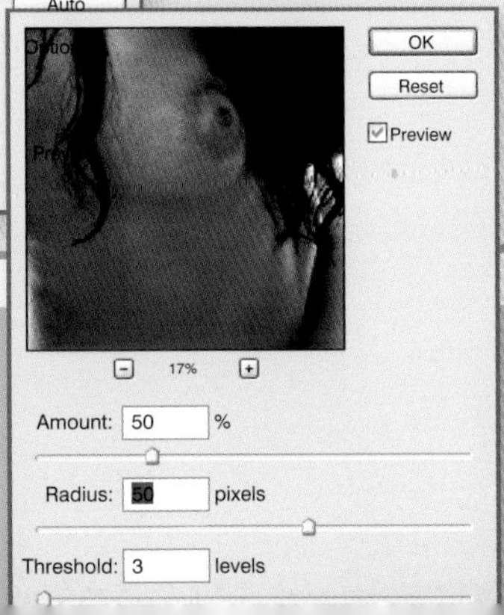

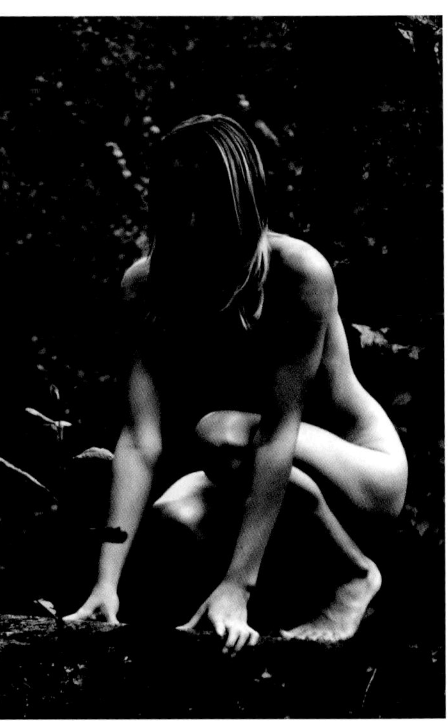

04 In this exterior shot from Mark Varley, we can see the figure well enough, with her smooth limbs placed against a riotous background of texture, but her face is hidden.

▲ To convert the "Tree" image to monochrome, the Channel Mixer was used, with the monochrome box ticked.

▼ Curves was used to slightly increase the contrast.

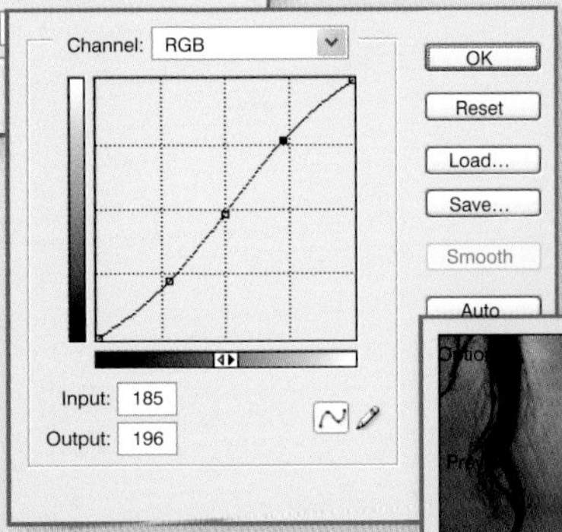

▼ The Unsharp Mask filter, with amount set at 50% and, crucially, the radius set at 50 pixels as well, was used to enhance the texture.

TOOLS AT A GLANCE
IMAGE > ADJUSTMENTS > CHANNEL MIXER
IMAGE > ADJUSTMENTS > CURVES
IMAGE > ADJUSTMENTS > SHARPEN > UNSHARP MASK

ABSTRACT SHAPES

Forget about the face and personality when we talk about abstract shapes; here, the aim is to illuminate body parts and show them in complete isolation. By removing the personality from the picture, the viewer can concentrate on just the form, texture, and lighting. Abstract pictures are usually shot in monochrome, because the reason for shooting them is to prune the picture right back to absolute fundamentals, and color can be a diversion.

SETTING IT UP

In the closeup shot opposite, the light is on the other side of the model, at 45 degrees. The 105mm lens is 6 feet (1.8m) away at f/8. The composition is simple: the model lifts her arms up and stands against the black background. The key is positioning the light so it illuminates only the edge of the figure.

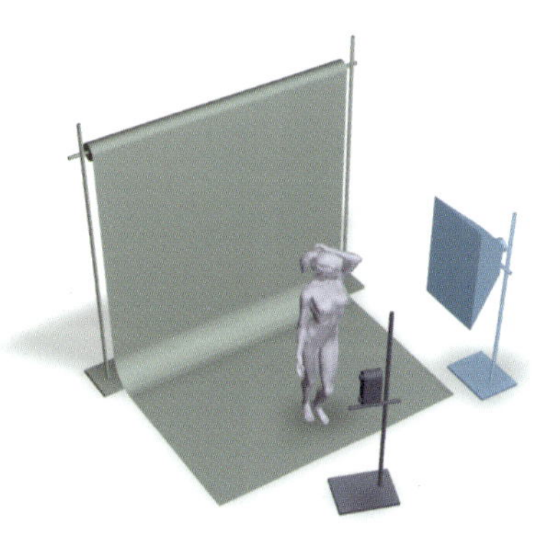

01 Stephen Haynes has concentrated on the rear view here, shot in a high-key style. The addition of the hand adds uncertainty to the picture.

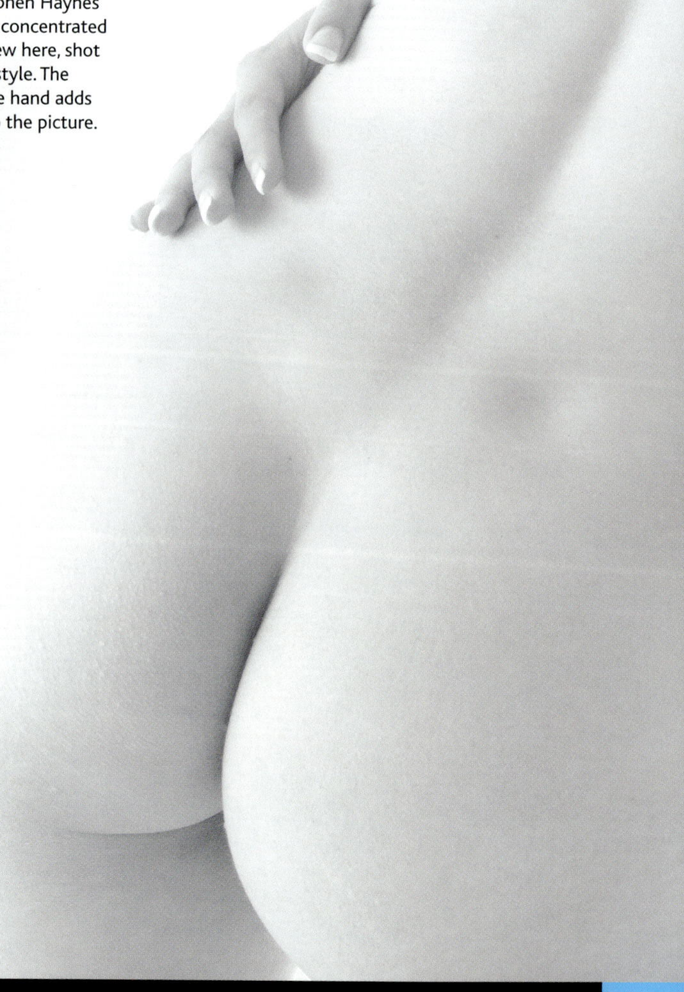

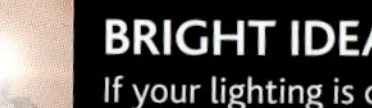

BRIGHT IDEA
If your lighting is covering too much area, use a barn door attachment to narrow the beam, or bounce it off a reflector and use that to direct the light.

PHOTO EDITING

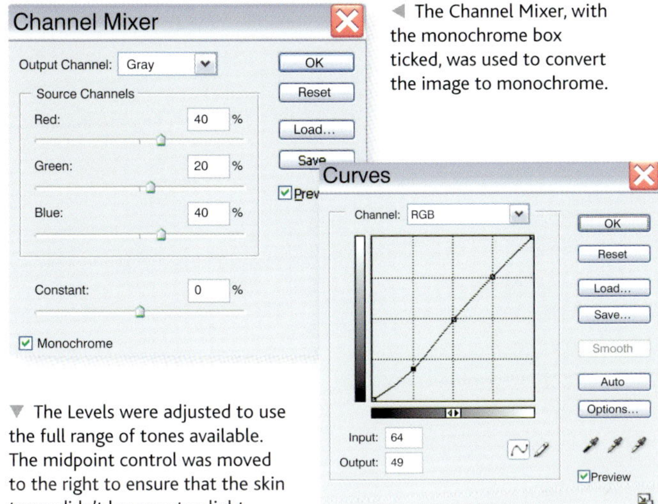

◀ The Channel Mixer, with the monochrome box ticked, was used to convert the image to monochrome.

▼ The Levels were adjusted to use the full range of tones available. The midpoint control was moved to the right to ensure that the skin tones didn't become too light.

▲ The Curves function was run so that the highlights and midtones were locked in position, but the shadows were deepened slightly.

▼ With subtle lighting revealing detail and shape along the edge of the figure, this is a classic abstract nude study from Björn Oldsen. It's all about the shape and the progression from dark, to revealing light, to dark again.

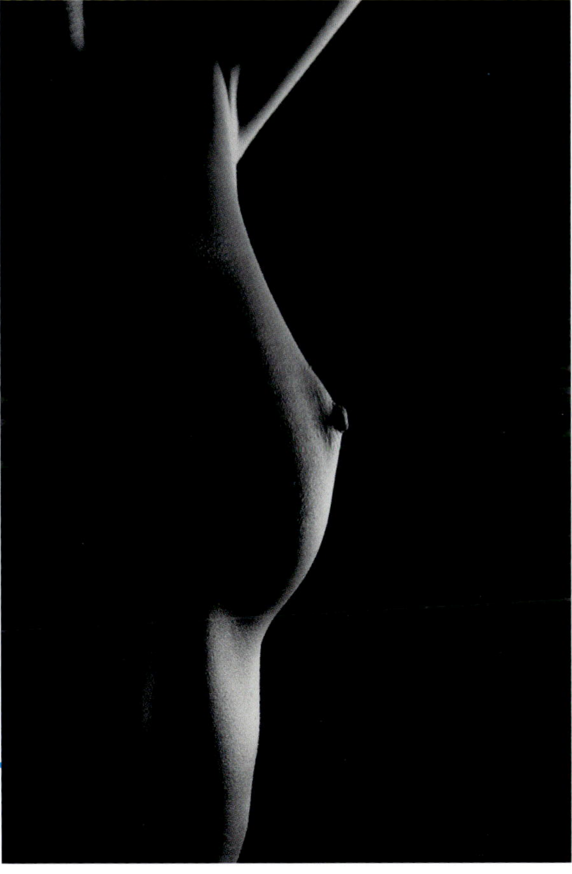

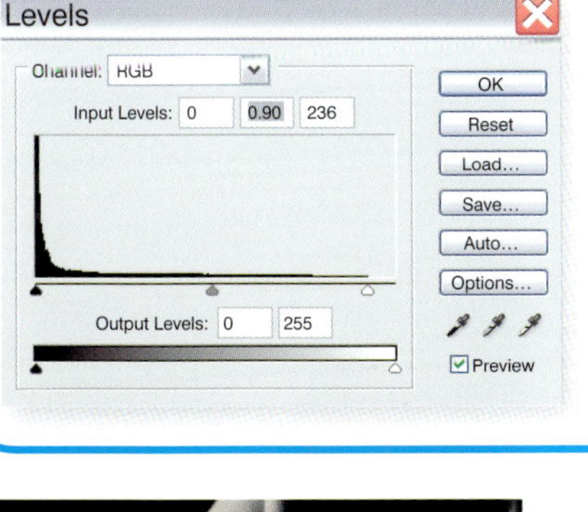

02 This mysterious image with edge lighting revealing a curved shape was shot by Eric Kellerman. It is full of unanswered questions—is the subject leaning through a doorway, going somewhere, or trying to stop something? It is presented in a very graceful style with the gentle loop of the leg, torso, and arm.

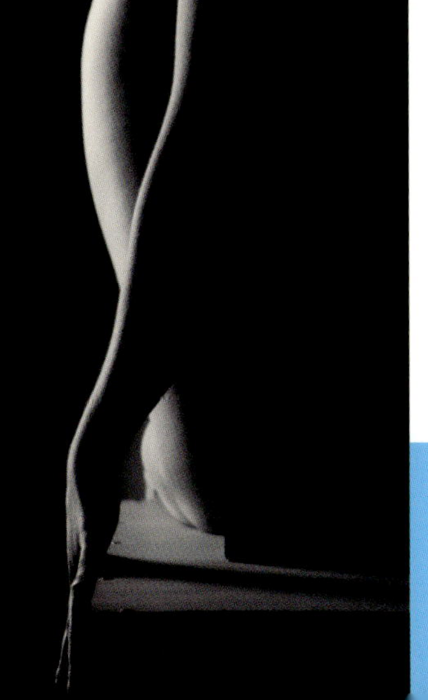

TOP TIP

Electronic flash can be difficult to place accurately with subtle shots, so if the unit has a modeling light, turn it on and use that for more precise positioning.

TOOLS AT A GLANCE
IMAGE > ADJUSTMENTS > CHANNEL MIXER
IMAGE > ADJUSTMENTS > LEVELS
IMAGE > ADJUSTMENTS > CURVES

ASSIGNMENT: BODY PART ABSTRACTS

As part of an artistic project between you and a college student, you have been tasked with shooting a series of body part nude shots. As the subject does not want to be recognized, you cannot include the face, but must concentrate instead on the various elements of the body. Look to find light and shadow and interesting shapes in your composition.

SETTING IT UP

Set up a black background to shoot against, and put one key light off to one side. Take a meter reading from this at, say, f/11. This will help remove any background ambient light. Position a reflector on the other side of the subject's area so that it bounces some light back and provides fill on the opposite side of the figure. The subject can then move and pose in the area between them. Use a 105mm lens, or a medium telephoto lens so that you can get closeup shots while standing about 10 feet (3m) away.

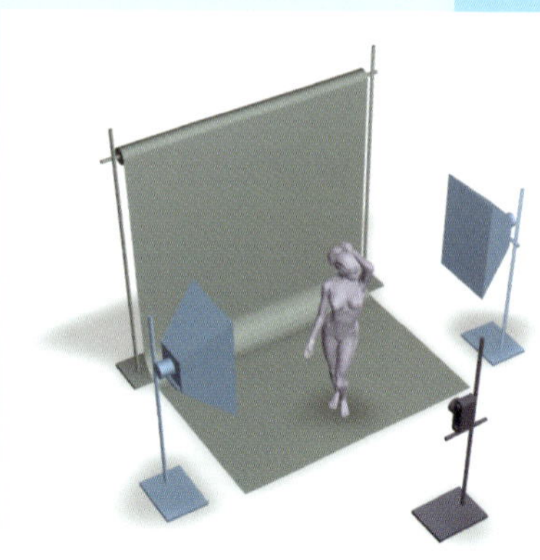

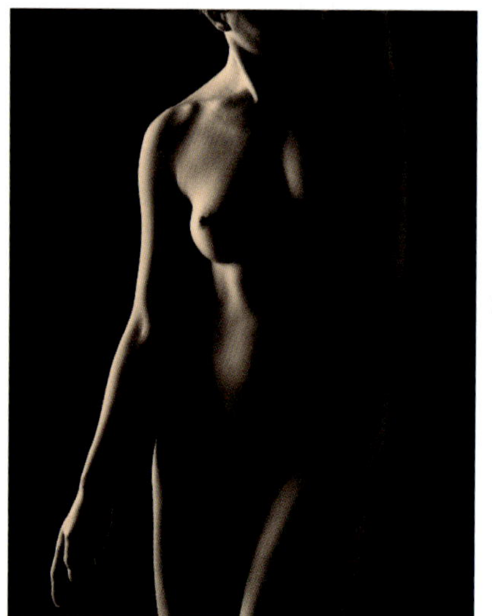

01 It's good to start off with a fuller view, importantly excluding the head in this shot. That way you can see where the light will fall on the model.

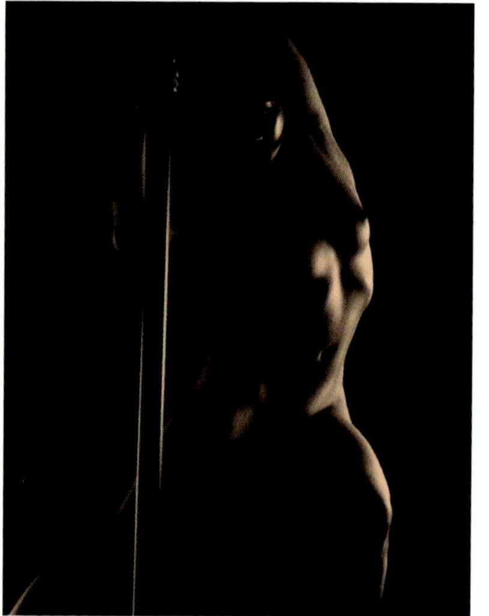

02 The subject has a pole to pose against here, which helps add interest and structure to the composition. The light bouncing back from the reflector turns the model and pole into shadowy silhouettes.

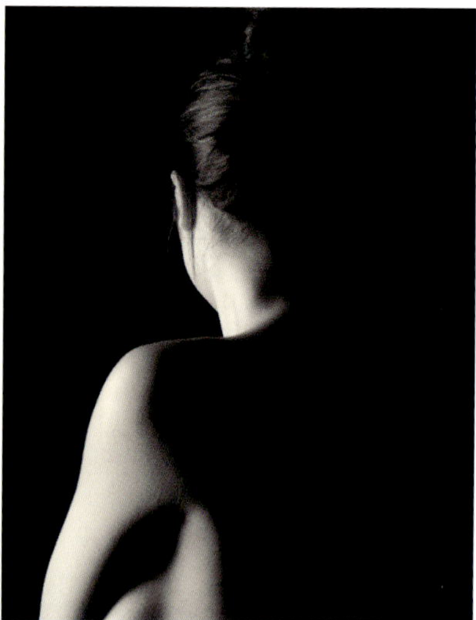

03 With her hair tied up, the model presents the smooth surfaces of the expanse of her back and shoulders.

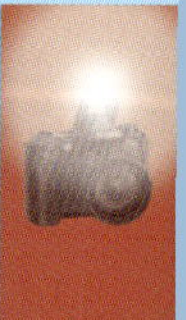

PHOTO EDITING

▶ In this final picture in the series (which were all shot by Eric Kellerman), the reflector has been moved close in to light the fingertips. The position of the hands creates a series of interesting shapes set against the angles of the model's legs.

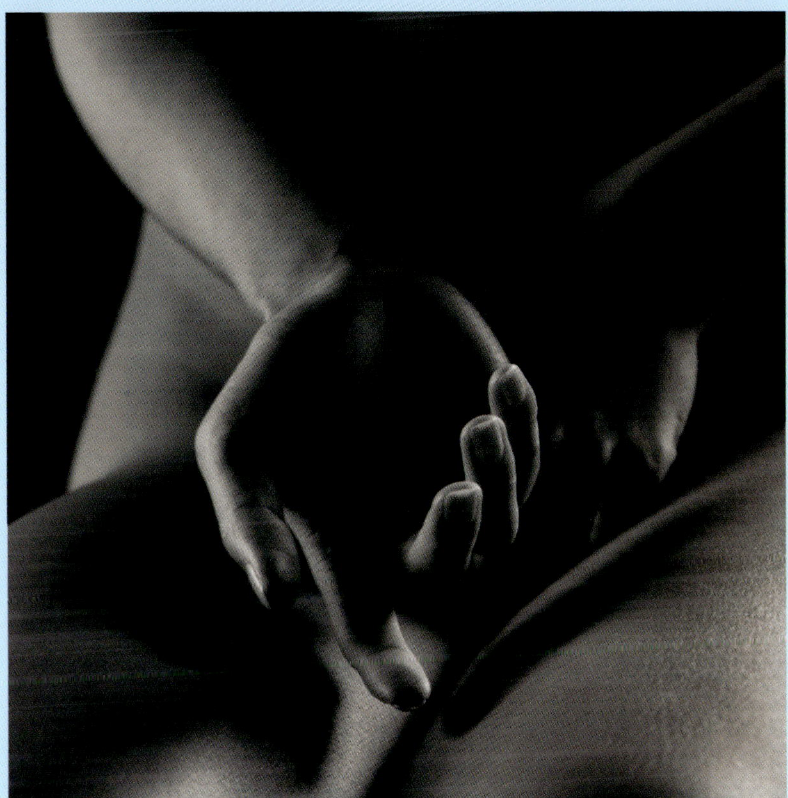

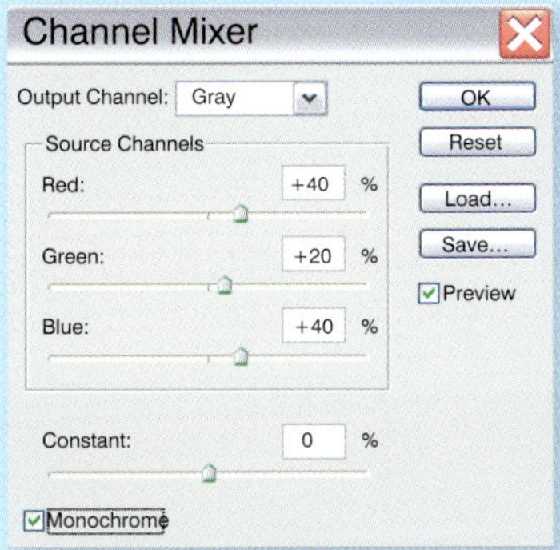

▲ The image was converted to monochrome using the Channel Mixer.

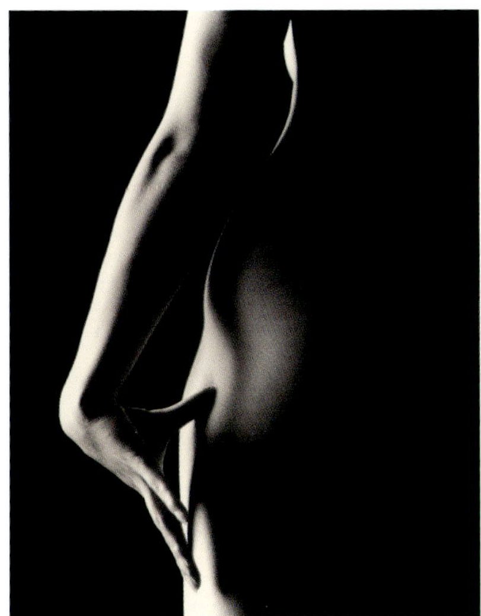

04 This shot just about shows the buttocks, but the emphasis is on the hand shape and the light and shadow patterns that this makes. It gives the image an attitude and style all by itself.

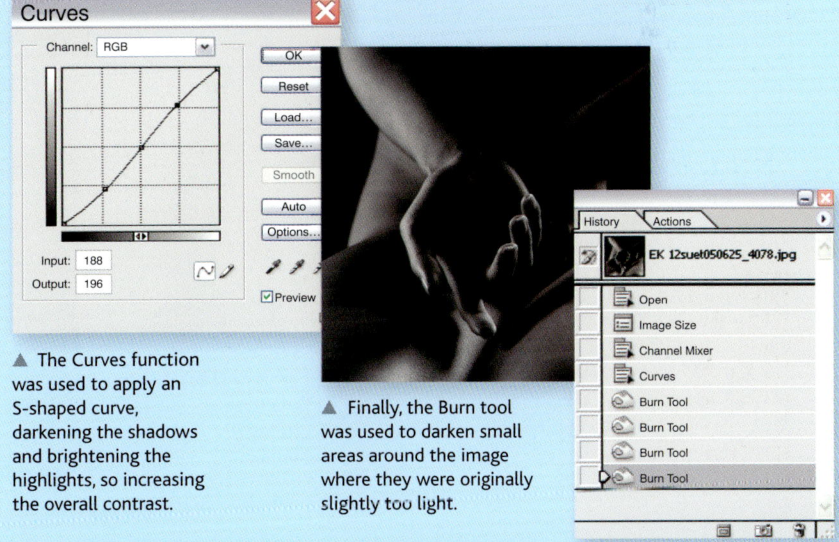

▲ The Curves function was used to apply an S-shaped curve, darkening the shadows and brightening the highlights, so increasing the overall contrast.

▲ Finally, the Burn tool was used to darken small areas around the image where they were originally slightly too light.

TOOLS AT A GLANCE
IMAGE > ADJUSTMENTS > CHANNEL MIXER
IMAGE > ADJUSTMENTS > CURVES
BURN TOOL

USING PROPS

Props can be used to put nervous subjects at ease and to give them something to do with their hands. The other reasons for using props is to give a flavor to the scene, to add to the atmosphere, or to enhance the composition. The props can be placed in the scene without being used by the subject. In this case, they are there as set decoration. Flowers, vases, paintings, and antiques can all be used for effect. Often, the prop can be the whole point of the image, being the lead element that focuses attention, or it can be a device that adds meaning.

SETTING IT UP

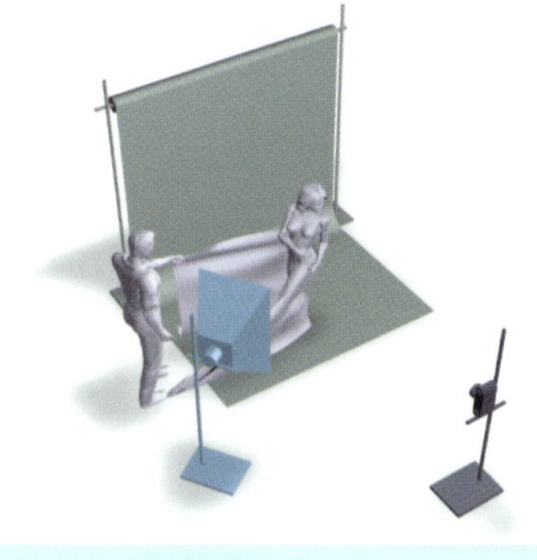

In the main picture here, the key light is just to the left of the camera, lighting up the subject and the fabric, and allowing the right side of the picture to fade to shadow. The fabric is pulled tight around the back of the subject and is held off-screen. The camera is around 12 feet (3.6m) away, with the focal length set to around 50mm.

TOP TIP

When adding a prop to a scene, check how bright and reflective it is; it might stand out more than you expect, and dominate the scene.

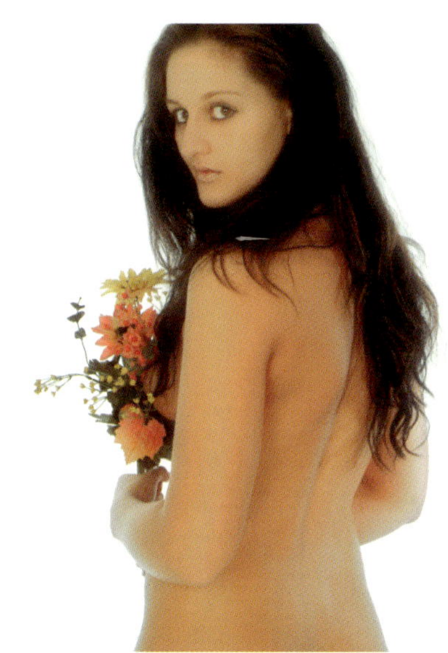

01 If your subject is nervous, give them something to hold. A bunch of flowers kept this model from fidgeting.

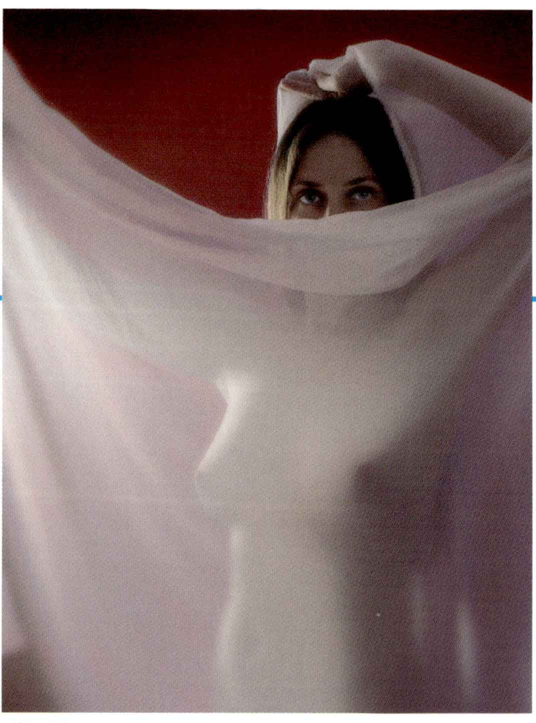

02 Fabrics are great to play with and can be used to diffuse light. As Stephen Haynes demonstrates here, fabric and lighting can be used to focus attention on the model's eyes, giving the picture a dramatic element.

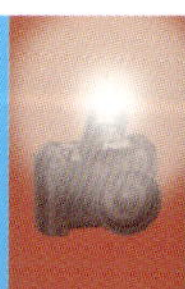

BRIGHT IDEA

Bring a few bits and pieces to a shoot and try the same shot with different props. Then check out which one worked best on screen.

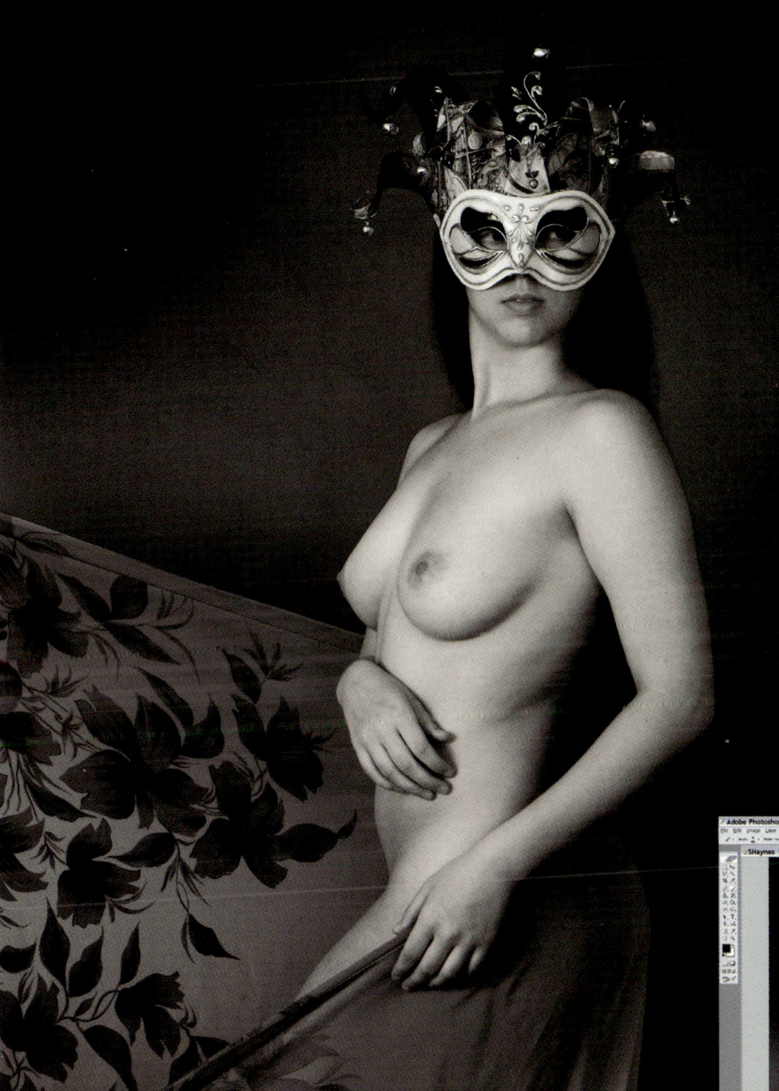

PHOTO EDITING

◀ The use of masks and fabrics lifts this picture by Stephen Haynes right out of the ordinary, giving it a Renaissance or Venetian feel. The fabric is pulled tight to the subject, creating areas of pattern, while the mask provides baroque decoration and hides the face.

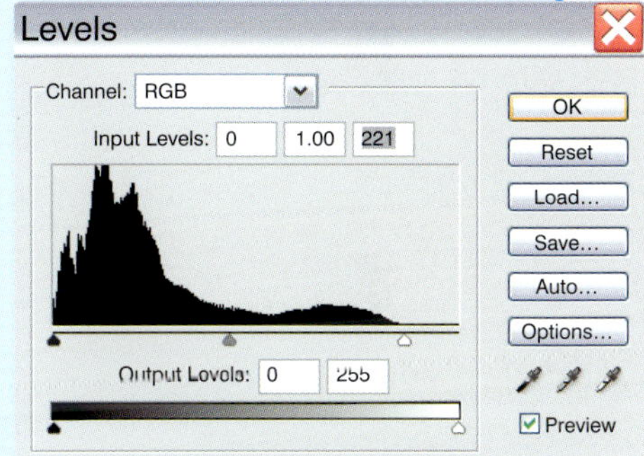

▲ The Levels were adjusted to ensure all the tonal range was used.

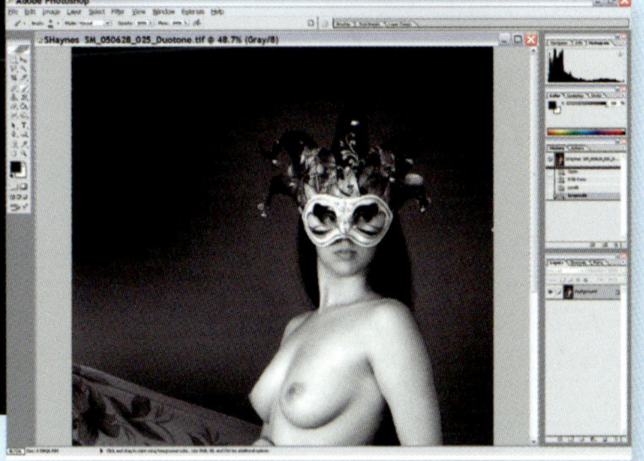

▶ The image was converted to grayscale mode, discarding the color information for the next step. You cannot go directly from RGB to duotone.

▶ A duotone was applied by changing the mode to duotone and selecting black and a light sepia color.

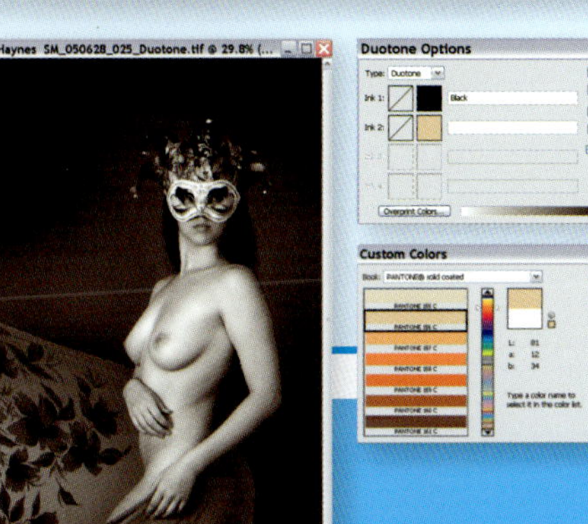

TOOLS AT A GLANCE
IMAGE > ADJUSTMENTS > LEVELS
IMAGE > MODE > GRAYSCALE
IMAGE > MODE DUOTONE

ASSIGNMENT: VEILS

You've been commissioned to shoot some nude studies of a model for her portfolio. She's new to modeling and in clothed studies has found it difficult to know what to do with her hands and arms. You must use a prop to give her something to do. For our shoot, the prop is a length of golden fabric, as the color complements the model's skin-tone. Your assignment is to produce a set of three-quarter-length studio shots featuring the model interacting with something so she doesn't look awkward.

SETTING IT UP

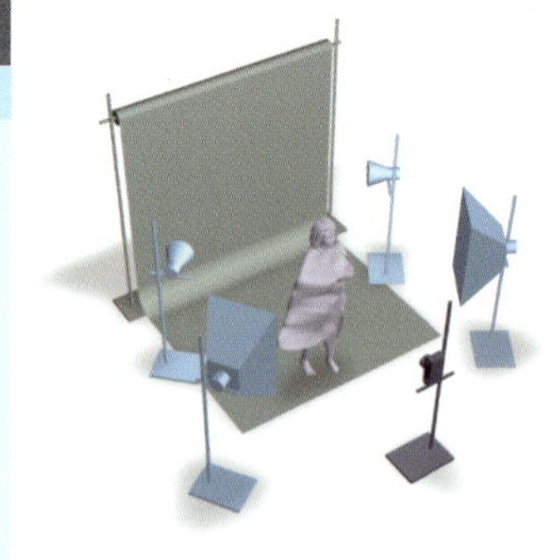

This is relatively easy to set up. Position flash units with softboxes to the left and right, at 45 degrees of the camera. Meter these for a power reading of f/11. Further down the set, use two smaller lights, on either side, to fire at the white background, using no diffusion. Set the power on these to f/16. This will ensure the background is rendered white. Stand 10 feet (3m) back from the model with a 50mm lens. Your model can now move around freely in the middle, which should help her relax.

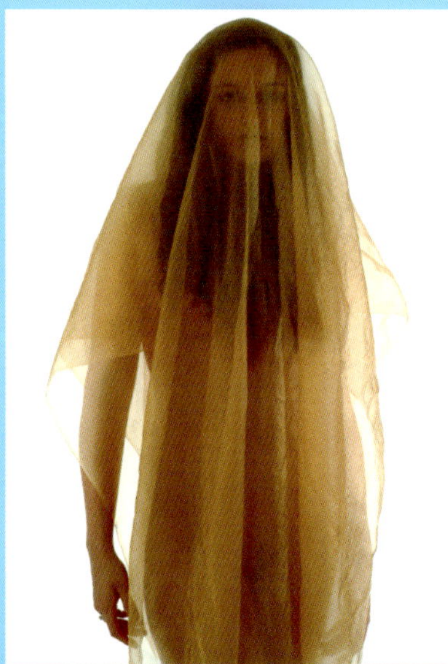

01 With a subject who might be tense, it's a good idea to try out ideas that are wacky or funny. The aim is not to get a great shot but to lead the subject into the shoot. Remember; with digital, it isn't costing you anything. Here the model placed the fabric over her head and adopted a solemn look.

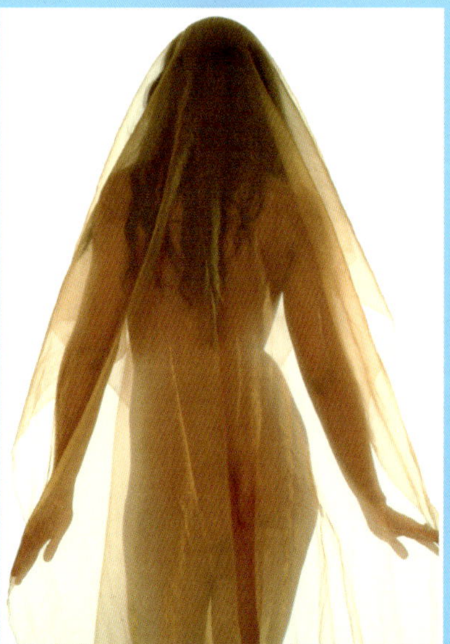

02 Here the model is asked to move around, moving her hands out so that they are interacting with the fabric. This is already better than the last shot.

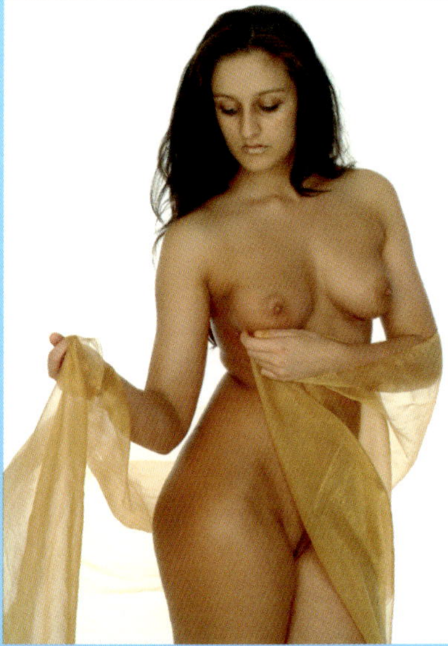

03 Now more relaxed, the model is asked to wrap the fabric around her torso. This gives the hands and arms something to do, leading to natural poses. Watch the head though, as she may start looking at the fabric or the prop.

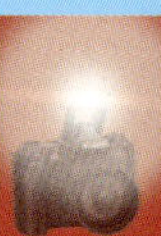

BRIGHT IDEA

If you are stuck for a prop to use on location, try a candle. You will need a tripod because of the low light levels, but the warm glow will add to the picture.

PHOTO EDITING

▶ This is the best of the shots. The fabric is wrapped around the model, but flows away from the direction in which she is looking. She is now not posing directly for the camera, but wrapped in a golden swathe of fabric.

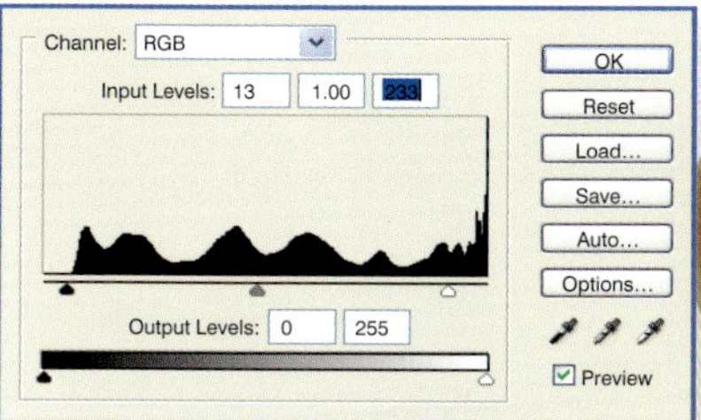

▲ Levels was used to ensure that the background was completely white, by moving the control carat on the right in a small amount.

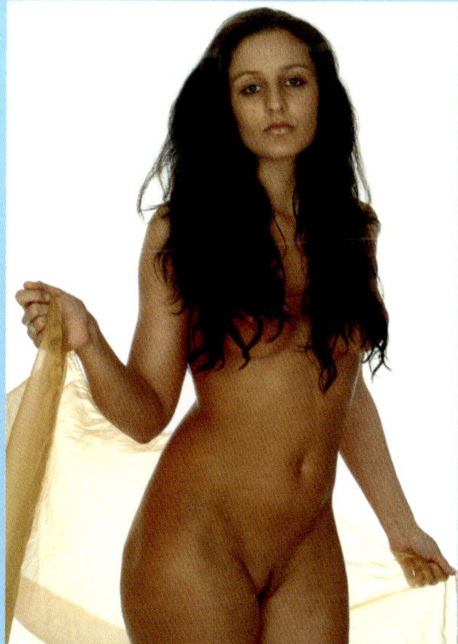

04 Now we're fully engaged with the shoot, the background light shines back through the fabric, and the model feels confident enough to look directly into the camera.

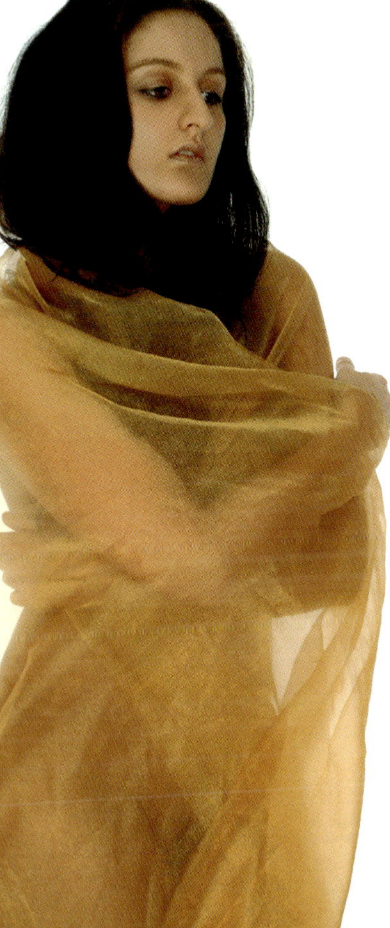

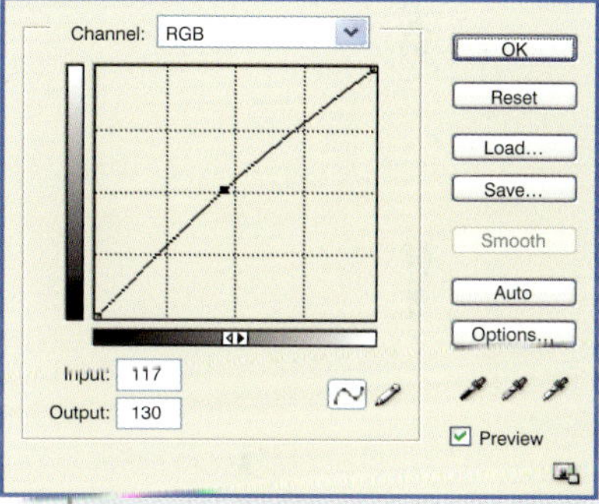

▲ The body and fabric were then brightened, bringing out the color more, by using Curves and just pulling the line upward.

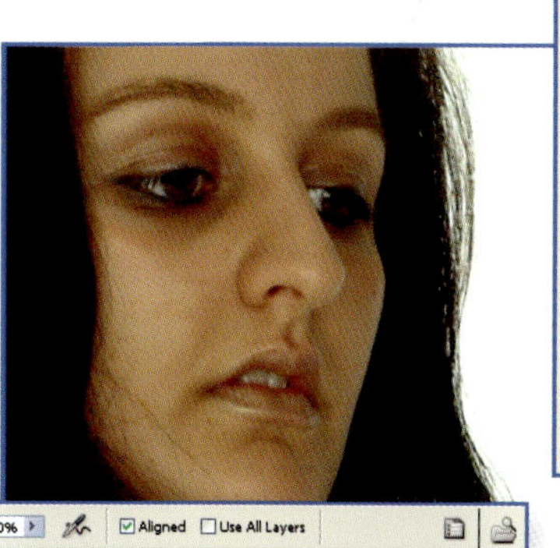

▲ The Clone Stamp tool in the lighten mode at 100% opacity was used to remove the loose hairs across the face. Then the mode was changed to normal and the opacity set to 20% to smooth out blemishes.

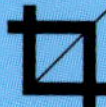

TOOLS AT A GLANCE
IMAGE> ADJUSTMENTS > LEVELS
IMAGE > ADJUSTMENTS > CURVES
CLONE STAMP

NUDES TOGETHER

The nude study can be one of form and abstract shapes, but when a second figure is added, the element of human interaction comes into play. This can be between the figures themselves, or simply in the interpretation by the viewer who draws meaning and inference, regardless of what may or may not be the case. There is also a large difference between adding a male and a female character to the composition, which can affect how the two figures interact.

SETTING IT UP

The key element in this picture was the tight composition and arrangement of the figures. The lighting consisted of two flash heads, one on either side of the camera at 45 degrees. The figures were arranged on a dark fabric against a black background. The key light on the right was set to f/11 power, while the second light on the left was set to f/9.5. The camera lens was set at 75mm on a 28–105mm lens so a tight crop could be achieved from around 10 feet (3m) away.

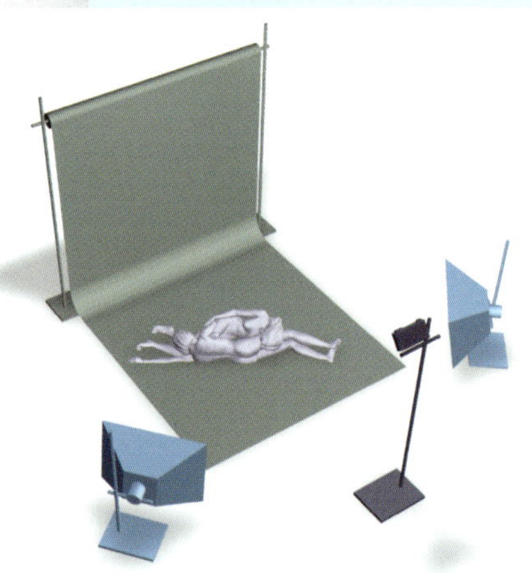

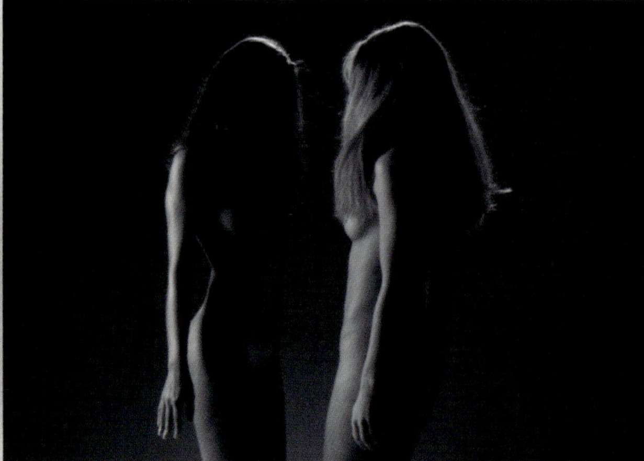

01 The first of a pair of images from Björn Oldsen shows two female figures facing each other. The meaning here is ambiguous. Is this a confrontation? The fact that the models' faces are hidden adds to the mystery.

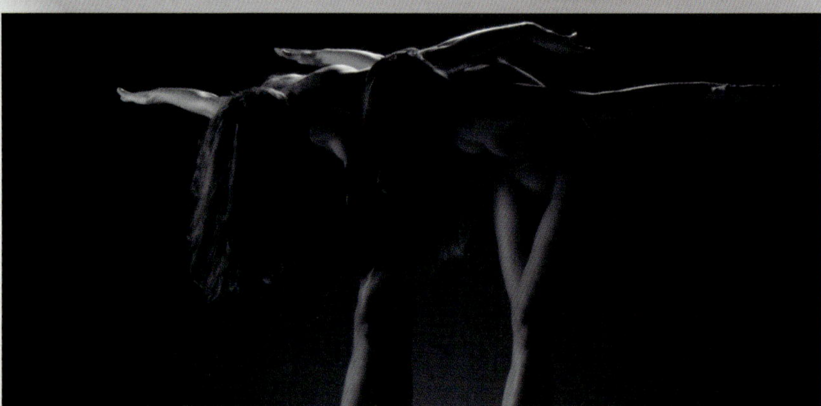

02 In this second image from Björn, the two figures pose together. This is far less mysterious because it is an obvious, deliberate pose, with the two subjects forming a graceful image. The hidden faces are now part of the imagery and the overall effect is far more traditional.

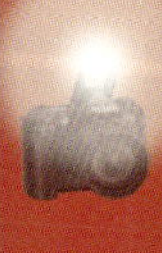

BRIGHT IDEA

If your subjects are becoming nervous, then start with darker lighting schemes and with the subjects well apart. As the shoot progresses and they become more confident, get them to move closer together.

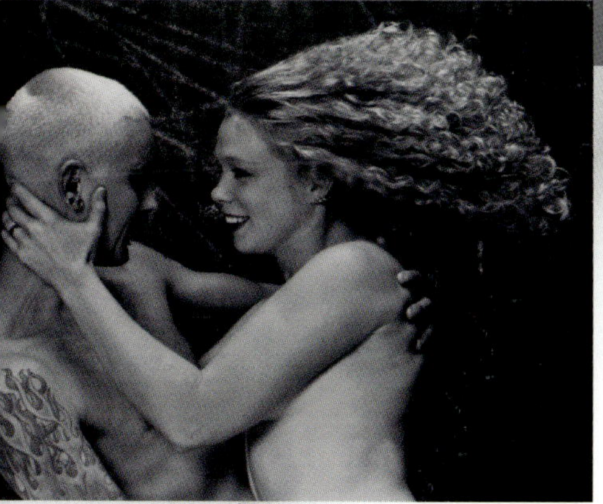

PHOTO EDITING

▶ Stephen Haynes' picture is like a nude representation of Yin and Yang, with the subjects gracefully curving around, one ending where the other starts.

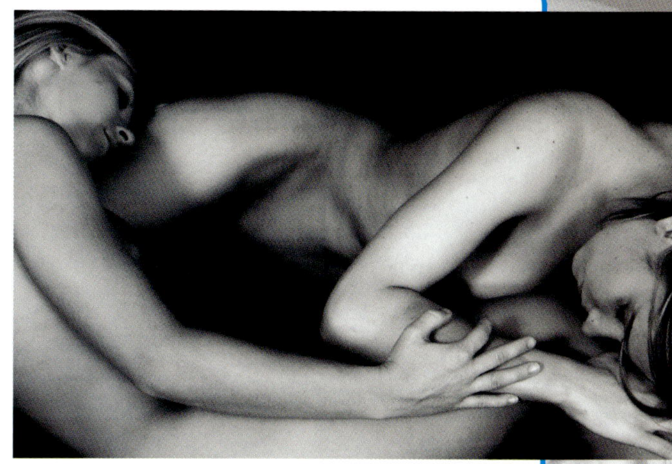

03 When the figures interact, it adds a whole new level of interest and intrigue because of how we perceive relationships. Alan Cockburn's picture could be an advert for hair products because it is so stylized and the figures are so happy. Getting male and female subjects to get this close while naked without looking uncomfortable requires skill on the photographer's part and experience on the models'.

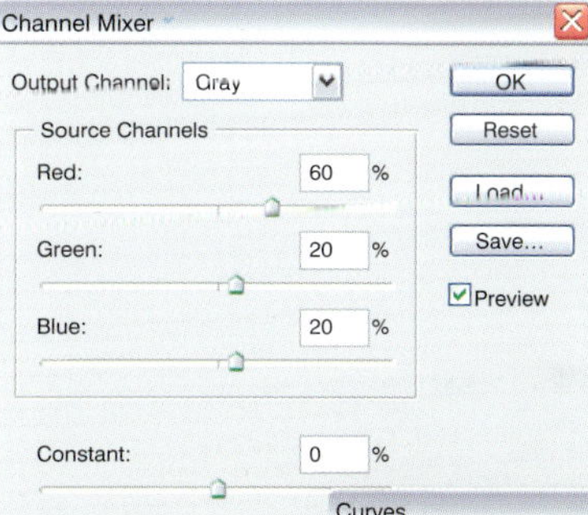

◀ The Channel Mixer was used to convert the image to black and white, with a high red component to get very white skin tones.

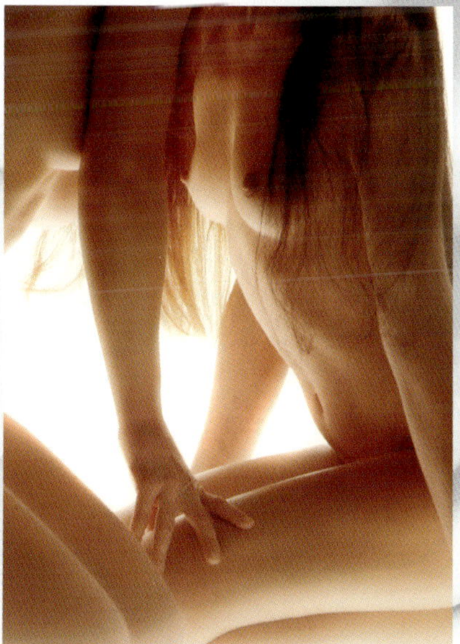

04 In this image from Björn Oldsen, the cropping of the subjects' heads is a nod toward classical nude photography that concentrates on the models' form rather than their personalities.

◀ The Curves function was used to darken the shadow areas, while control points held the midtones and highlights in place.

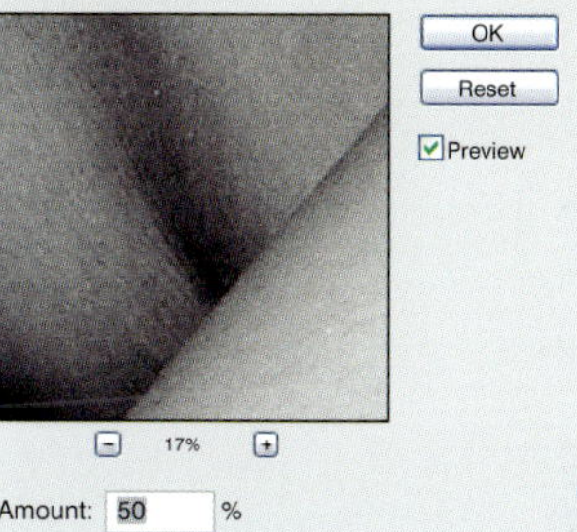

▶ Finally, the Unsharp Mask filter was used to add sharpness and bring out textures without making the image too crisp.

> **TOP TIP**
> To give your subjects greater room to move and give them the illusion of privacy, use a telephoto and stand 20–30 feet away.

TOOLS AT A GLANCE
IMAGE > ADJUSTMENTS > CHANNEL MIXER
IMAGE > ADJUSTMENTS > CURVES
FILTER > SHARPEN > UNSHARP MASK

ASSIGNMENT: SHOOTING COUPLES

To put your photographic and social skills to the test, this assignment is a tough one. You have to start with a male model and get him into the swing of posing naked in the studio. Pose a couple of photos with a lighting scheme that shows his muscle definition. Then add a female model and get the two to work together, contrasting the sleeker lines of the female form and more muscular attributes of the male. Your challenge is to get them to interact to produce a powerful image that plays on the dynamic between the male and the female.

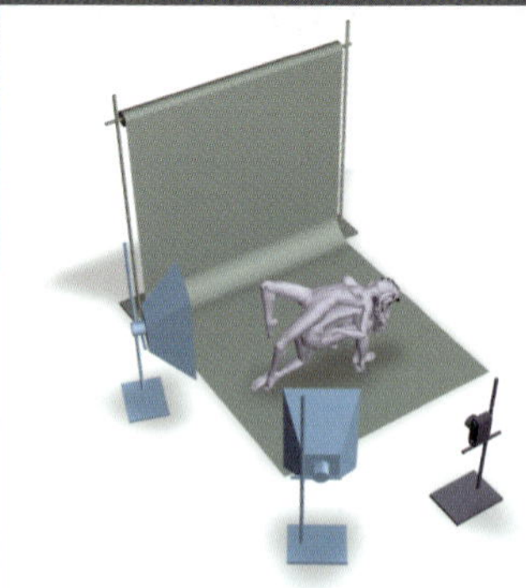

SETTING IT UP

The lighting scheme needs to produce defined shadows on the subjects, but not be so precise that a little movement will ruin the effect. This means you should forget about a small hair light and only use one if it will cover a wide area. In the main image from the series by Alan Cockburn, the key light is behind the subjects at 45 degrees and to the left, with a fill light to the left and in front of the subjects. The camera lens is 28mm shot from around 12 feet (3.6m) away.

TOP TIP

After you have shot all the regular ideas, try some more unusual ones where depth of field becomes an issue and one of the subjects is in focus and the other is behind them and out of focus.

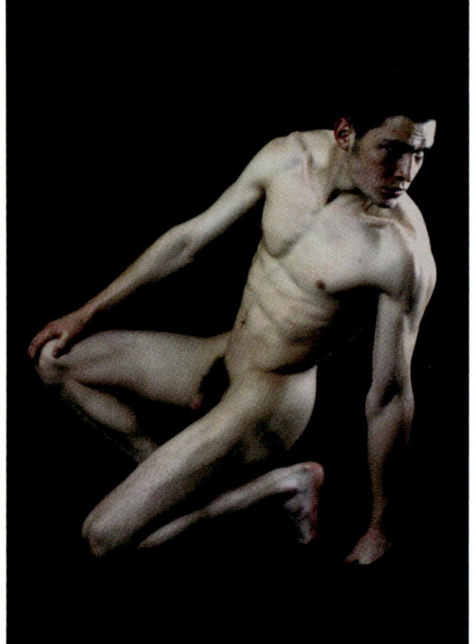

01 To start with, the key light was on the right-hand side behind the subject. He is looking into it while his torso is angled across the beam of the fill light so that chest definition is acquired.

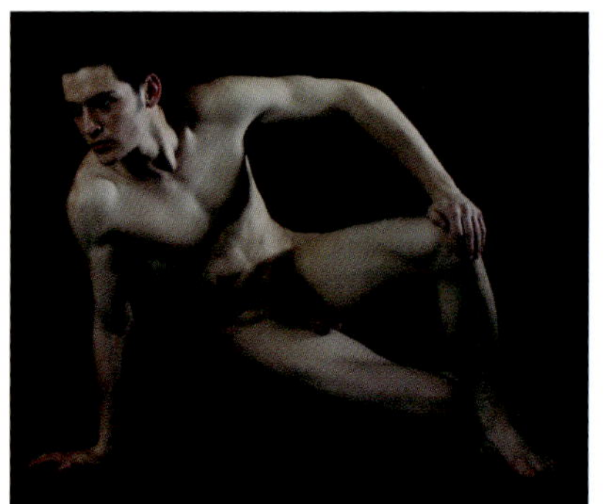

02 After turning around and stretching in the opposite direction, it became obvious that there were some deficiencies in the lighting scheme, as the raised left arm threw a distinct shadow over the chest. However, after a few poses on his own, the model was ready to interact.

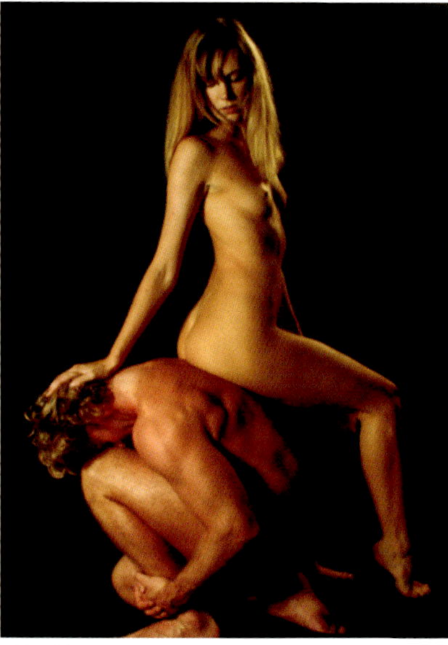

03 This was a shot from a previous session and is included here to show you what not to shoot. The subjects should interact, but not in a way that looks awkward, as this couple does.

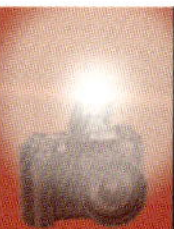

BRIGHT IDEA

The easiest way to find a couple to pose together is to ask models who they have worked with, or who they know that they can work with. Finding a couple who are at ease together makes shooting far easier than two uncomfortable people who have never met.

PHOTO EDITING

▶ This is the winning picture, allowing the powerful male to be a sturdy prop for the curves and athletic form of the female. The lighting scheme allows highlights to show on the upper surfaces of the female model while plunging the head areas of both into shadow.

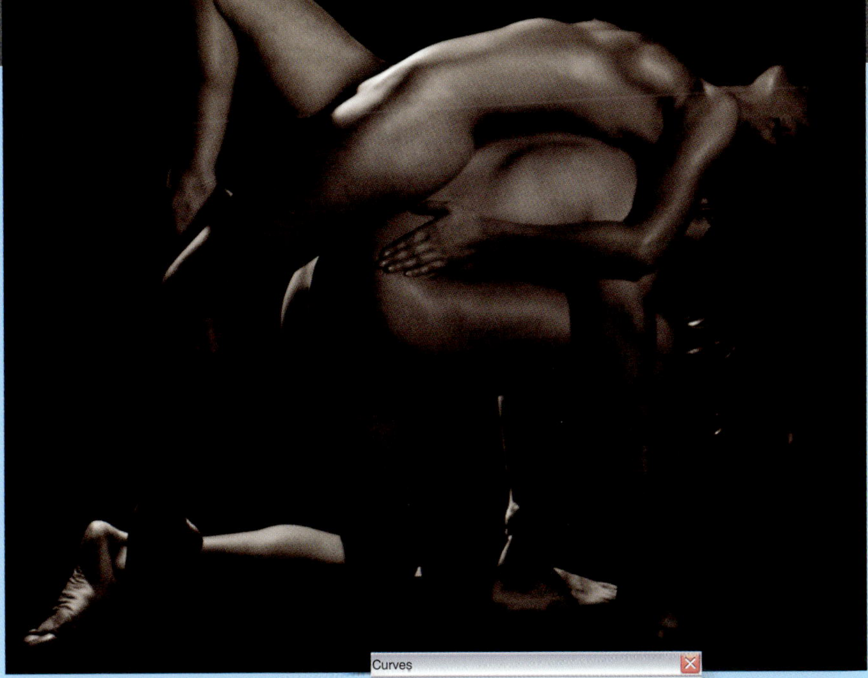

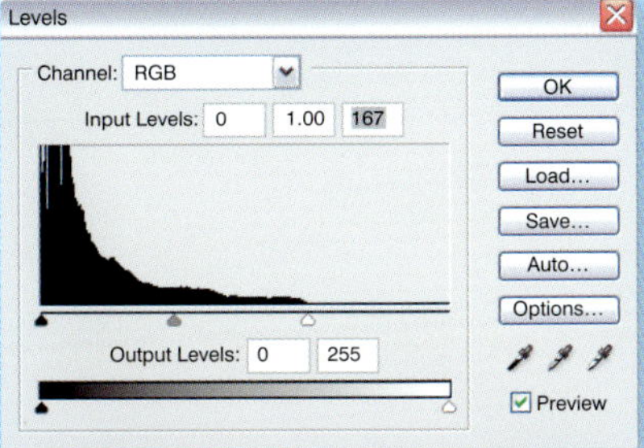

▲ The picture was underexposed from the regard of using all the available tones. A Levels Adjustment Layer was applied to amend this.

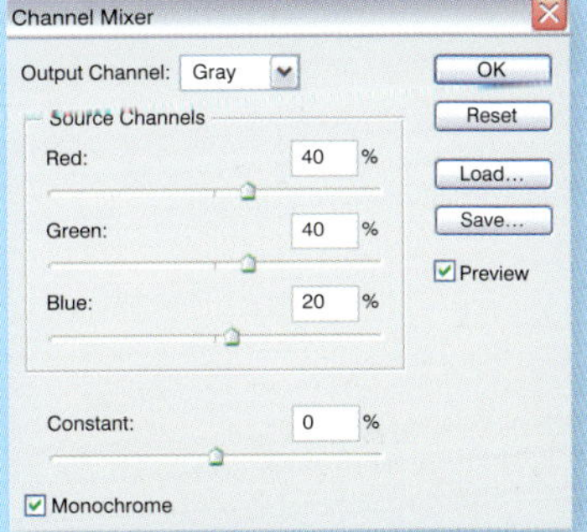

▲ Conversion to black and white was carried out with the Channel Mixer.

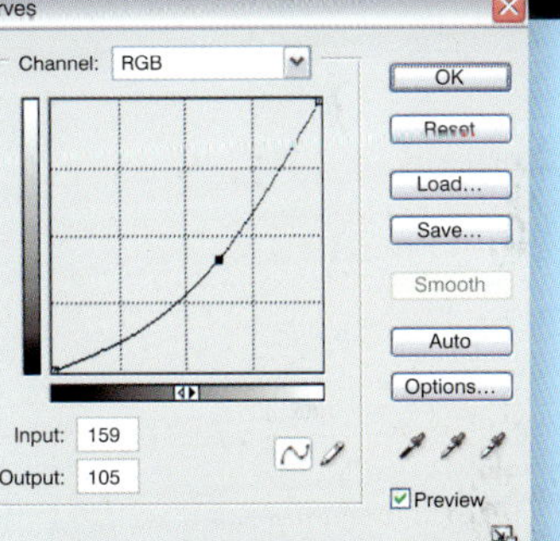

◀ The image was too bright so Curves was used to substantially darken all tones, particularly the middle ones.

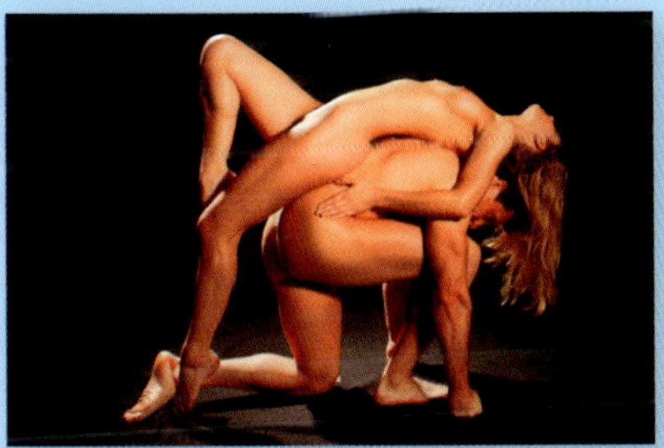

▲ The Crop tool was used to produce a more square composition that was tighter to the subjects, avoiding wasted space on the sides.

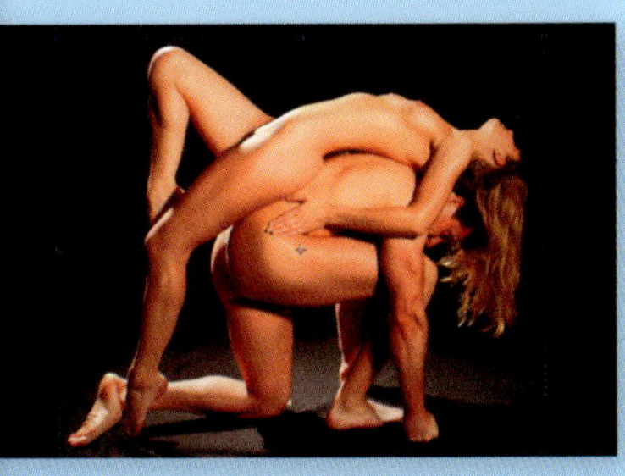

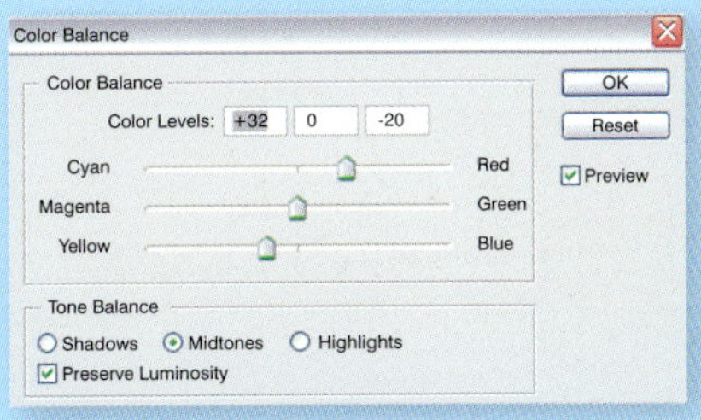

▲ The Color Balance control was then used to add yellow and red tints, giving a sepia-like effect.

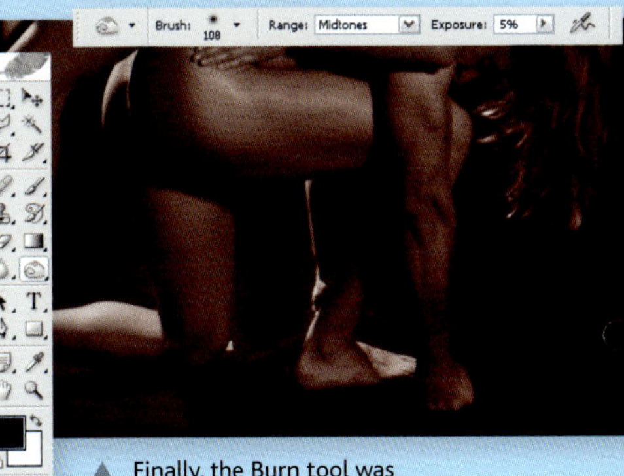

▲ Finally, the Burn tool was used to darken areas around the feet of the models on the floor to make it more subdued.

⌗ TOOLS AT A GLANCE

LEVELS ADJUSTMENT LAYER
CROP TOOL
IMAGE > ADJUSTMENTS > CHANNEL MIXER
IMAGE > ADJUSTMENTS > COLOR BALANCE

IMAGE > ADJUSTMENTS > CURVES
BURN TOOL

INSPIRATIONS: THE BEST OF PORTRAIT STYLES

The stunning shots shown here illustrate some of the themes that we have touched on in this chapter. Notice how powerful an image can be even if the model's face is not included. Moody, dramatic lighting, and the imaginative use of settings also work powerfully.

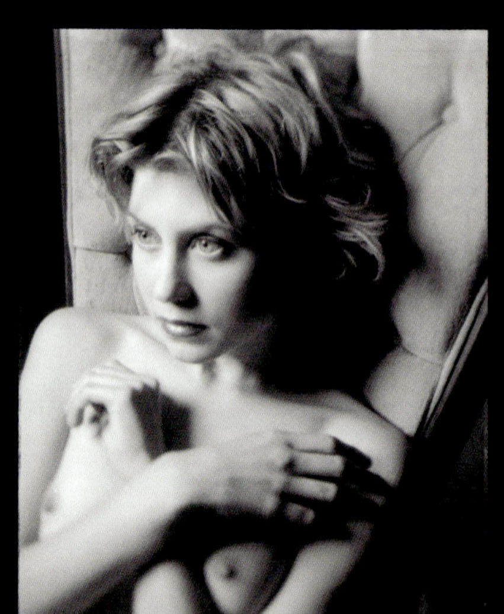

▶ This head-and-shoulders shot from Dan Howell manages to cram detail and subtle lighting into a very small area, making for an interesting closeup shot.

▼ Sheer brilliance comes from Stephen Hughes with this rendering of a nude as a work of sculpture. The high-key lighting and pale skin combine to give an almost plasterlike finish, while the pose and cropping are straight out of classical art.

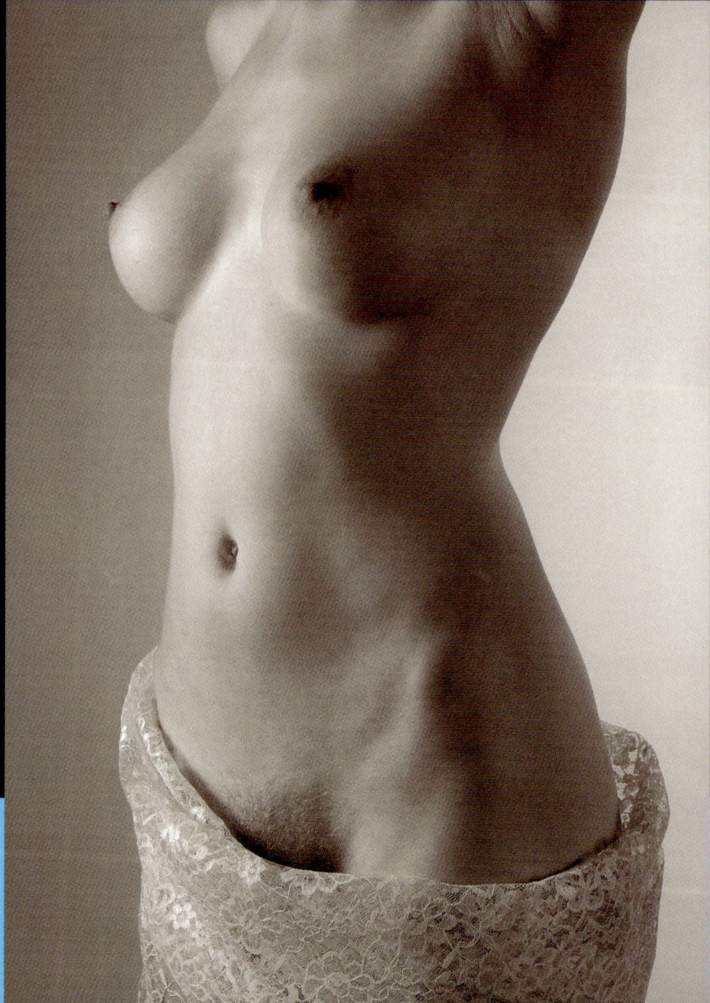

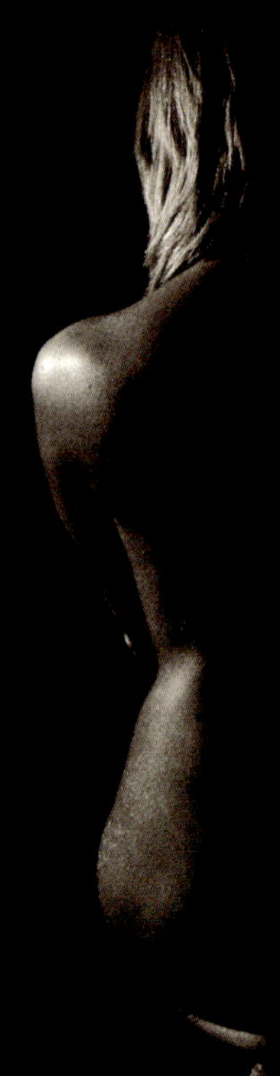

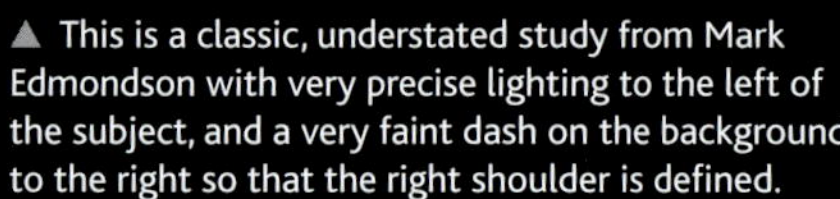
▲ This is a classic, understated study from Mark Edmondson with very precise lighting to the left of the subject, and a very faint dash on the background to the right so that the right shoulder is defined.

▼ This is an active twist on the three-quarter-length shot by Björn Oldsen. While all of the figure is visible, by having the subject kneeling, the height is reduced, while the angles of the legs and arms suggest movement and action.

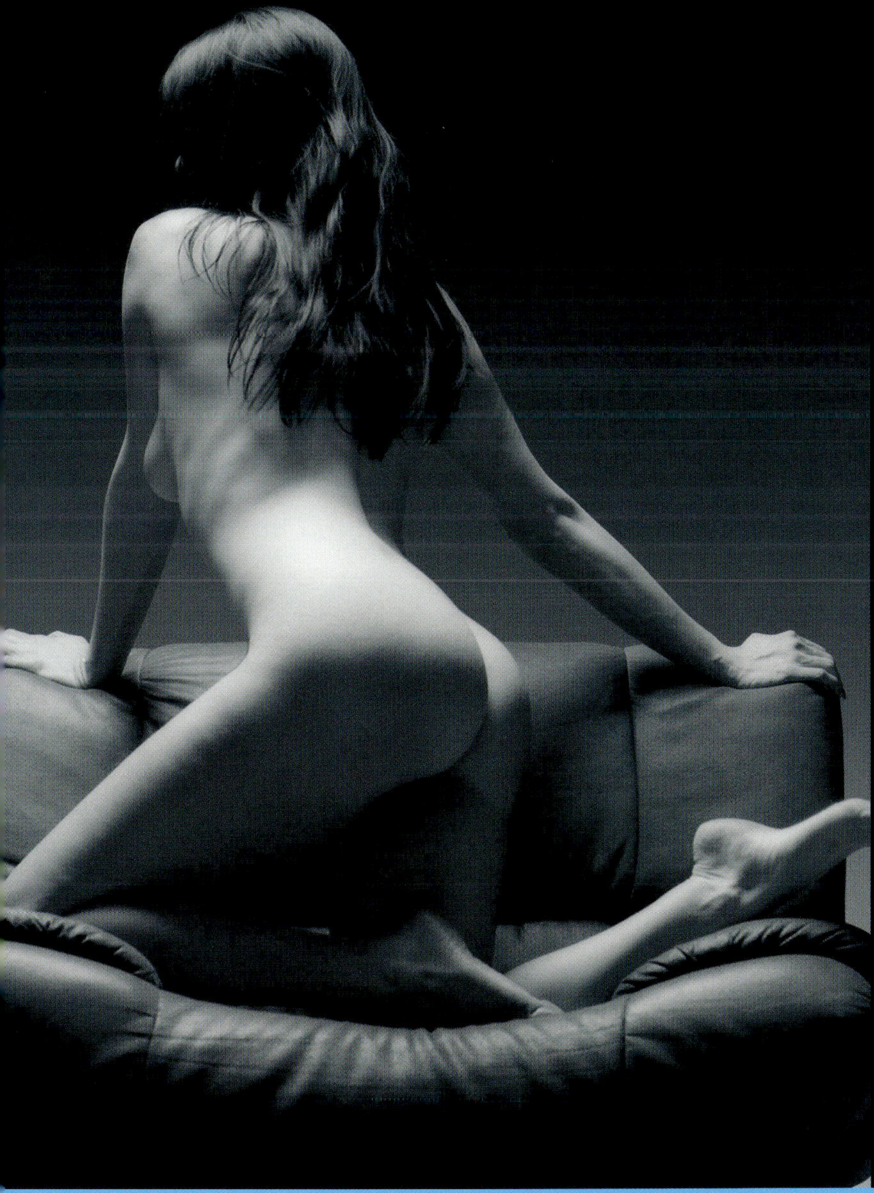

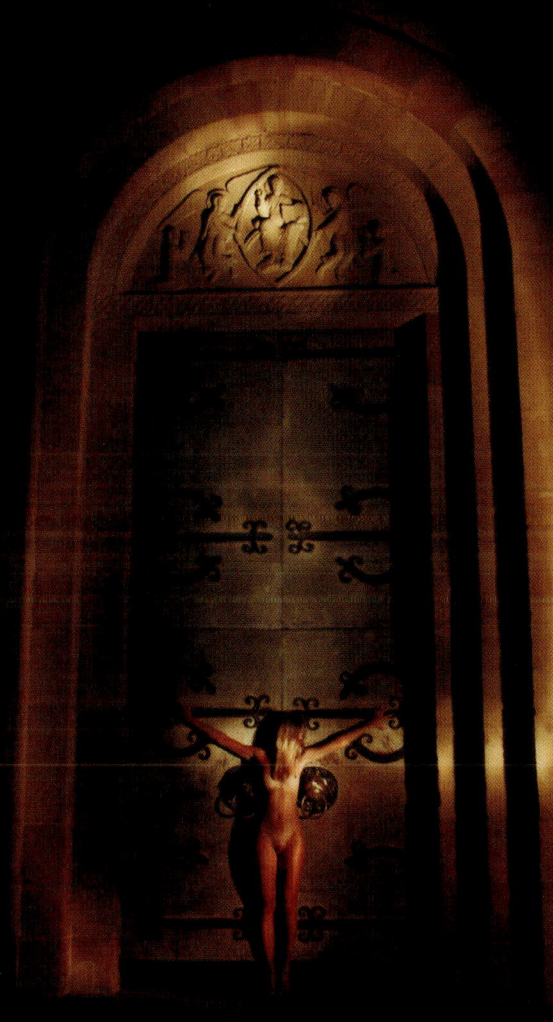

▲ Another image from Björn. The wonderful lighting perfectly suits the ornate decoration on the door and frame, allowing it to dominate the seemingly insignificant nude figure at the bottom.

4 LOCATION SHOOTS

Break out from the everyday confines of the studio and inspire yourself by working with the environment, nature, and the elements. Shooting on location can add drama, interest, and a narrative in a way that studio shots simply cannot compete with. This way of working poses more of a creative challenge, but rise to it and see what you can achieve.

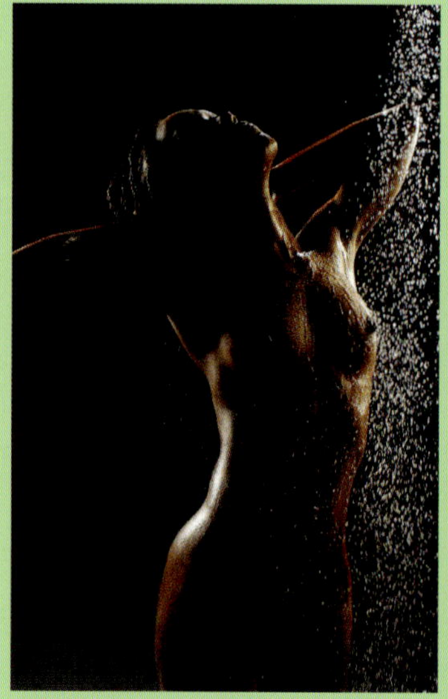

▲ Shooting movement. The dynamic element of moving water offers an exciting creative avenue to explore.

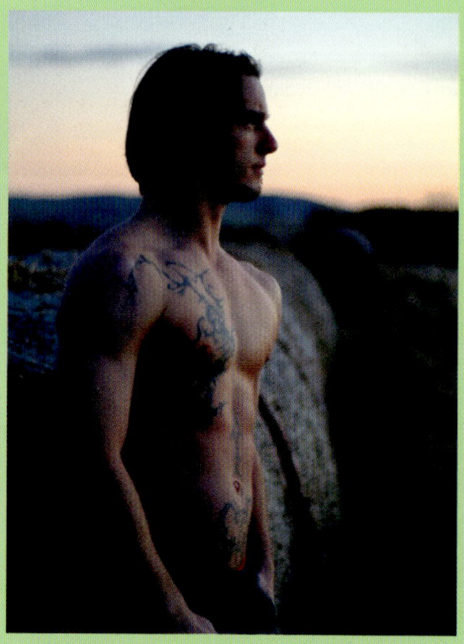

▲ Assignment: rural locations. A countryside locale and the dying sun make for a striking and warm-hued image.

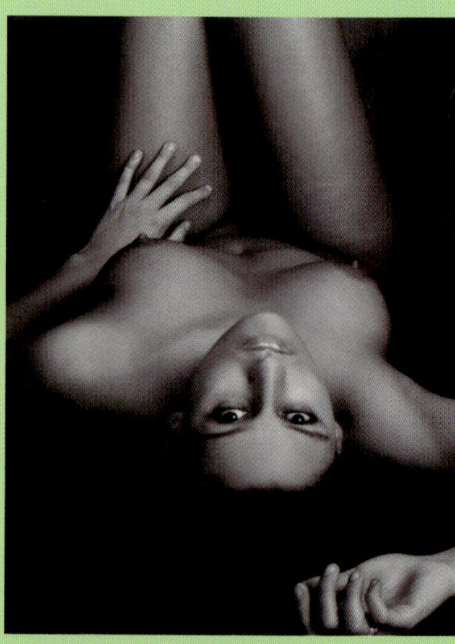

▲ Unusual viewpoints. Add an extra element to your location photography by experimenting with poses and camera position.

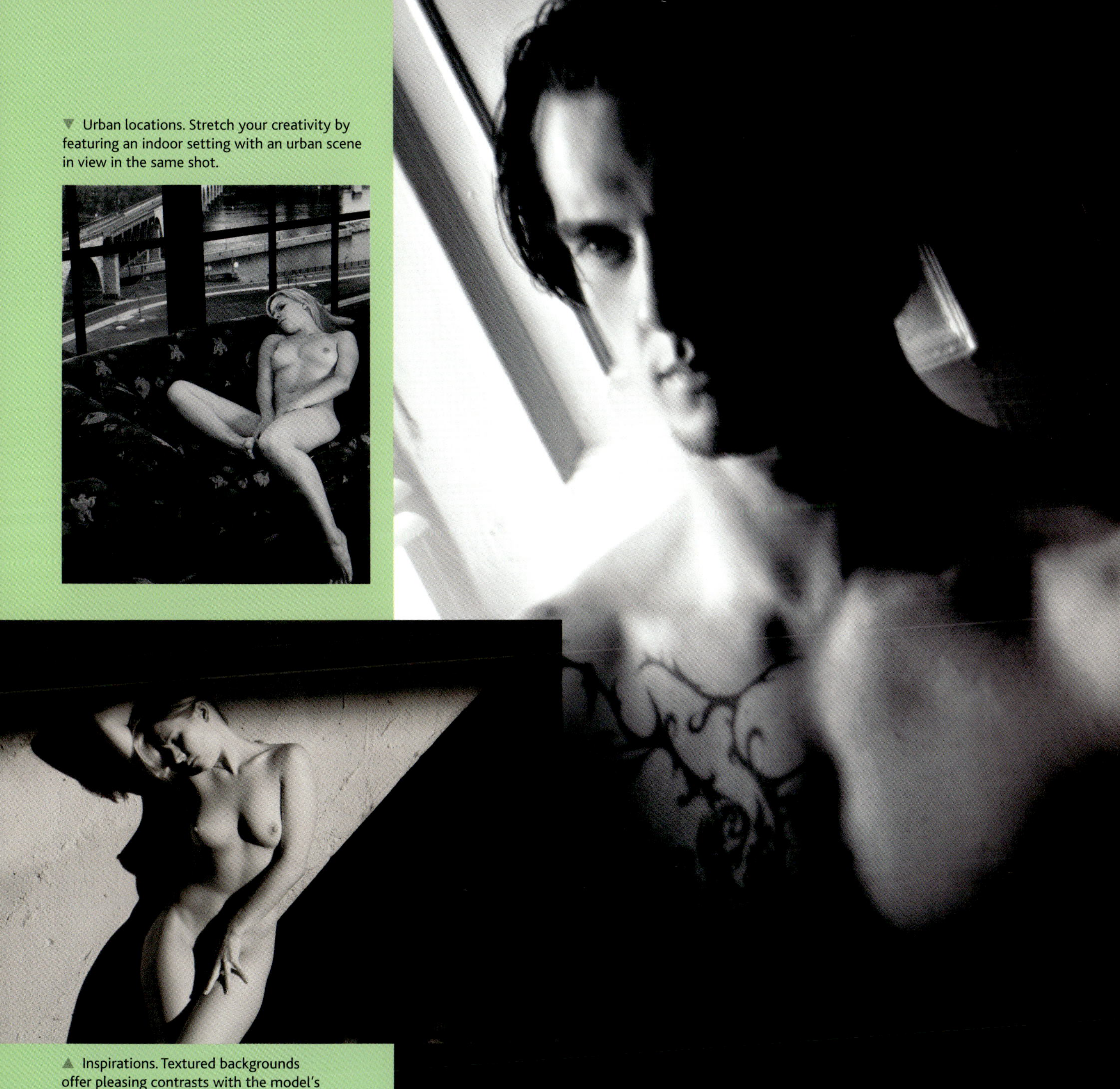

▼ Urban locations. Stretch your creativity by featuring an indoor setting with an urban scene in view in the same shot.

▲ Inspirations. Textured backgrounds offer pleasing contrasts with the model's smooth contours.

INTERIOR LOCATIONS

The studio is fine for standard photographs and abstract closeup shots, but beyond that, everything starts to look rather similar. Shooting outside is great, but dependent on weather, people, and accessibility. The best place to shoot nudes with interesting backgrounds and settings is on location, but inside. Make use of decorative backgrounds and modern or antique furniture—but make sure your model and poses are compatible with the prevailing atmosphere.

SETTING IT UP

This shot was taken in a piano room with bright afternoon sunlight outside. To avoid the model being plunged into shadow, an umbrella and flash was set up to the left, facing 45 degrees at the model. The aperture was set to f/5.6 and the shutter speed to 1/125 sec. A wide-angle lens of 18mm (27mm effective on the digital camera) was used to ensure that the entire scene was captured. The camera was about 20 feet (6m) away.

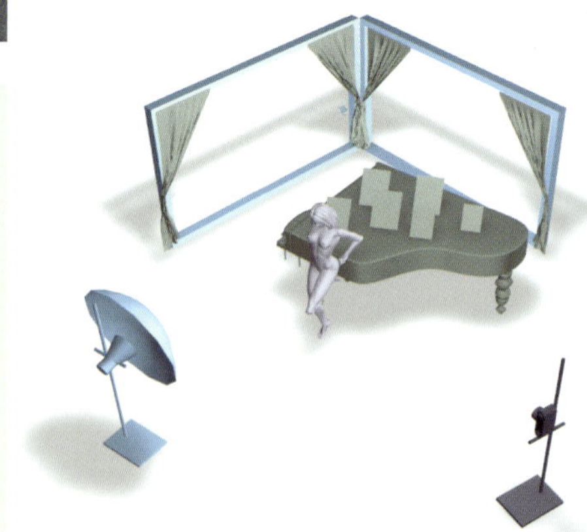

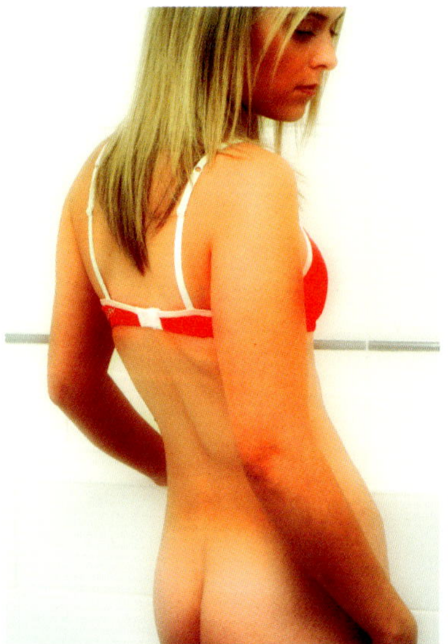

01 Everyone's house has a bathroom, and if it is tiled completely in white or a single color, you can create minimalist compositions. The other advantage is that they tend to have a lot of light, so you can shoot bright, high-key images with ease.

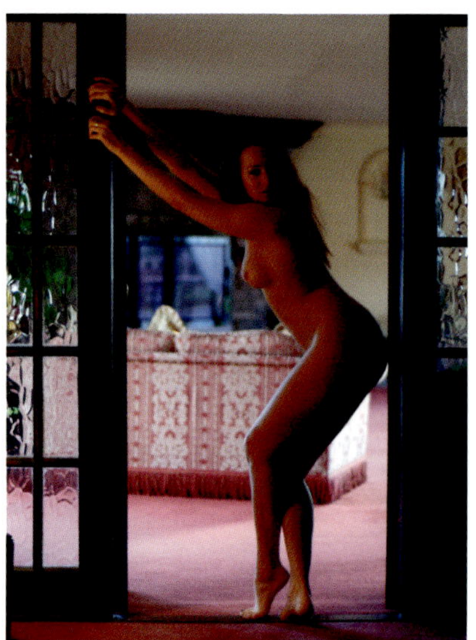

02 While people might be impressed with your large-screen plasma TV, it doesn't make for a great centerpiece to an image, unless you shoot creatively against it. Instead, use doorways and entrances into this communal entertainment space.

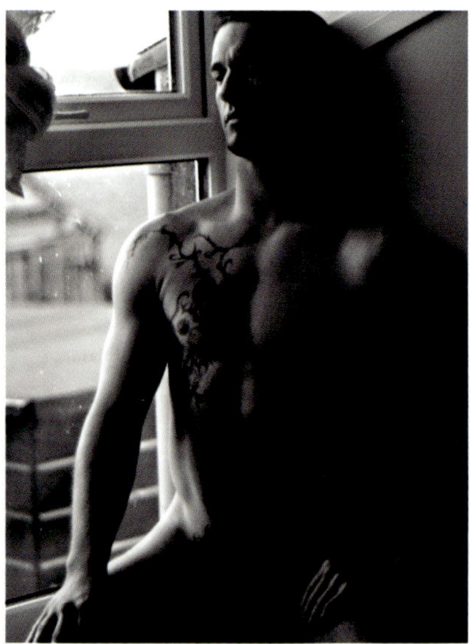

03 If you set your subject against a window, your reward is a fantastic play of light and shadow across the subject. Don't shoot in bright sunlight because there is too much contrast. This image used a reflector to the right to ensure that there was some definition across the chest because the subject was turned right away from the light.

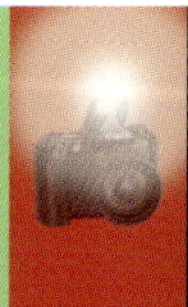

BRIGHT IDEA
People often have one room in their house that is a particular favorite in terms of content and style; ask around to see whether you can use one for a shoot.

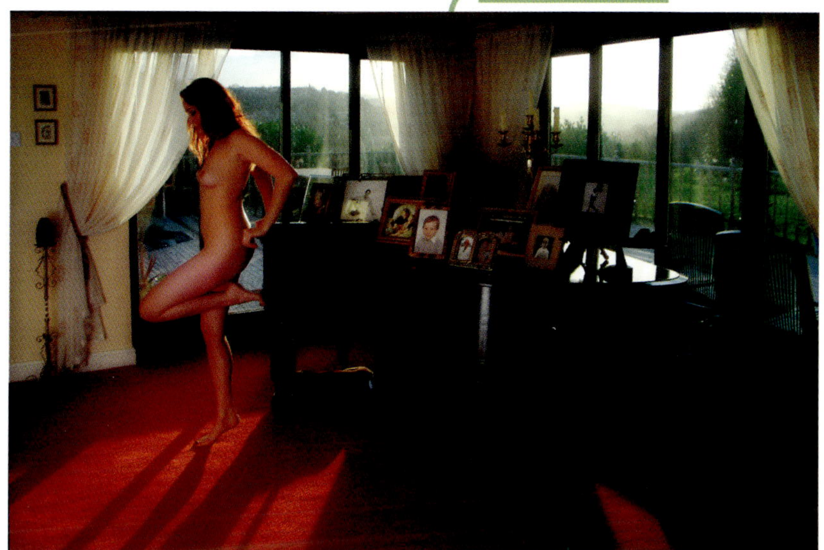

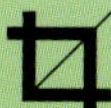

04 When shooting in a bedroom, either pick an interesting feature, shoot using dark and dangerous lighting, or create a more unusual composition, as we have here.

PHOTO EDITING

◄ The idea behind this shot was to show the model leaning against her own piano stacked with family photos. I wanted to place the model within the environment, without concentrating on her. The wide-angle was used so that the full spread of light through the windows could be seen.

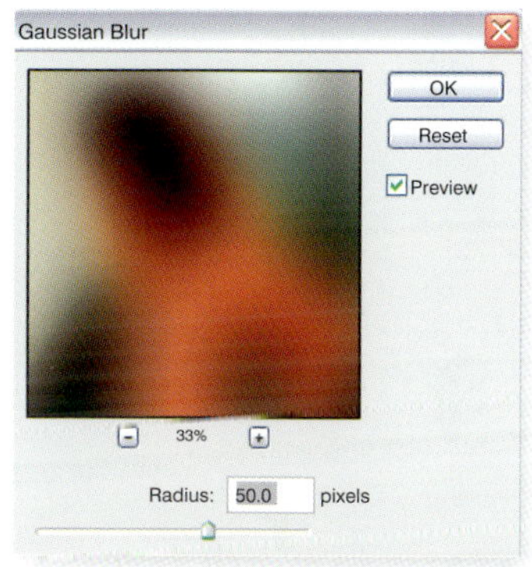

▲ Curves was used to darken the shadows and brighten the highlights, particularly so that the streaks of light on the carpet would stand out more.

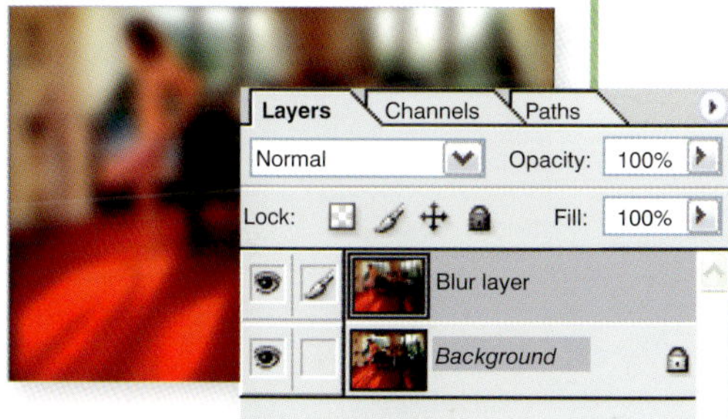

▲ A duplicate layer was created and then the Gaussian Blur filter run on it with a strength of 50 pixels. The Duplicate Layer blend mode was changed to overlay, which increased the color saturation.

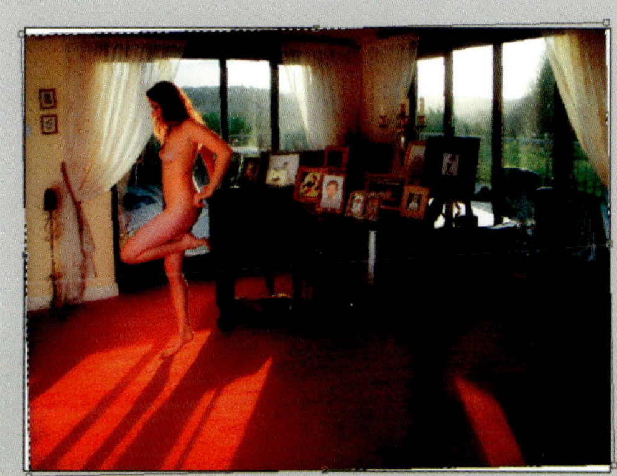

◄ The image was slightly unbalanced so it was selected with Ctrl+A and then rotated to a straighter orientation.

TOOLS AT A GLANCE
IMAGE > ADJUSTMENTS > CURVES
DUPLICATE LAYER
FILTER > BLUR > GAUSSIAN BLUR
EDIT > TRANSFORM > ROTATE

ASSIGNMENT: SHOOTING INDOORS

Most of the time, shooting inside is easier than shooting outside. There's no bad weather, passersby, landowners, dirty roads, garbage, or even the police to contend with. It's a comfort zone, which is why for this assignment using an indoor location, we're going to give you a hard time. Your task is to shoot a series of pictures inside a house, without using the bedroom, bathroom, or kitchen. They are too easy, as they are full of props. Instead, concentrate on available light and creating emotion using the other spaces available.

SETTING IT UP

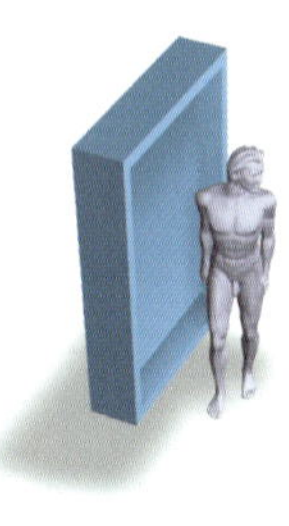
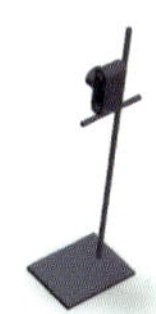

While some of the pictures in this series use a handheld Metz flashgun fired and bounced off the ceiling, the main picture does not. It features only available window light in the late afternoon. The lens is a 50mm—not just for the lack of distortion it causes, but because it has a maximum aperture of f/1.8, allowing the background to be thrown out of focus. The shutter speed using that was 1/90 sec, enough to shoot without a tripod. The shooting distance was about 10 feet (3m).

01 We're shooting on a staircase here, with light coming from a skylight above. The subject sits on the landing while the camera position is on the floor above looking down. A Metz flashgun was used to supply additional light by firing at the ceiling and bouncing it downward, mixing in with the natural light. In this shot, the model looks contemplative.

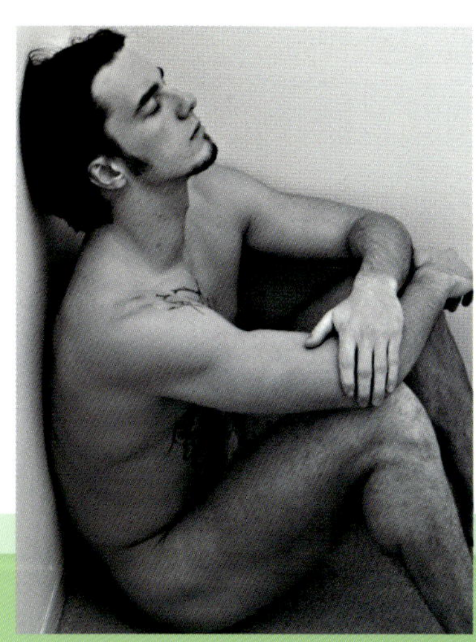

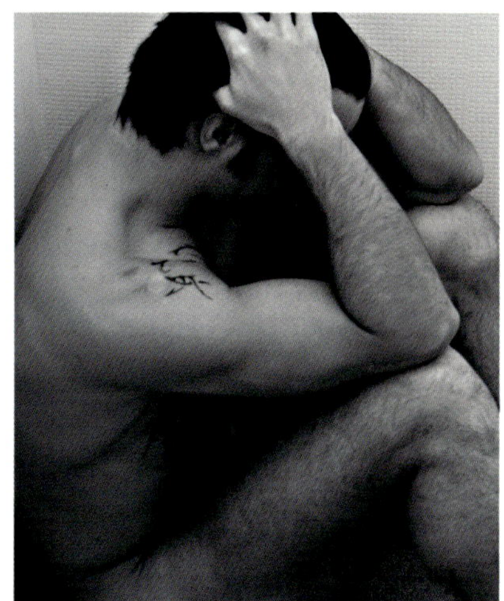

02 Now we're trying to express a little more emotion, with the subject holding his head in hands. The shot was taken with a 150mm focal length to get close in.

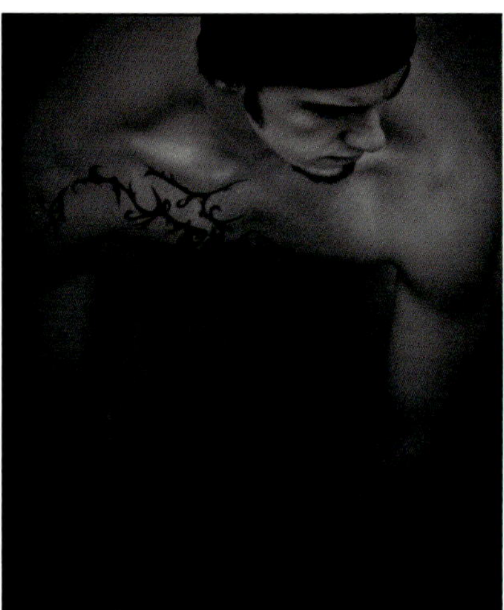

03 The subject has turned around and now sits on the top step of the landing. The expression is broody and angry, so the picture was darkened to make it suit the expression.

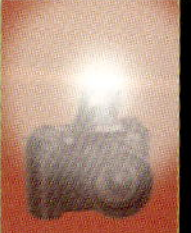

BRIGHT IDEA
Have you got a toolshed? Try posing your subject in there as an alternative to the more obvious indoor locations.

PHOTO EDITING

▶ This was the best shot of the series. Using the diffuse light coming through the blinds, the torso was angled so that there was shadow definition on the torso and stomach, while the model's left side descended into blackness. The exposed nature of the shot contrasts that vulnerability with the model's powerful physique. The subject's head was turned away deliberately so that it was completely in shadow.

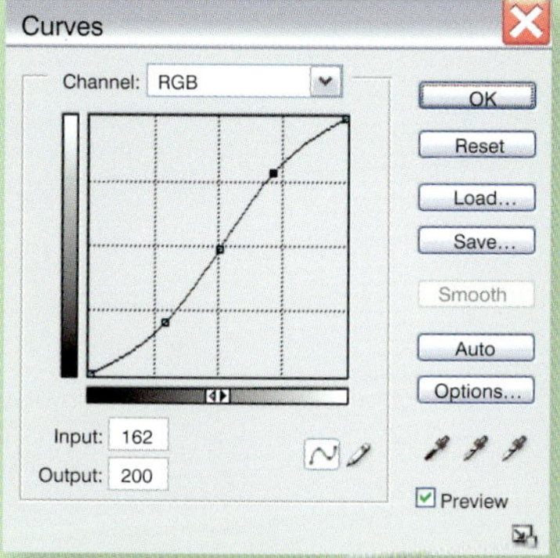

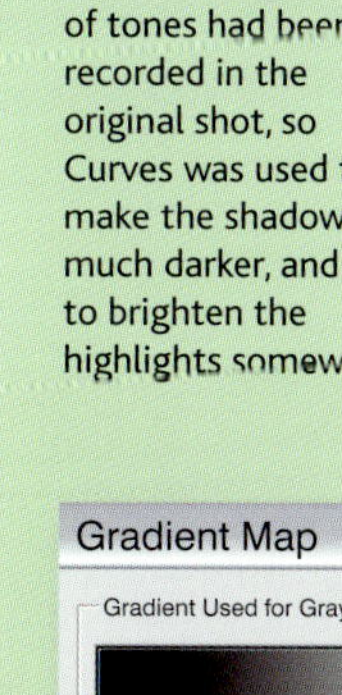

▲ A full range of tones had been recorded in the original shot, so Curves was used to make the shadows much darker, and to brighten the highlights somewhat.

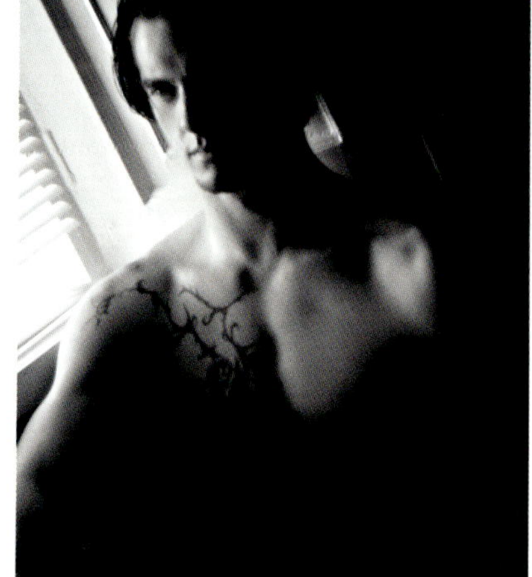

04 In the lounge was a window with Venetian blinds, and with late evening light coming through almost horizontally, it created great areas of darkness and mystery. The subject looks thoughtful, too.

▲ The image was converted to monochrome with a black–white Gradient Map. It was cropped slightly.

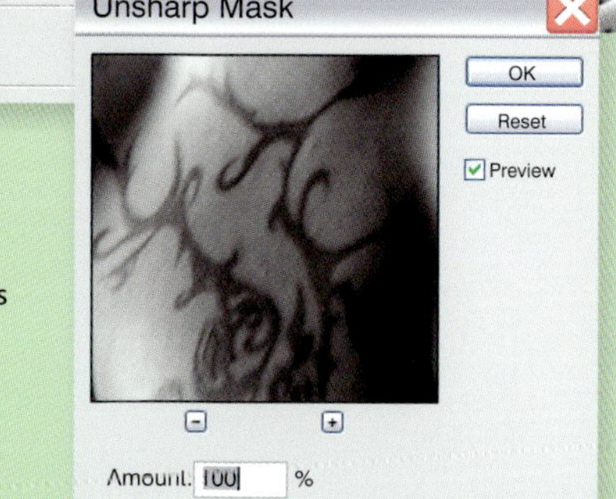

◀ The Unsharp Mask filter with an amount of 100% was used to bring out the details and sharpen the image up. Finally, a keyline border was added.

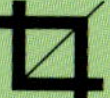

TOOLS AT A GLANCE
IMAGE > ADJUSTMENTS > CURVES
IMAGE > ADJUSTMENTS > GRADIENT MAP
CROP

FILTER > SHARPEN > UNSHARP MASK
CANVAS SIZE

URBAN LOCATIONS

In and around a city, town, or industrial site, there are interesting and contrasting backgrounds to shoot against. You can use the grime of post-industrial decay to contrast with smooth skin, or go for an incongruous combination of well-known location and nudity. The trouble with urban locations is that the more popular, well-known, or busy they are, the harder it is to have a successful shoot.

SETTING IT UP

The key point to the shot opposite is the incorporation of an interior scene with the lighting from outside. To get this to work, the light from both has to be very similar. If shooting on an average bright day, interior light on its own is unlikely to be strong enough, so a flash unit with a diffusing softbox should be used. Set the light meter to incident or reflected light rather than flash or ambient. Set the shutter speed to 1/125 sec and meter from the light coming from outside. The result is the aperture setting. Set the aperture and speed settings in manual mode and connect the camera to a flash unit. Set the power on the flash unit so that it is rated at the same aperture. You will need to change the light meter to flash cord or ambient mode to get the power output from the flash head right.

01 Privacy is always a problem when shooting in urban locations, unless you can find an abandoned or little-used industrial location. Here the shoot took place in an abandoned warehouse. This provided lots of textured backgrounds, broken windows, and natural light.

02 Shooting in the city is fraught with difficulties; at best, people get in your way, and at worst, prevent you from shooting. The more popular or famous the location, the harder it is. However, you can still shoot with very famous backdrops. This series of shots on London's Westminster Bridge, against the Houses of Parliament, was possible only with a minder keeping tourists out of shot.

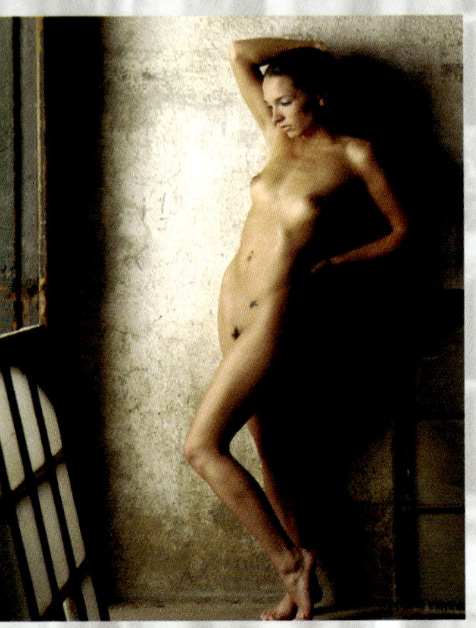

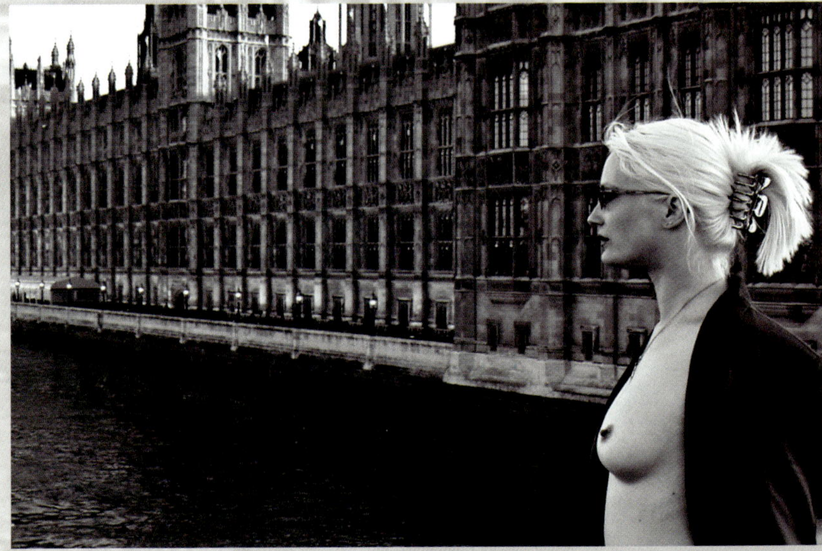

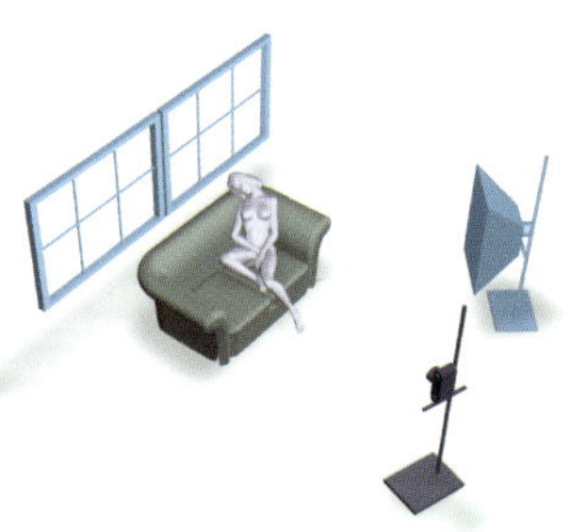

BRIGHT IDEA

Ports and docks were busy in the nineteenth and most of the twentieth century, but as cheap overseas labor cut into the workforces of Westernized countries, and other forms of transport took over, these waterside industries fell into decay. They now make excellent background locations for nude photography.

TOP TIP

The main point about shooting in an urban environment is that you can show it against the subject, so use an aperture of a least f/8 in your shots.

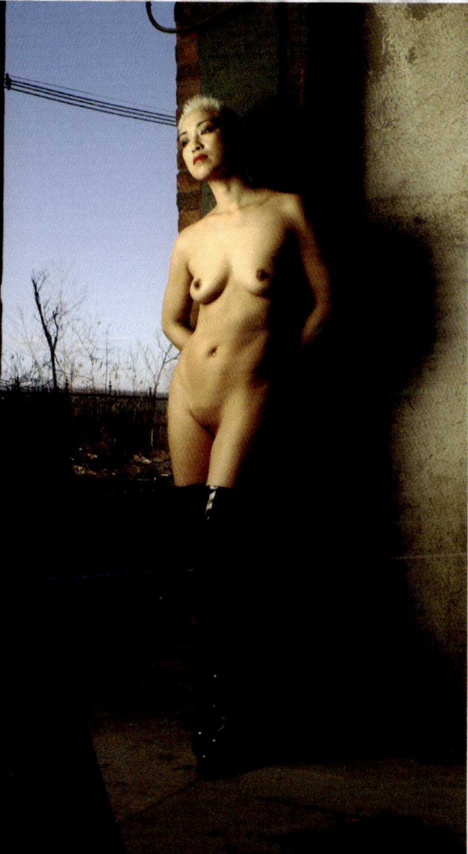

03 The lure of the open air in an urban location adds an element of danger and ambiguity to the imagery. Here, the subject poses in the doorway of an abandoned industrial building with a road outside.

PHOTO EDITING

▶ This picture by Stephen Haynes is a brilliant combination of interior comfort with the unyielding city elements of river commerce, roads, industry, and bridges. The model was lit by a flash unit to the right side of the camera. A narrow aperture was used so that, although the point of focus was on the model, the background in the far distance through the window remained sharp.

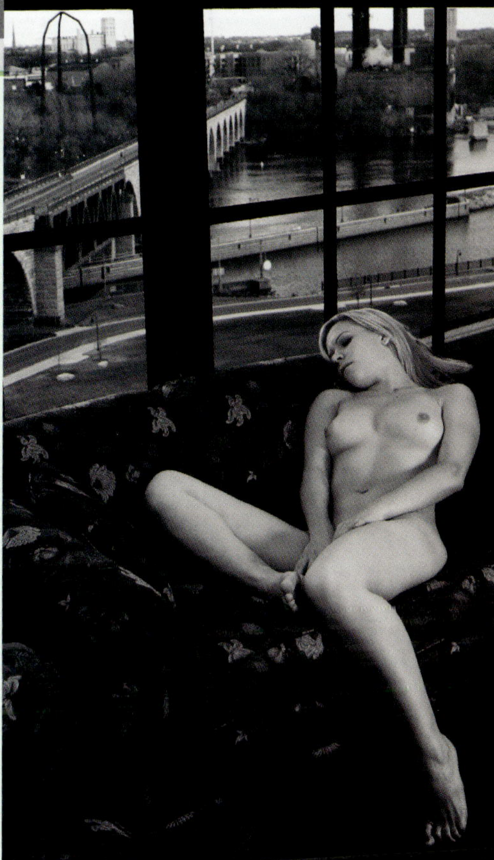

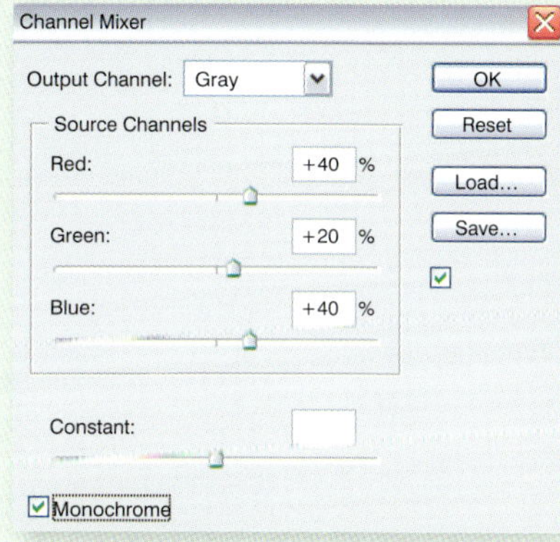

▲ The Channel Mixer was used to convert the image to monochrome, giving a good tonal range throughout.

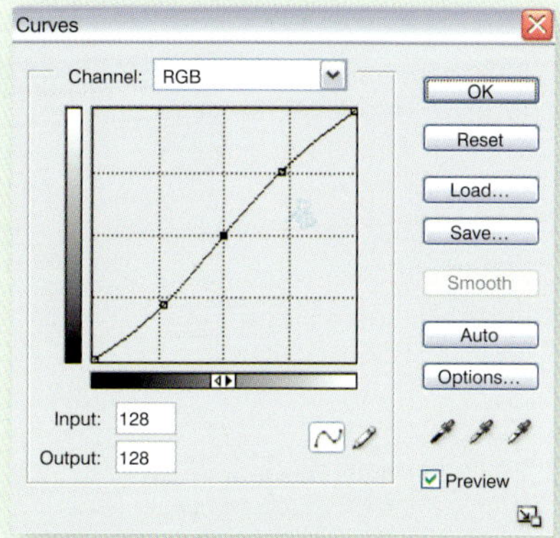

▲ The shadows were darkened and the skin tones lightened with the Curves control.

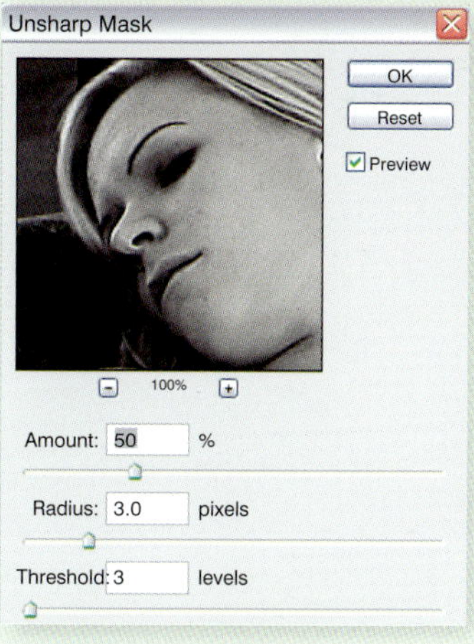

▲ A final level of sharpening was applied using the Unsharp Mask and a 50% amount setting.

TOOLS AT A GLANCE
IMAGE > ADJUSTMENTS > CHANNEL MIXER
IMAGE > ADJUSTMENTS > CURVES
FILTER > SHARPEN > UNSHARP MASK

ASSIGNMENT: SUBURBAN GARDENS

At a suburban property you expect to find some sort of garden, whether it's a small yard or a few rolling acres. Your assignment is to find a garden that has views or features that would make for an interesting range of photos. Go outside just after sunset so the light in the sky isn't bright, and shoot in five different locations around the garden, aiming for five different poses as well. There's no flash allowed on this one either—you have to pose the model with respect to the available light.

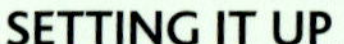
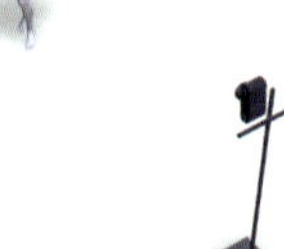

SETTING IT UP

How you set each shot up depends on where you are in the garden, how much space there is, and what aspect of the background you want to include. For the main picture, a 50mm lens was used from about 15 feet (4.5m) away with the aperture wide open at f/1.8. This ensured a fast enough shutter speed and also minimal depth of field. Center-weighted metering was used to meter from the subject so that the slightly brighter sky didn't cause underexposure.

TOP TIP

Shooting at high ISO ratings because of the low light creates colored digital noise that can ruin a picture, but not if you convert it into monochrome.

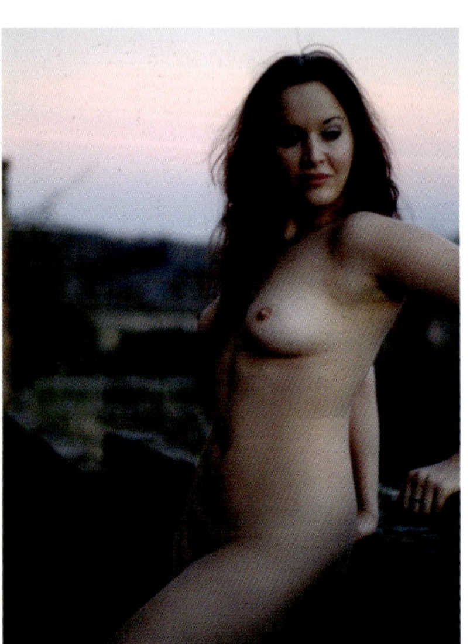

01 With the model perched on the garden wall, this picture captures the evening colors while the subject faces into the light. This means that the scenery behind, which is in shadow, is much darker, making the subject stand out more.

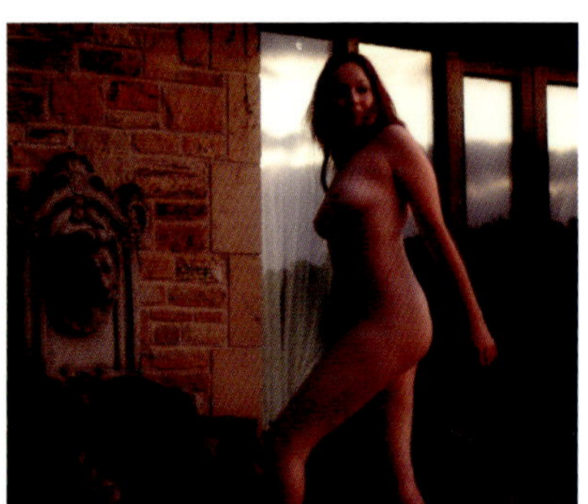

02 The composition here is rather messy. The model pose is interesting, as she focuses on something off-screen. However, by placing her dead center and awkwardly climbing over the garden feature the whole thing looks unbalanced with little dynamism.

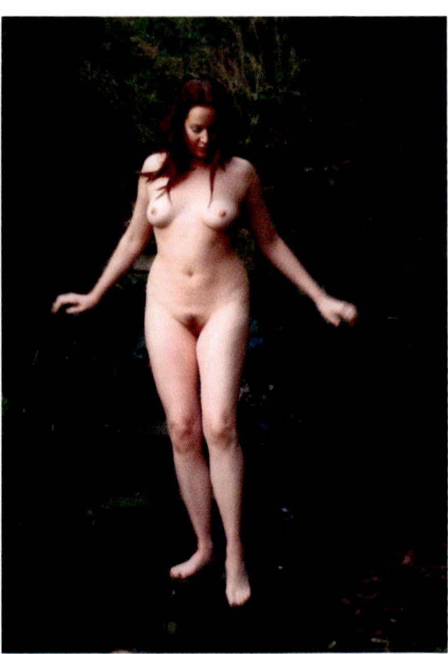

03 This was shot as fast as the camera could manage as the model stepped down. There was a garden light behind some of the foliage, which is why the model looks nice and bright while the surroundings look dark and gloomy.

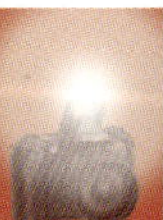

BRIGHT IDEA

Set the camera up on a tripod, set a narrower aperture such as f/22, and this will create a longer exposure. Ask your model to move around and he or she will blur while the background remains sharp.

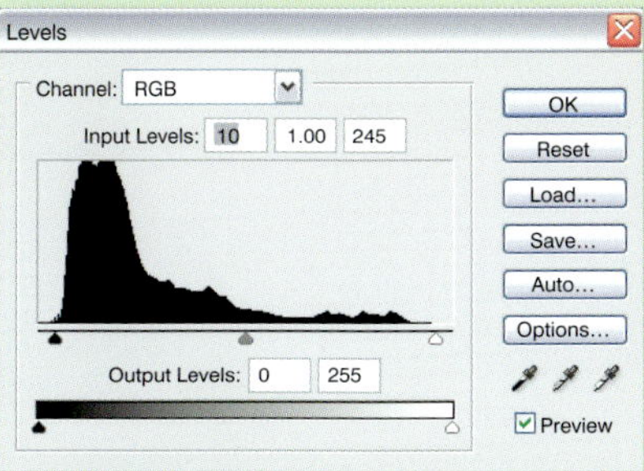

▲ The picture used most of the tonal range available—any later in the day and the histogram would have been much more narrow; any earlier and the contrast would have been too great. The Levels command was used to fill out the range.

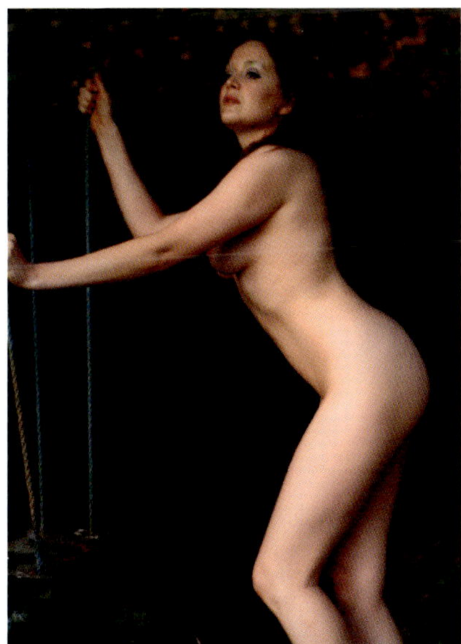

04 In another corner of the garden was this old swing. Unfortunately, it was overgrown, making it hard to get to barefoot, so most of the poses didn't look good. This was the best, but the moldiness of the rope put the model off holding on to it, resulting in a grimace.

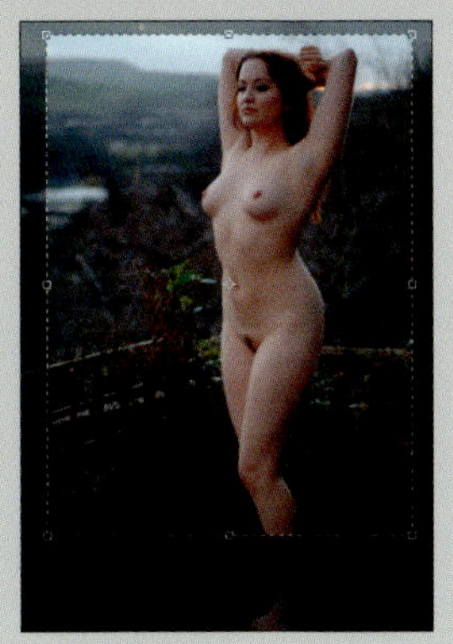

▲ There was just too much of the legs at the bottom, so the decision was made to use the Crop tool to limit it to just below the knee.

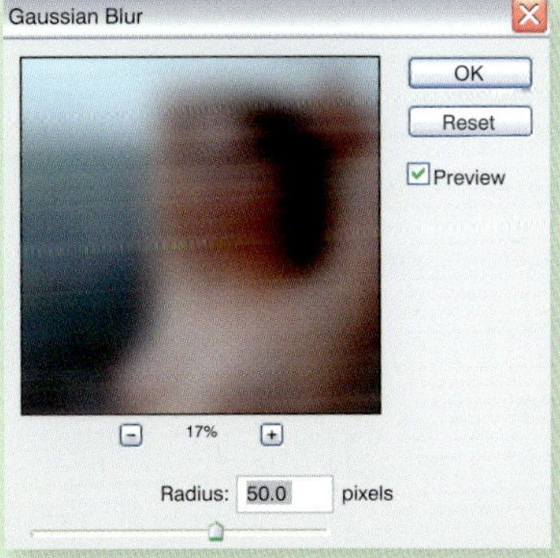

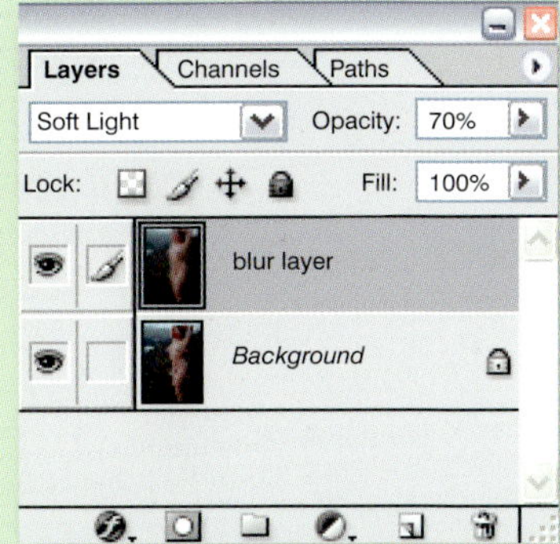

▲ A Duplicate Layer was created and a 50-pixel Gaussian Blur applied to it. The blend layer was changed to soft light and the opacity reduced to 70%. This added a soft, warm range of colors to the image.

PHOTO EDITING

▼ Over on a raised wooden patio with her back to where the sun had set, the model stretches out in a classic pose. One advantage of this is that it pulls everything up and defines the ribcage. Center weighted metering was used to ensure that the model was well exposed, and the immediate foliage and the valley in the distance were dark and atmospheric.

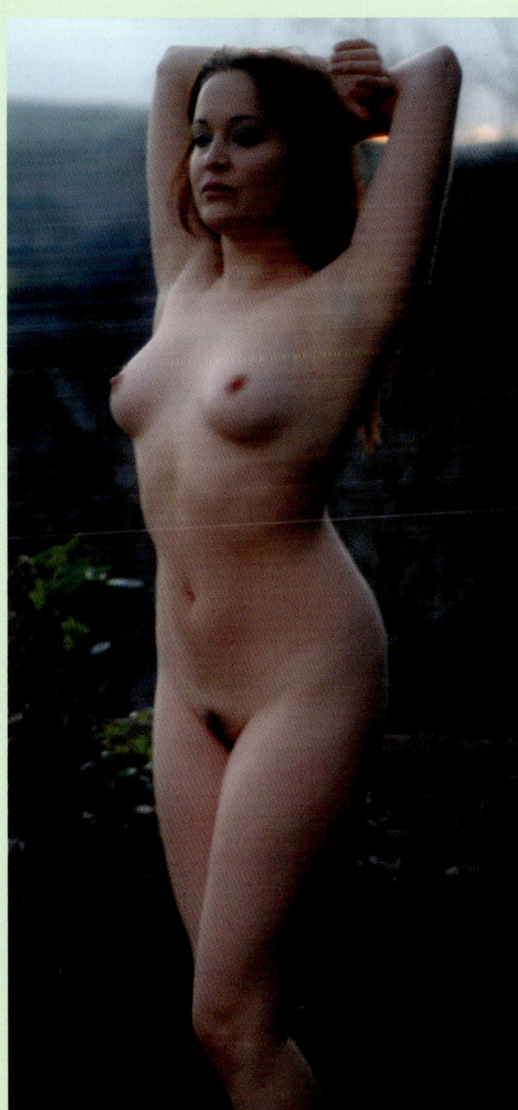

TOOLS AT A GLANCE
IMAGE > ADJUSTMENTS > LEVELS
CROP TOOL
DUPLICATE LAYER
FILTER > BLUR > GAUSSIAN BLUR

SHOOTING IN THE COUNTRY

There's no doubt about it: the combination of fresh air, pleasant surroundings, and a nude model can make for great photography. The countryside is the ideal location to shoot nudes, both in terms of privacy, and also for setting the figure against an attractive backdrop. The main points to contend with are the weather and the lighting. If you can bring flash equipment or reflectors to the scene, then your ability to control the exposure hugely increases your chances of a successful shoot.

SETTING IT UP
The countryside image opposite was shot with a Nikon D100 digital SLR, a 24–70mm short telephoto lens, and very cleverly, used fill flash, bounced down from a

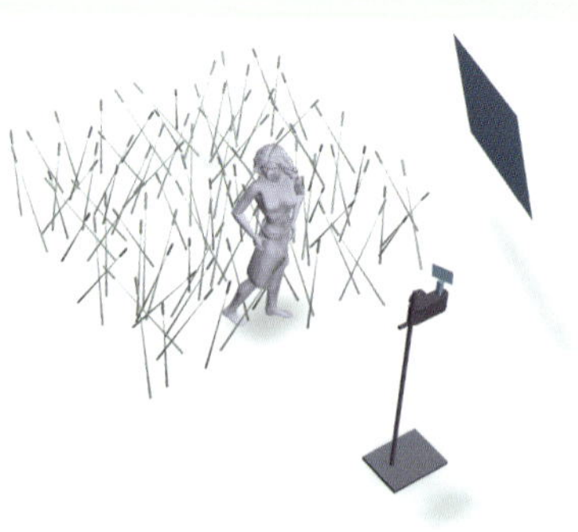

reflector held above head height. This ensured the light on the model appeared to come from the sky, though was in fact artificially supplementing the daylight to make the model stand out from the background without casting ugly shadows.

01 A field of long grass on a warm summer day. Get in close as the model wanders through the fields. This was shot just as she unconsciously started playing with the strands of grass.

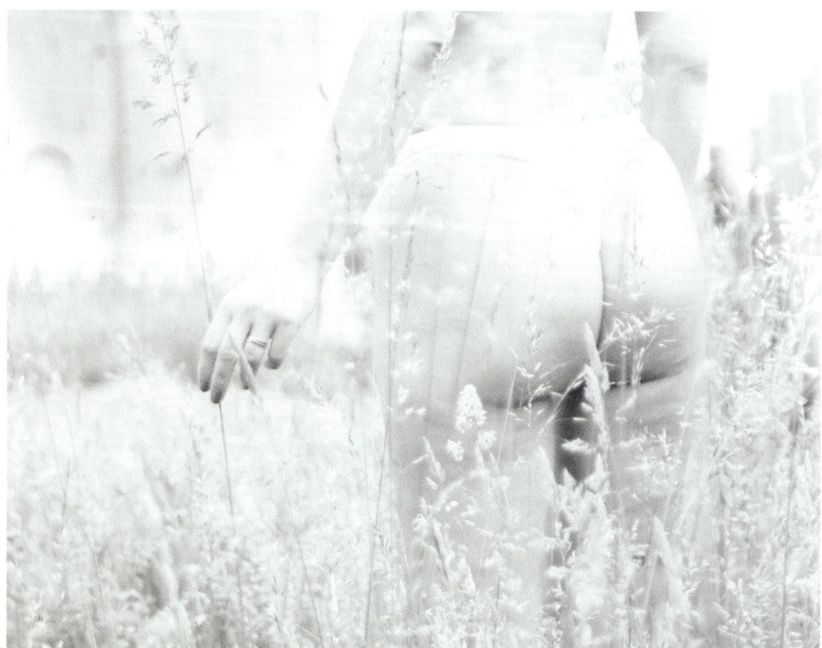

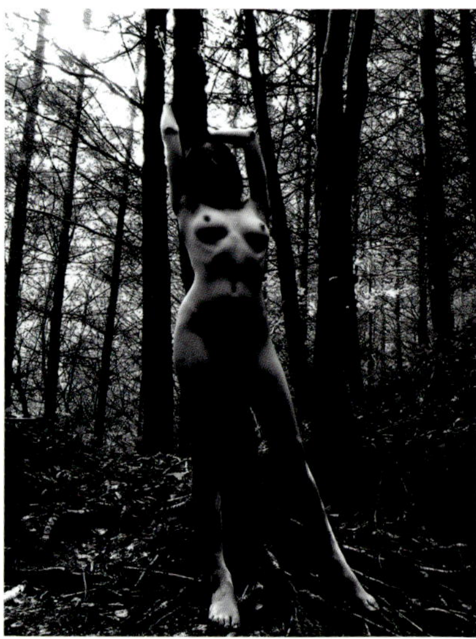

02 Shooting in woods offers a great deal of privacy. Here, Mark Varley has maximized the impact of tall tree trunks by using a wide-angle lens and shooting from low down. The perspective exaggerates the length of the model's legs and makes the trees tower up to the heavens.

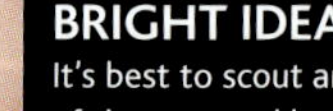

BRIGHT IDEA
It's best to scout an area out first before shooting there, but if this is impossible, get a map of the area and look for historical or abandoned buildings, towers, farms, rivers, and fields as potential sites.

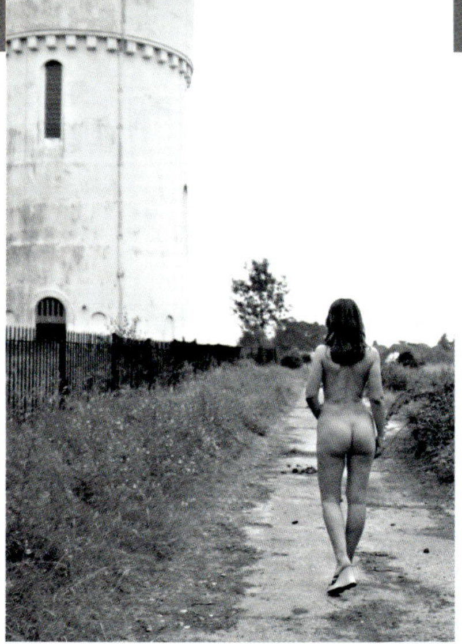

03

Any interesting structures can add to the narrative of the photo. Here, the model wanders down a farm track, while to the left looms an enormous water tower.

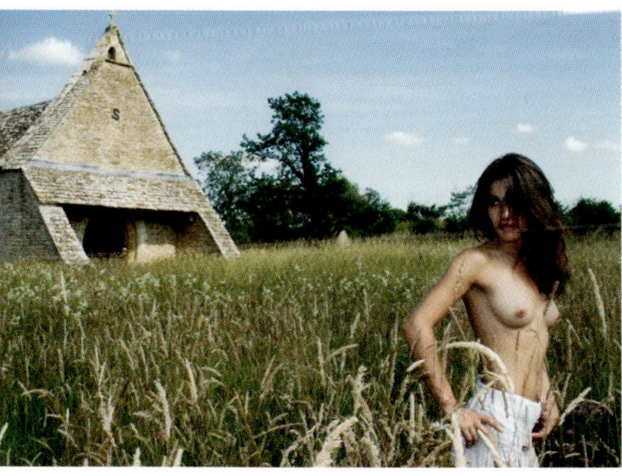

04

This is the color original of the image on the right.

TOP TIP

Check the surface types when shooting outdoors. Anything reflective can bounce too much light back to the camera meter and fool it. Set Exposure Compensation to −0.5EV to compensate.

PHOTO EDITING

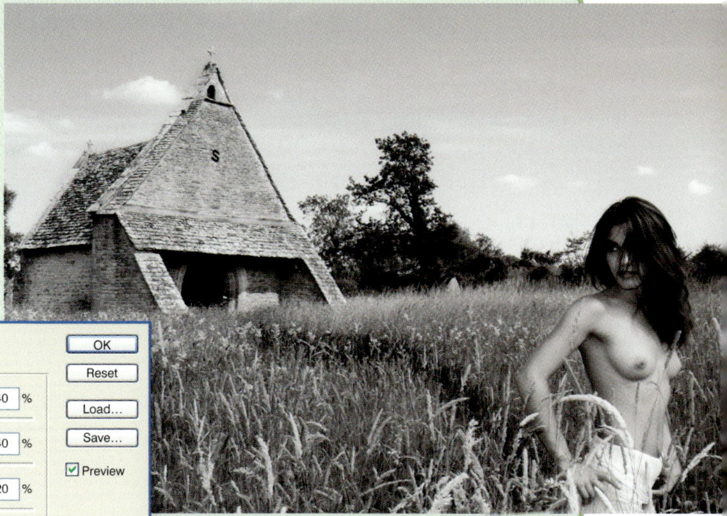

▶ Simon Young called this photo "Late for Church." It shows a model wandering through a field of hay, with an old church in the background.

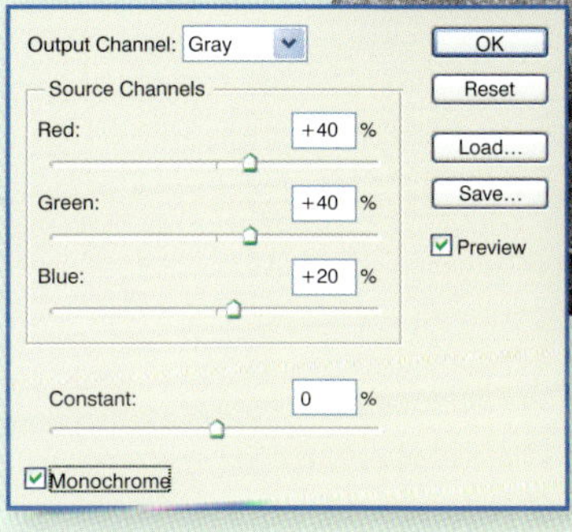

▲ First the image was converted to monochrome using the Channel Mixer.

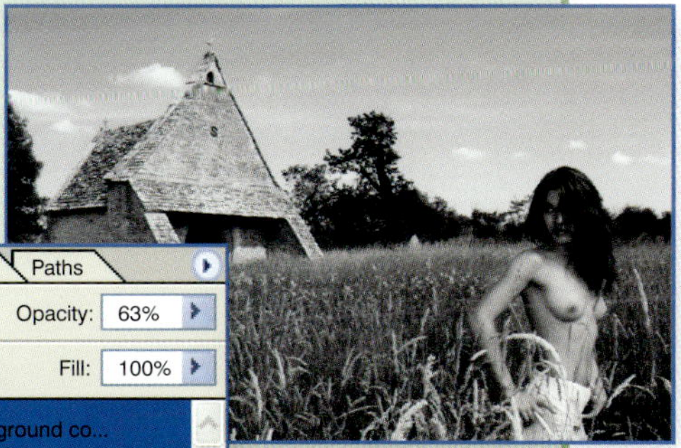

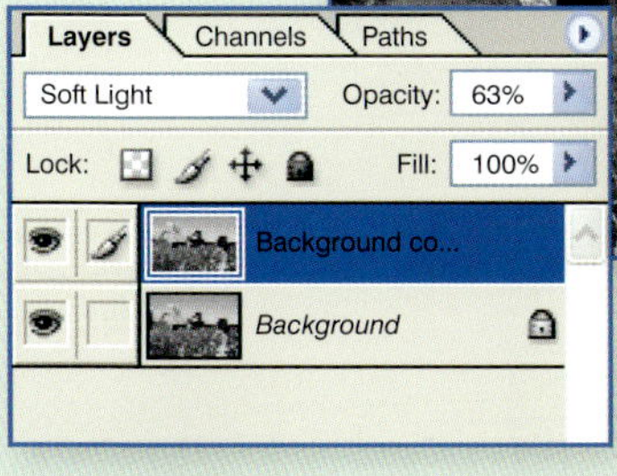

▲ Then the hay was given more contrast by using a Duplicate Layer set to soft light.

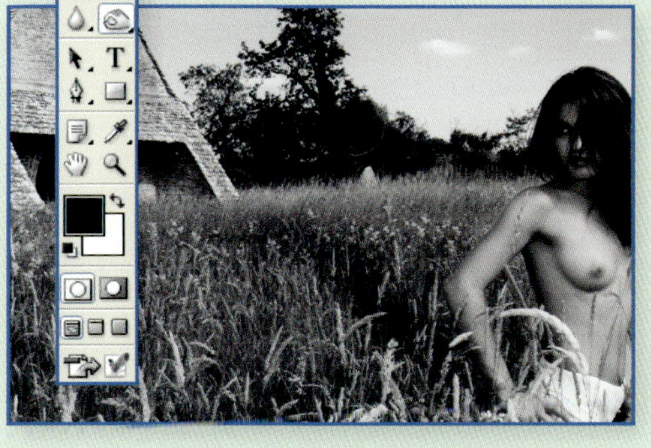

◀ Finally, the Burn tool was used to trace the path through the hay and make it far more prominent.

TOOLS AT A GLANCE
IMAGE > ADJUSTMENTS > CHANNEL MIXER
DUPLICATE LAYER > SOFT LIGHT
BURN TOOL

ASSIGNMENT: RURAL LOCATIONS

On this assignment to the country, we're going to give you something different to do. We want you to use a male model, the shots have to be topless, and you have to find a photogenic location. You have to show off the physique of the subject but, just to make life a little more interesting, we want you to shoot this at sunset so that there is color in the sky, but light levels are falling. You must judge when you can shoot in the ambient light and when you need fill-in flash. Anything shot with full-strength flash can go straight in the trash.

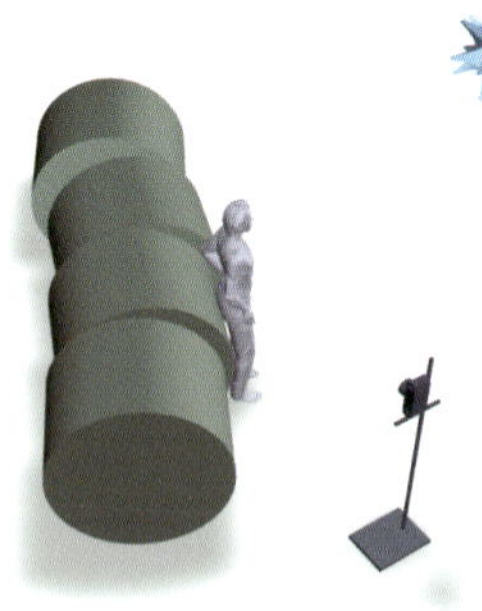

SETTING IT UP

It's easy to capture the subject when they are facing into the light. Open the aperture right up, use center-weighted metering and focus on the subject. Shoot using ambient light. When they stand with their back to the sky you need to use fill-in flash or they will be too dark. Use zone metering so that sky is read, not just the person, as it is important to capture the color. You can shoot these images with a 50mm lens, either closeup or from further back. Don't shoot using 35mm or wider or you'll distort the features.

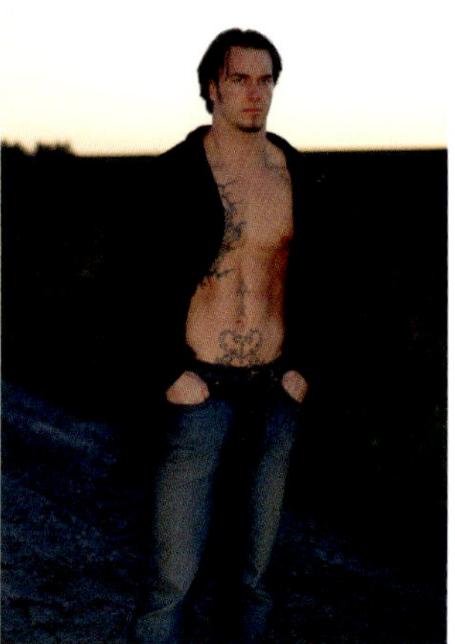

01 This is here to show you what not to do. The feet have been cut off for no reason. It isn't a three-quarter-length shot; it's just wrong. The subject is close up, but the pose doesn't work and the background is as dull as it could be. The sky has lost most of its color, too.

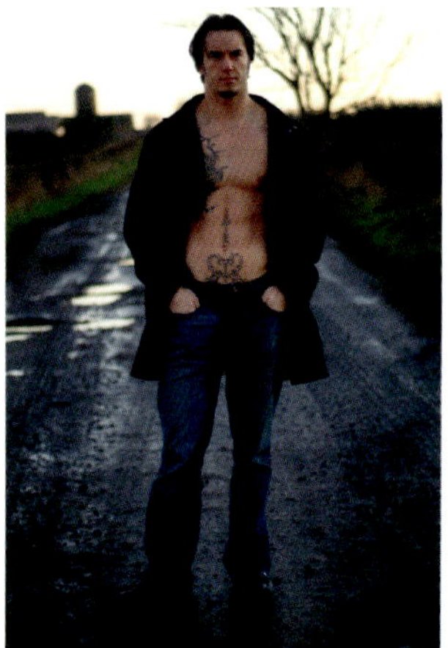

02 This is how that first shot should have been taken. There is enough road at the feet of the subject, and the track heading into the distance adds depth. The buildings on the horizon add interest. The frontal shot shows plenty of attitude, too.

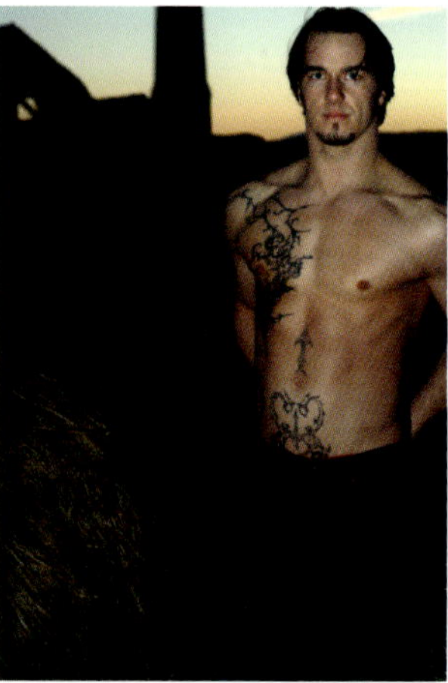

03 Next to the dirt track was a row of hay bales, with a ruined mill in the field behind. This shot uses fill-flash to light the subject while recording the background skylight. The ruin adds interest on the horizon. It is rendered as a silhouette but, crucially, doesn't cut across the back of the subject.

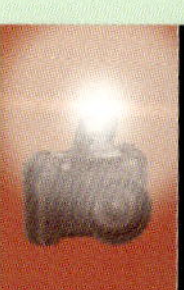

BRIGHT IDEA

Not got a reflector? A large piece of white card will work just as well. Also, light will bounce back off a white wall, so stand against one and have your subject face toward it.

PHOTO EDITING

▶ This is how to shoot that last image. The model stands facing into the light while the row of hay bales behind him disappears into the distance. The wide aperture (f/1.8) ensures that the bales don't detract attention from the subject, and the sky is full of the subtle tones of sunset. The pose also fits in with the environmental conditions.

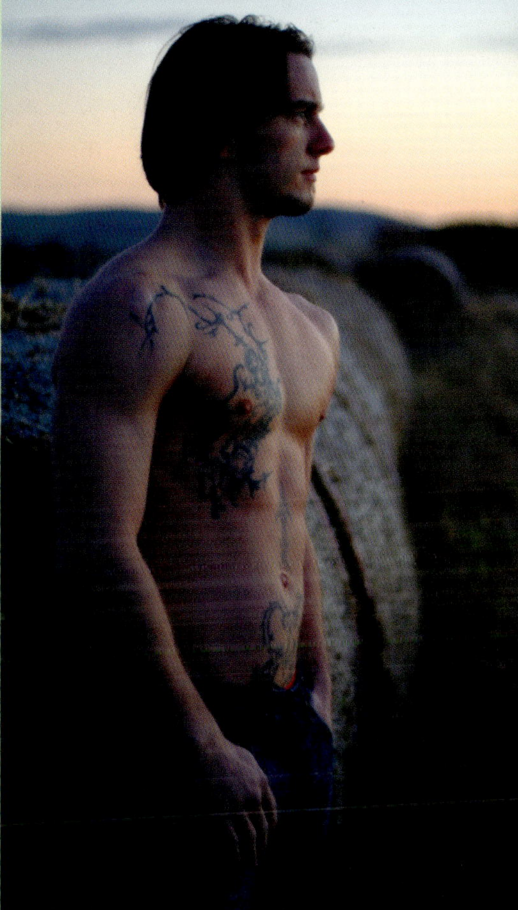

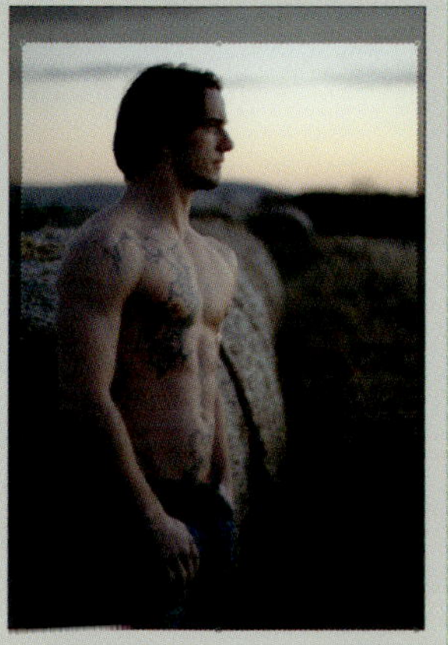

◀ There was a little too much spare room at the top of the picture. While I didn't want to crop into the head because it's important to show the environment, the Crop was used to remove just a small slice.

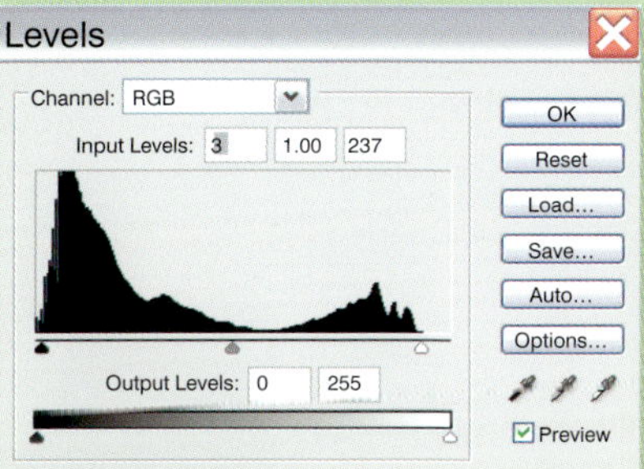

▲ The full range of tones was not being used as the light was fairly subdued, so Levels was applied to stretch the range out.

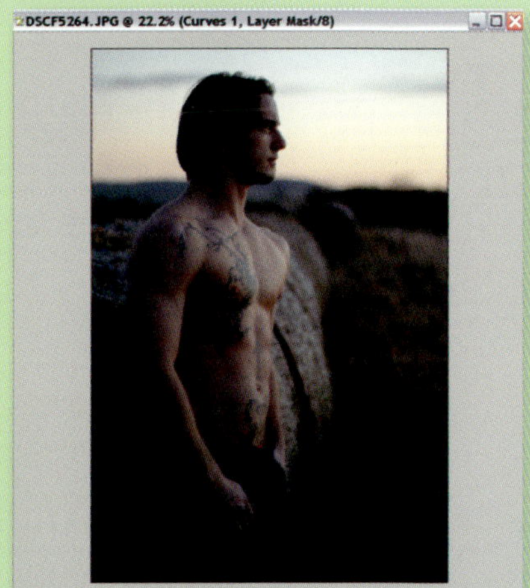

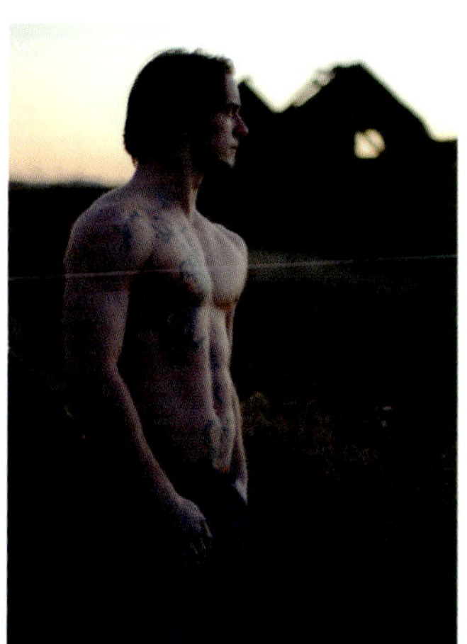

04 The subject faces into the light here so that just the ambient light can be recorded. The angle doesn't really work, though; there is depth to the image, but it seems cluttered because the head overlaps the ruin in the background.

▲ A Curves Adjustment Layer was then used to darken the shadows around the hay bales while lightening upper surfaces. The mask was painted on where the figure is so that it wasn't affected by the adjustment.

▼ A Duplicate Layer was created and the Gaussian Blur filter applied. The blend mode of this layer was changed to color. This was to increase the color saturation of the original layer, but in a subtle way, without increasing digital noise.

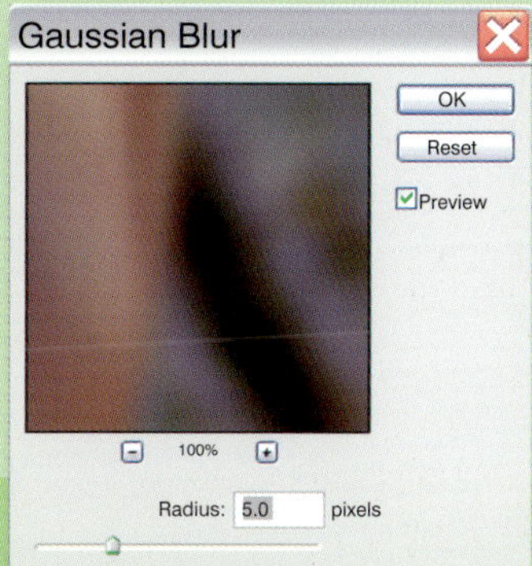

TOOLS AT A GLANCE

CROP
IMAGE > ADJUSTMENTS > LEVELS
CURVES ADJUSTMENT LAYER

DUPLICATE LAYER
FILTER > BLUR > GAUSSIAN BLUR

UNUSUAL VIEWPOINTS

One of the ways to help create a different look to a nude study is to work toward an unusual viewpoint. This can mean using a telephoto lens and zooming in, a wide-angle lens and placing the subject within the environment, or using the characteristics of a wide-angle lens to get close to the subject and distort the perspective. By taking a more unusual viewpoint, there will undoubtedly be images that are consigned straight to the trash, but those that work should give a fresh and unexpected look to a classic pose.

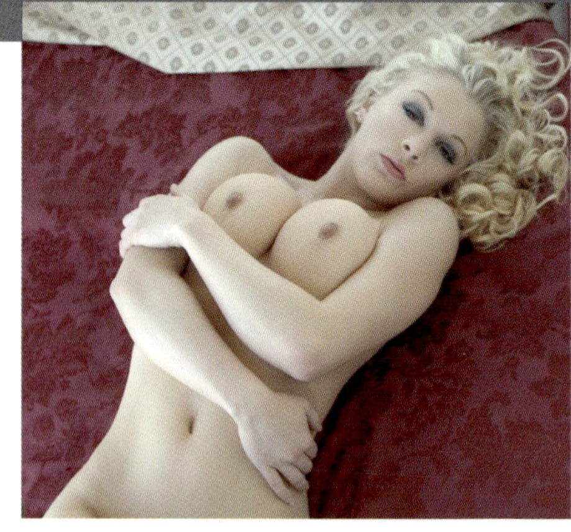

▲ In this shot, the camera is high above the subject. A 50mm lens is used to get close in, without incurring any of the distortion of a wide-angle lens.

SETTING IT UP

There is one key light in this shot, set up with an umbrella so that it throws light over a large area from one end of the bed to the other. Careful positioning and metering were required to ensure the spread of light was even from end to end. The light was metered at f/5.6, so the camera was set to that aperture and 1/125 sec shutter speed to sync with the light.

An 18–50mm (27mm–75mm) wide-angle zoom lens was used at the widest setting, so that shots could be taken from all around the bed.

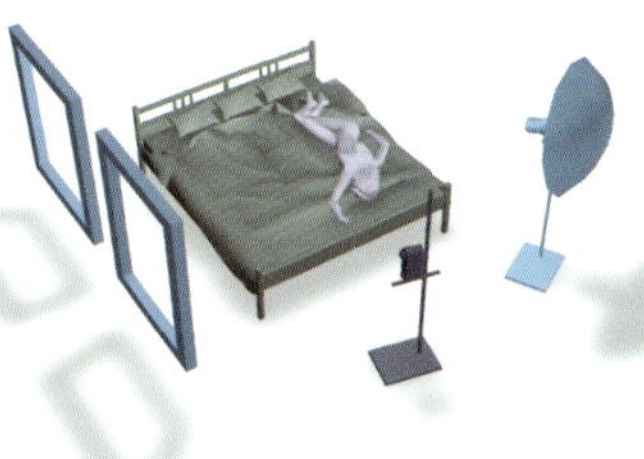

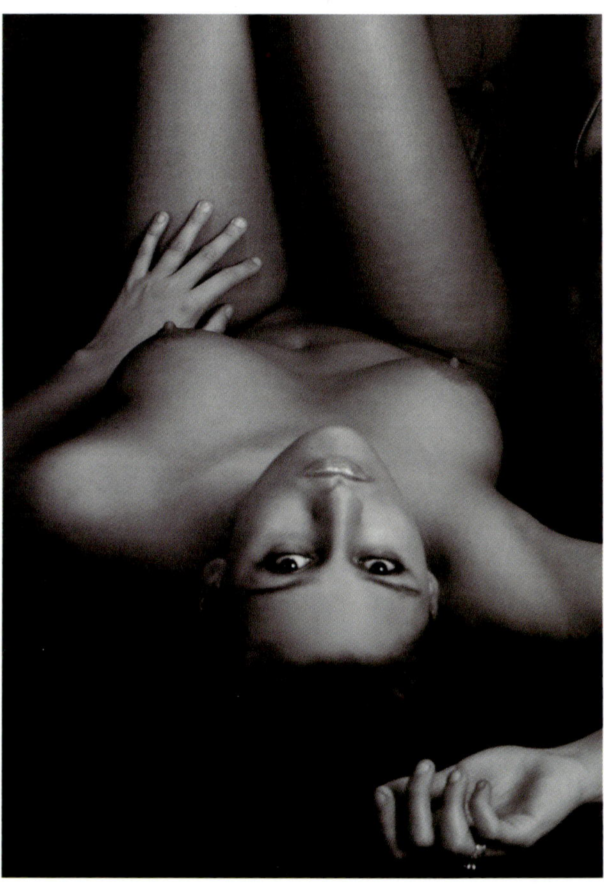

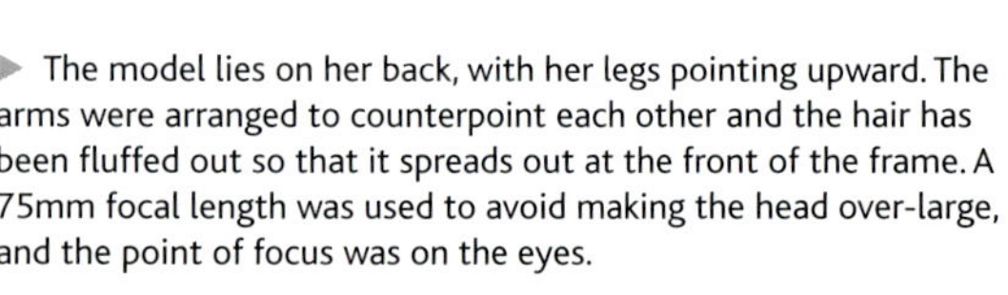

▶ The model lies on her back, with her legs pointing upward. The arms were arranged to counterpoint each other and the hair has been fluffed out so that it spreads out at the front of the frame. A 75mm focal length was used to avoid making the head over-large, and the point of focus was on the eyes.

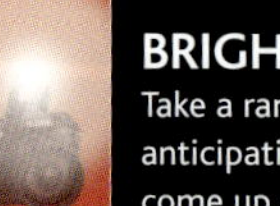

BRIGHT IDEA

Take a range of lenses to a nude photo shoot. After you have captured the shot you were anticipating, try out the opposite type of lens and change your position to see if you can come up with a radically different alternative.

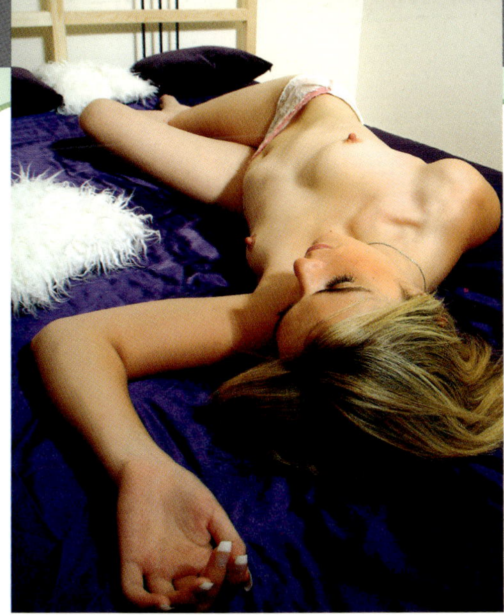

01
For these two shots, the wide-angle lens was used to deliberately distort and exaggerate the pose. The model is lying down on the bed with one arm and her hair leading toward the camera. The pose leads the viewer into the picture and off into the distance.

02
Although using the same setup as the last shot, this one is very different. The model lies across the top third of the image and an arm falls down the vertical third on the left. The lens distortion makes it very long and adds to the slightly surreal look.

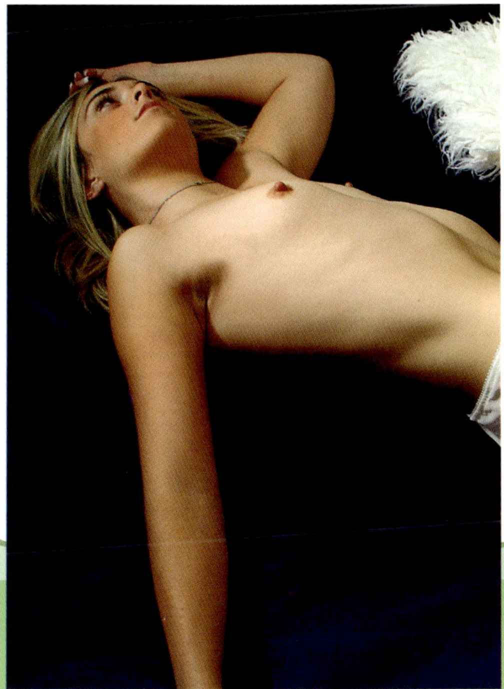

PHOTO EDITING

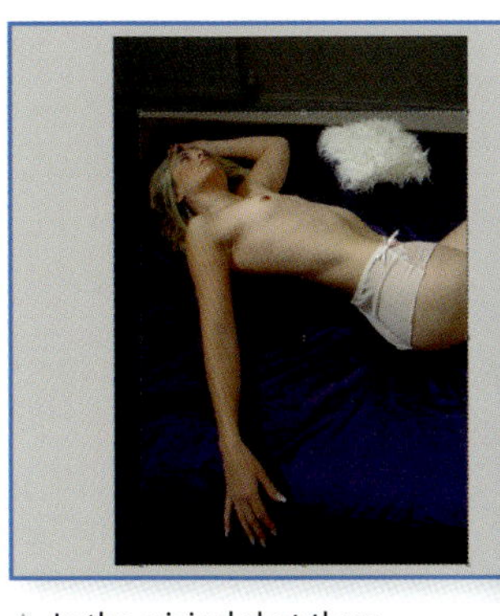

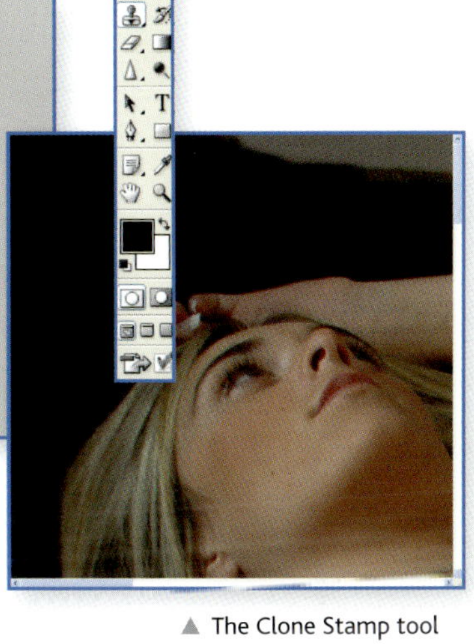

▲ In the original shot there was a little too much room at the top. The radiator was not attractive, so was cropped out.

▲ The Clone Stamp tool was used to extend the bed cover so that it filled in the gap at the top of the picture.

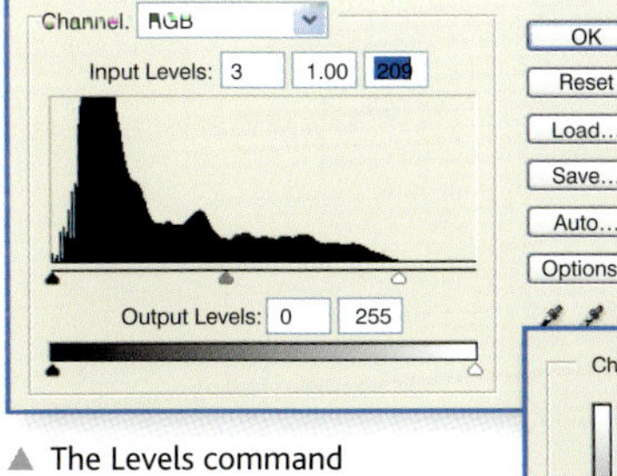

▲ The Levels command was used to stretch the tonal range out.

▼ Curves was used to darken the purple and lighten the highlights.

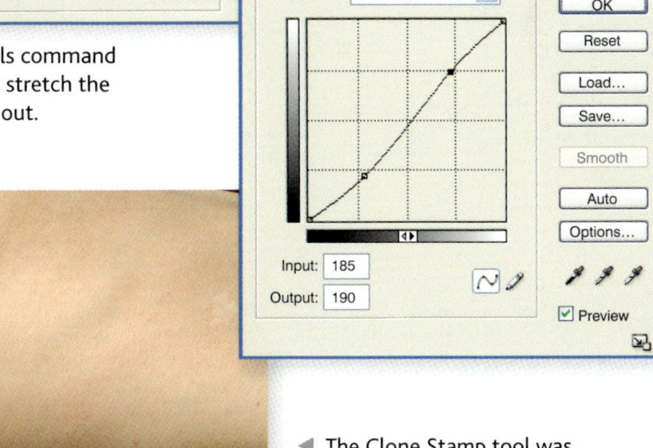

◄ The Clone Stamp tool was used again, set to lighten mode at 100% opacity, to carefully remove underwear marks and blemishes.

TOOLS AT A GLANCE
CROP
CLONE STAMP
IMAGE > ADJUSTMENTS > LEVELS
IMAGE > ADJUSTMENTS > CURVES

BACKGROUND TEXTURES

As models tend to have nice smooth skin, one interesting thing you can experiment with in your photography is to contrast that smoothness with background textures. It doesn't matter what those textures are; simply work with the contrast between the skin and the environment. You can look for natural textures, such as tree bark, leaves, grass, stone, and rocks, or manmade ones such as buildings, cars, or sumptuous interior furnishings.

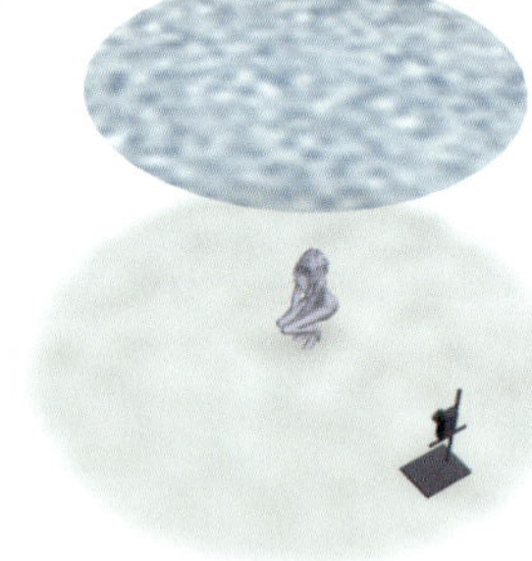

SETTING IT UP

The model was crouching down on the other side of a little pond in a wood, with a pathway leading up and away behind her. The lens was a 50mm, giving an effective range of 75mm on a digital SLR, with the aperture wide open at f/1.8 to throw the background into soft focus. The camera was about 10 feet (3m) away and soft, diffuse light was coming from overhead through the trees.

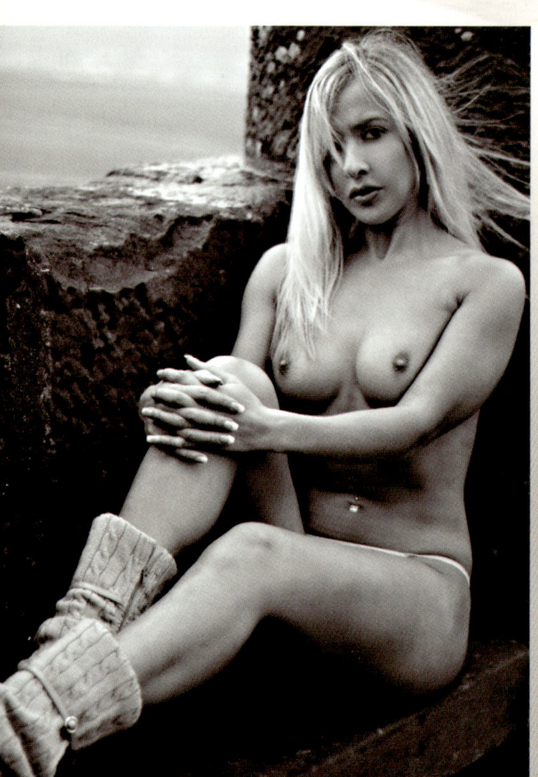

01 The textures here are from the rough-hewn stone platform that the model is sitting on. With cold, windy weather, it provides a forbidding environment.

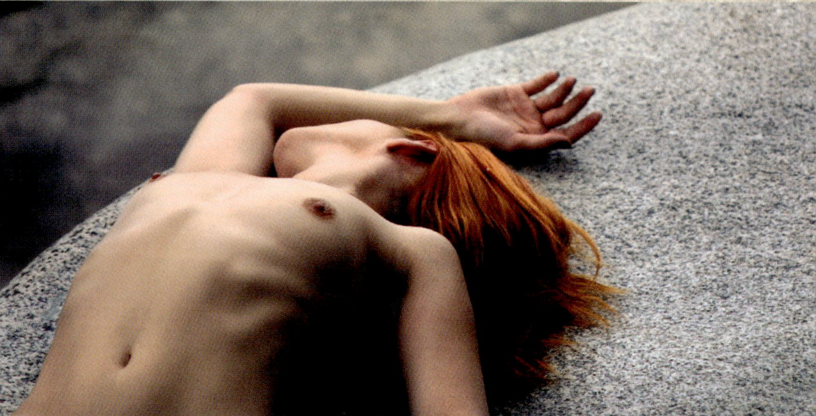

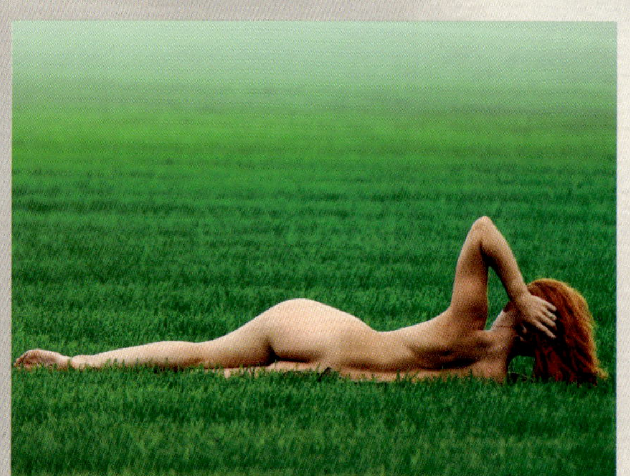

02 This shot by Stephen Haynes uses stone textures, but in a completely different way. The model is relaxed and the shot contrasts her skin tones with the rocky textures beneath her.

03 Stephen shot this image with a telephoto lens. The aperture was as wide as possible to avoid camera shake. The depth of field is quite limited, resulting in a pleasing blur of green into the distance.

BRIGHT IDEA

Stuck for a background texture? Look around the house, or go to a soft furnishing store, and see if you can find a large rug with lots of tousled hair for the subject to pose against.

PHOTO EDITING

▽ With the end of fall, all the leaves came down from the trees in this wood, making the background to the picture a riot of leafy textures to contrast with smooth skin. The model was asked to crouch down so that the steps to the path leading away were in the background.

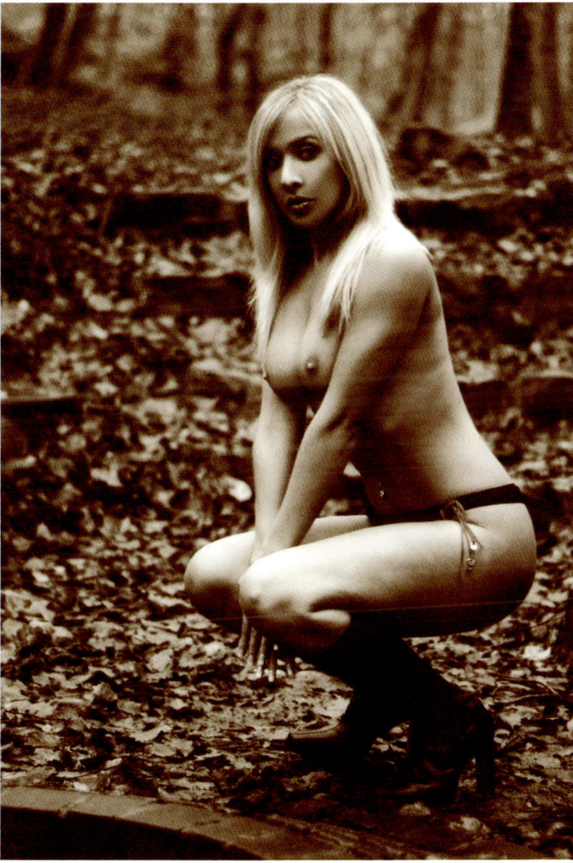

▷ The image was rather flat so the levels were adjusted to spread out the tones and increase the contrast.

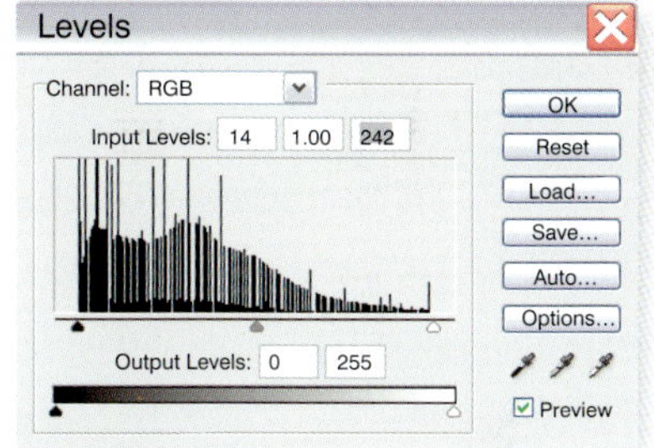

▽ The image was converted to monochrome using a black–white Gradient Map.

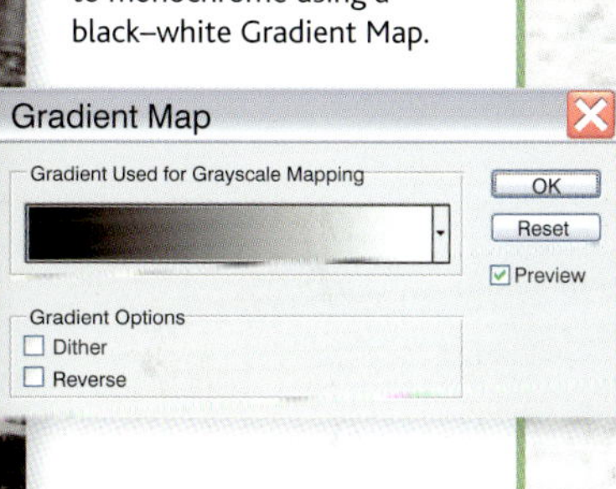

◁ The Clone Stamp tool was used in lighten mode with 100% opacity to remove some underwear marks and blemishes.

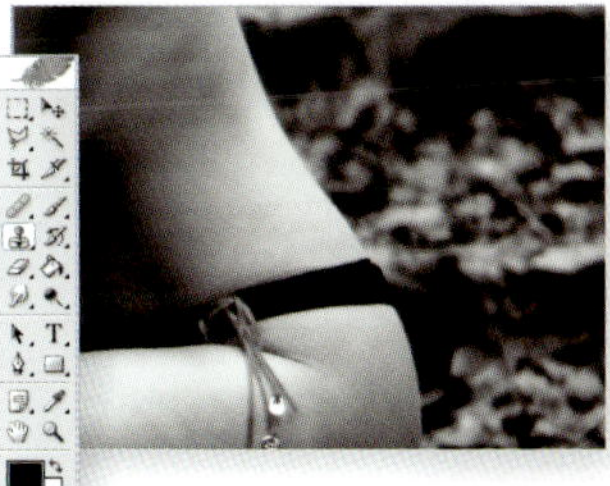

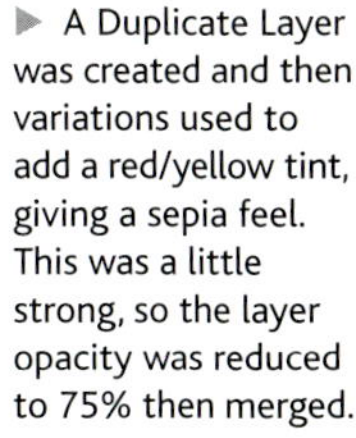

▷ A Duplicate Layer was created and then variations used to add a red/yellow tint, giving a sepia feel. This was a little strong, so the layer opacity was reduced to 75% then merged.

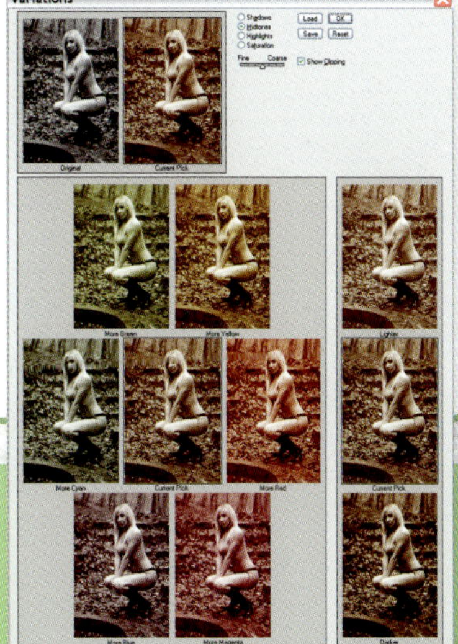

TOP TIP

Use a narrow aperture of, say, f/22 if you want all the textures to be as sharp as the subject, or f/4 or wider if you want to capture the overall feel of textures in the background.

TOOLS AT A GLANCE
IMAGE > ADJUSTMENTS > LEVELS
IMAGE > ADJUSTMENTS > GRADIENT MAP
IMAGE > ADJUSTMENTS > VARIATIONS

CLONE STAMP
DUPLICATE LAYER

SHOOTING MOVEMENT

Photography usually deals with split seconds, but for artistic purposes you can stretch that out to whole seconds. Instead of pin-sharp instants in time, you can capture a progression of movement. When you combine other elements, like water, using a fast shutter speed has the opposite effect. What is seen as a smooth flow is frozen into individual droplets and streams as it cascades onto the subject. Even slight image blurring, where the subject or the camera move when the shutter speed isn't fast enough, can lend artistic flair to nude images.

SETTING IT UP

This is the setup for the subject under the shower. It's a studio shot, and the first point to be made is to keep electrics away from any running water. The model stood in a pool, and the water was poured from a sprinkler by someone on a ladder to the right. There are two powerful lights (tungsten floods) on either side of the model, but also slightly behind so that she is almost backlit. The key point is to get the light to shine through the water. The aperture was set to f/8 on the camera, as this is what was metered using the built-in spot meter. The shutter speed was 1/640 sec, which was the top speed of the Olympus camera used. Although it had a built-in zoom, it was set to an equivalent focal length of around 75mm.

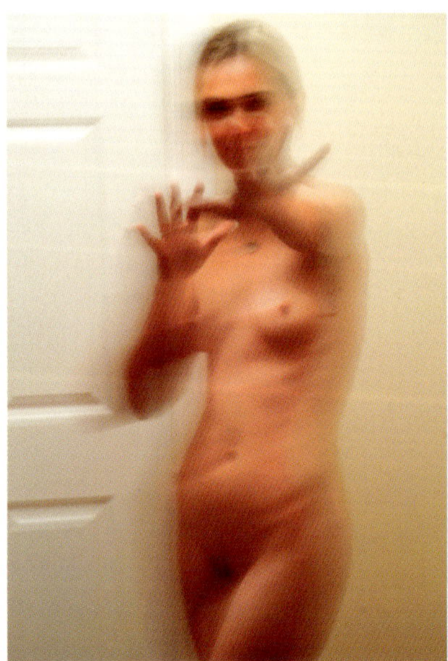

01 In this first shot, you can see the effects of a long exposure. This was two seconds, when the subject was moving around. She was asked to wave her hands about so that the image would be deliberately foggy.

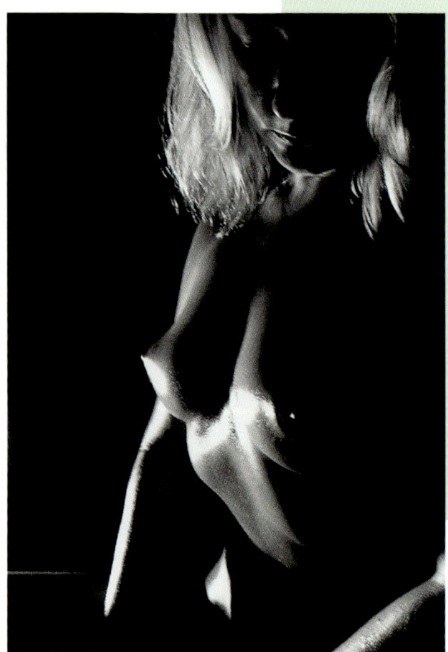

02 This shot from Mark Varley uses two powerful 500w tungsten lamps and a shutter speed of 1/150 sec. However, some camera movement while taking the shot has made a slight double image. This camera-shake effect can give artistic flair to a nude portrait, although it would be unacceptable in a landscape image.

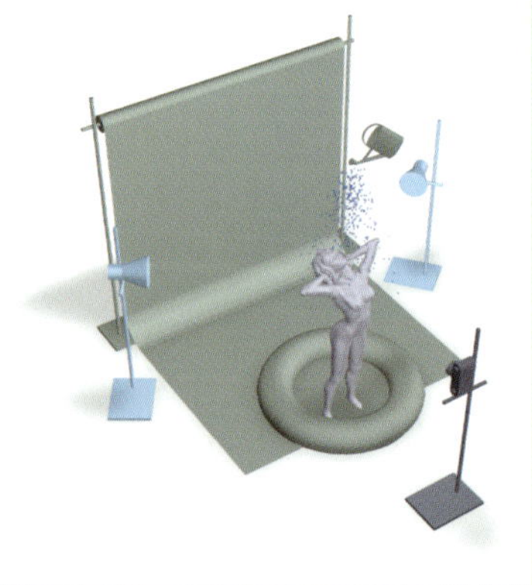

TOP TIP

To keep the background sharp while the subject moves about during a long exposure, mount the camera on a tripod.

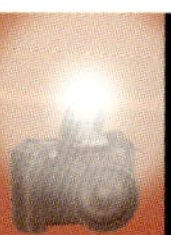

BRIGHT IDEA

Try keeping the model still and moving things around them, such as lights, candles, and flashlights, to create unusual lighting effects.

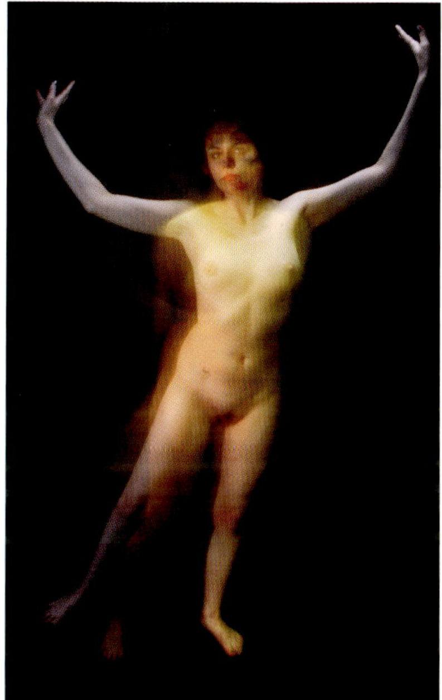

PHOTO EDITING

▶ When you introduce water into a composition with a model, the creative possibilities of playing around with the shutter speed are magnified. Here, the rushing water has been frozen in position with a fast shutter speed by Björn Oldsen, which also captures the model splashing underneath the shower.

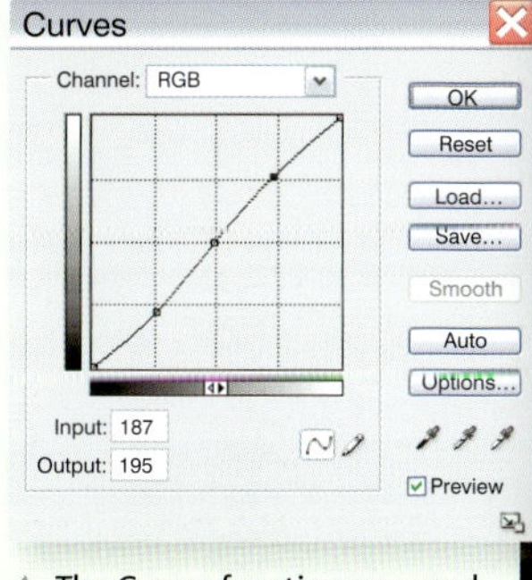

▲ The Curves function was used to darken the shadows and to make the water droplets shine a little more brightly against the background.

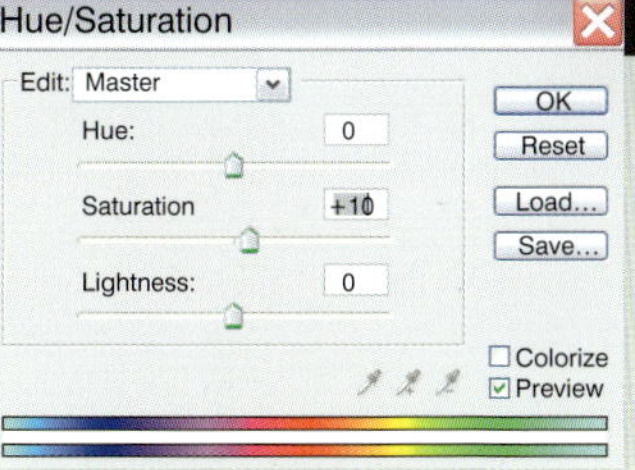

▲ The saturation of the image was tweaked with Hue/Saturation to make it look a little warmer on the skin tones.

▶ To make the water droplets stand out further, the Unsharp Mask filter was used with a 50% amount setting.

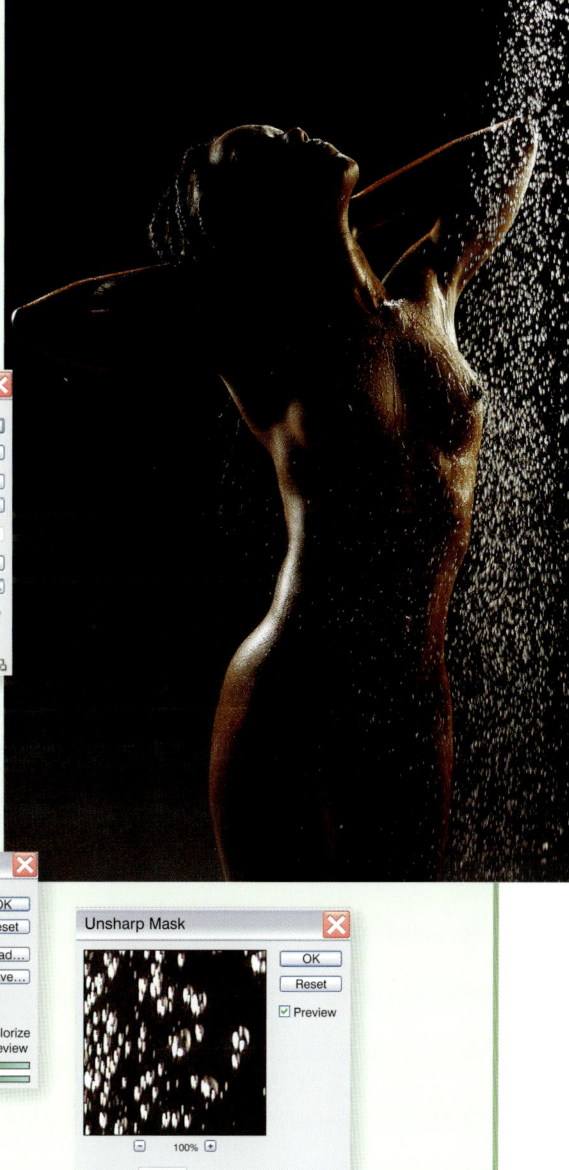

03 This was a tricky shot to set up because the area the model stood in was illuminated by fairly weak modeling lights. She stands against a black background. Firstly, what was required was a shutter speed of around 4 sec. This was dialled into the camera in Shutter Priority mode. The background light was metered and this gave an aperture reading of f/4. However, I wanted the background to be dark, except for where the light was hitting the model. So the single flash unit and the camera were set to f/8. The model was asked to start dancing and moving with the opening of the shutter, then, toward the end of the exposure, the electronic flash was triggered with an infrared remote. The result is ghostly yellow trails from the tungsten modeling lights on the model during the long exposure, and the model frozen in place when the flash fired.

ASSIGNMENT: THE DANCER

Your assignment on movement comes from a classically trained ballet dancer and model who wants a series of graceful nude portraits, showing off both her figure and her ability to go through a variety of poses. Because she will be moving around, there must be a large enough environment for her to do so, and you must shoot from further away than perhaps normally required. To that end, only a very large studio would be suitable, and a location shoot would be preferable.

SETTING IT UP

Location and lighting are everything, as the subject must be able to move freely without you worrying about where the light is. This location—the top floor of a converted warehouse in New York—is ideal. Light comes from two large windows, with a dark corner behind the subject so that she stands out in the light. The lens is around 105mm with the camera 20–30 feet (6–9m) away. An aperture of f/8 ensures enough depth of field as the dancer moves, and the natural light ensures a fast enough shutter speed to freeze the moving subject.

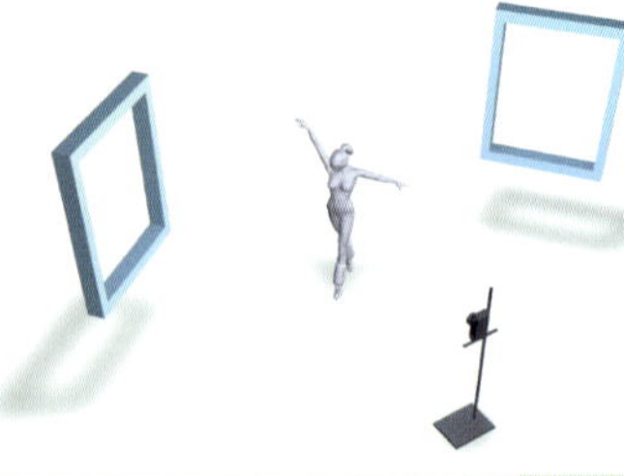

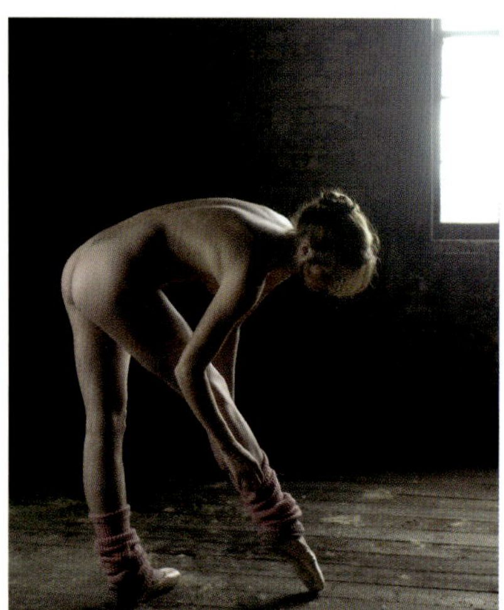

01 The opening shot here shows the subject extending her legs to put her legwarmers on. The pose is a good one to show the initial stage of dancing. Be wary of the light coming through the windows, as this will cause flare and underexposure if it is in the shot and the camera meters for it.

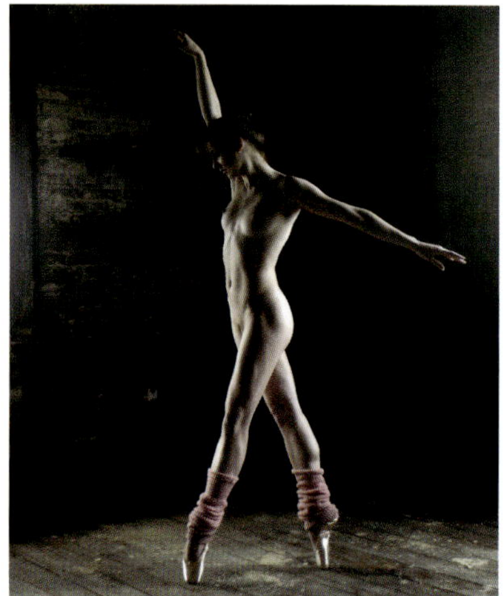

02 This is a great action shot as the dancer goes up on the points of her toes, showing off her fantastic athletic ability and control.

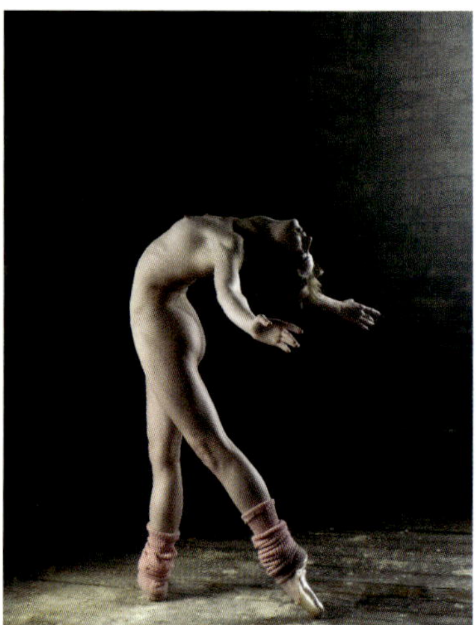

03 This graceful shot shows off the flexibility of the subject as she bends back, arms extended. You can make the decision to crop any pictures later—the priority is to capture the movement.

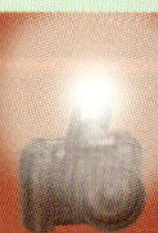

BRIGHT IDEA
Using fill-in flash could help if it's a little too dark to capture the shots properly. Don't use normal on-camera flash as it will ruin the atmosphere.

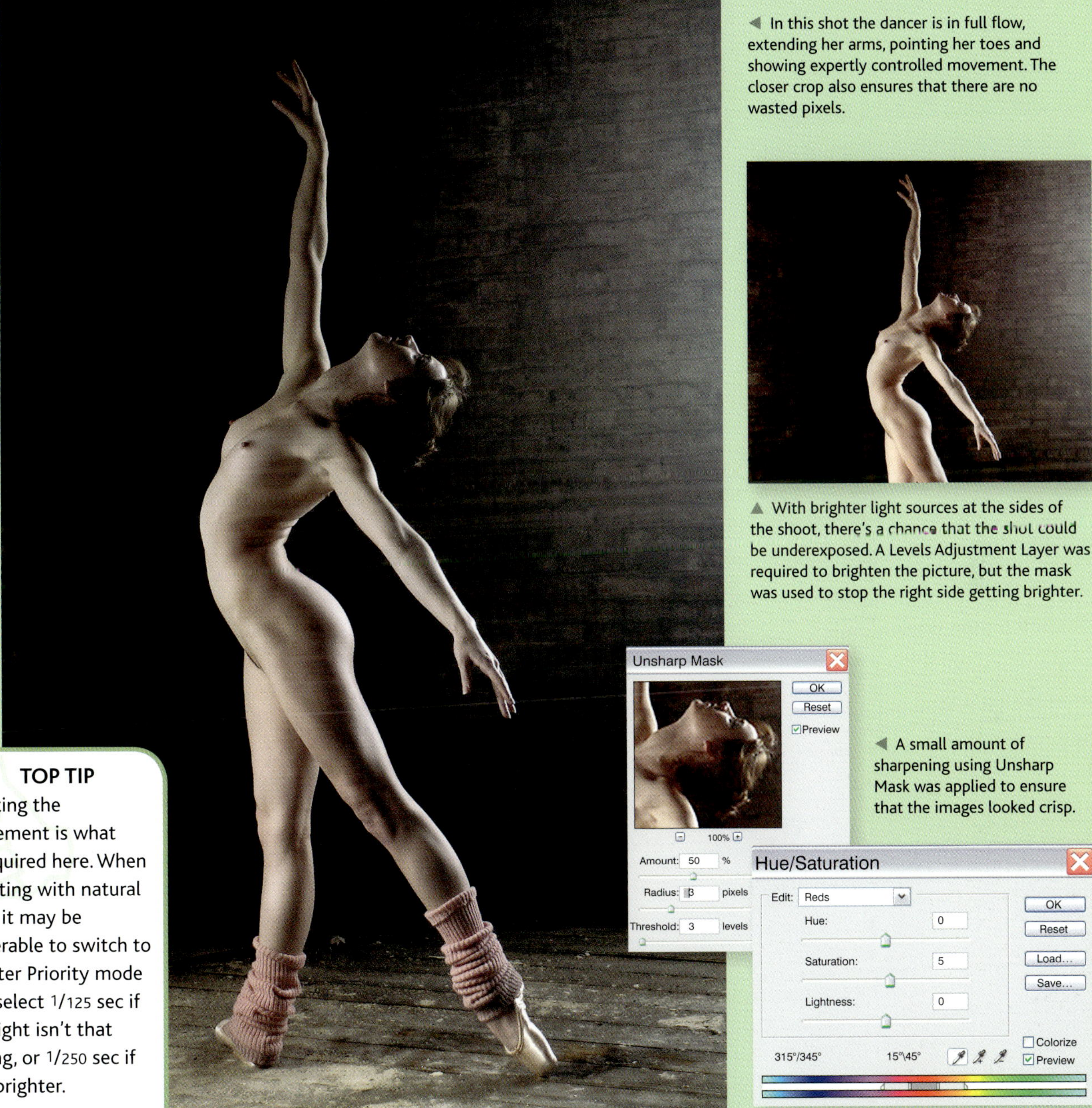

PHOTO EDITING

◀ In this shot the dancer is in full flow, extending her arms, pointing her toes and showing expertly controlled movement. The closer crop also ensures that there are no wasted pixels.

▲ With brighter light sources at the sides of the shoot, there's a chance that the shot could be underexposed. A Levels Adjustment Layer was required to brighten the picture, but the mask was used to stop the right side getting brighter.

◀ A small amount of sharpening using Unsharp Mask was applied to ensure that the images looked crisp.

▲ The saturation of the yellow and red colors in Hue/Saturation was increased by 5% to make the skin tones a little warmer.

TOP TIP
Freezing the movement is what is required here. When shooting with natural light it may be preferable to switch to Shutter Priority mode and select 1/125 sec if the light isn't that strong, or 1/250 sec if it is brighter.

TOOLS AT A GLANCE
LEVELS ADJUSTMENT LAYER
FILTER > SHARPEN > UNSHARP MASK
IMAGE > ADJUSTMENTS > HUE/SATURATION

INSPIRATIONS: THE BEST OF LOCATION SHOTS

When shooting portraits outside, the environment can be part of the photographic narrative, lending a meaning in conjunction with the styling of the person in it. Or, the scene can place and identify the subject, putting them into context. Finally, there might just be a nice background to shoot someone against. All these things are elements in a successful location shoot.

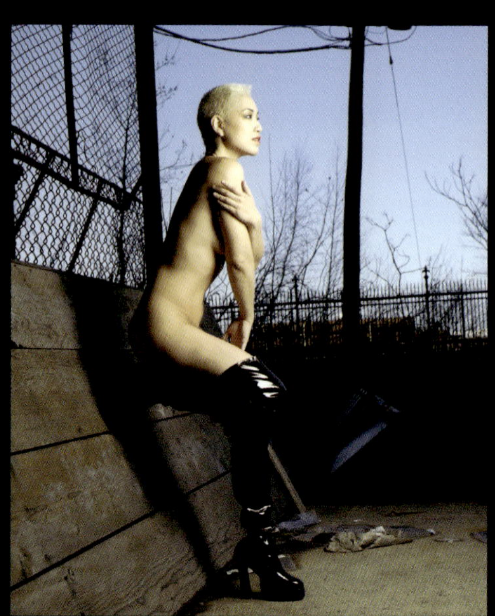

▶ A disused bus shelter in an abandoned industrial complex offered both grime and decay with a modicum of privacy for Dan Howell's shot on a clear, cold morning.

▼ There are multiple light sources in this picture, shot with a 50mm lens from some 25 feet away. The camera AWB is set for the electronic flash that was used to light the model, while bluer light from outside comes through the window and yellow light can be seen in the background from a table lamp in the hallway beyond.

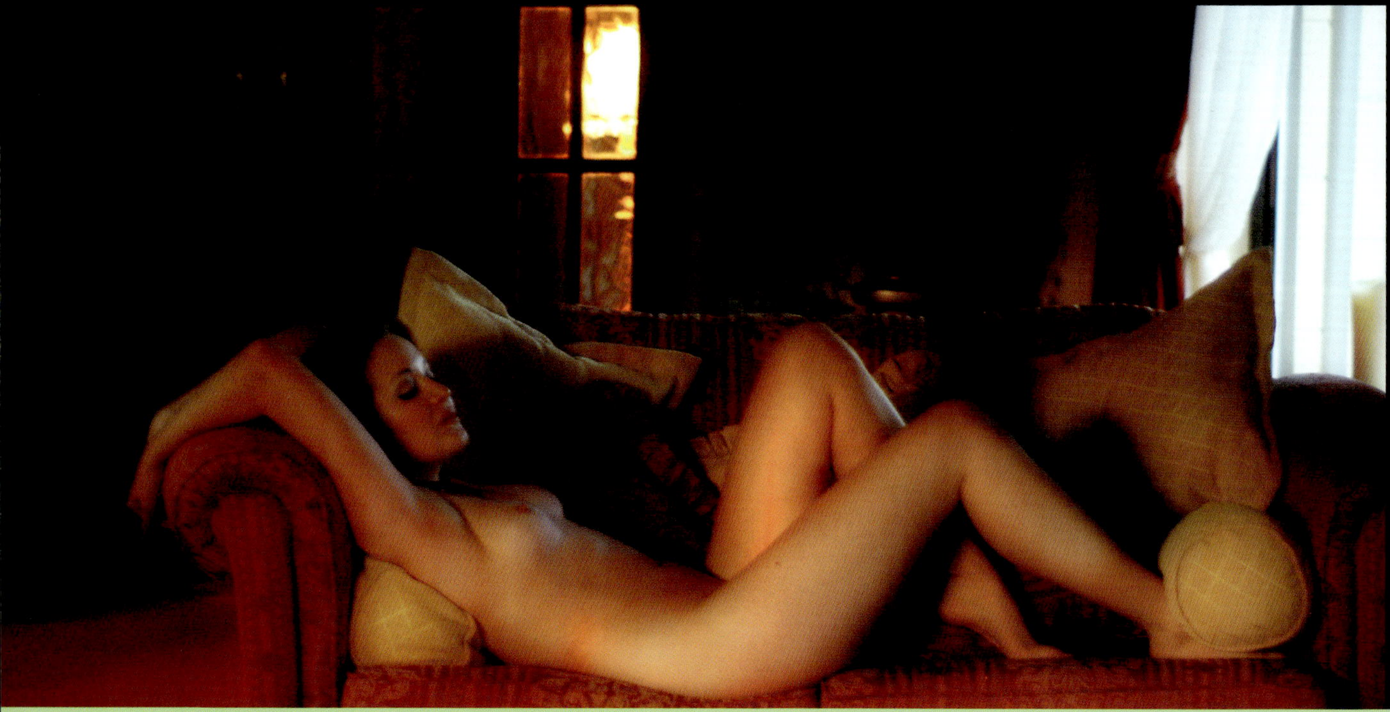

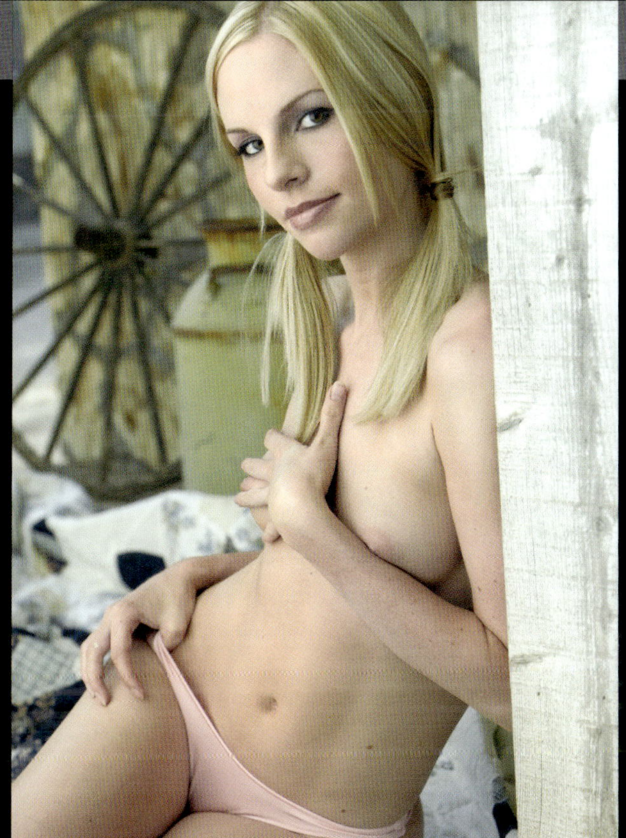

◄ This outdoor shot by Dan Howell uses a fresh and natural-looking model against a country, almost Western-style background. Rather than contrasting, these elements complement each other.

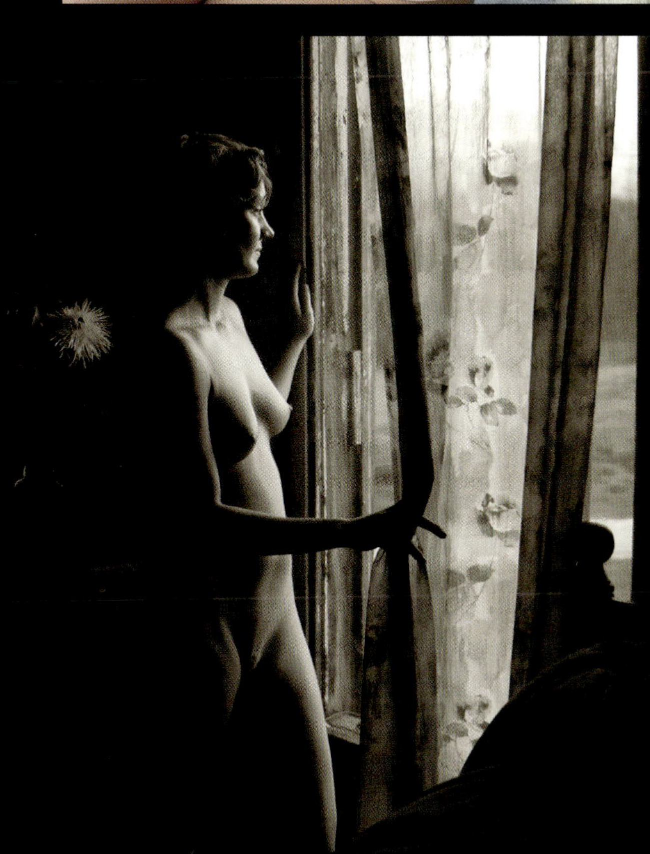

◄ An old house with a rotting window frame, worn furniture and traditional style bed and net curtains perfectly suits the sepia toning in this image from Dale Lehmer.

▲ The harsh contrast of midday is normally to be avoided, but Stephen Haynes exploits it wonderfully here. The diagonal of the bridge support separates black from white, framing the model in the blazing glare.

5 LIGHTING STYLES

How you light a scene, whether from natural sources, or from artificial lights on location or in the studio, sets the entire look and mood of a photo. While the styling and pose of the subject either need to fit in with the lighting scheme you have created, or make a striking contrast with it, lighting and composition are your number-one concerns. In this chapter we look at different types of lighting and how to use framing devices to aid in the composition.

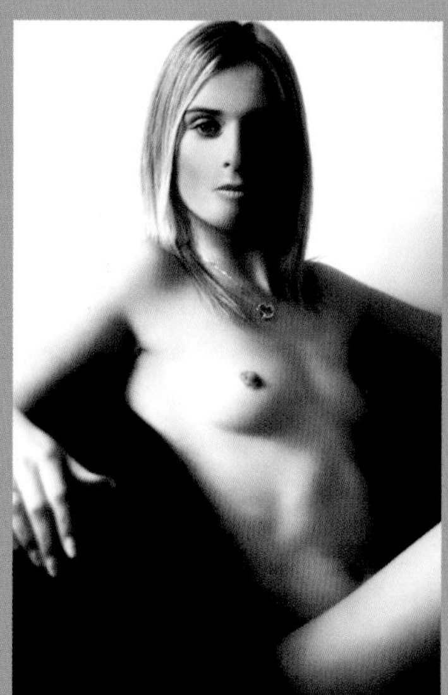

▲ Assignment: window light. Your first challenge of the chapter demands that you create a series of photos using only light from a window.

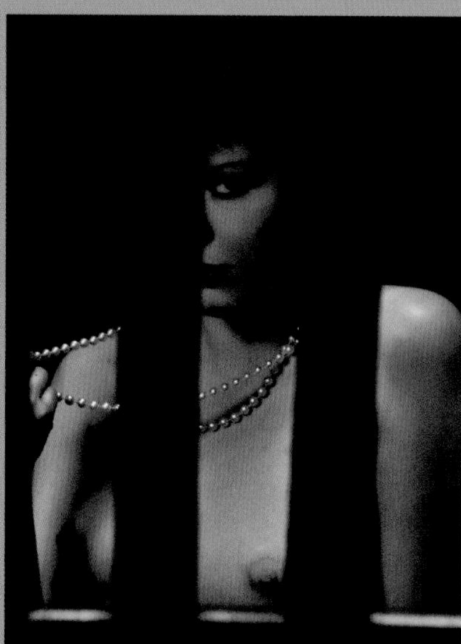

▲ Silhouettes: render the subject as an outline, or use the outlines of other objects to obscure your subject.

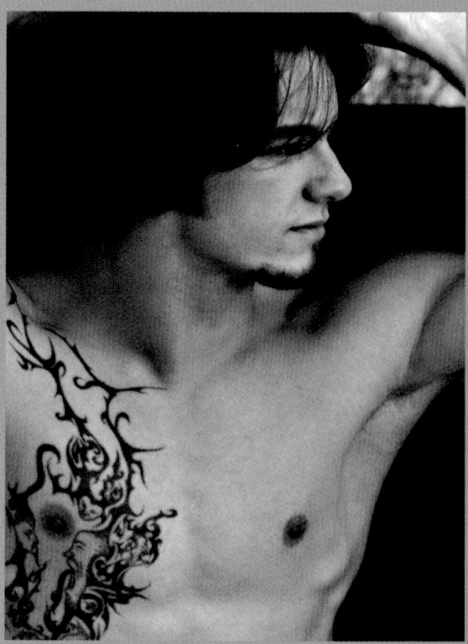

▲ Assignment: work the frame. Get your subject to move and work within a rigid frame.

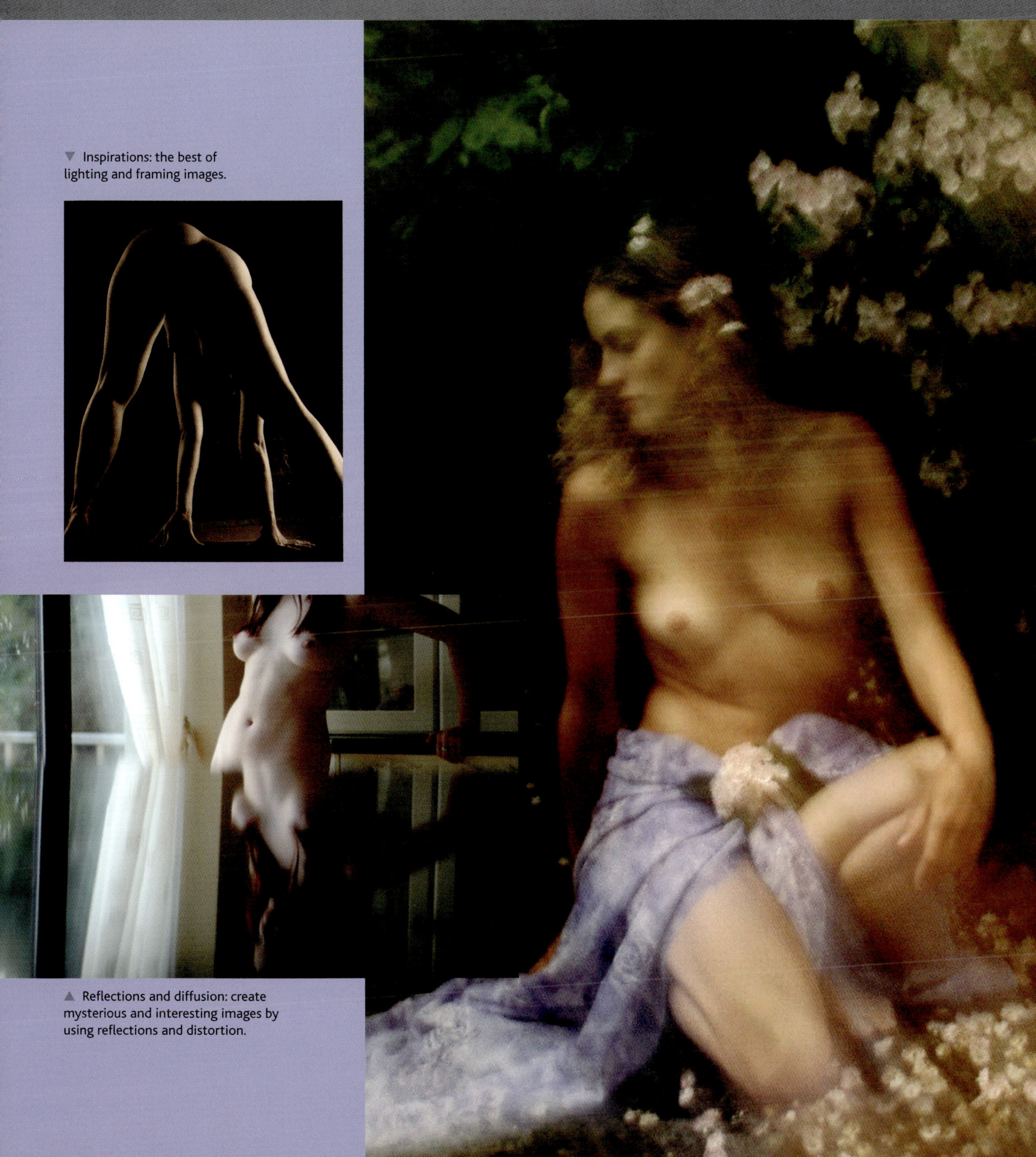

▼ Inspirations: the best of
lighting and framing images.

▲ Reflections and diffusion: create
mysterious and interesting images by
using reflections and distortion.

USING DAYLIGHT

The great thing about daylight is that it's available, free of charge, and you can use it outside or indoors. Available light offers a host of opportunities for trying out different types of photography. The bad news, however, is that natural light is changeable and unreliable. It isn't yours to command, and there's no dial to make it brighter, darker, or less contrasty. However, you can be skilful, and manipulate light how you want it. Think about where you position your subject, determine how the light is going to be reflected and refracted, and where the shadows will fall.

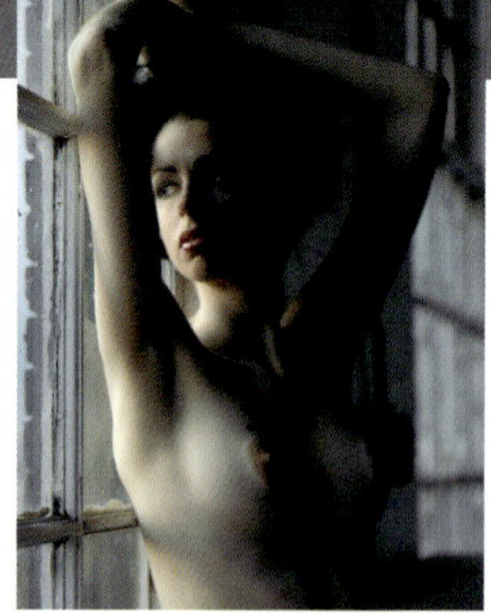

01 Window light on cloudy days offers a source of wonderfully diffuse light that the subject can look into without squinting. Here, the model is framed by the window she looks out of and a second one further down the room.

TOP TIP

If you want the subject to be perfectly visible, and accept the bright window light behind burning out lots of detail, then use spot metering and read off the subject's skin in an area in shadow.

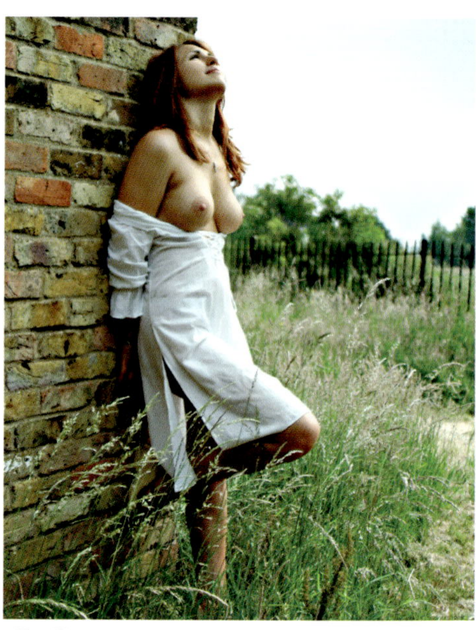

02 Daylight means working outside as well. Particular care must be taken in bright, sunny conditions, and also even if there is cloud cover. While there may not be any ugly shadows, it will be hard for the subject to look up into the sky if it is very bright.

SETTING IT UP

Using window light is about as easy as it gets in photography. It was cloudy here, which is ideal for photography because there are no harsh shadows and unrecordable levels of contrast. In this shot the model sat on a couch, with the window light to the left. This threw half of her face into gentle shadow and left patterns of shadow and highlights on her torso. The aperture was f/1.8 for very shallow depth of field, and the 50mm lens and camera were 10 feet (3m) away.

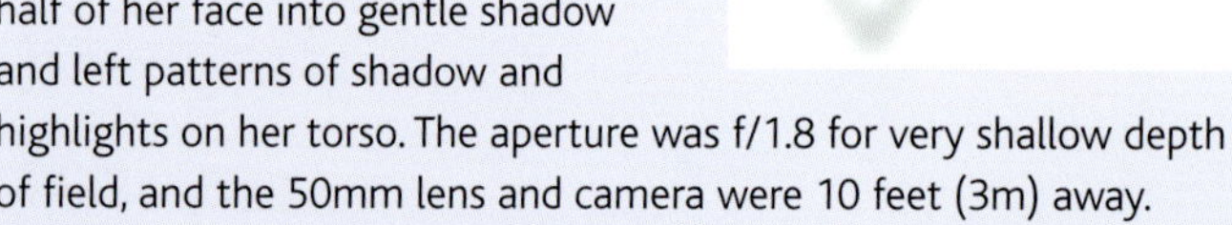

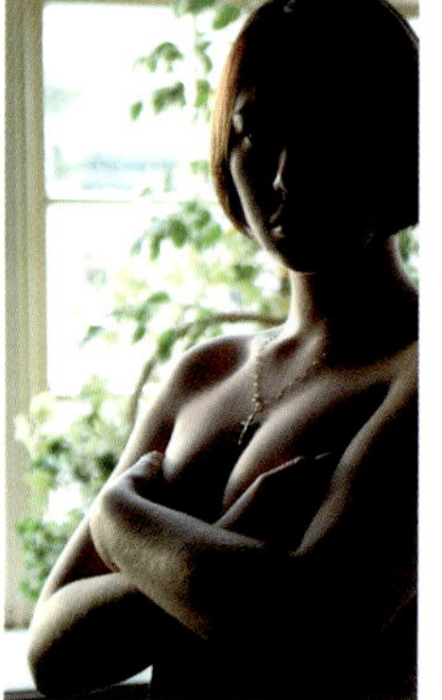
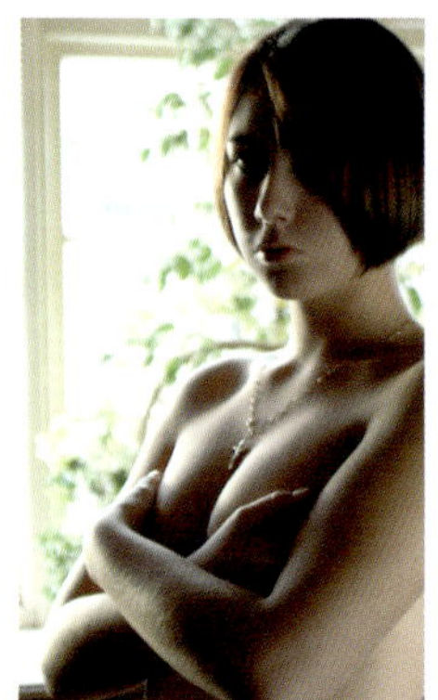

03 You can control how daylight is used in your images, as these shots show. The one on the left simply uses regular daylight; center-weighted metering off the skin tones was used to ensure that the figure was not rendered as a silhouette. In the image on the right, a portable flash unit was introduced, set at a lower power setting than that provided by the window light. The result is that it has brightened up this side of the image, revealing the model's face, without losing all the shadow detail.

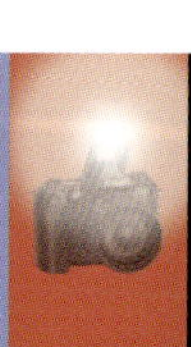

BRIGHT IDEA
Brighten up dark areas on the other side of the daylight source by using a reflector. Silver ones give a clean finish, whereas gold ones provide a more healthy glow to the subject.

PHOTO EDITING

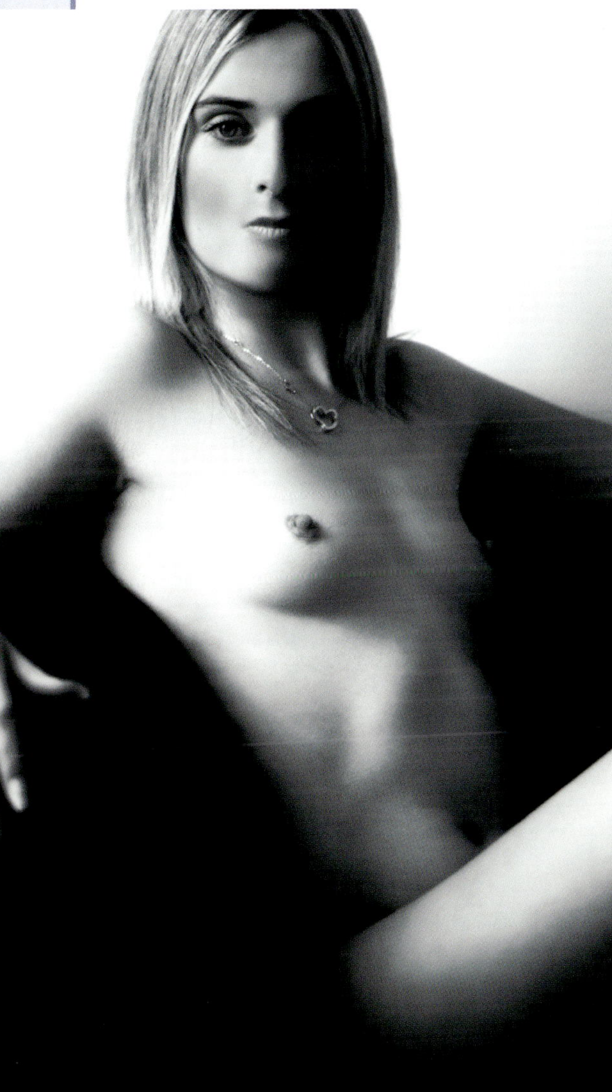

▲ In this photo, the model relaxes in the corner of a couch while the window light to the left provides soft, diffuse illumination. This, on a cloudy day, allows shadows to form where detail is still apparent. All you have to do in such favorable conditions is align the model with respect to the window light.

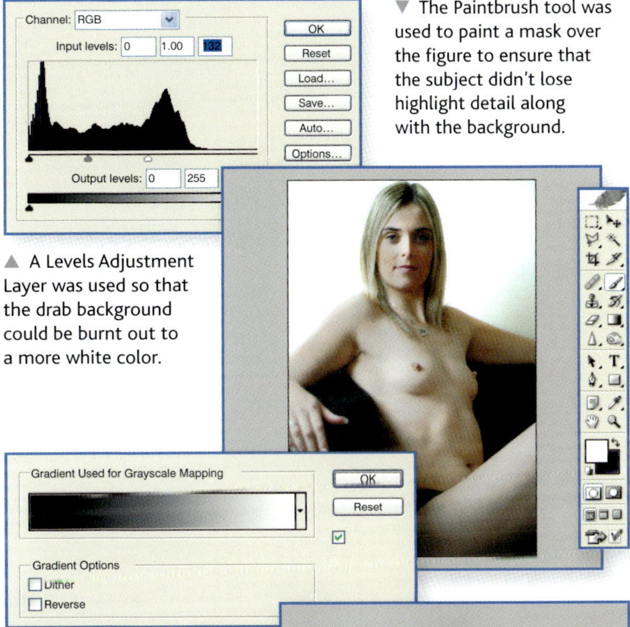

▲ A Levels Adjustment Layer was used so that the drab background could be burnt out to a more white color.

▼ The Paintbrush tool was used to paint a mask over the figure to ensure that the subject didn't lose highlight detail along with the background.

▲ A black–white Gradient Map was then used to convert the image to monochrome.

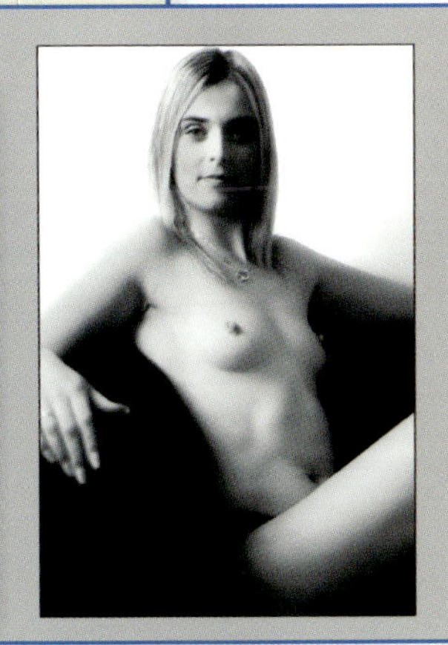

▶ A duplicate layer was created and this was blurred with the Gaussian Blur filter. The level blend mode was set to overlay and the opacity reduced to 50%. This added more shadow and finer graduation between light and dark areas.

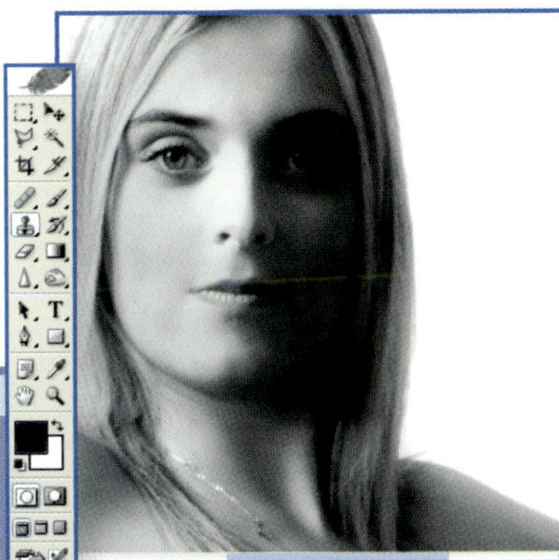

▶ The Clone Stamp tool at 20% opacity and normal blend mode was used to smooth out skin imperfections and give a deliberately flawless look.

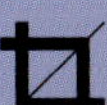

TOOLS AT A GLANCE
LEVELS ADJUSTMENT LAYER
IMAGE > ADJUSTMENTS > GRADIENT MAP
IMAGE > ADJUSTMENTS > BLUR > GAUSSIAN BLUR

PAINTBRUSH
CLONE STAMP

ASSIGNMENT: WINDOW LIGHT

Your assignment is to make use of daylight comes from a gallery. They have commissioned you to take a series of photographs of a trained dancer. The criteria are that she must be able to demonstrate her athletic ability, and you must use only sunlight to light her with. If you can include shadows and patterns from windows, all the better. The pictures must retain interest as a series, yet all stand up on their own merit.

SETTING IT UP

Set the model in late evening sunlight, filtered through a window so you get plenty of shadow effects. Stand 10–15 feet (3–4.5m) away and use a short telephoto lens (28–70mm) to zoom in and frame different lengths of shot. Zone metering should be fine, but if there's a tendency to lose highlights, use center-weighted metering and take the reading from the model's skin.

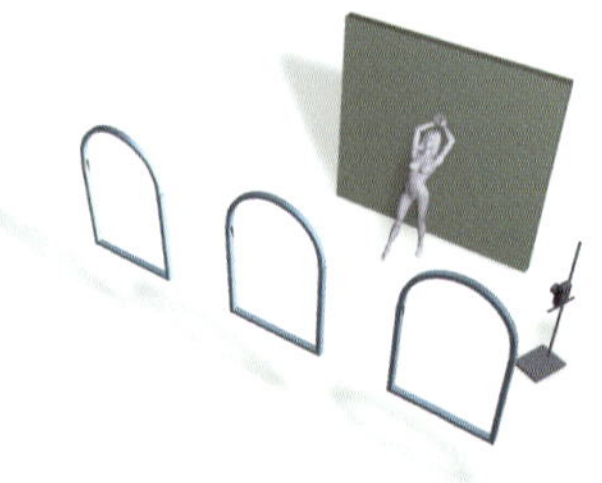

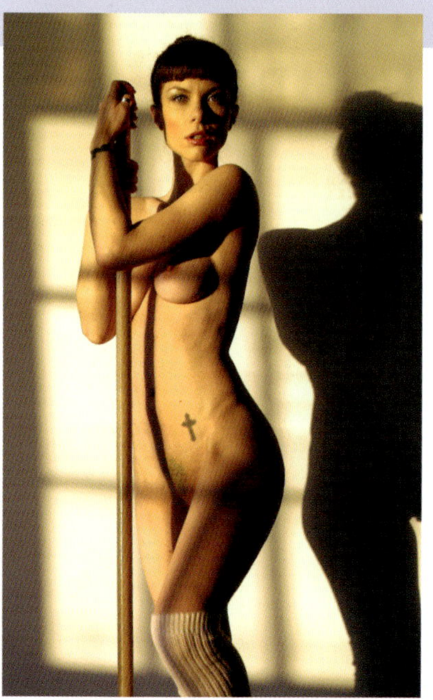

01 The model can use a pole as a prop to get the session started. The light from the window frames the subject well here.

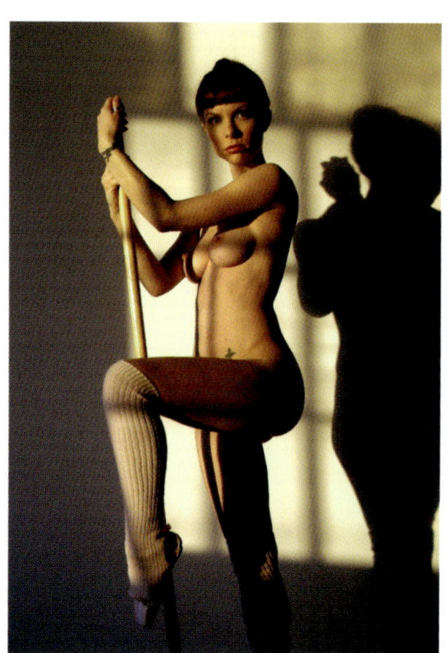

02 In this shot, the model shows more of her athletic ability by holding the pose with her leg held out. With shadows from the window frame and from herself on the wall behind, there is plenty of visual interest.

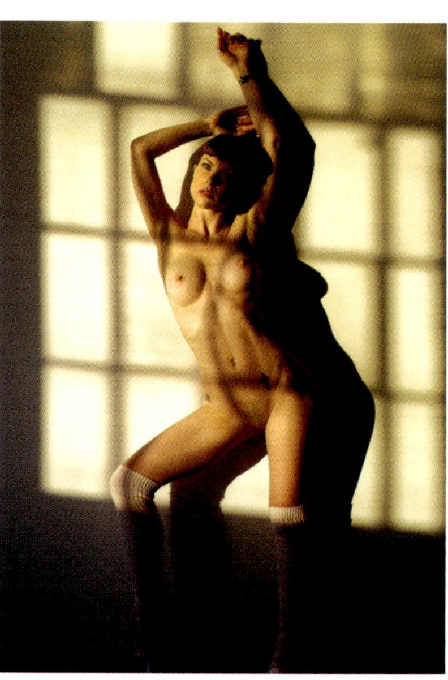

03 Here, the subject looks framed by the shadows from the window. The pose is languid, but the pointed toes allude to the model's dancing ability.

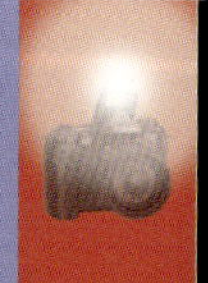

BRIGHT IDEA

If you have an interesting background, such as a textured wall, but the sunshine doesn't fall on it, use a large reflector to bounce light in that direction.

PHOTO EDITING

▶ This is the best of the session. The pose is all about the athletic ability of the dancer. There are patterns from the windows combining with gorgeous late evening sunshine, and the angle of the shot makes it the most dynamic as well.

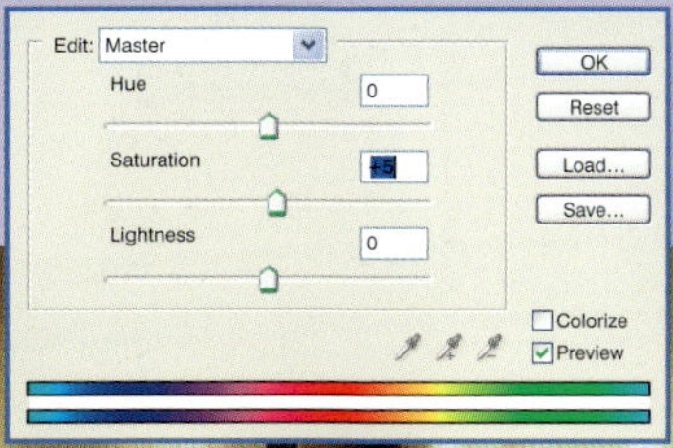

◀ The saturation was tweaked by 5% to boost the colors just a little.

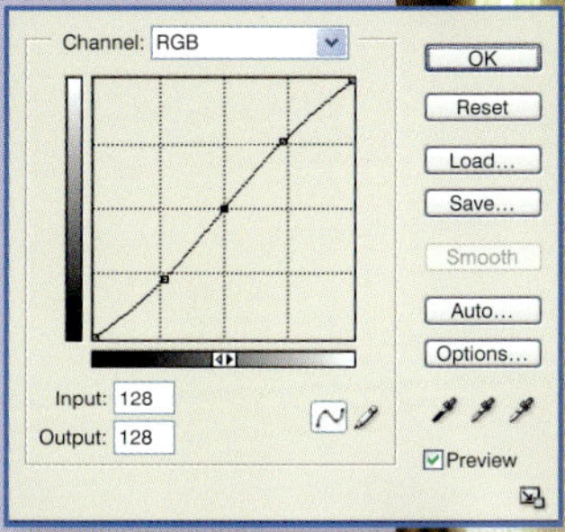

◀ The Curves tool with an S-shape curve was used to enhance the contrast of the image a little.

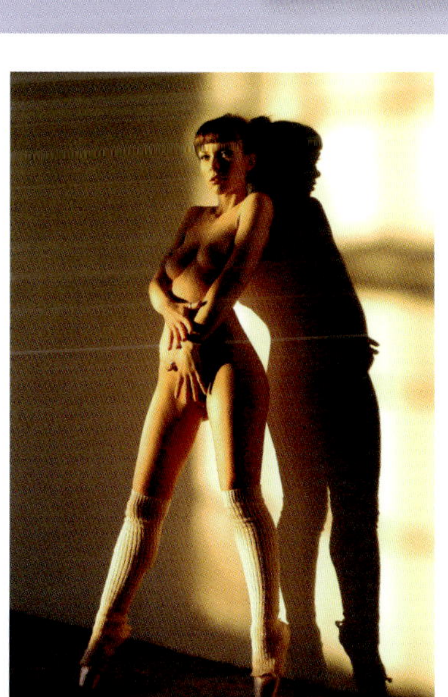

04 The reflection from the window frame has become quite diffuse, leaving a general shape and spray of colored light. Standing on point in her ballet shoes, the model's legs look wonderfully elongated.

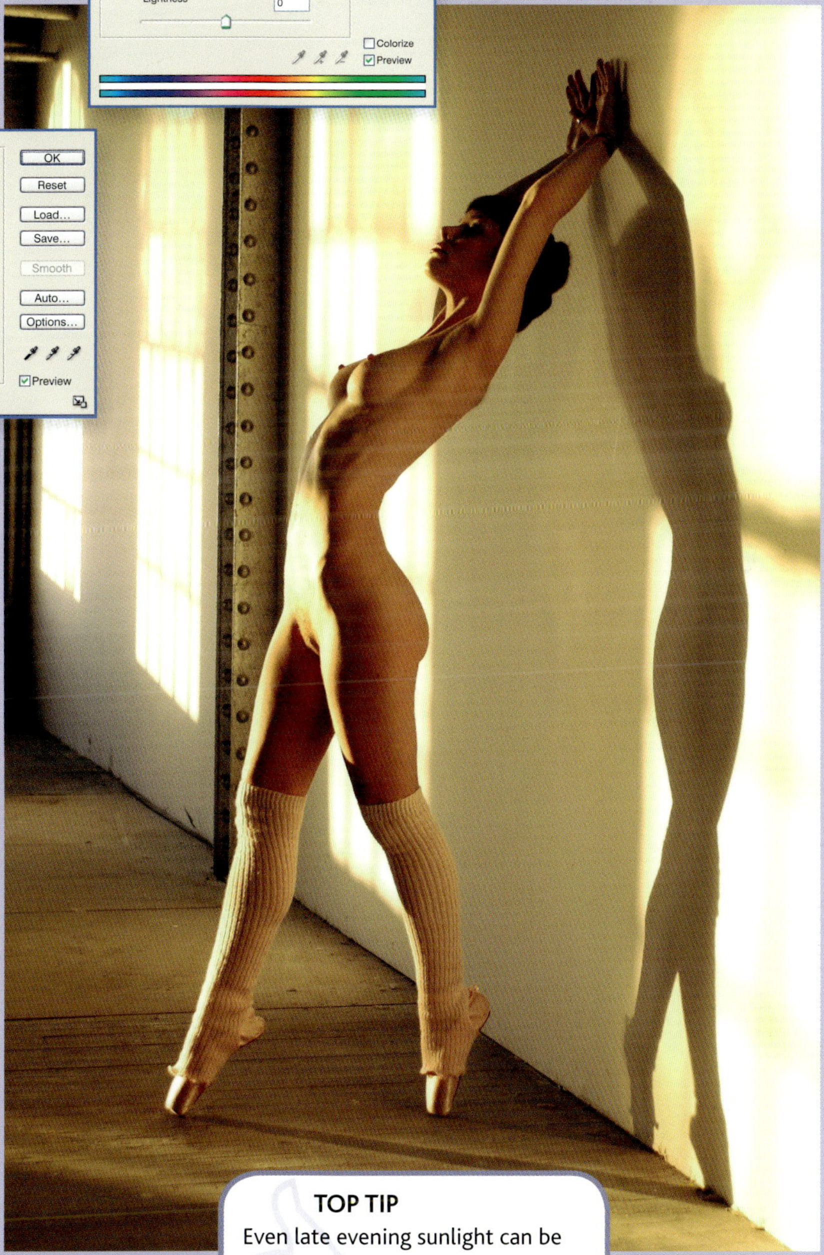

TOOLS AT A GLANCE
IMAGE > ADJUSTMENTS > CURVES
IMAGE > ADJUSTMENTS > HUE/SATURATION

TOP TIP
Even late evening sunlight can be quite bright, so an aperture of, say, f/5.6 should be possible to ensure the subject is in sharp focus, but that the far background is not.

SILHOUETTES

Given that a lot of emphasis in artistic nude photography is placed on composition and form, the silhouette is an obvious and much-used technique. The easiest way to shoot one is to place your subject against a bright background light and meter from the light area. The result is usually a fast shutter speed and the foreground (including the subject) rendered in shadow.

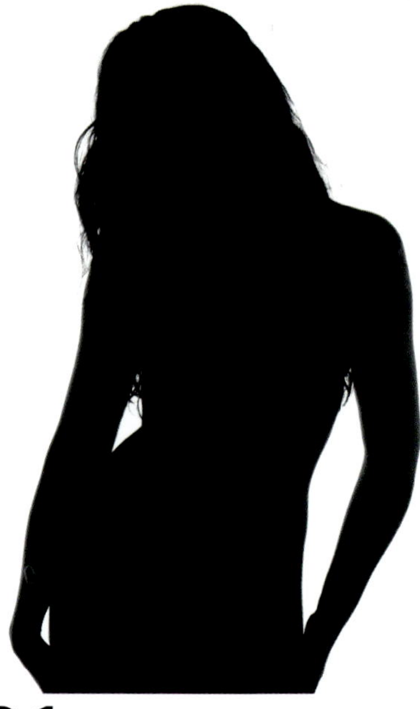

01 Shot in the studio, this is the simplest form of a silhouette shot. There are bright background lights but nothing firing at the subject herself. This turned her into a black outline, making the photo a study in form and little else.

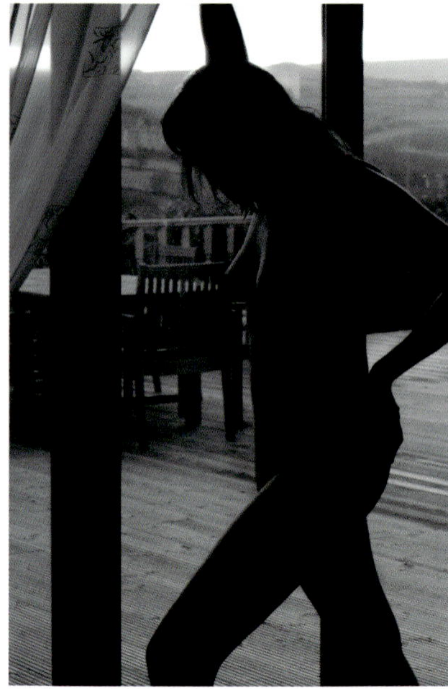

02 You don't have to turn people into complete outlines in order to use the general concepts of shooting silhouettes.

SETTING IT UP

This image began with the intention of framing the model with the elements of the chair. The chair was placed 6 feet (1.8m) in front of her and a 50mm lens used to shoot through it. A lens with a longer focal length could have been used as there is plenty of room on either side. The key light was a flash unit with a softbox off to the left of the camera. There was also a hair light suspended above. Light from the key light illuminated parts of the chair.

TOP TIP
Use spot or center-weighted metering and take a reading from the bright areas of the background to ensure a fast enough shutter speed to render it in shadow.

03 Doorways are obvious places of transit, whether the subject is coming in or going out. As the light outside is invariably brighter, it's easy to render the subject as a silhouette. The question then concerns the subject's relationship with the environment.

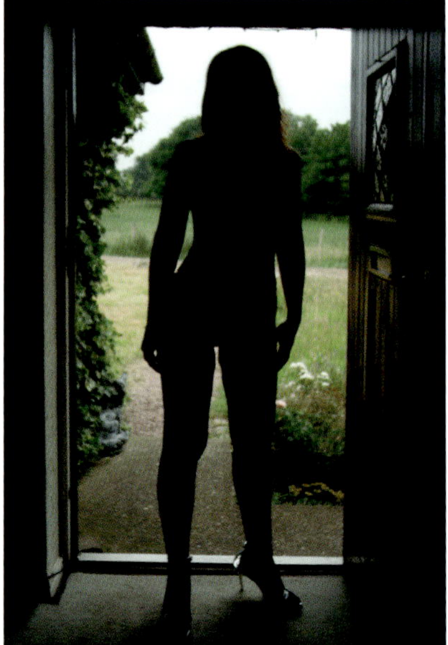

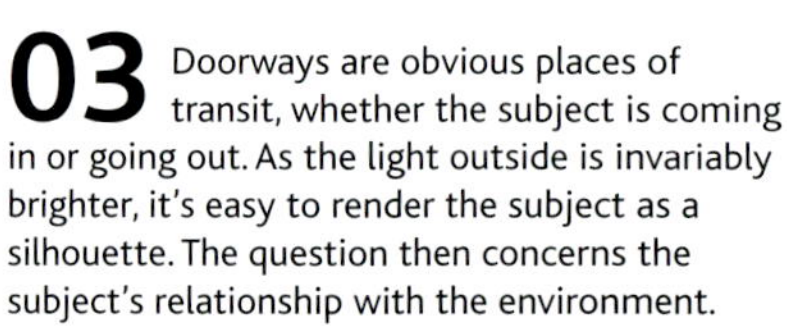

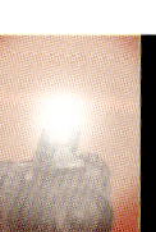

BRIGHT IDEA
If the background is not light enough to turn the foreground into a shadow, set up a flash unit to light it.

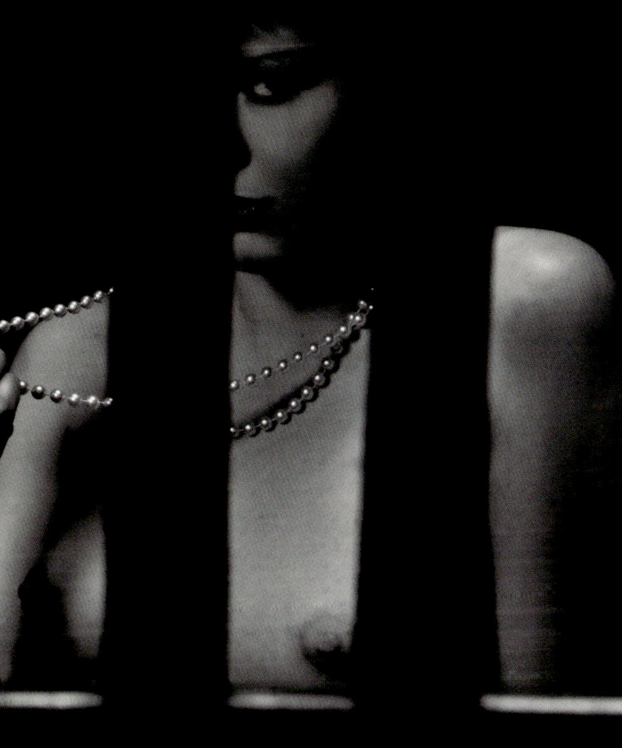

PHOTO EDITING

◄ While this started out as a framing device to put the model behind, it became apparent that darkening the chair frame to a silhouette would make it more effective. So, in this photo, it isn't the subject that is the silhouette, it's the framing device of the chair that is presented as a shadow.

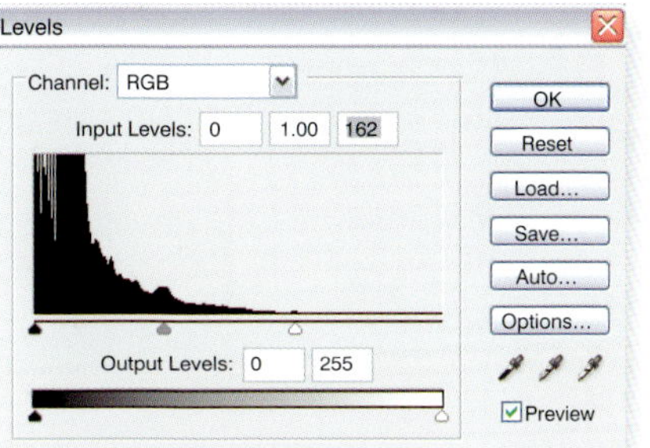

◄ As the image was very dark, the Levels were stretched out to use more of the tones. The primary aim of this was to make the subject brighter. The image was then converted to monochrome with a black–white Gradient Map.

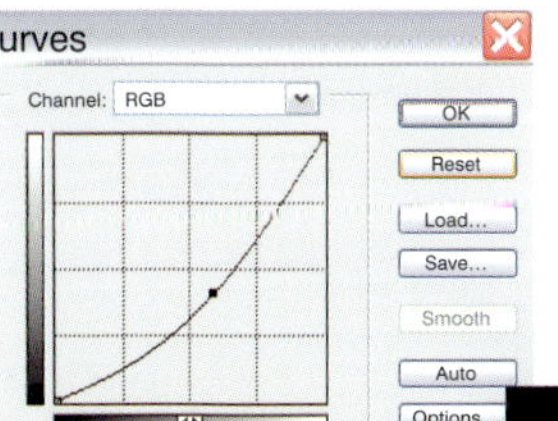

▲ A Curves Adjustment Layer was created to darken the struts of the chair and turn the foreground into a silhouette. The layer mask was painted in the gaps between the struts to retain the brightness in the picture.

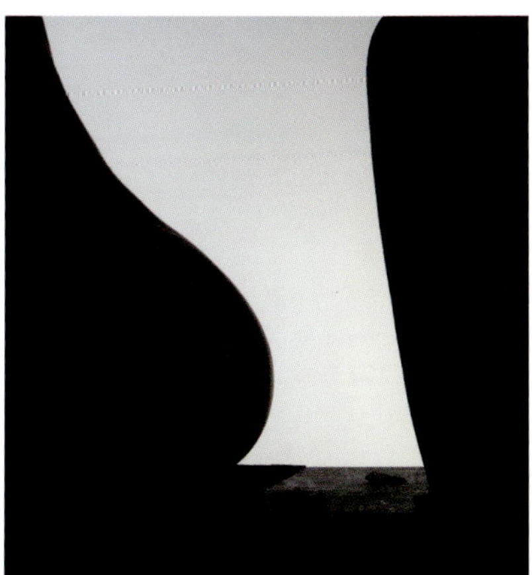

04 Eric Kellerman's image cleverly uses the shapes of his subject and a prop (a vase) to create a graphic image. As the picture is cropped at the top, all you can see are gentle curves opposite the back of the subject.

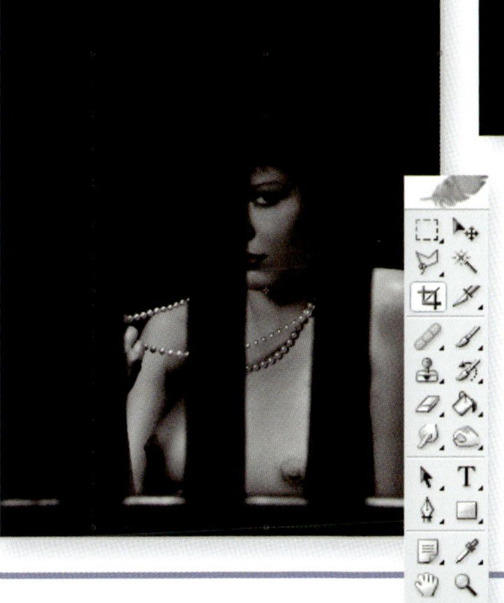

◄ The Crop tool was used to concentrate in on the action as there was too much wasted space.

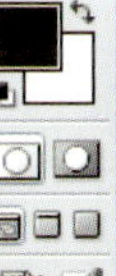

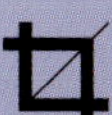

TOOLS AT A GLANCE
IMAGE > ADJUSTMENTS > LEVELS
IMAGE > ADJUSTMENTS > GRADIENT MAP
CURVES ADJUSTMENT LAYER
CROP TOOL

STUDIO FLASH OPTIONS

If you have never worked in a studio before, you could be forgiven for thinking that your lighting options were simply large lights with a softbox attached. However, there are far more alternatives than that, so you create a variety of effects to suit almost any situation you can devise. While some accessories and lighting types are more useful than others, it's the variety available that makes studio work so much more controllable.

SETTING IT UP

This is the setup for the main picture and shows the use of two main lights, fitted with softboxes. One is to the left, the other is slightly to the right of the camera, both set to f/8 power. This provides all-round light and, when used with a white background, allows the subject to be lifted out of their surroundings. The camera is around 10 feet (3m) back, with a 35mm lens capturing all of the model. The shutter speed is 1/125 sec, which is the typical synchronization speed.

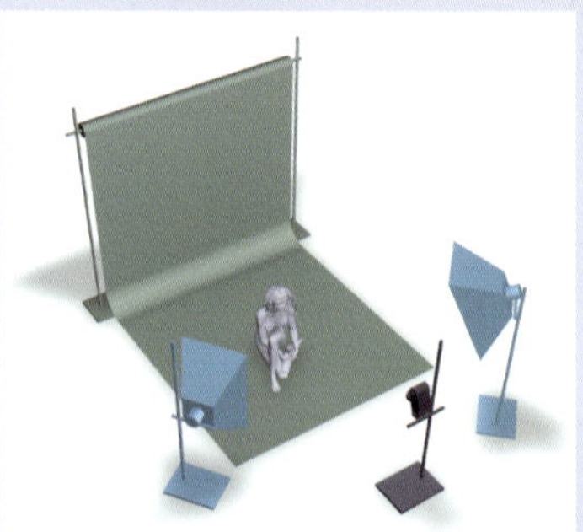

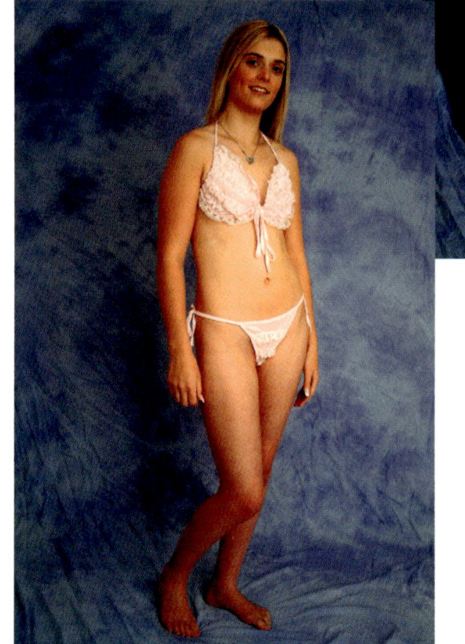

SOFTBOXES VS UMBRELLAS

In the studio, the softbox is king. It presents a large, even surface through which to diffuse the light from the electronic flash. The output is more even, there are fewer shadows, and it is easy to work with. A softbox fits on the front of the flash and is fired through. While most softboxes are square, there are also long and thin ones for creating narrow swathes of light.

An umbrella, typically, is fitted so that the curved side is facing the subject, the flash is facing backward into it, and the light then reflects outward. This makes it harder to position and the quality of the light isn't as good. However, if you don't need a powerful light setting, then you can also turn the entire thing around and fire the light through the umbrella at the subject. The light now is far more diffuse and casts very little shadow, though it is considerably weaker.

01 This picture shows the result if you don't diffuse your flash, or if you use a powerful tungsten lamp directly. Very harsh, deep shadows are the result.

02 Adding an umbrella and shooting through it gives very diffuse light, that casts only the weakest of shadows.

BRIGHT IDEA
Electronic flash is balanced to be the same color temperature as daylight, whereas constant tungsten light—even professional kits—are lower and will give a yellow cast to an image unless the white balance is set accordingly.

SNOOTS AND BARN DOORS

The snoot is a circular pipelike fitting that covers the flash and directs the light in a tight circle. Typically, the snoot is used on small lights for adding highlights to hair, but it can be used for dramatic effects as well. A barn door is an attachment that is used instead of diffusion, and features four movable plates. These can be arranged to restrict light in any of four planes, so that it only goes in certain directions. It is best used to control light on a background, rather than on the subject.

05 Mark Edmonson's image here uses two main lights fitted with softboxes in a typical studio setup. By using two lights, and with the subject sitting on the floor, all-round illumination is achieved.

TOP TIP

The main studio light is called the key light. Other lights, usually set on a weaker power, are called fill lights, as they add definition to areas that would otherwise be in shadow.

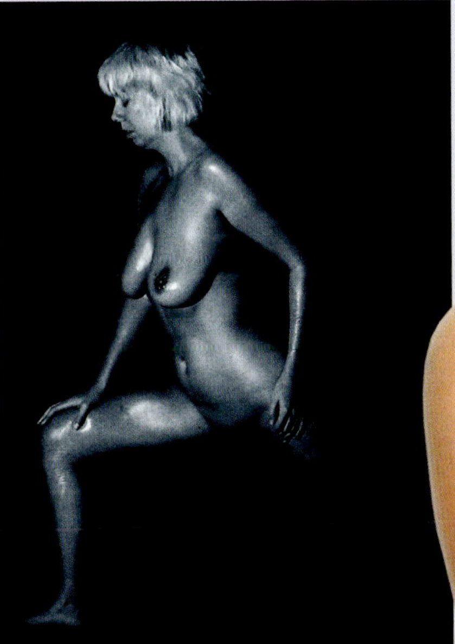

04 Mark Varley's image shows how using barn doors can restrict the light so that it cuts off at the trailing leg.

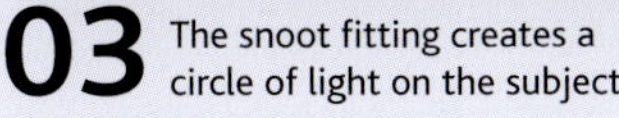

03 The snoot fitting creates a circle of light on the subject

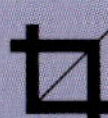
TYPES OF ATTACHMENT
SOFTBOX
UMBRELLA
SNOOT
BARN DOORS

ASSIGNMENT: STUDIO WORK

The main advantage of shooting in the studio is that you can control the environment and the lighting. Your studio assignment therefore is to shoot a series of artistic nudes featuring the model being lively and graceful, while surrounded by splashes of bright white light. To make things a little harder for you, you cannot shoot the face of the subject and the lighting must define the shape of the subject, not turn it into a high-key image.

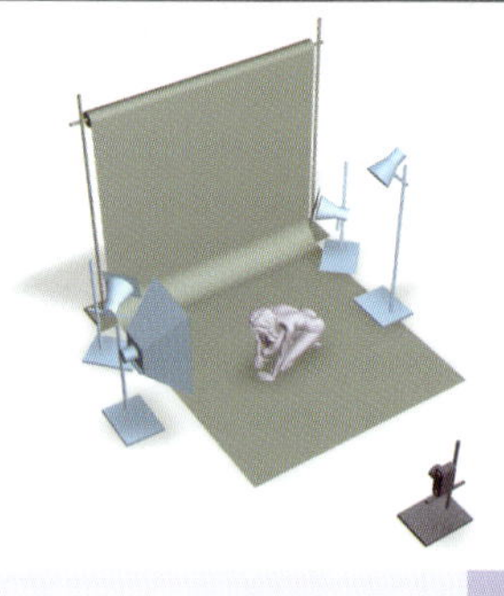

SETTING IT UP

You'll need a large white area, preferably with an infinity curve at the back. Use two lights with diffusers to aim at the background. Use the key light with a softbox to the left of the camera to shoot across the model. Place a secondary light behind the model on the right, pointed down to the ground. You will have to stay in the middle of the scene, to avoid shooting outside the backdrop. Use a 70–200mm telephoto lens to get closeup shots from 20 feet (6m) away. Set the key light to f/11, the rear lights to f/16, and the secondary light to f/8. Set your aperture to f/8, too.

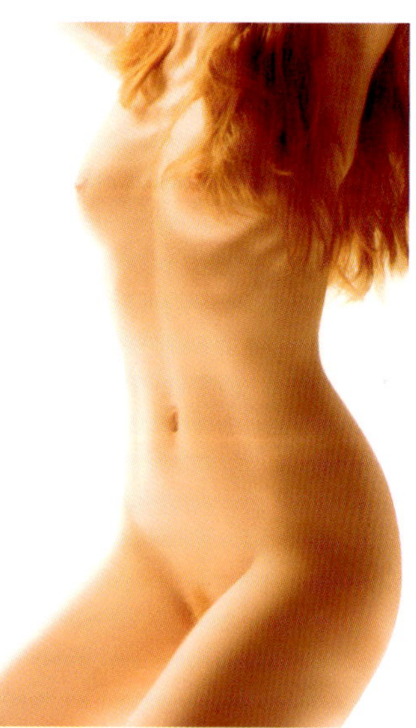

01 This is an excellent starting shot, showing off the slender physique of the model with masses of her red hair dropping down into the picture. The pose has been frozen as she jumped up and down—look at the angle of her legs—making for a very dynamic picture.

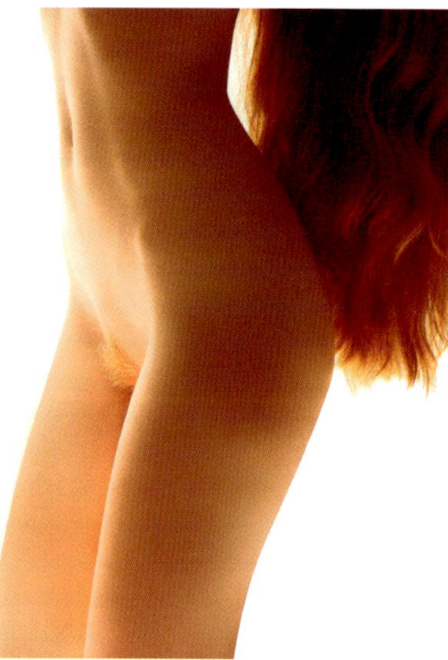

02 This interesting image features the model with her arms raised so that they are not in the shot and her head tilted back so that her hair cascades down her back like the mane of a horse.

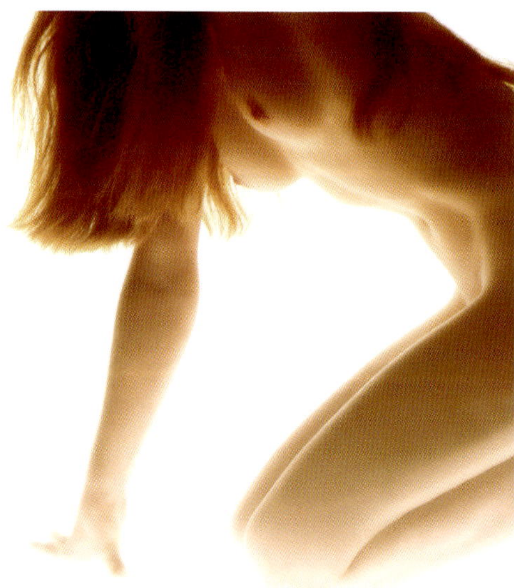

03 Now the model is on the floor, once again lifting an arm up out of the picture so that light from the key flash unit splashes across her midriff. Even in this pose, the feel is still one of movement and action.

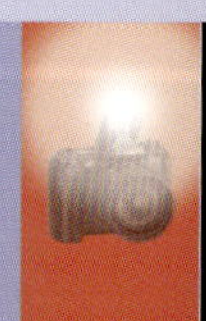

BRIGHT IDEA
Encourage the model to move and extend herself through a series of floor motions without pause. Keep firing as fast as you can and check the results afterward.

PHOTO EDITING

▶ This is a combination of the previous two images. The model's head hangs down so that her hair covers what little of her face is in the shot. Her hands pressed flat form a supporting shape for her torso as the light rushes across her form.

▶ The Curves tool was used to brighten the image across all tonal values, but to also shift the white tones right into pure white by moving the topmost carat along the top and left. The Hue/ Saturation filter was used to just increase the color saturation of the model.

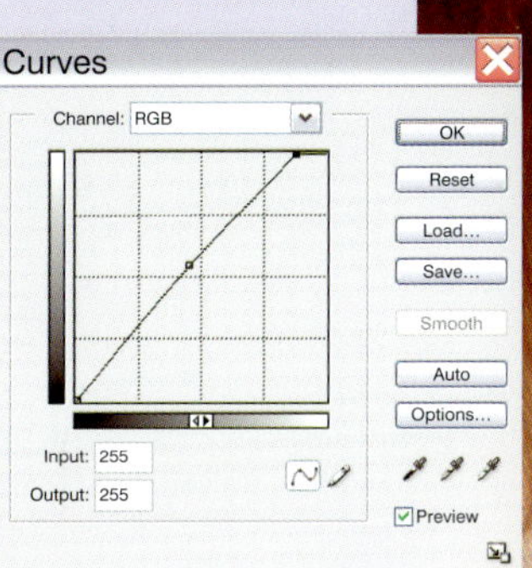

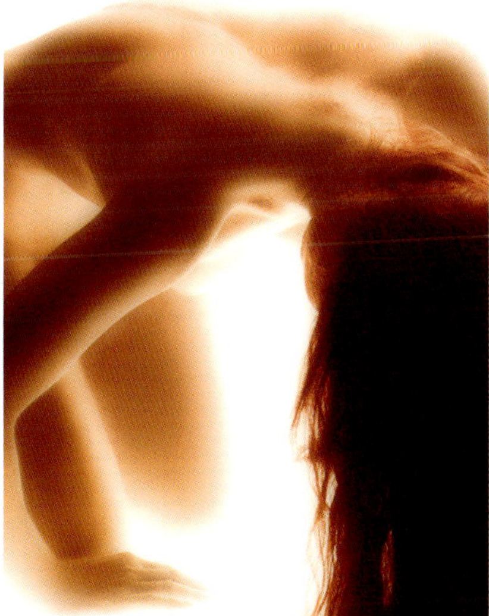

04 Björn Oldsen, who shot this entire series, here has got the model to dip her head so her hair covers the right side of the screen. The light from everywhere else puts highlights all over her torso.

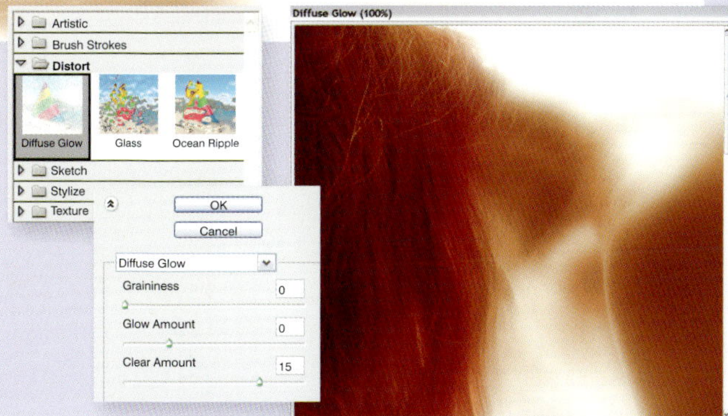

▲ The Diffuse Glow filter was run with a zero value for grain so that the white areas of the picture would literally glow with light. While not particularly necessary for the background, it ensured the floor was just as white and glowing.

TOOLS AT A GLANCE
IMAGE > ADJUSTMENTS > CURVES
IMAGE > ADJUSTMENTS > HUE/
SATURATION
FILTER > DISTORT > DIFFUSE GLOW

CREATIVE LIGHTING TECHNIQUES

One way to work creatively is to be imaginative with lighting. Whether this involves bouncing light back off surfaces, using reflectors, snoots, barn doors, or other accessories, try to be inventive. Look at the composition and imagine how you would light it normally, with one main key light at the front. Then try anything else that doesn't use that setup. Use colored filters, diffusion, rim lighting...let your imagination run wild.

SETTING IT UP

The main picture was shot in the hallway of an old factory, with grim lighting and peeling paint. It looks fairly spooky after sunset as there is no lighting in the corridors, which gave rise to the idea of creating the picture. The light at the front was a powerful handheld Metz flashgun, pointed at the floor to bounce the light upward. In the background, out of sight, was a small electronic flash unit with a yellow filter over the front. When the Metz gun fired with the camera, the slave cell in the other unit detected the light and fired in synchronization. The shutter speed was 1/125 to work with the flashgun, and the aperture f/5.6. This combined to remove any ambient light. The camera lens was a 50mm prime lens, being positioned some 12 feet (3.6m) from the subject.

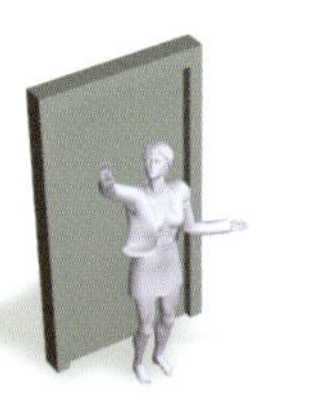
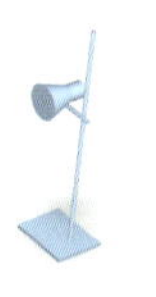
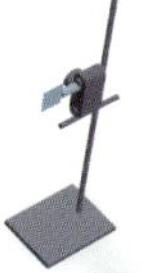

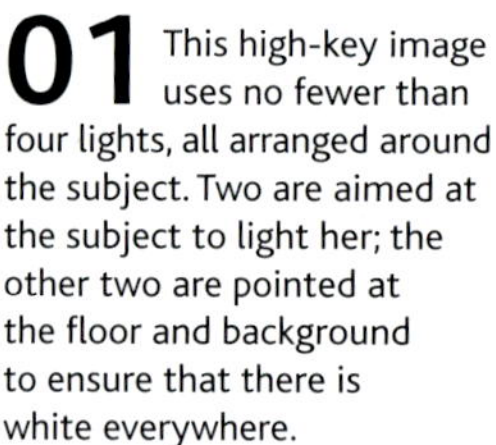

01 This high-key image uses no fewer than four lights, all arranged around the subject. Two are aimed at the subject to light her; the other two are pointed at the floor and background to ensure that there is white everywhere.

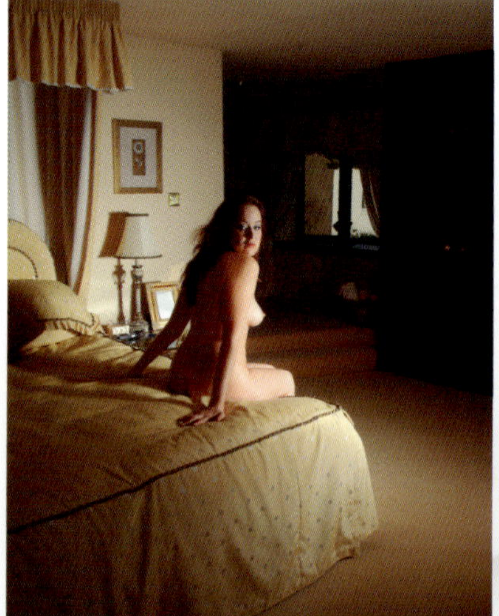
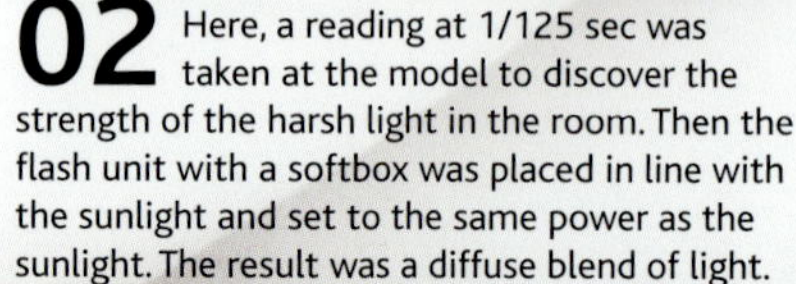

02 Here, a reading at 1/125 sec was taken at the model to discover the strength of the harsh light in the room. Then the flash unit with a softbox was placed in line with the sunlight and set to the same power as the sunlight. The result was a diffuse blend of light.

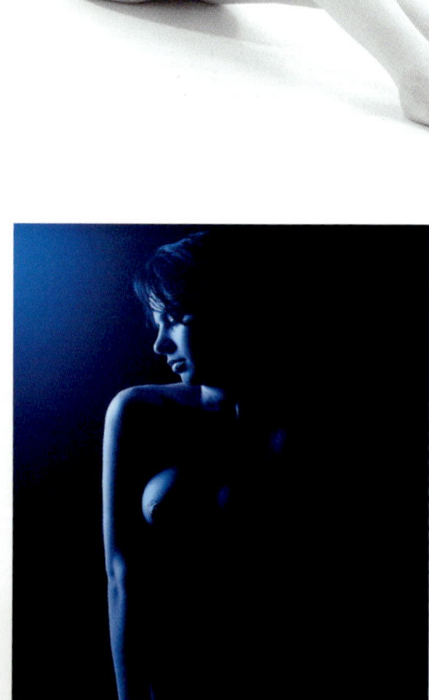

03 This image uses just one flash head, fitted with a blue gel filter to provide a burst of light in the top left corner, just behind the model. The face is turned into the light along with a bare outline of her figure.

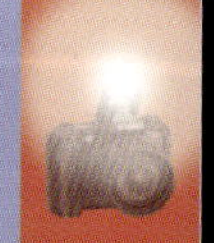

BRIGHT IDEA

Try combining ambient light with fill-in flash or diffuse flash. It helps if your flashgun can sync with the camera at a range of speeds and that it can detect that it is firing at a subject to help control the output.

PHOTO EDITING

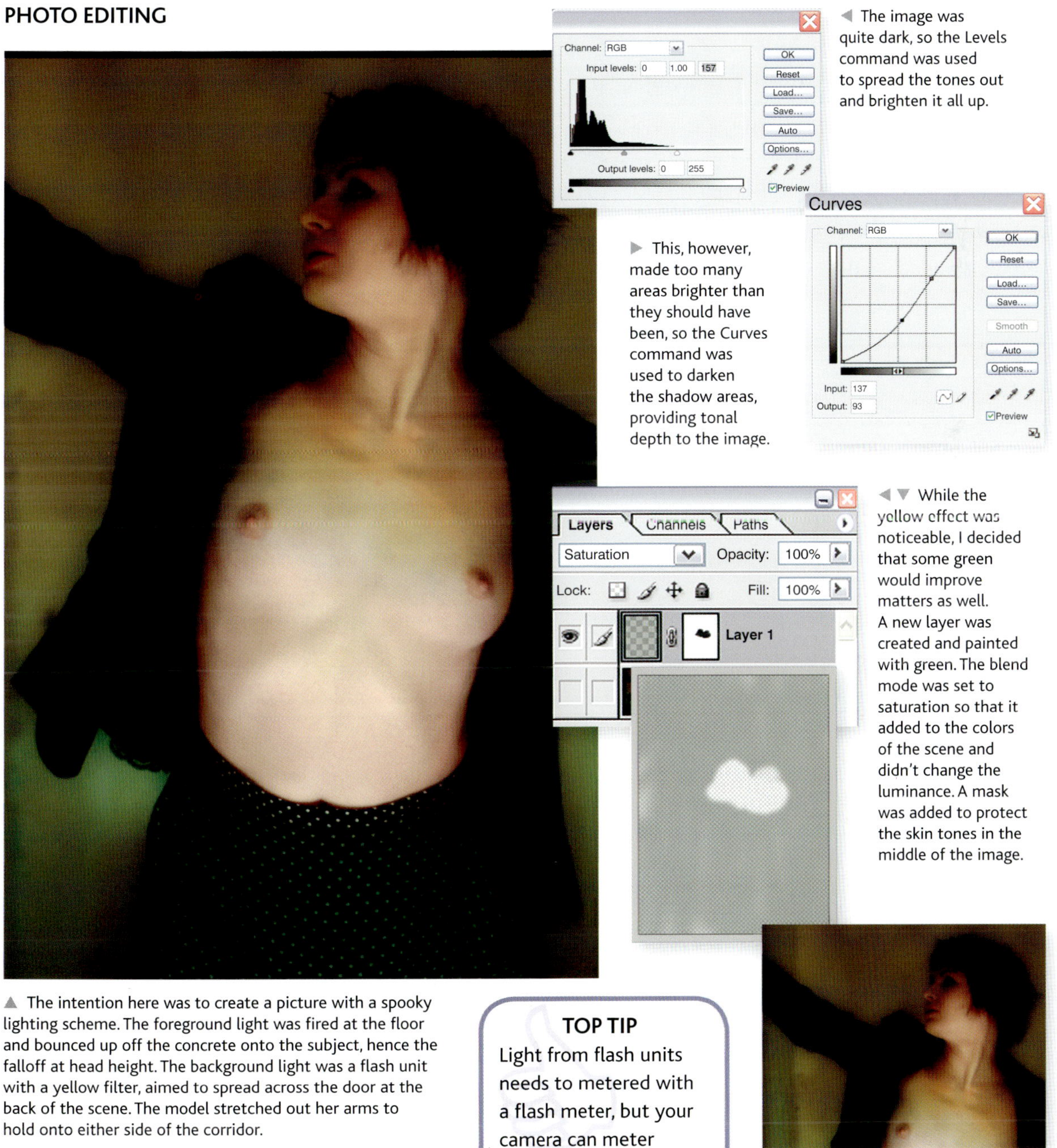

◄ The image was quite dark, so the Levels command was used to spread the tones out and brighten it all up.

► This, however, made too many areas brighter than they should have been, so the Curves command was used to darken the shadow areas, providing tonal depth to the image.

◄ ▼ While the yellow effect was noticeable, I decided that some green would improve matters as well. A new layer was created and painted with green. The blend mode was set to saturation so that it added to the colors of the scene and didn't change the luminance. A mask was added to protect the skin tones in the middle of the image.

▲ The intention here was to create a picture with a spooky lighting scheme. The foreground light was fired at the floor and bounced up off the concrete onto the subject, hence the falloff at head height. The background light was a flash unit with a yellow filter, aimed to spread across the door at the back of the scene. The model stretched out her arms to hold onto either side of the corridor.

TOP TIP

Light from flash units needs to metered with a flash meter, but your camera can meter scenes lit by tungsten or ambient light itself.

TOOLS AT A GLANCE
IMAGE > ADJUSTMENTS > LEVELS   PAINTBRUSH
IMAGE > ADJUSTMENTS > CURVES   LAYER MASK
NEW LAYER

ASSIGNMENT: USING COLOR LIGHTING

Your creative assignment here is to produce a spread of images that use color imaginatively. The color, though, has to come from the lighting. You can pick any color you like, but it has to work with the scene. This means that you can either fit a colored gel to the lighting unit, or try something fancy using the camera's white balance control, in conjunction with other lighting, to produce a color cast in part of the image.

SETTING IT UP

Here, there is a flash unit to the right, fitted with a diffuser and a blue gel. This is pointed downward to light the model and the rug. The key flash is to the left and is fitted with a large softbox to ensure the light spreads out evenly. A window behind adds an extra, whiter, lighting element. The camera is set to the power of the key flash (f/16). The blue light is set to f/11. The camera is 15 feet (4.5m) away, fitted with a 28–70mm telephoto.

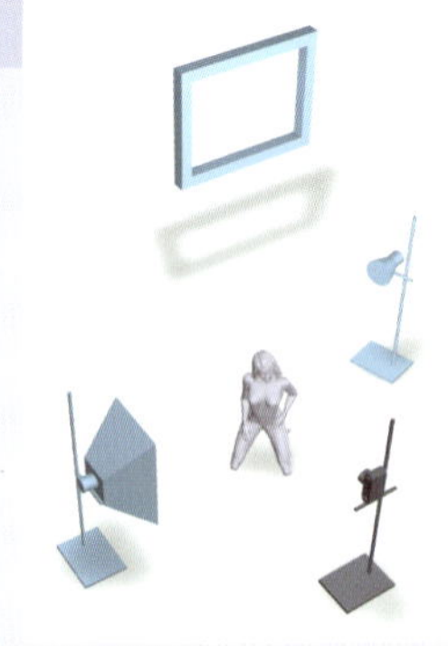

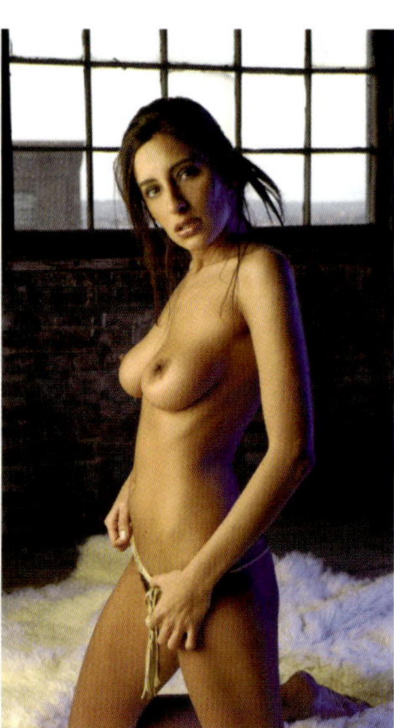

01 There's a nice pose here. The lighting works well, with the background behind the subject taking the blue cast, while the front is lit by the main flash. The model's head stands out with the window behind as well, giving a good mix of colors.

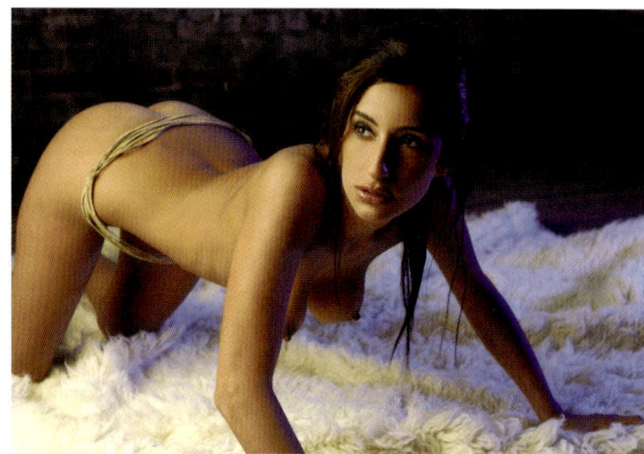

02 The model has moved round so that the main light hits along her torso and the right side of her head and arm are defined by the blue light. The window isn't in this shot, so it makes the image more shallow in terms of composition but it still works.

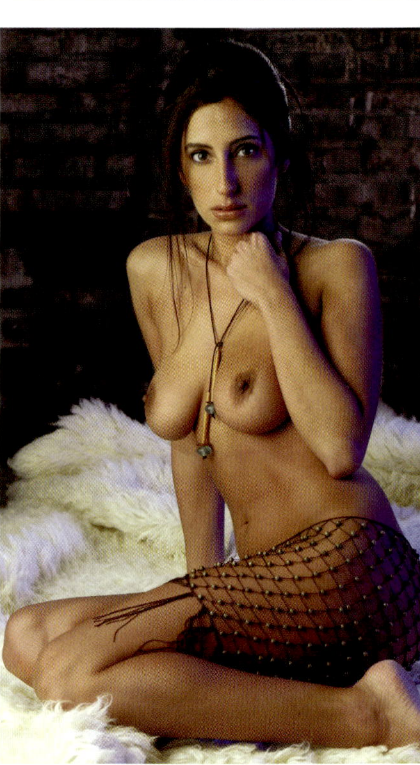

03 Here, the secondary lighting from the blue unit is much more subtle and, overall, this shot lacks the creative flair of the other images.

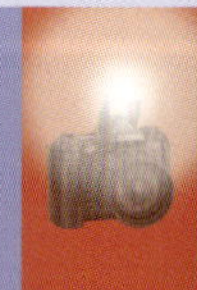

BRIGHT IDEA
Tungsten lights give a natural yellow glow, but the effect from professional units is far more pleasant than that from the bulb in the ceiling. Try shooting with a tungsten lamp and the AWB set to normal daylight to record the effect.

PHOTO EDITING

▶ Here, all the elements are brought together with the beaded skirt prop working well. The window is in the shot but doesn't detract as it is not right behind the model's head. The key light makes the model stand out from the darker brickwork behind, while to the right the blue light covers the floor and provides splashes of light along her features.

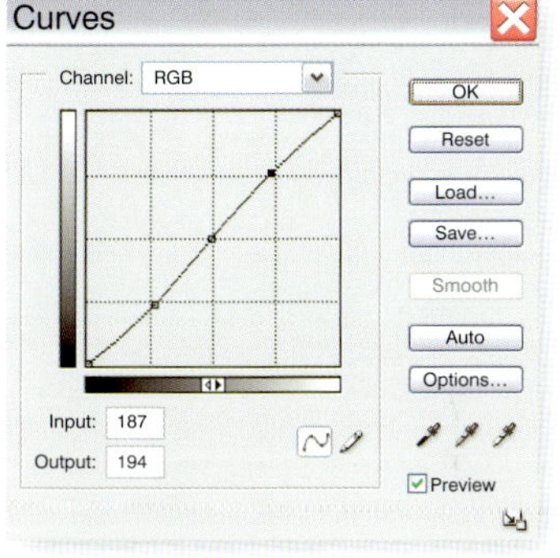

◀ The Curves command was used to increase the contrast in the image a little.

▶ The saturation of the yellow skin tones was increased slightly to make them look a little warmer with Hue/Saturation.

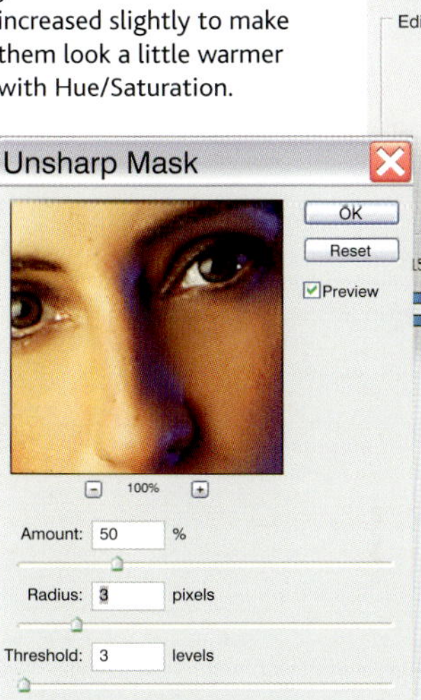

◀ A small amount of sharpening was added with the Unsharp Mask filter to make the features stand out.

> **TOP TIP**
> The automatic white balance will work off the area that you focus on. If this has the color, then you will need to switch to a manual white balance setting to avoid it being negated.

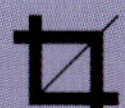

TOOLS AT A GLANCE
IMAGE > ADJUSTMENTS > CURVES
IMAGE > ADJUSTMENTS > HUE/SATURATION
FILTER > SHARPEN > UNSHARP MASK

REFLECTIONS AND DIFFUSION

When we enter the world of reflections and diffusion, the narrative takes on an interesting twist. Reflections can show what is not directly in the view of the camera, both hiding and revealing. Diffusion is also a means of playing with the image, placing the emphasis on another element within the photo, while keeping the nude in shot to create an atmosphere of mystery.

01 Simon Young's image uses a standard mirror reflection composition with the added interest that the model's exposed breast can be seen only in the reflection.

SETTING IT UP

The main image was shot in a room by a window. The reflective surface in the foreground was a piano; it was polished down to make it reflective. A 50mm lens was used with the aperture wide open at f/1.8. The point of focus was the subject. Then the composition was moved slightly to include as much of the foreground as possible. It meant quite a tight shooting angle. Center-weighted metering was used to ensure that the light from the window didn't cause underexposure.

TOP TIP

Someone stood right in front of a mirror is likely to be rendered sharp in both reality and reflection. However, the wider the aperture and the further they stand away from the reflective surface, the more out of focus one of the images will be.

PHOTO EDITING

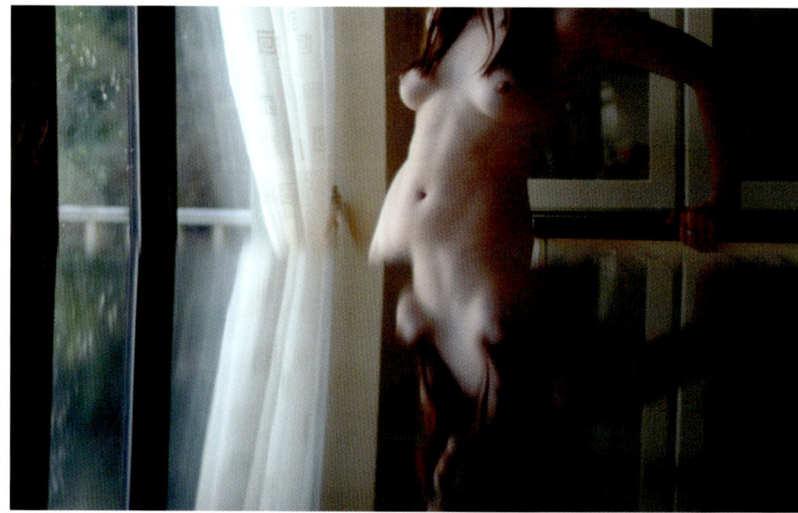

This image takes everything from the previous shot and maximizes the possibilities of the reflection. The image is split in half; crucially, the head is missing from the direct image and can be seen only in the blurry reflection, giving the image a sense of mystery.

BRIGHT IDEA

Find a large glass vase and fill it with water and small but brightly colored flower petals. Now shoot your subject though it.

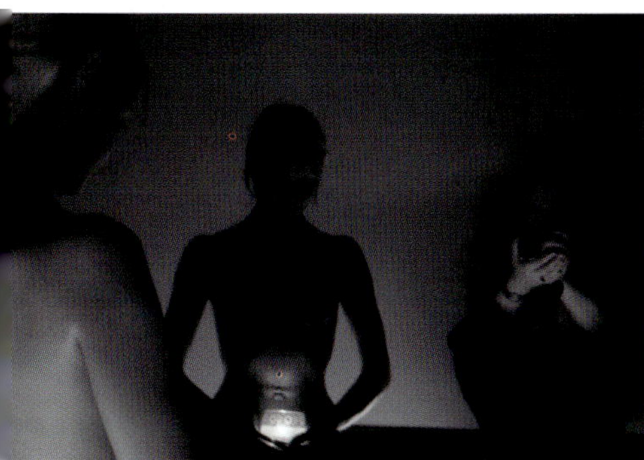

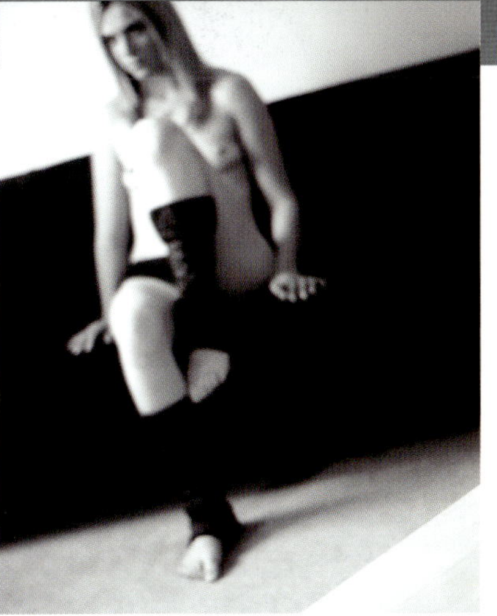

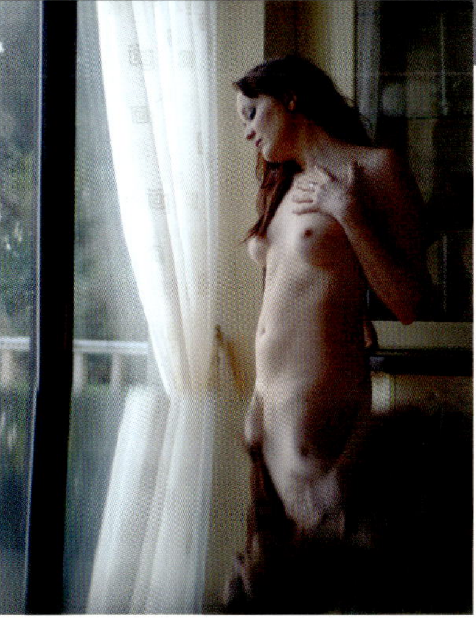

02 There's an awful lot going on in this photo by Mark Varley. The model is holding a candle in a bowl, which can be seen in the large mirror. The light level is very low, but the photographer himself is also clearly seen in the reflection. This gives the photo another level of discussion—why is the photographer in view, and what is happening in the image?

03 This is diffusion rather than reflection. A wide-open aperture and focus on the corner of the table in the lounge means that the subject can be seen as a blurred figure in the background. The strong diagonal lines of the black couch and the raised leg give the picture a sense of dynamism.

04 The polished surface of the piano was used to provide a level of interest across the bottom third of the picture. The focal length of the reflection was longer than that of the subject because the point of focus was on the subject. With the maximum aperture of f/1.8 giving shallow depth of field, the result was a pleasingly blurry reflection.

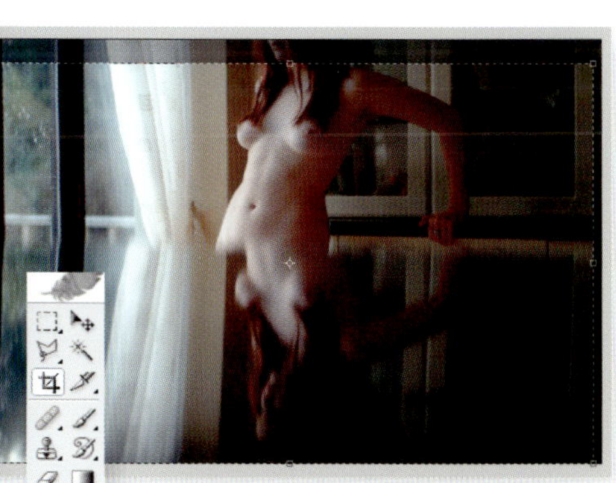

▲ While the image was shot with the intention of being able to see the model's face only in the reflection, there's a little extra at the top. The Crop tool was used to trim out the model's lips.

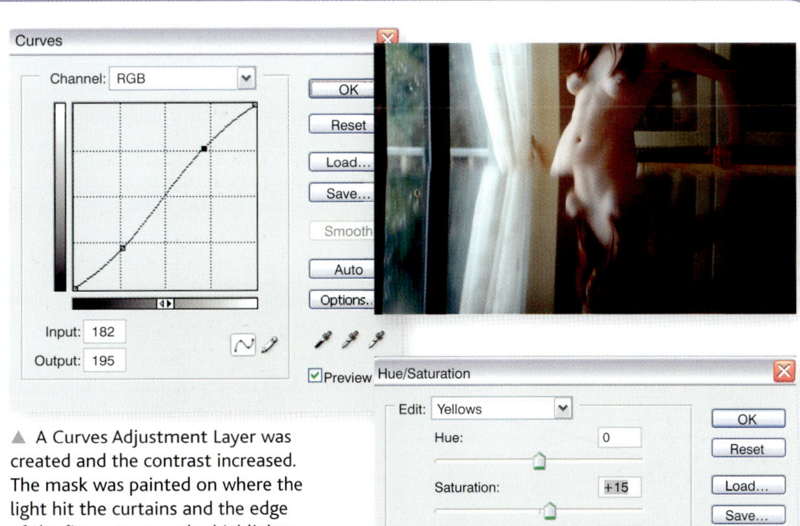

▲ A Curves Adjustment Layer was created and the contrast increased. The mask was painted on where the light hit the curtains and the edge of the figure to stop the highlights burning out.

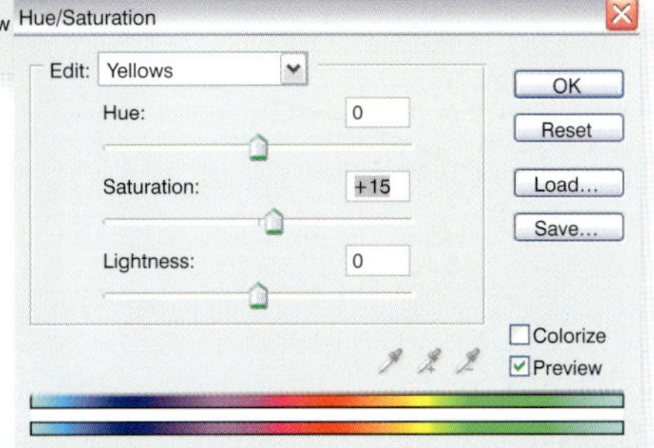

▶ The saturation of the image was increased to spruce the colors up a little.

TOOLS AT A GLANCE
CROP TOOL
CURVES ADJUSTMENT LAYER
IMAGE > ADJUSTMENTS > HUE/SATURATION

EXTREMES: HIGH AND LOW KEY

High key and low key are the extremes of lighting. High-key images contain mainly light tones, whereas low-key images contain mainly darker tones. This isn't to say that a high-key image cannot contain black and a low-key image cannot contain white. They usually don't, but they can, and will make more dramatic pictures when they do.

SETTING IT UP

To set up the main image opposite required some deft positioning of the lights. There is a large window providing plenty of daylight, and this is what is illuminating the model. The light on her was metered at f/5.6. To the left of the scene is a large flash unit with a softbox; this is pointing at the background and set to f/16. The camera is around 10 feet (3m) away, set at an angle, with a 35mm focal length.

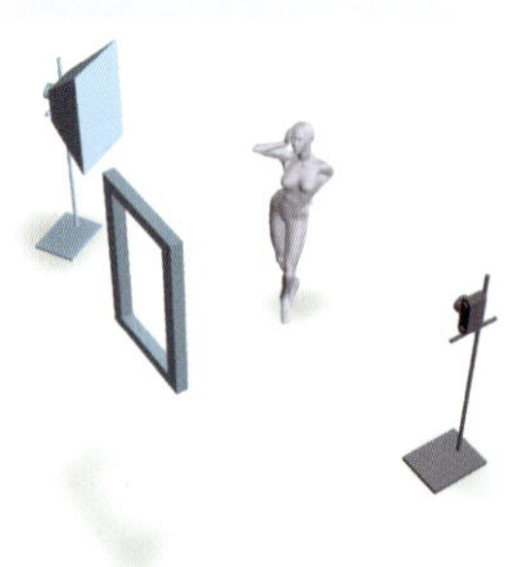

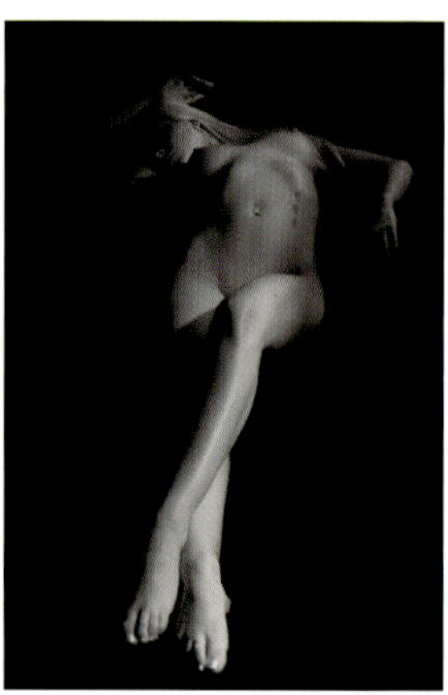

01 This is a traditional low-key image, where the lighting has been arranged to strike the limbs of the model, and little else. Dark fabrics help soak up the light and, as the pose leads away from the camera, the image gets darker.

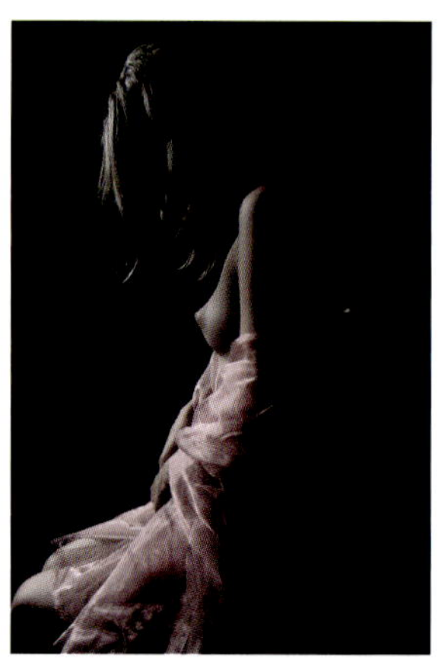

02 This low-key image takes the concept of directed lighting further. The studio background is black, the camera is side-on to the subject, and the only light is 90 degrees to the left of it. The light illuminates the front of the model, pointing down, but the camera is positioned so that only part of her body is visible and behind her is a vastness of dark.

03 This high-key shot has been significantly overexposed so that the background is pure white and the skin tones are very light. Note how the hair, which is a dark shade in reality, is now a gray tone.

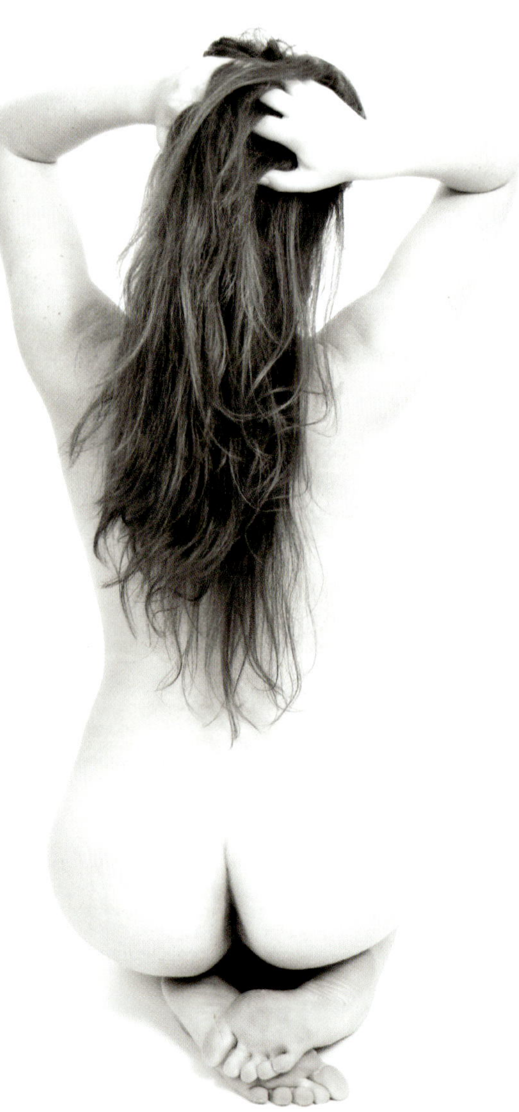

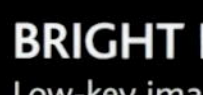

BRIGHT IDEA

Low-key images can be created in Photoshop by using levels and curves, or the lighting filter, or by adding a layer containing black and using a layer mask to block it off, revealing just the elements you want visible.

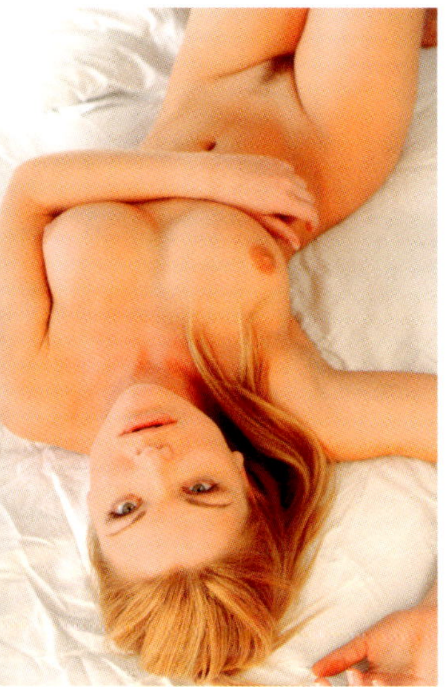

04
This looks like a high-key image because the bedding is white and the model is blonde and fair-skinned. Examining the histogram in fact shows a range of tones. It would take very little image manipulation, though, to make this very light and pale.

TOP TIP

To generate a high-key image when using studio flash, take the meter reading for the aperture setting for a normal exposure. Then stop down to wider apertures by perhaps one or two stops to let in more light and create a brighter image.

PHOTO EDITING

▼ This is a deceptively clever picture and shows that high-key does not always mean having no dark colors. A flash unit overexposes the background, while natural window light illuminates the model, who poses with real style. Her black attire stands out dramatically against the high-key background.

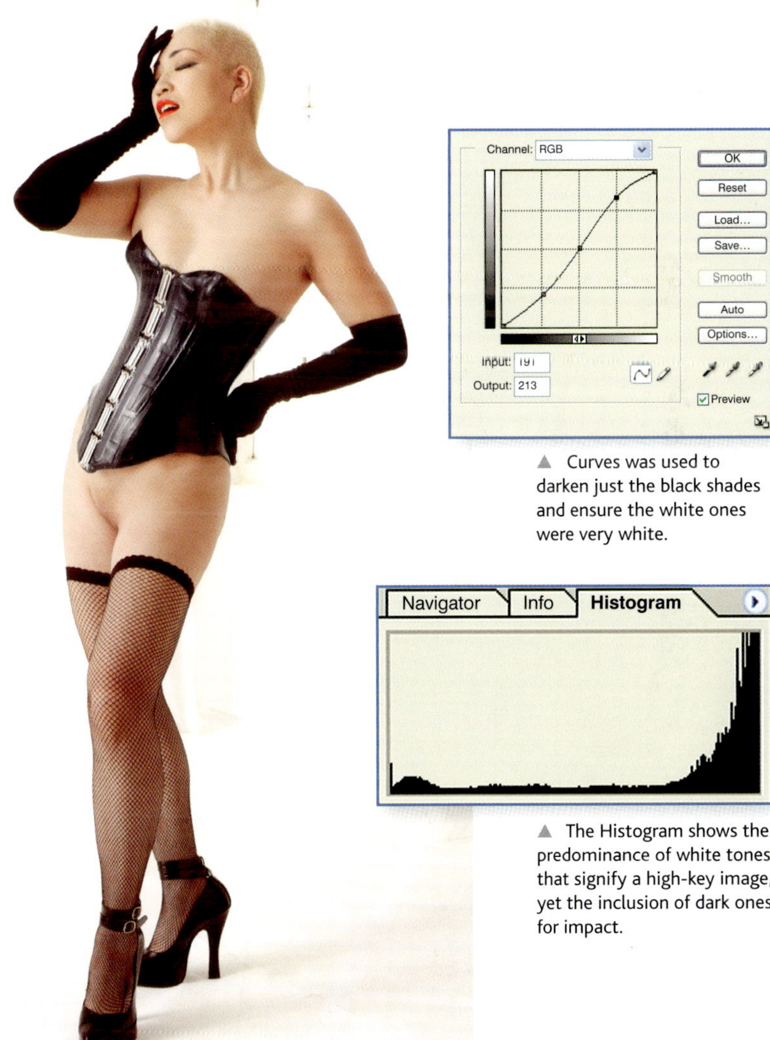

▲ Curves was used to darken just the black shades and ensure the white ones were very white.

▲ The Histogram shows the predominance of white tones that signify a high-key image, yet the inclusion of dark ones for impact.

ASSIGNMENT: LOW LIGHTING

This is an assignment into the world of low lighting on location. You are tasked with producing a series of nudes on location, after the sun has gone down. You are allowed to bring a portable tungsten lighting unit if you have one; otherwise flashlights and car lights will have to suffice. Street lighting is not allowed as you must find a location that will be dark without your lights. A tripod would be handy. See what variety of shots you can produce under these conditions, mixing blurred movement with background light in the sky.

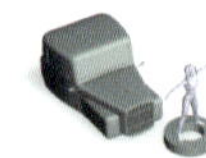
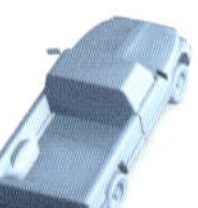

SETTING IT UP

For this setup, the location is an old car wreck in the countryside. The lighting is provided by the headlight of the car carrying everyone to the scene. A wide-angle lens of 35mm was used to get everything into the shot, and the camera was about 20–30 feet (6–9m) away from the subject. A tripod was used with an aperture of f/2. The shutter speed was only 1/4sec.

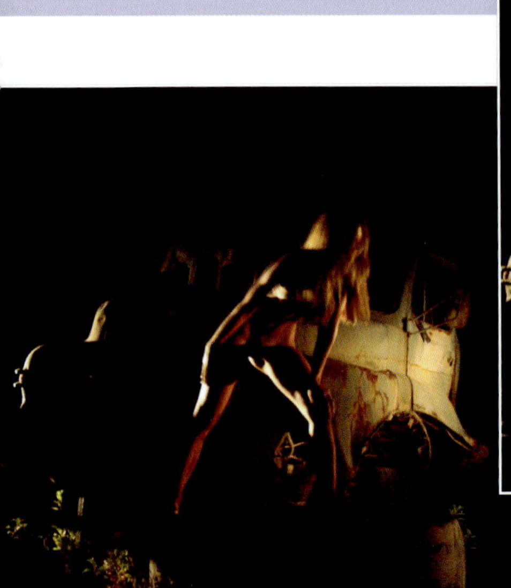
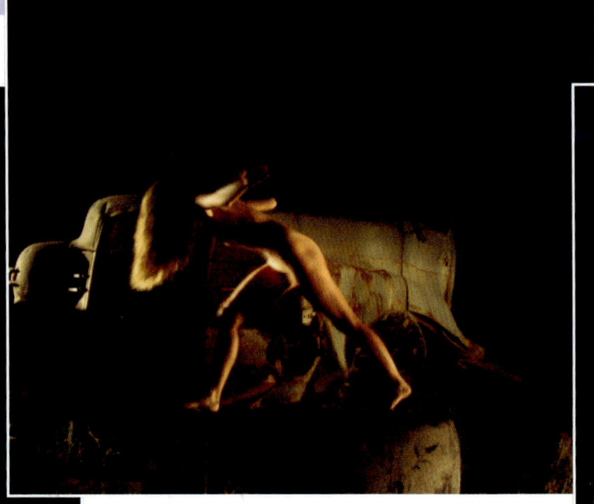
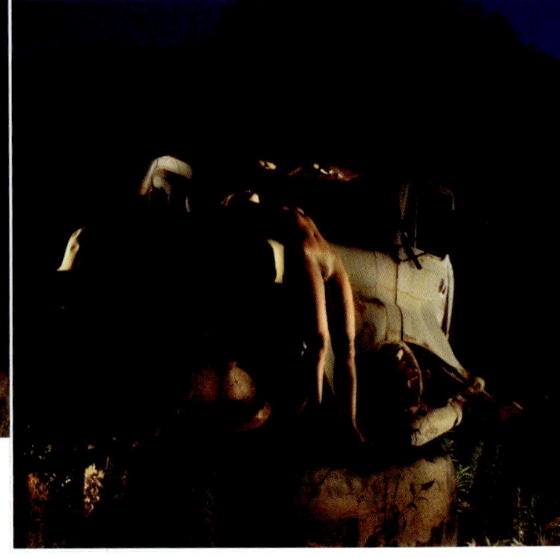

01 To start with, Björn Oldsen, who shot this series, zooms in to 100mm to get a closeup of the car and subject. Another car to the left provided extra illumination. The model is blurred as she was moving slightly during the exposure.

02 Here, the model is walking over a large, abandoned tyre, arms out as though flying. The composition on this one is a little off, as everything is happening on the left and the right is completely empty.

03 With the extra lights on the other side of the wreck, the shape of the car has been defined, allowing the model to throw herself back into the gloom. Some light in the sky has been recorded in this shot.

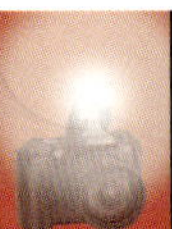

BRIGHT IDEA
With low light levels it's very easy to get long exposures. Increase the aperture to f/16 to obtain a long shutter speed, then ask the model to move around a little.

TOP TIP
To get more shutter speed so that you can freeze the subject or use the camera handheld, ramp up the ISO rating to 400 or 800.

PHOTO EDITING

▶ Exposure compensation of +1EV has been used here so that the sky is recorded as brighter. The other car lights have been switched off and the main car has been moved closer and angled so that it covers the front of the wreck with light. Standing back, the shot now encompasses the wreck, the surroundings, and the blue night sky.

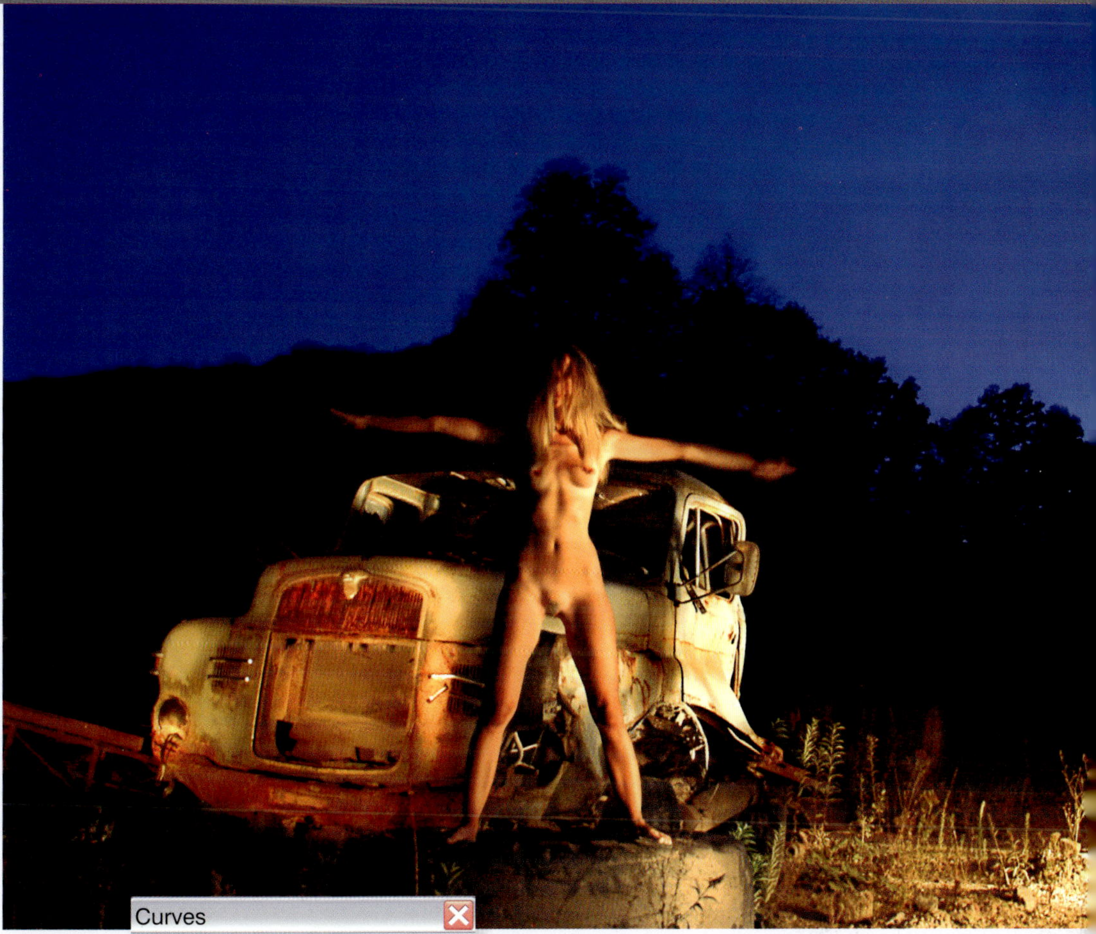

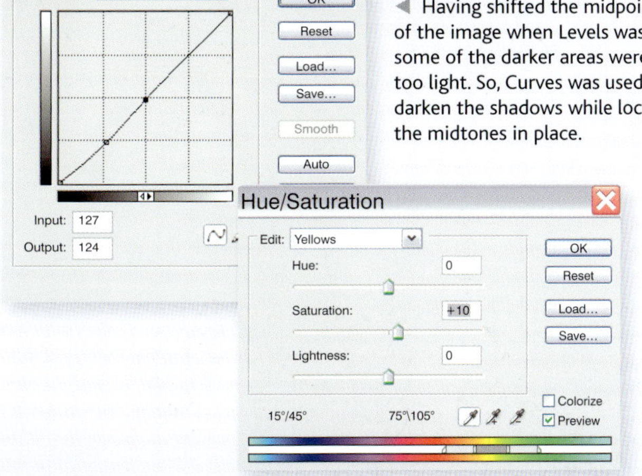

◀ Having shifted the midpoint of the image when Levels was used, some of the darker areas were then too light. So, Curves was used to darken the shadows while locking the midtones in place.

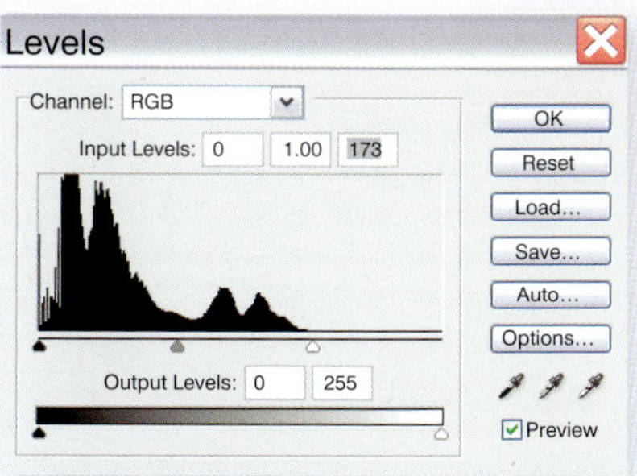

▲ Firstly, the Levels were adjusted as the image was underexposed and half the available tones weren't being used in the picture. This has the effect of instantly brightening the sky.

◀ To give the picture a richer color on the model's skin, the Hue/Saturation control was used to increase the saturation to the yellow tones. The image size was interpolated larger for printing.

TOOLS AT A GLANCE
IMAGE > ADJUSTMENTS > LEVELS
IMAGE > ADJUSTMENTS > CURVES
IMAGE > ADJUSTMENTS > HUE/SATURATION
IMAGE > IMAGE SIZE

FRAMING THE SUBJECT

Framing the subject means not just getting the model in the viewfinder and framing the composition with it, but using elements within the picture to hold the shot together. It can also add a narrative, depending on what the frame is and what it is doing. The more imaginative you are about how framing devices can be made to work, the more varied the composition and creative the results. There are many different ways to frame a subject than just making them stand in a doorway.

SETTING IT UP

The camera is virtually directly above the subject in this shot, so while a relatively wide angle of 35mm was used, because the subject is flat to the plane of the camera, there is little distortion. The light comes from a tungsten lamp to the left side, fitted with a diffuser, which gives a very soft spread of golden light. As the light level was quite low, it resulted in a lower shutter speed than normal.

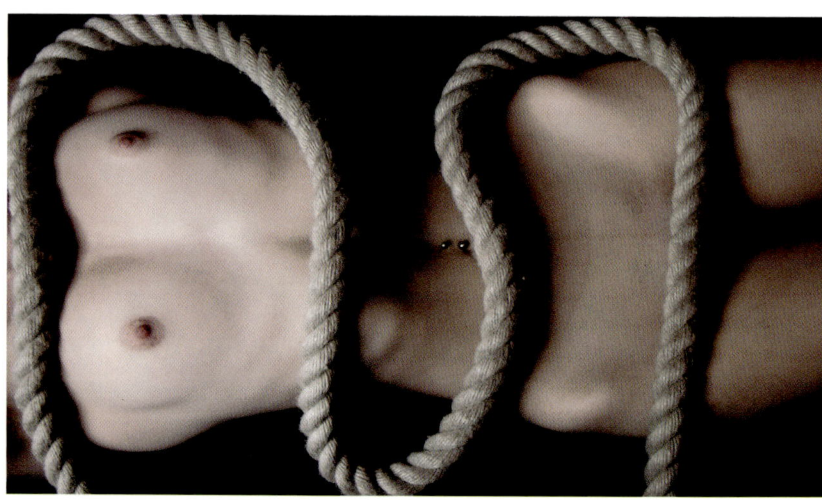

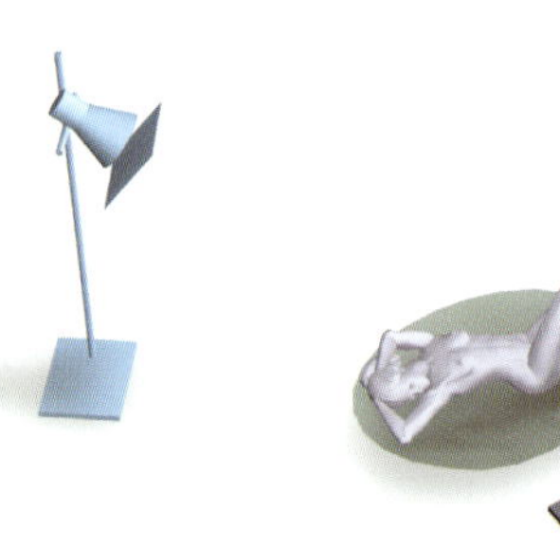

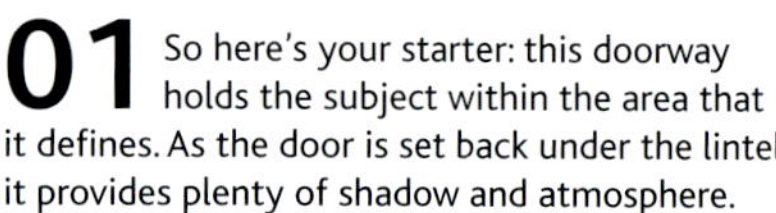

02 Mark Varley's image changes things around by shooting from above and using the framing device—a piece of rope—to lie on top of the subject, framing her in position underneath.

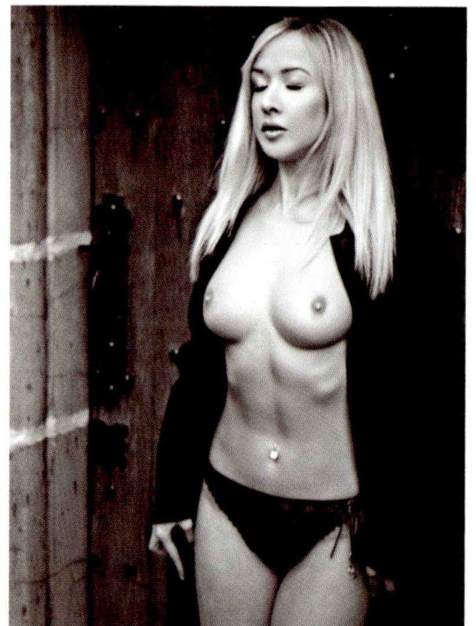

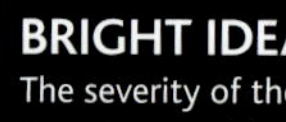

01 So here's your starter: this doorway holds the subject within the area that it defines. As the door is set back under the lintel it provides plenty of shadow and atmosphere.

TOP TIP

As you usually want the framing device to be seen, if it is in the background, don't shoot with a lower aperture than f/5.6 or the effect may be lost.

BRIGHT IDEA

The severity of the frame and how constricting it is will influence the feel of the picture. Experiment with the model shrinking within the framing device, and breaking the edges of it.

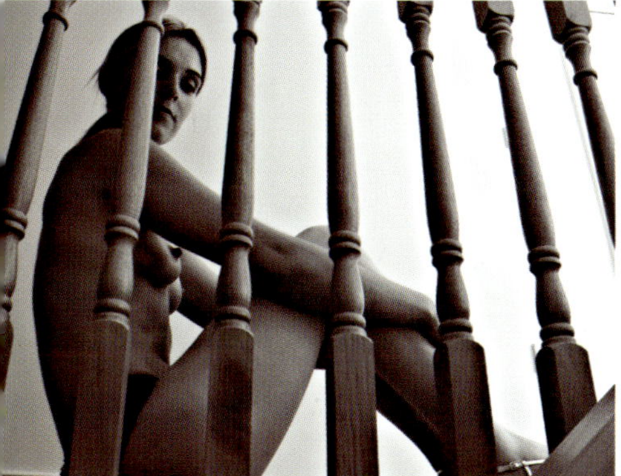

03 Here, the frame is provided by the balustrade of a staircase. The picture has been shot from below with a wide-angle lens, to deliberately distort the perspective.

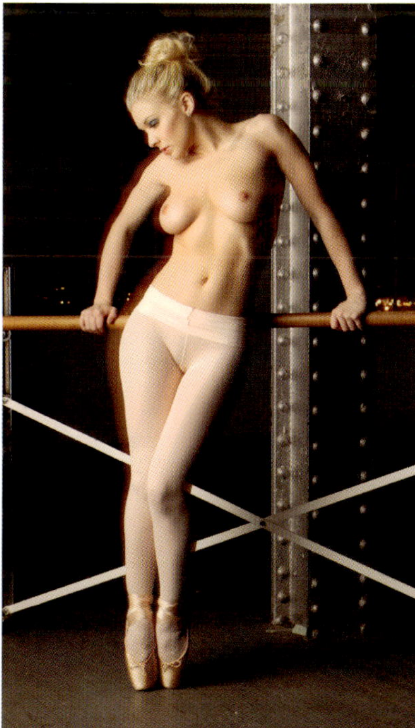

04 Now we have the frame, provided by both the pillar and the crossing metal and wood elements, behind the subject. These hold the picture from the back, giving it a rigid feel that is counterpointed by the model being able to move about freely.

PHOTO EDITING

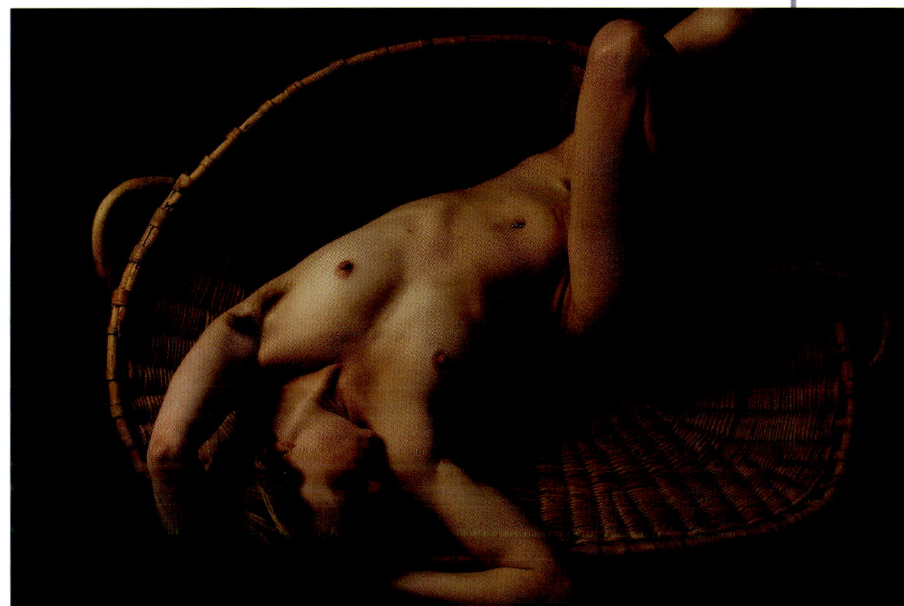

▲ This gorgeous picture from Stephen Haynes combines many of the ideas in the other pictures by using the basket to frame the subject and hold her, yet allow her to break the edges of the frame in places. The soft golden light perfectly complements the color of the basket and warms the skin tones, giving the picture a very relaxing feel.

▼ The Curves were adjusted to ensure that the shadows were dark enough and that there were sufficient highlights.

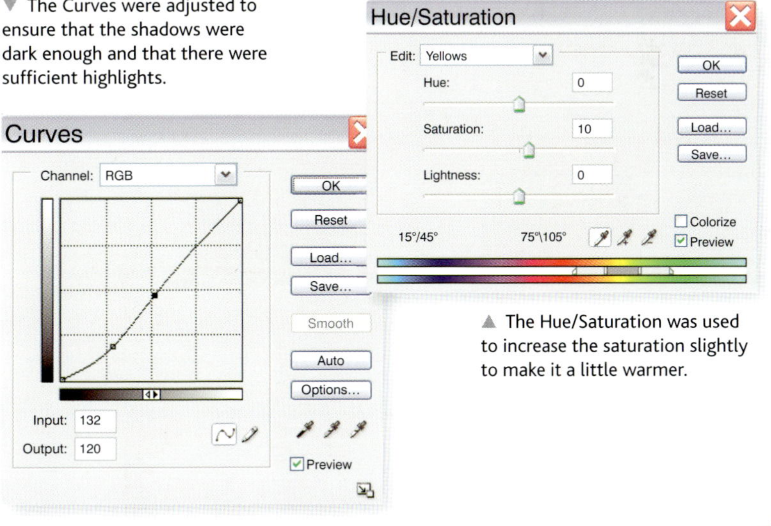

▲ The Hue/Saturation was used to increase the saturation slightly to make it a little warmer.

ASSIGNMENT: WORK THE FRAME

The purpose of using framing devices is to constrain the contents that might otherwise be too freeflowing, or to give structure to a picture, contrasting the rigidity of the frame with the fluidity of the subject. You can also create frames and have the subject break out of them. In this assignment, your task is to use a doorway as a frame. You must work the subject so that he or she is both confined by and trying to break free from the structure around them.

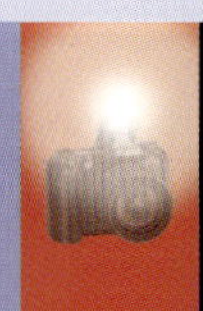

SETTING IT UP

Find yourself a good doorway frame to work with and look into the background beyond for reflective objects. Also ensure that any windows don't compete for attention. In front of the subject and to the right, set up a flash unit with an umbrella, but fire the flash through it. You will need to set the flash to maximum power to get enough light to scatter through, but it will avoid unpleasant shadows in the doorway and keep the aperture down so that there is not much depth of field and nothing behind the doorway will be in sharp focus. Stand 10 feet (3m) back and use a 50mm lens or thereabouts to focus in on the subject.

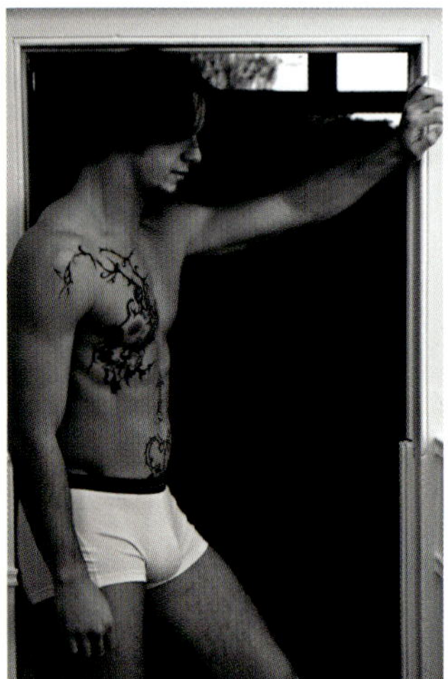

01 One reason for placing the light to the right of the camera was so that there were no reflections back from the window—bear that in mind when setting up your shot. As the subject has turned in toward the light, most of his torso is illuminated, contrasting with the dark shadow behind.

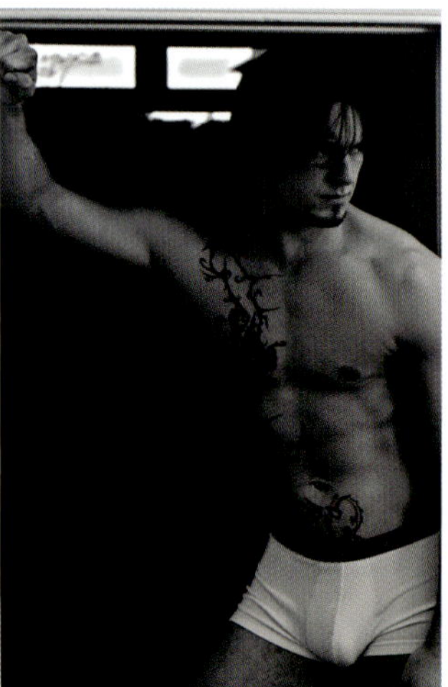

02 Switching the subject around so that the light falls across the torso gives it more shadow definition. The point about shooting males is to celebrate well-defined physical characteristics and to show the emotional aspect of the male character.

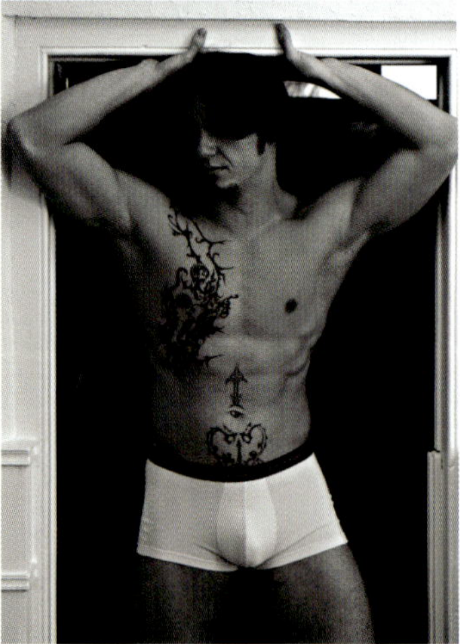

03 The use of the elbows here breaks out of the frame, while the main torso is still confined within it. The expression is like a tamed lion, and the gripping thumbs at the top of the picture also show confined power.

BRIGHT IDEA
Want to try something different but within the overall concept? Shoot outdoors using a small archway into somewhere like a country house garden or a cemetery.

▶ Pulling back just a little makes all the difference. The side and top of the doorway are visible, allowing it to frame the subject. The model's posture is now one of breaking free from the constraints of the surroundings with the chest more prominent and the face staring aggressively into the light source.

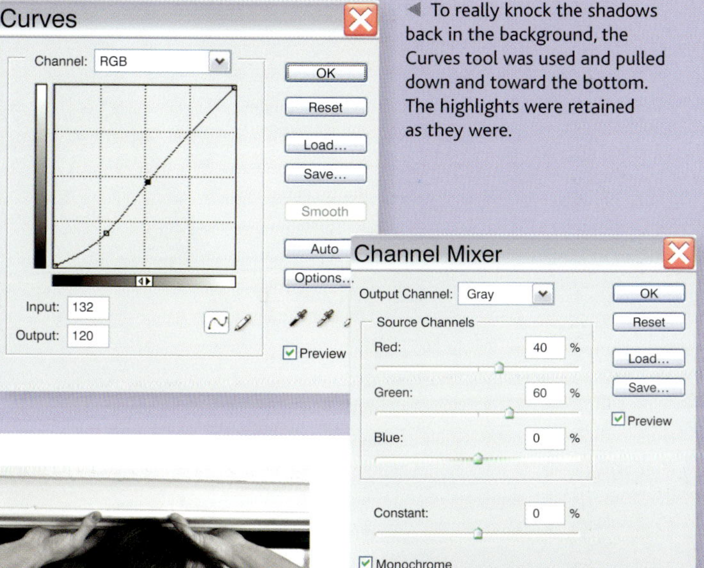

◀ To really knock the shadows back in the background, the Curves tool was used and pulled down and toward the bottom. The highlights were retained as they were.

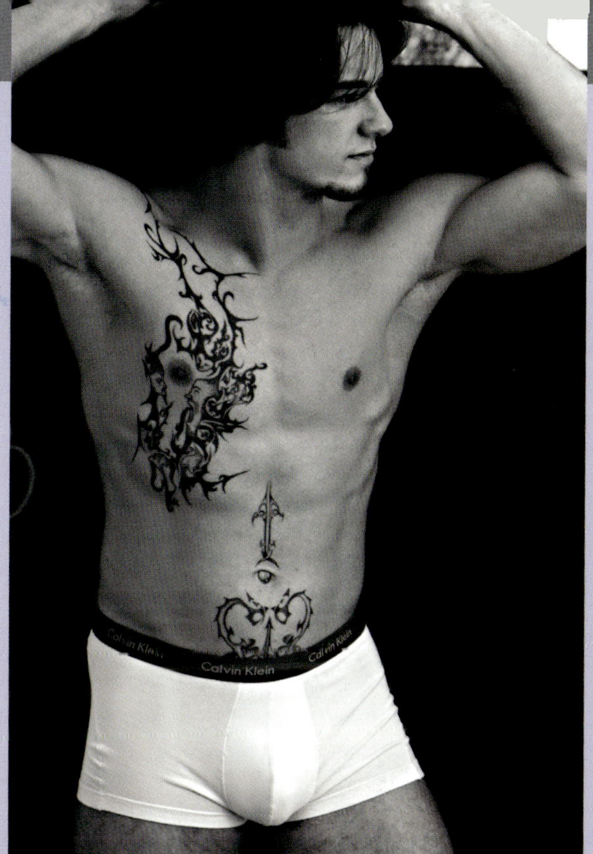

▲ The image was converted to black and white using the Channel Mixer with these fairly unusual settings. The red channel represents the skin tones, but by using the green channel for everything else, the shadows were kept in the background.

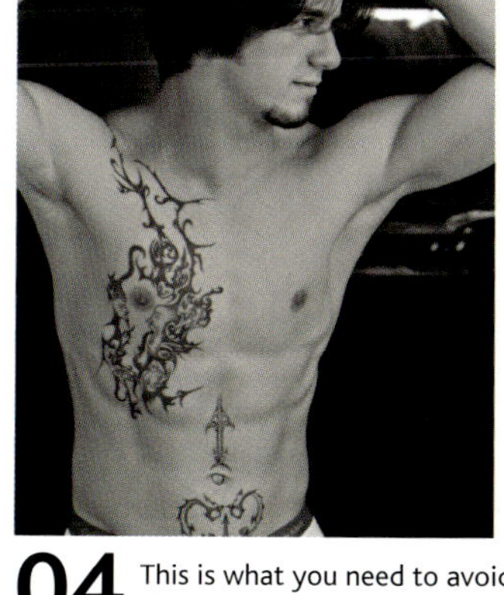

04 This is what you need to avoid. The camera has wandered too close to the subject so that the arms aren't really doing anything and the sides of the frame have been lost. The sense of confinement or breaking out is missing.

▶ A Duplicate Layer was created and the Unsharp Mask filter run to add large amounts of contrast along the edges and detail. This also tends to make bright highlights in odd places so a layer mask was added. The paintbrush was then used to paint on the mask in areas such as the end of the nose to block the effect. The layers were then merged.

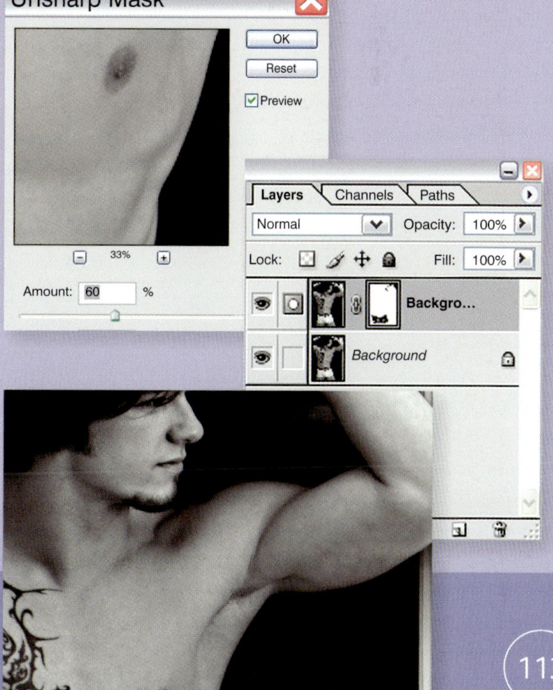

TOOLS AT A GLANCE
IMAGE > ADJUSTMENTS > CURVES
IMAGE > ADJUSTMENTS > CHANNEL MIXER
DUPLICATE LAYER
FILTER > SHARPEN > UNSHARP MASK

INSPIRATIONS: LIGHTING STYLES

When shooting portraits outside, the environment can be part of the photographic narrative, lending a meaning in conjunction with the styling of the person in it. Or, the scene can place and identify the subject, putting them into context. Finally, it might just be a nice background to shoot someone against. All these things are elements in a successful location shoot.

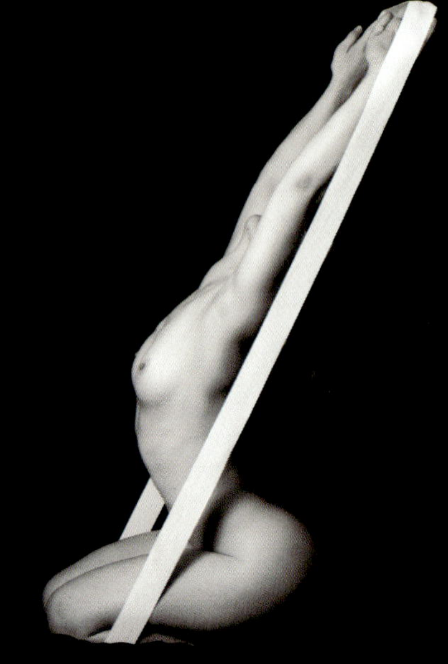

▶ The framing for this image by Stephen Haynes is provided by the fabric stretched around and held out by the subject herself. The diagonal slash of the fabric holds in the subject, making for a more interesting composition than a side-on shot with no depth would normally offer.

▼ In Eric Kellerman's clever image, lighting is used very subtly in a darkened studio. A combination of narrow aperture and fast shutter speed to sync with the lights ensured that no background ambient light was recorded. This left the lighting to two lights, placed a good distance away on either side, providing rim lighting on the subject in the middle.

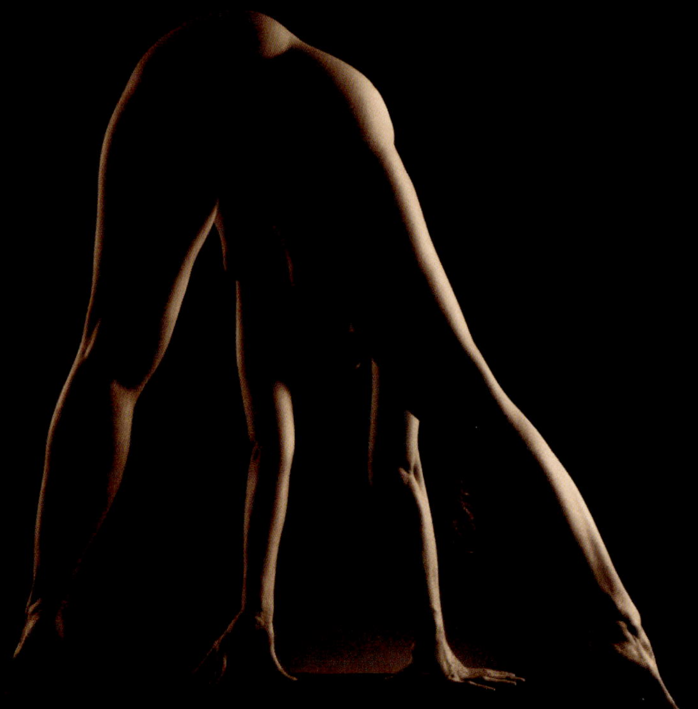

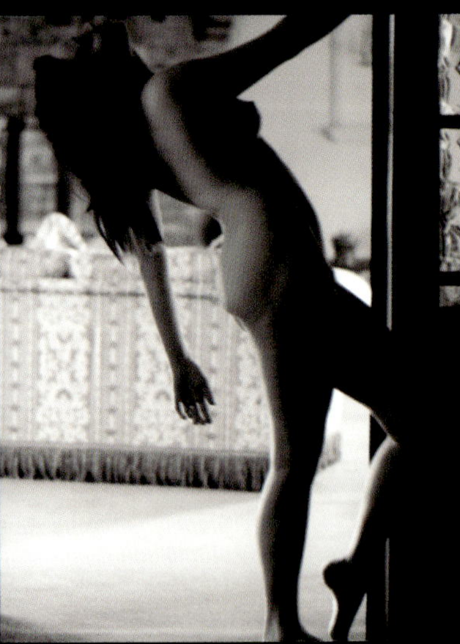

▲ This image is backlit, and there is also weaker illumination at the front on to the model from a flash unit and umbrella. The flash was fired through the umbrella to give a more diffuse, but weaker, light than normal. The frame is provided by the sliding doors to the room beyond, which the model is hanging from.

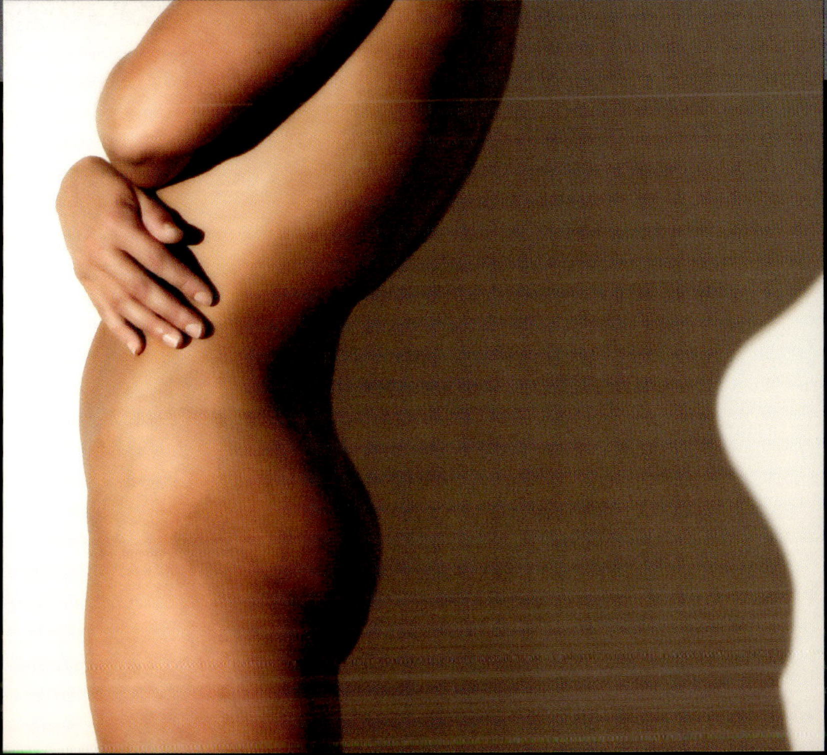

◀ This Stephen Haynes image is all about the bold, striking shadow that falls behind the subject. The shadow reveals a knot of muscle in the leg, though this wasn't apparent on the leg itself when shooting the picture.

▼ Dale Lehmer shot this gorgeous photo with a modest digital SLR with a fixed lens. The movement effect you can see was created in-camera by panning in low light during the exposure. The composition was arranged so that the light caught the white fabric, enclosing the model in a swathe of color.

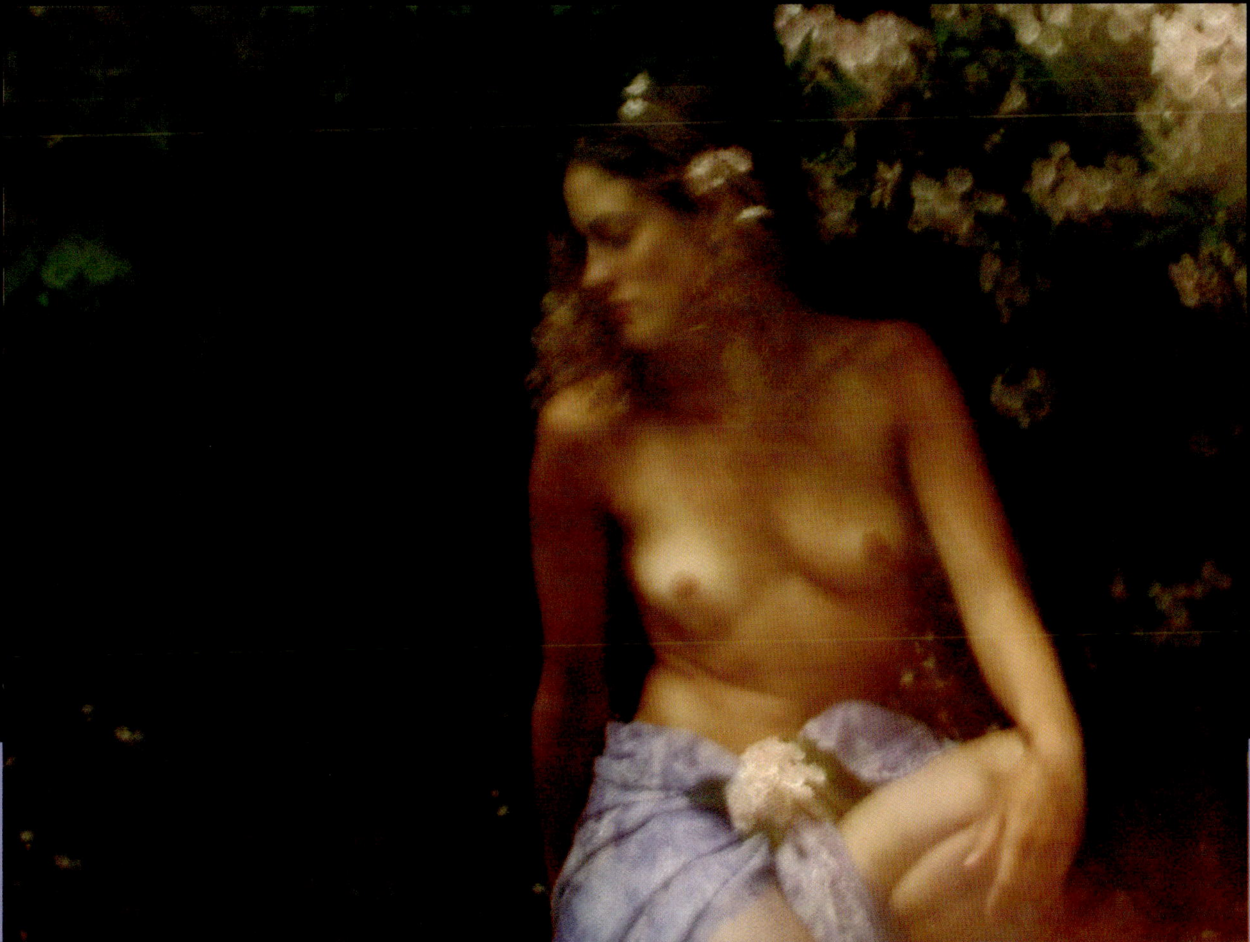

6 IMAGE EDITING

The power of image editing means that the digital photographer can do everything from correcting and enhancing colors and contrast, to removing flaws, creating new works of art, and applying tones and ageing effects. Being digital, the original image is usually color, so converting to monochrome is very important in artistic nude photography. There are lots of different looks that can be achieved. You now have the power; all you need to supply is the imagination.

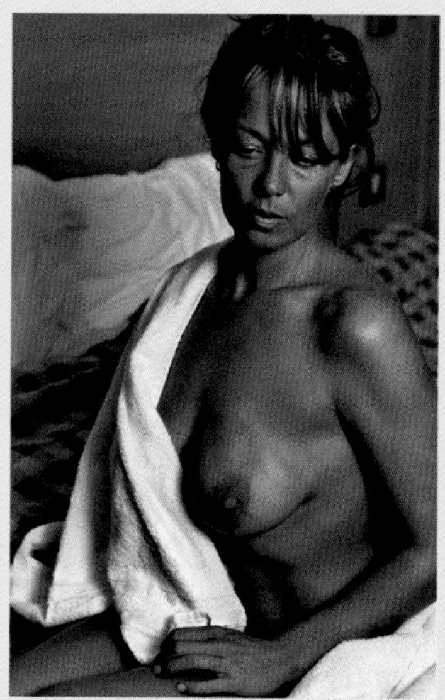

▲ Moody monochrome. Magnify a brooding atmosphere by implementing a harsh monochrome effect.

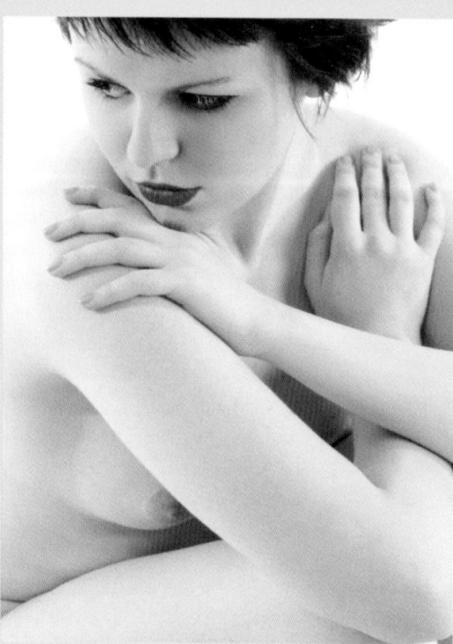

▲ Subtle shades. When a light, airy touch is required, forsake contrast in favor of pleasing tones in your imagery.

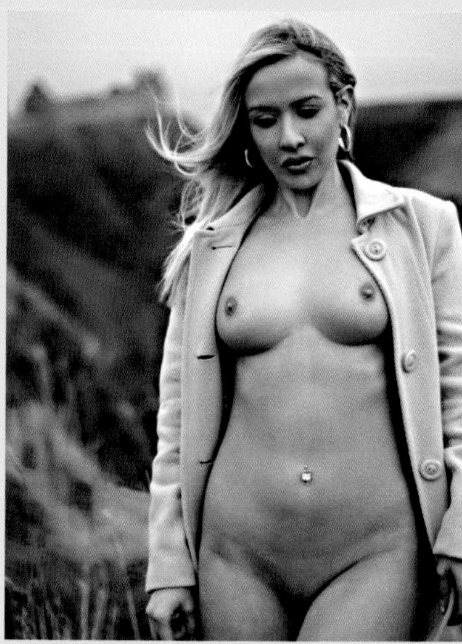

▲ Cleaning up images. You'll always need to remove some unwanted element in the background when you shoot on location.

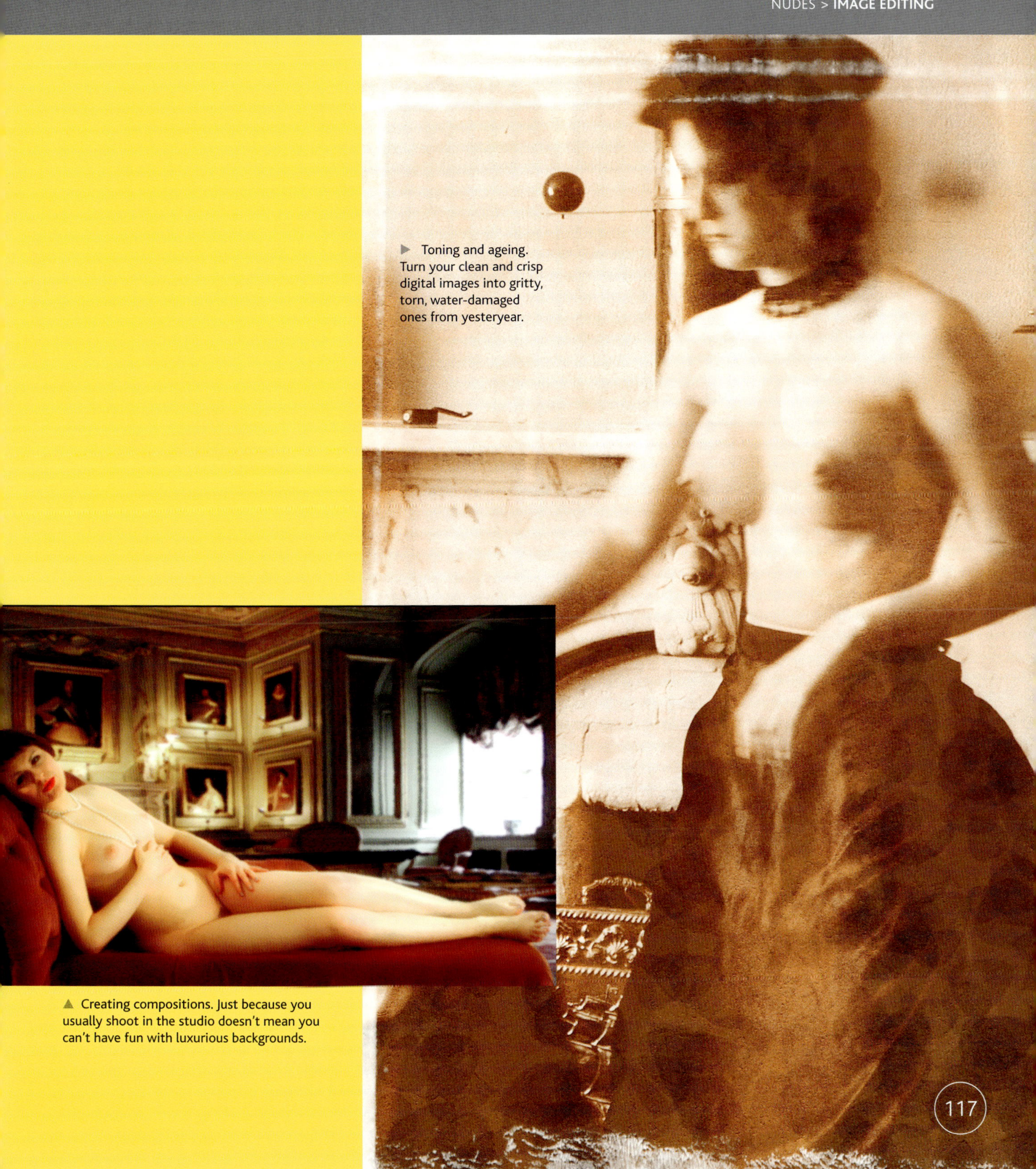

▶ Toning and ageing. Turn your clean and crisp digital images into gritty, torn, water-damaged ones from yesteryear.

▲ Creating compositions. Just because you usually shoot in the studio doesn't mean you can't have fun with luxurious backgrounds.

MOODY MONOCHROME

There are different ways you can approach monochrome: the delicate, subtle transition of tones, or the harsh contrast with extra grain thrown in. Some subjects suit the subtle approach, others the more dramatic. Certainly, the older the subject, even with nudes, the more powerful the high-contrast option becomes as it shows up the subject's imperfections. This can make them look more human than a glossy fantasy vision.

SETTING IT UP

This type of picture is easy to set up. Stand about 6 feet (1.8m) back with a 50mm lens, or a short telephoto, and place one flash head to the right of the camera. Set the flash on a low power so that you get a fairly shallow depth of field—this was f/4 at 1/124 sec.

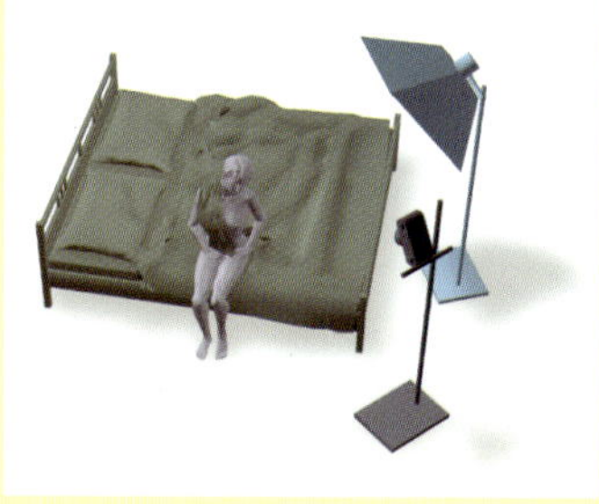

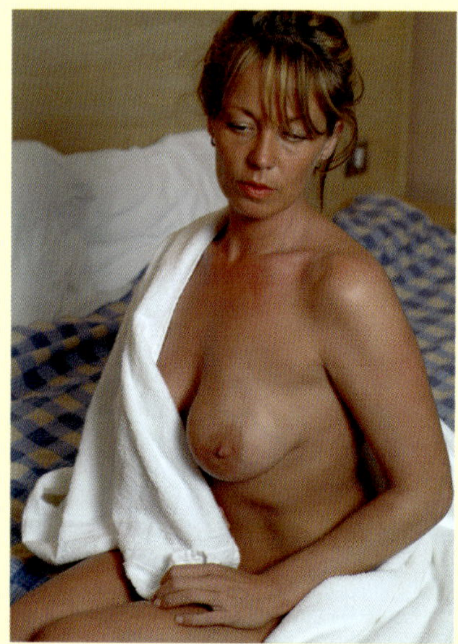

01 This is the original image and the starting point for the project. The typical digital SLR image is flat straight out of the camera.

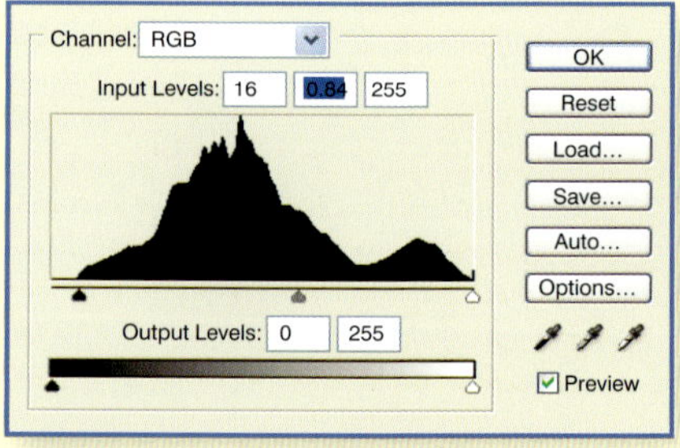

02 The first task, therefore, is to spread the tones out using Levels. The center point was also moved to the right to make the image darker.

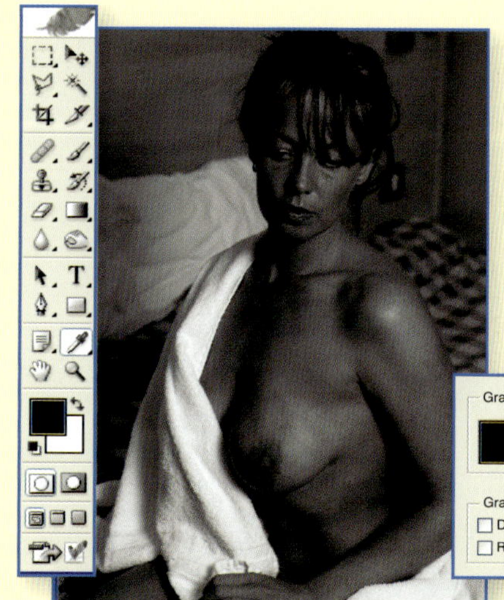

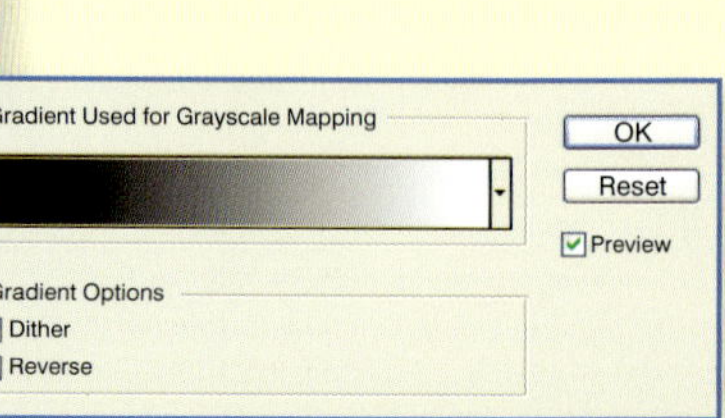

03 One option of monochrome conversion is the Gradient Map using a black–white gradient. While this gives a very accurate spread of tones, we wanted more contrast from the start.

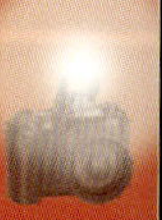

BRIGHT IDEA
Try bouncing light onto the subject from the wall or ceiling to get diffuse lighting with no awkward shadows.

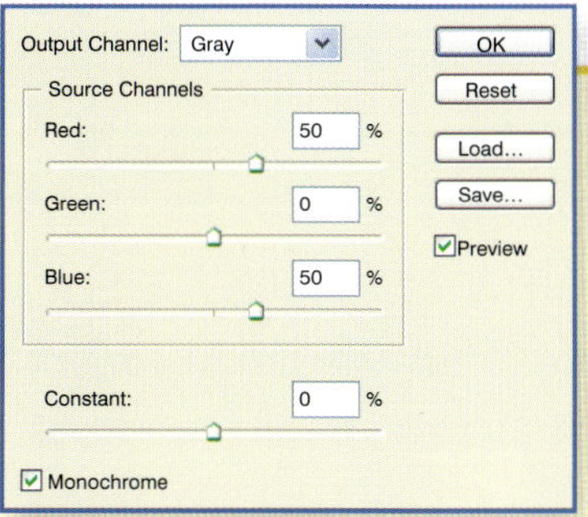

04 In this case, the Channel Mixer was used instead. The monochrome box was ticked and entries of 50% for red and blue gave the image as much contrast as possible to start with.

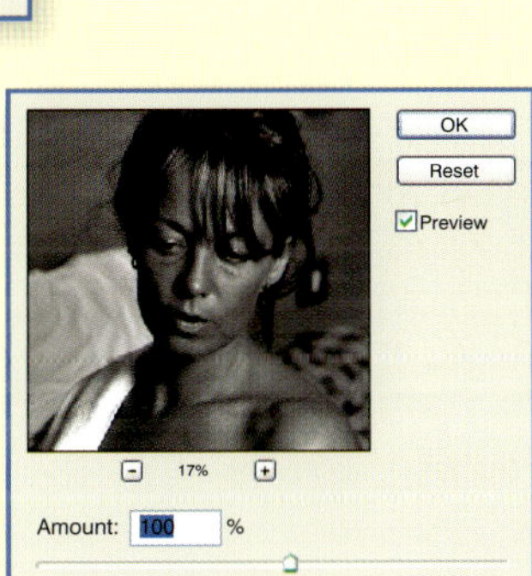

05 A duplicate layer was created, then the Unsharp Mask filter run. The settings were 100% amount and 100% radius. This has the effect of giving the image a huge contrast boost, based on the edges in the photo.

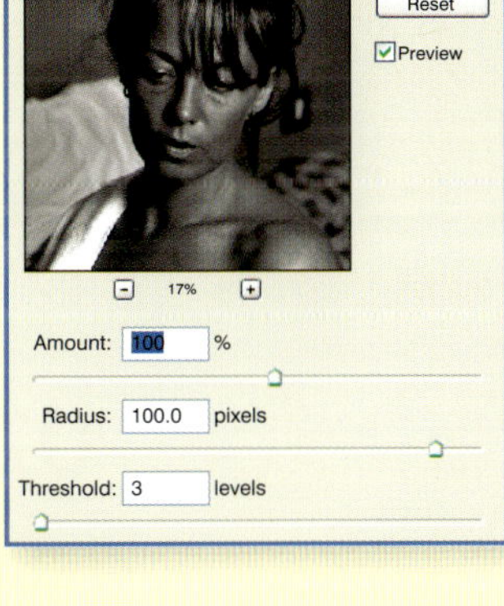

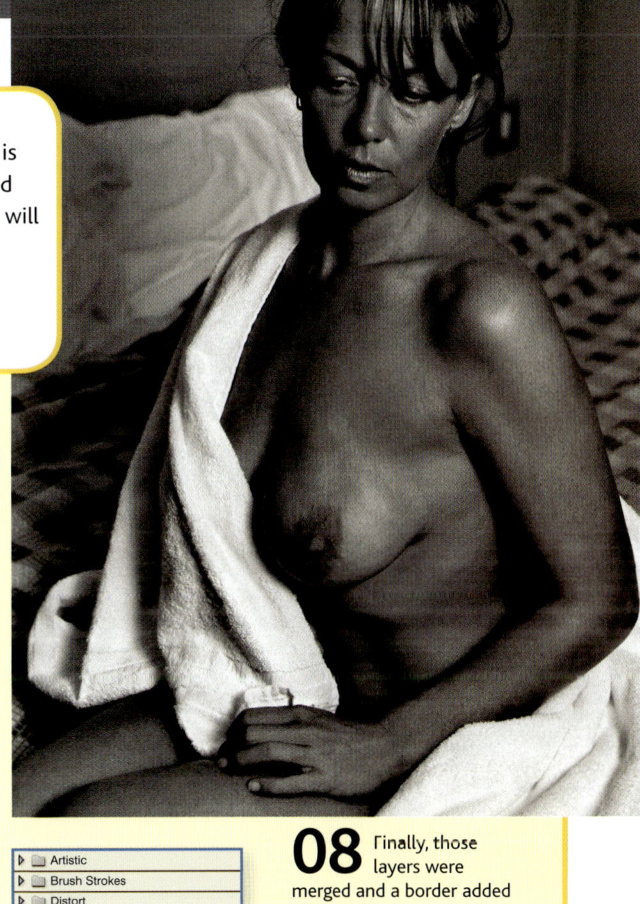

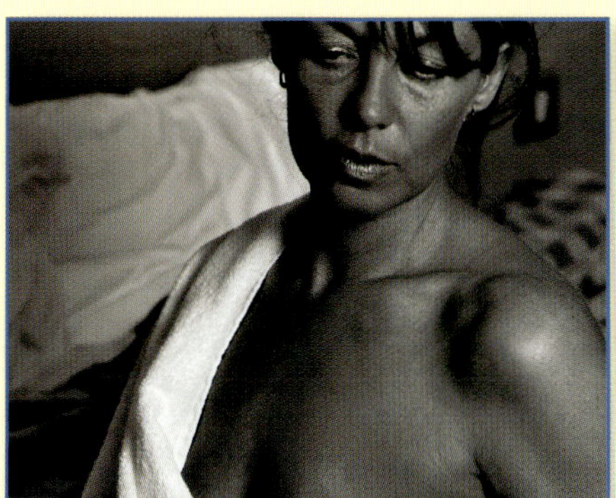

06 This can also blow highlights, as happened on the towel. A layer mask was added to this duplicate layer, a black paintbrush selected, and the opacity set at 20%. Then the missing detail on the towel was painted back in by masking this layer.

07 Those layers were merged and then another duplicate layer was created. Then the Grain filter was run and normal grain with a reasonable high amount of contrast was added. Note that this is colored, so the blend mode of the duplicate layer was set to luminance.

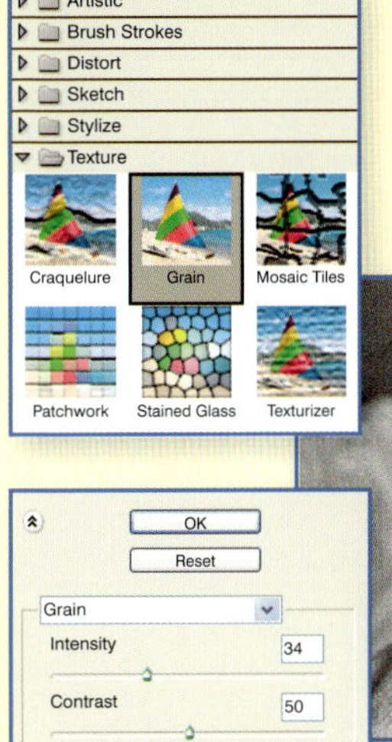

08 Finally, those layers were merged and a border added for the high-impact, high-contrast nude shot.

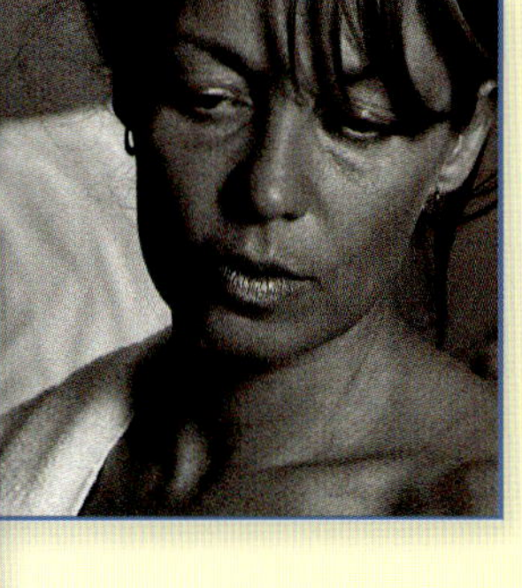

TOOLS AT A GLANCE

IMAGE > ADJUSTMENTS > LEVELS
IMAGE > ADJUSTMENTS > GRADIENT MAP
IMAGE > ADJUSTMENTS > CHANNEL MIXER
FILTER > SHARPEN > UNSHARP MASK

LAYER MASK
FILTER > TEXTURE > GRAIN
IMAGE > CANVAS SIZE

SUBTLE SHADES

Digital editing allows you to create a range of different imagery from one original shot. It also lets you develop an image in the way that the master printers of the chemical era did, when developing made all the difference in the final image. Artistic nudes particularly suit the style of delicate tones in monochrome images. Light, airy, and esthetically pleasing is the aim. It is often better to ensure that you get an even exposure than try to produce a high-key image in-camera, as most digital cameras don't have much tonal latitude and you may lose highlights that cannot be recovered.

SETTING IT UP

Here, two smaller flash lights with diffusers on the front were pointed at the background, toward the floor, set at f/11. The key light, with a large softbox, was to the left of the camera, pointed across at the front of the model. The camera aperture was set to f/9 (digital SLRs have more control over aperture selection than manual cameras) and 1/125 sec to sync with the lights. The lens was a 50mm to avoid distortion, shooting from around 6 feet (1.8m), getting close in to the subject, who sat on the floor.

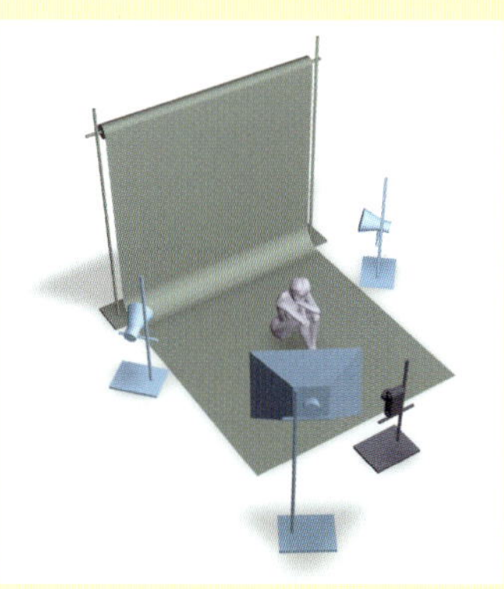

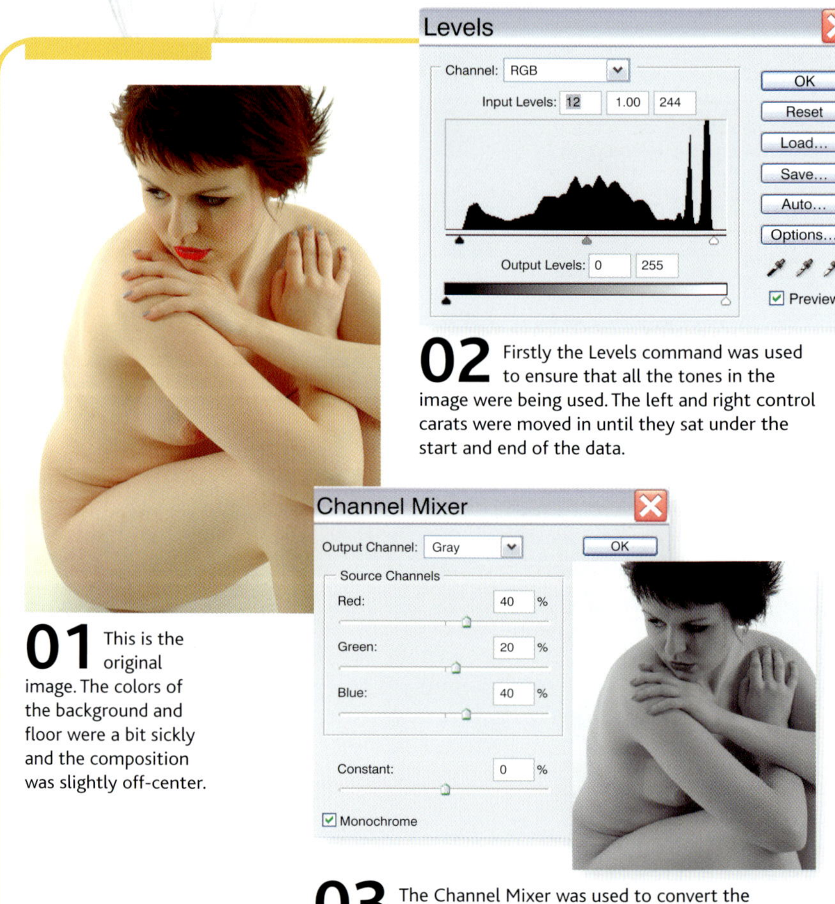

02 Firstly the Levels command was used to ensure that all the tones in the image were being used. The left and right control carats were moved in until they sat under the start and end of the data.

01 This is the original image. The colors of the background and floor were a bit sickly and the composition was slightly off-center.

03 The Channel Mixer was used to convert the image to monochrome. While using a 100% red channel automatically gave a whiter skin tone, splitting the percentages as they were enables the figure to be differentiated from the background a little more.

BRIGHT IDEA
Use a reflector to bounce light back into dark areas on a figure, particularly if arms or legs are crossed and pulled up. This will enable you to get more even tones.

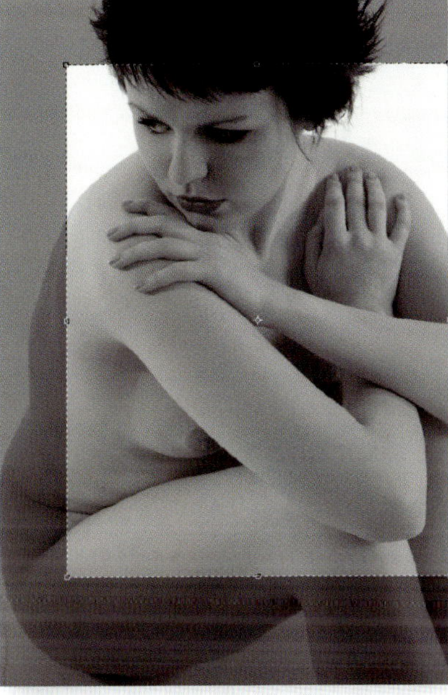

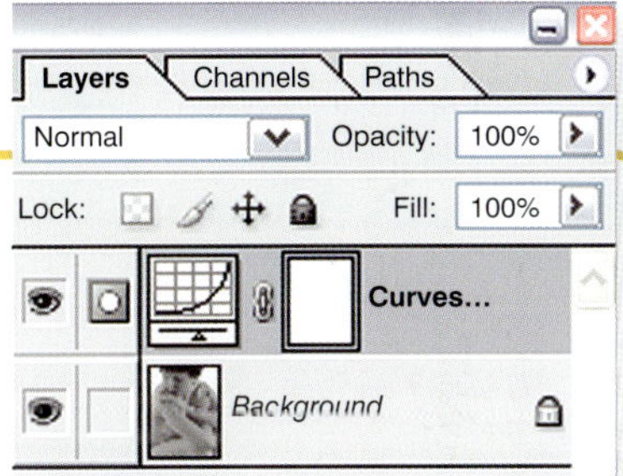

04 The Clone stamp tool, using the lighten blend mode at 100% opacity, was used to remove marks from tight clothing. The key is to sample from an area that is the same tonal brightness as the one you are painting over. It was easier to do this now, rather than later when the image was brighter.

06 The Crop tool was used to tighten up the composition and remove the wasted area down the left side of the screen. The head was cropped into to provide focus on the face and eyes.

08 The paintbrush and a 100% black color was selected and the opacity of the brush set at 15%. The layer mask in the layers palette was clicked on to ensure it was selected. Then the outlines of the figure, the lips, and some of the hair were painted over. This masked off the effect of the curves adjustment. The layer was then merged.

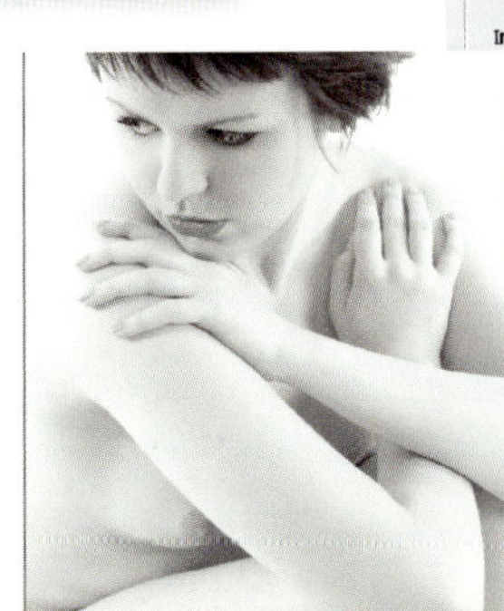

05 The opacity of the clone brush was reduced to 20% and the blend mode set to normal. The brush was used to remove an annoying shadow and highlight just under the eye on the right and to smooth out blemishes on the face.

07 A Curves Adjustment Layer was created. The curve itself was dragged up and left to substantially lighten the tones across the image.

09 This is the final image with a 20-pixel black keyline border added using Canvas Size.

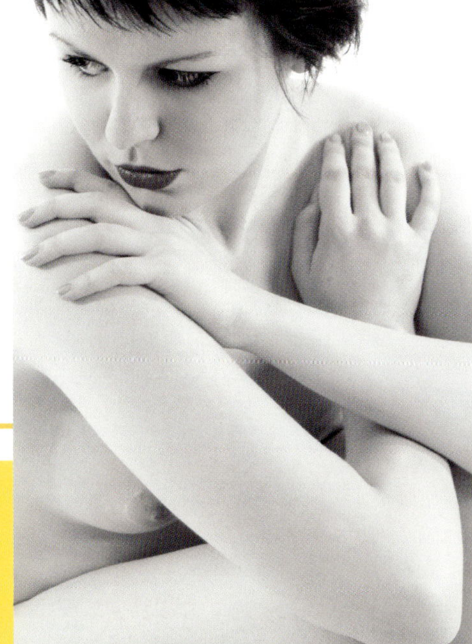

CLEANING UP IMAGES

With digital photography, there is always some tweaking that needs doing. You might need only to make a subtle adjustment to the tonal range, the contrast, the sharpness, or the color saturation of an image. On the other hand, you might have some more complex problems that need to be addressed. When you are shooting nudes on location, for example, you will have little control over the elements and environment. You might be able to pick up any stray pieces of garbage, but it will be a little harder to remove a fence or a lamp post if it happens to be exactly where you want to take a shot. In this project, both the mundane and the more difficult problems are tackled.

SETTING IT UP
When the original was shot, it was both very cold and wet, with a light rain being made worse by the strong wind blowing right at the poor model. The resulting image is flat and lacking in contrast. It was destined to be turned into monochrome anyway, and that metal wiring in the bottom half of the picture did nothing for it.

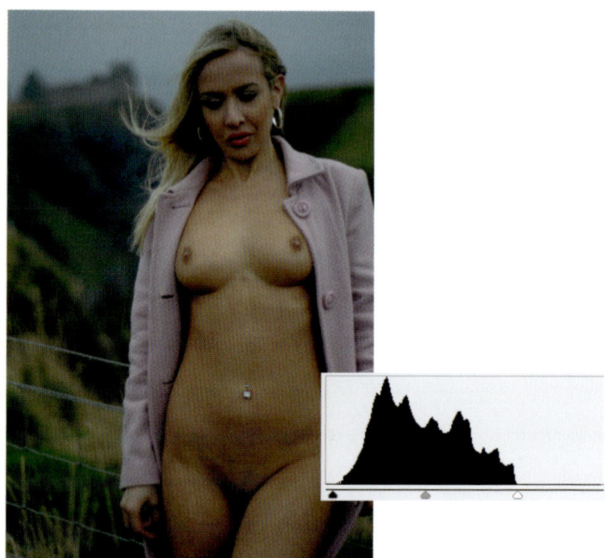

01 The first step was to adjust the levels. This shows a histogram of the image data and reveals that some darker tones were missing, along with a lot of brighter ones. By dragging the right carat in from the end to where the histogram ends, the tonal range is made use of.

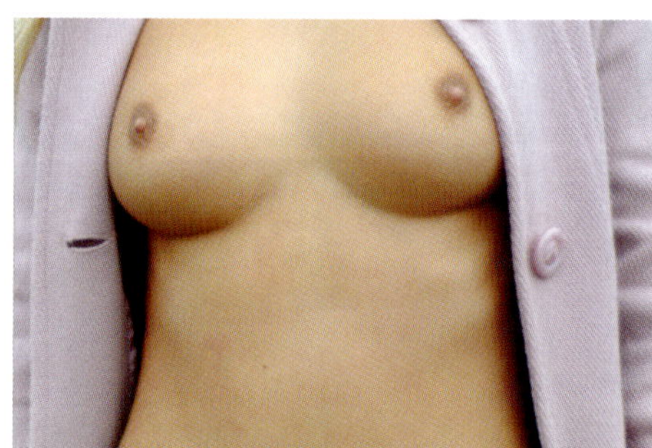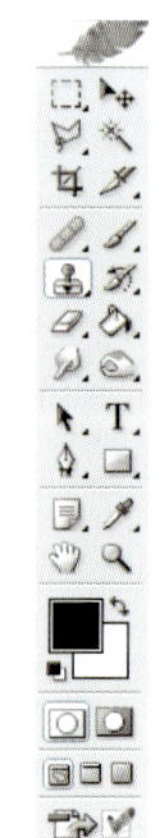

02 There are always blemishes, underwear marks, freckles, and so on that need removing. Here, the Clone Stamp brush was selected and the blend mode set to lighten. The opacity was set to 100% as a lower one would soften the areas tackled. With a blend mode of lighten, it means that only those pixels in the target area that are darker than the ones in the sampling area will be replaced. It allows you to remove blemishes without placing an obvious large white circle on the skin. You must, however, sample from a skin area that is the same tone as the target area.

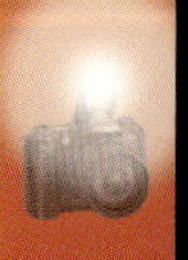

BRIGHT IDEA
When using the Clone Stamp brush, you must try to avoid repeating patterns. If you spot any, go back to that area and sample and clone in some new texture to break it up.

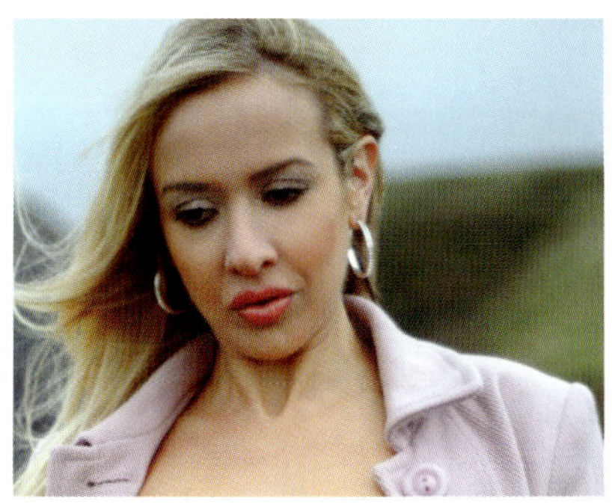

03
The Clone Stamp opacity was set to 18% and the blend mode set to normal. This combination was used to remove shadows under the eyes, lines on the forehead, and the excessive grimace of the cheeks caused by the grim weather.

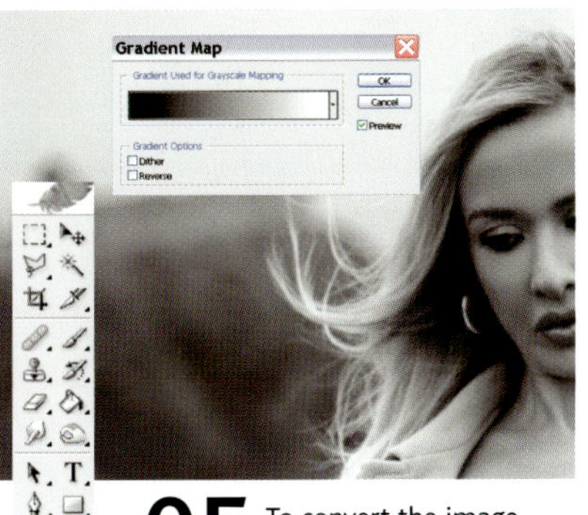

05
To convert the image to black and white, the foreground colors were set to those shades respectively, and the Gradient Map was applied.

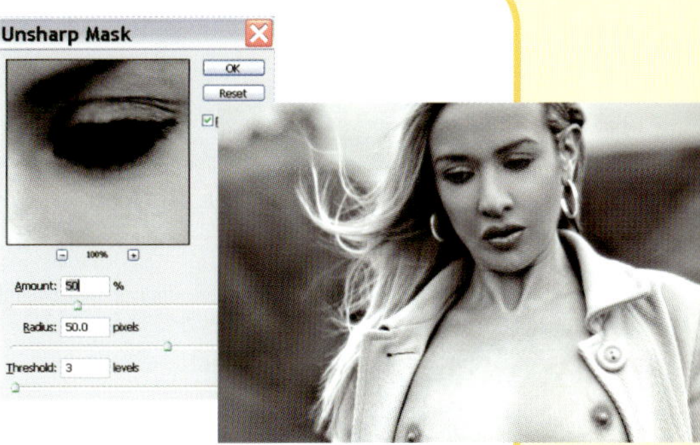

07
Those layers were merged and a duplicate layer was created. Unsharp Mask was applied to the top layer with settings of amount: 50% and radius: 50. This added heavy contrast to the scene but made the eyes too dark. A layer mask was added to this layer, and black painted on the mask to block the Unsharp Mask effect on the eyes and parts of the face.

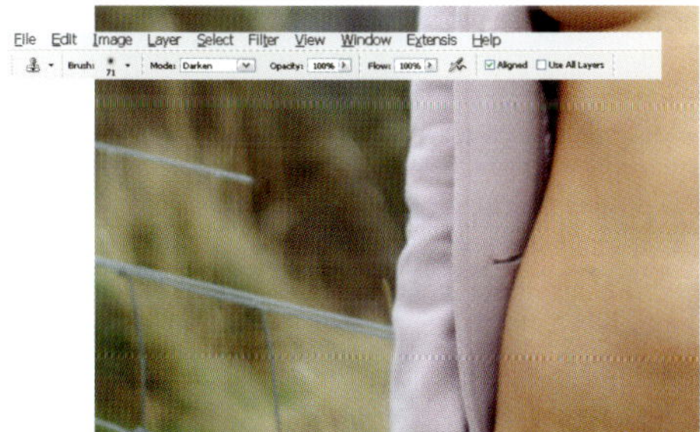

04
To remove the metal wire from the fence, the blend mode of the clone brush was set to darken, because the wire is light in tone. The opacity was set to 100% again. The sample areas were taken from whatever direction the underlying tone was going in. This is certainly easier if the background is out of focus.

TOP TIP
Using the clone brush at 20% causes it to smooth out texture. Use it to even out the complexion and remove flaws, but be careful—overuse will result in a plastic skinlike finish.

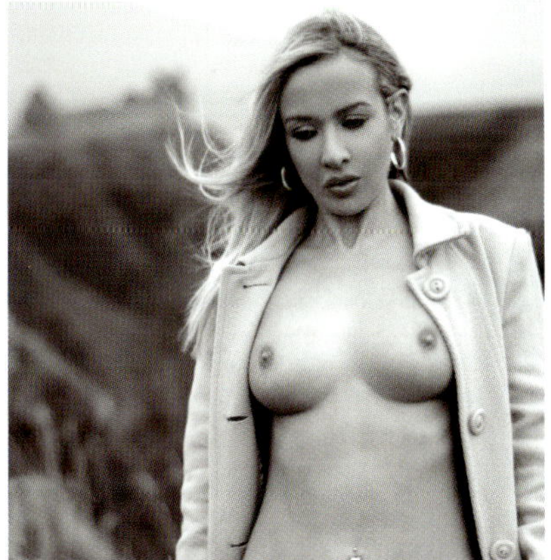

06
This had the effect of shifting the levels around so that the image was darker in mono than it was in color. A Levels Adjustment Layer was created. This was stretched out as before, and the paintbrush used to paint over the sky area. This paint was added to the layer mask, not the picture, and blocked the effect of the levels adjustment. This was so that the sky remained dark and gloomy, not bright and white.

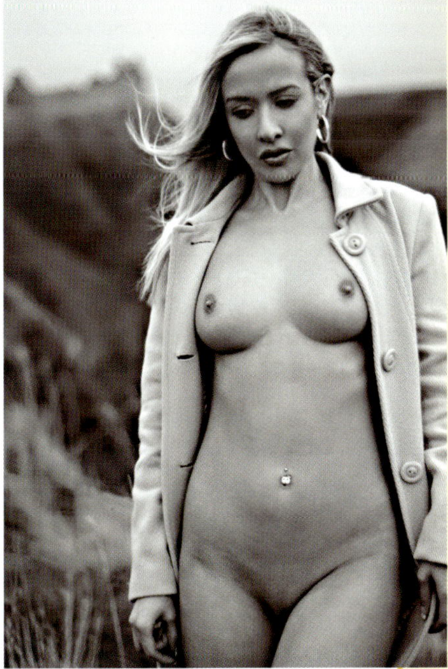

08
All layers were then merged and a 20-pixel black border added with the Canvas command.

TOOLS AT A GLANCE
IMAGE > ADJUSTMENTS > LEVELS
CLONE STAMP
IMAGE > ADJUSTMENTS > GRADIENT MAP
LEVELS ADJUSTMENT LAYER

FILTER > SHARPEN > UNSHARP MASK
LAYER MASK
CANVAS

TONING AND AGEING

It's a curious irony of digital imaging that we love to take clean digital images and distort, decay, color, and degrade them so that they don't look shiny and new any more. The detractors miss the whole point of this process, much as they miss the whole concept of digital photography. It isn't that you are trying to pretend or pass off an image as one that is old, but rather that you are creating an image that has the atmosphere and style of an old image for the purposes of creating a narrative or generating an emotion.

SETTING IT UP

To set up a picture like this, with a view to visiting destruction upon it at the image-editing stage, pay a visit to your local fancy dress shop. That provided the outfit, while my front room came up with the Victorian fireplace. Use available light—here, it is coming from a window through net curtains. Shoot from a distance away with a 140mm lens. Use a narrow aperture to get a long shutter speed so that movement from the subject will blur. Something like f/16 will work. This will make the background too sharp, but given the amount of damage that is going to be inflicted, this isn't critical.

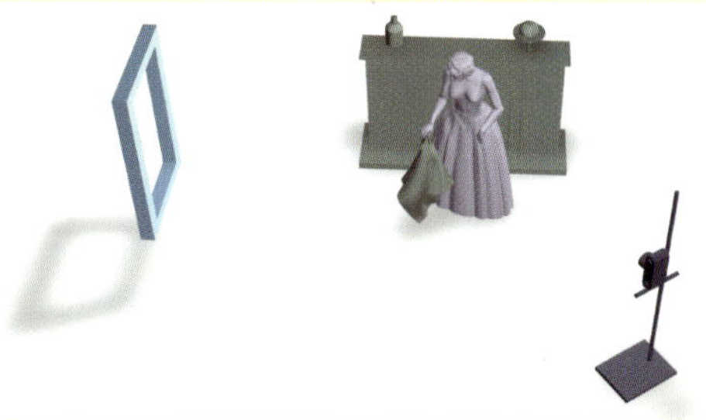

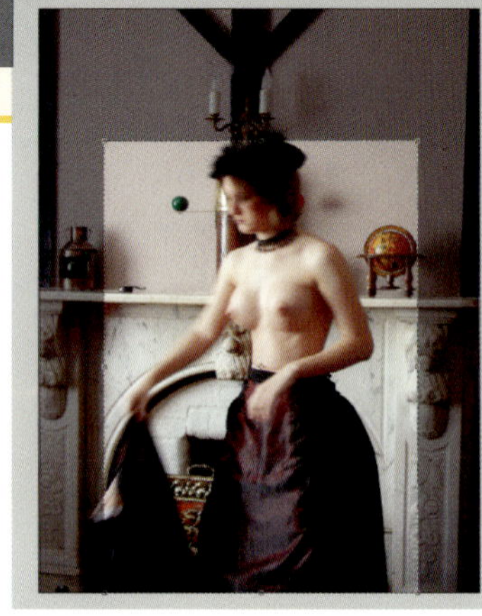

01 The original image has too much spare space around the top of the picture and also some modern artifacts such as those light bulbs. Judicious use of the Crop tool solved both these problems.

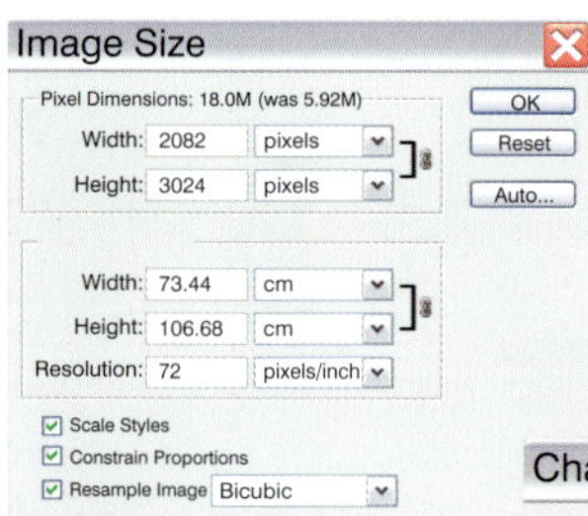

03 The image was converted to monochrome using a fair spread of values from each channel in the Channel Mixer. It was important not to have too much contrast.

02 The resulting image was interpolated back up to the required size by using Image Size. While not acceptable for images generally, it is fine here because the final image will not be sharp anyway.

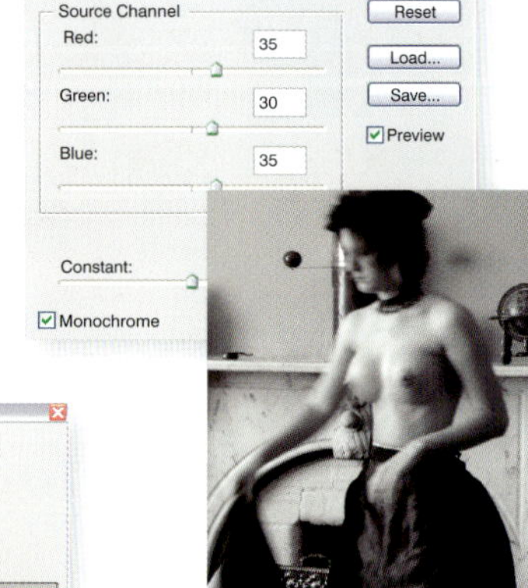

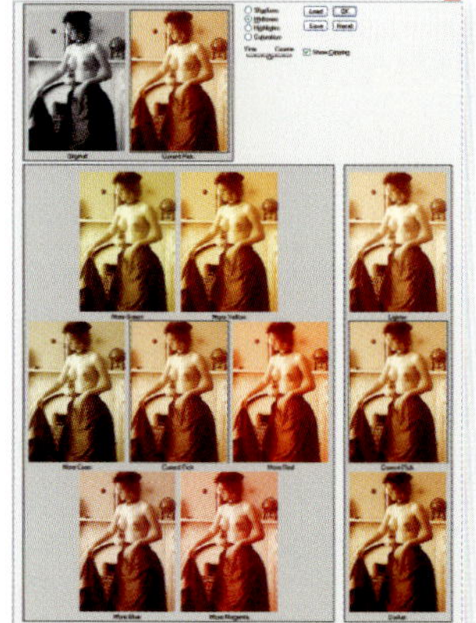

04 Variations was used to add two lots of red and two lots of yellow to form a sepia tint. You could also convert the RGB image to grayscale, and from there to a duotone where you can pick a specific color blend.

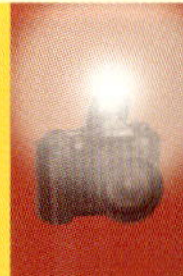

BRIGHT IDEA
To get a longer shutter speed without the need for a very narrow aperture and hence lots of depth of field, fit a neutral density filter to cut down on the incoming light. Alternatively, reduce the ISO rating to under 100 if possible.

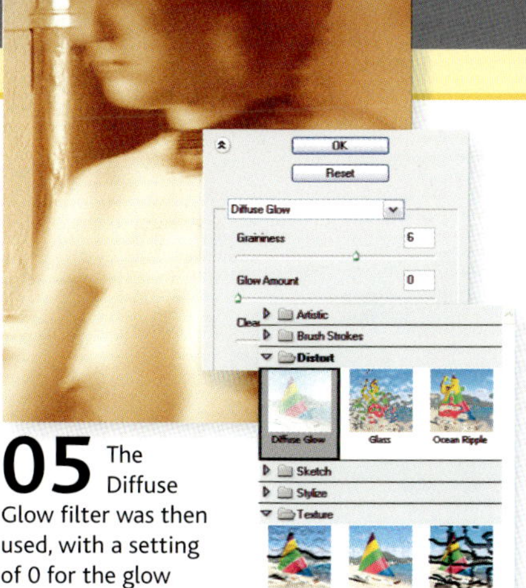

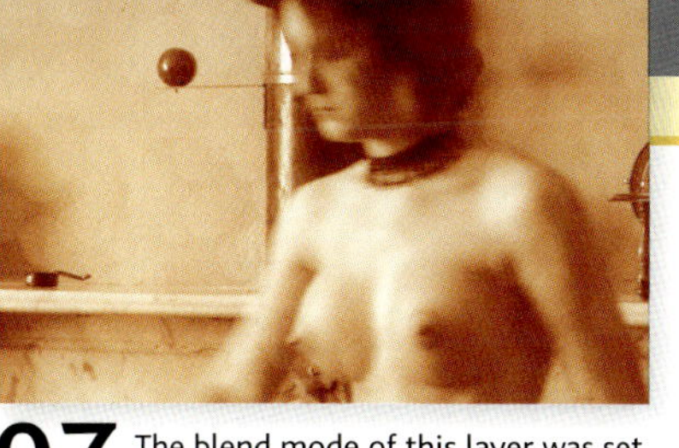

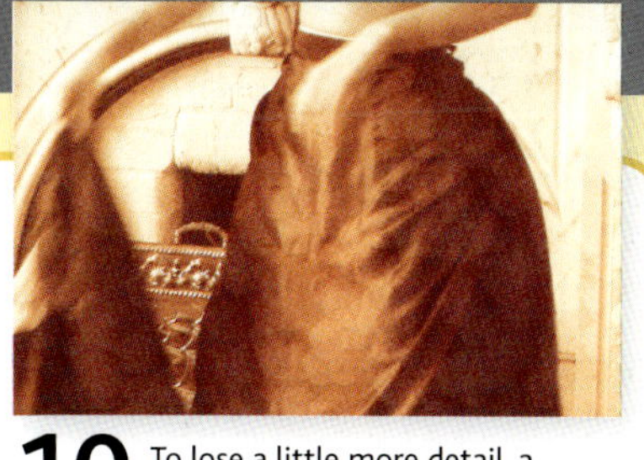

05 The Diffuse Glow filter was then used, with a setting of 0 for the glow amount. 6 was entered for the grain and 4 for the clear amount. This added grainy noise in the same shades as the sepia tint—the grain filter itself adds colored noise.

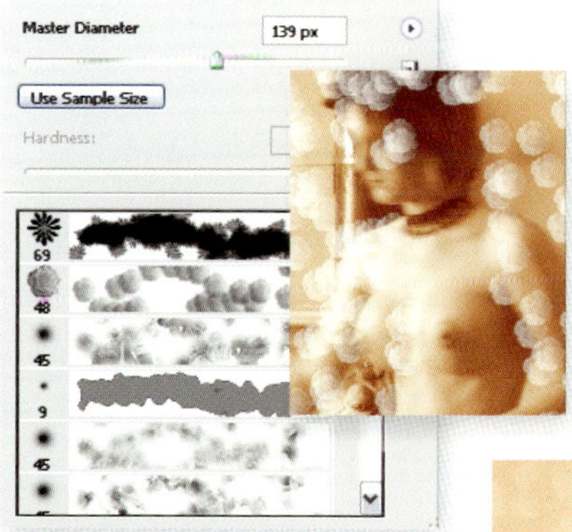

07 The blend mode of this layer was set to multiply and the opacity reduced to just under 50%. The eraser was selected and set to 28% opacity. It was used to smooth out the effect in the lighter areas in the top left and right of the image. It is supposed to look like faint water damage.

10 To lose a little more detail, a duplicate layer was created and the blend mode set to screen. The opacity was reduced to just under 50%.

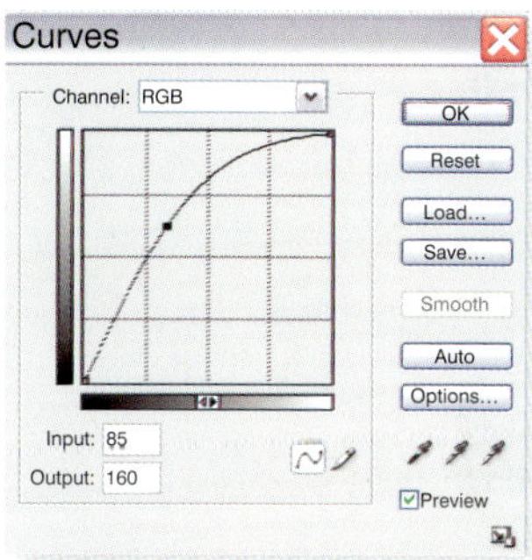

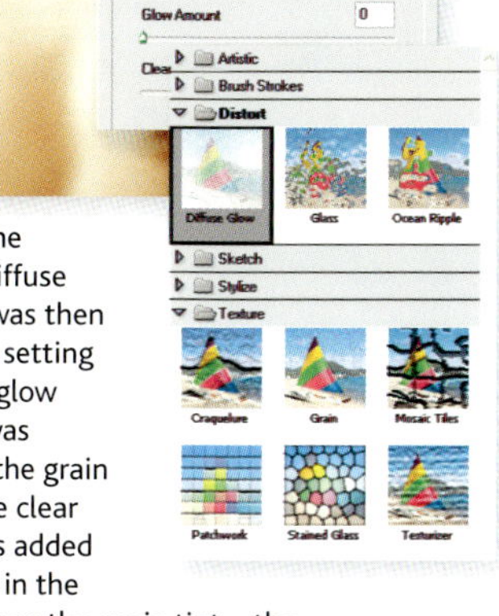

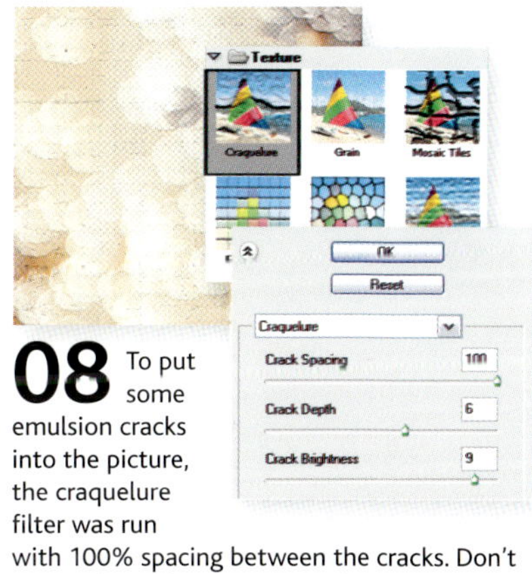

06 A duplicate layer was created and paintbrush selected. The special effect brush set was loaded and the rose petal brush selected. The brush size was increased to roughly double, and white selected as the color. This was then painted onto the duplicate layer.

08 To put some emulsion cracks into the picture, the craquelure filter was run with 100% spacing between the cracks. Don't worry about the preview window as this is simply the multiply layer in its natural state, not what the image actually looks like. The layers were then merged.

11 Finally, Curves was used to lift the tones into a lighter spectrum across the board, and a plug-in distressed edge filter was used to finish the image off.

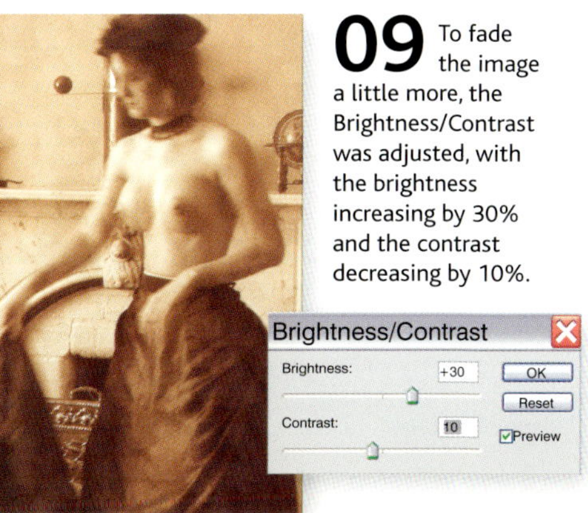

09 To fade the image a little more, the Brightness/Contrast was adjusted, with the brightness increasing by 30% and the contrast decreasing by 10%.

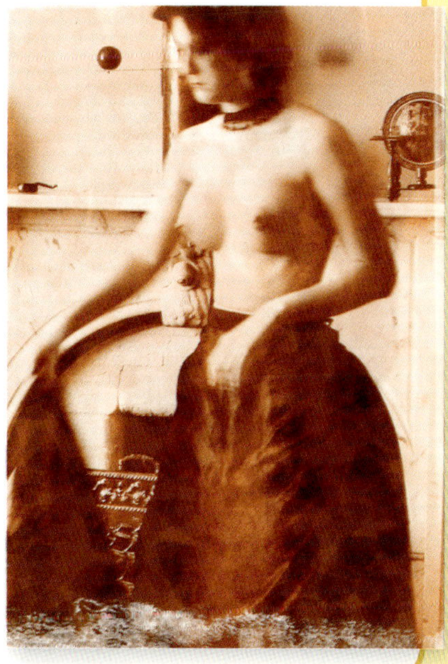

CREATING COMPOSITIONS

There are those who like to assert that creating compositions is an entirely modern phenomenon of computers and digital photography. This is not quite true; great painters thought nothing of painting people in scenes when they were, in fact, studied in the studio. The early photographers would happily press parts of images together to create new ones, and trickery abounded. However, while misleading the viewer is not the intention here, there is also a rich history of simply posing people in front of backdrops, not to pretend that they were actually there, but to make for an interesting picture. That's what we're looking at in this project.

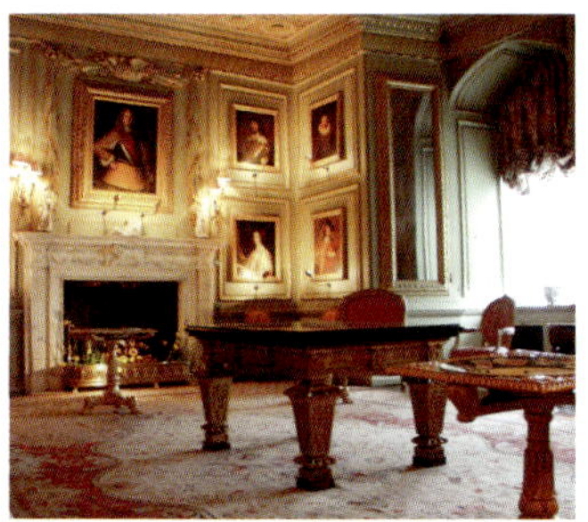

◄ This is a snapshot from a country house that was taken at a high ISO rating on a point-and-shoot camera.

◄ This was shot in the studio against a white background, with the purpose of making it easier to create a composition.

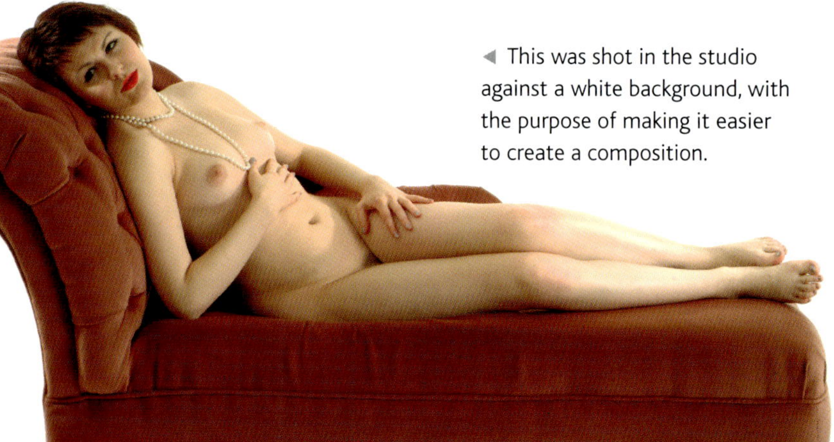

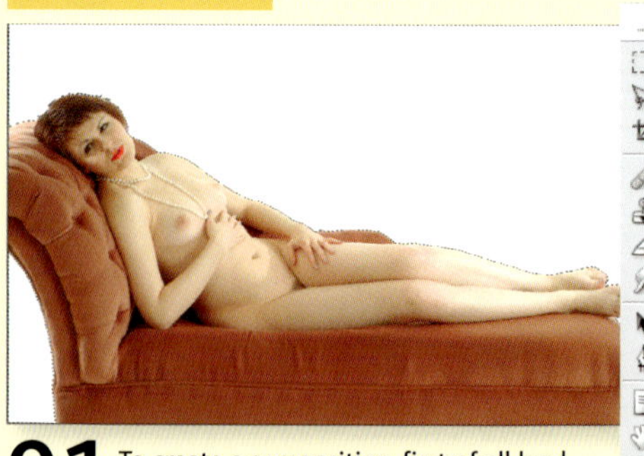

01 To create a composition, first of all load the picture with the white background. While you could use a layer mask to reveal the background, with all that white the magic wand is a time-saver. Set the tolerance to 20% and click in the white areas. Then go Select > Modify > Expand and enter a value of 1 pixel.

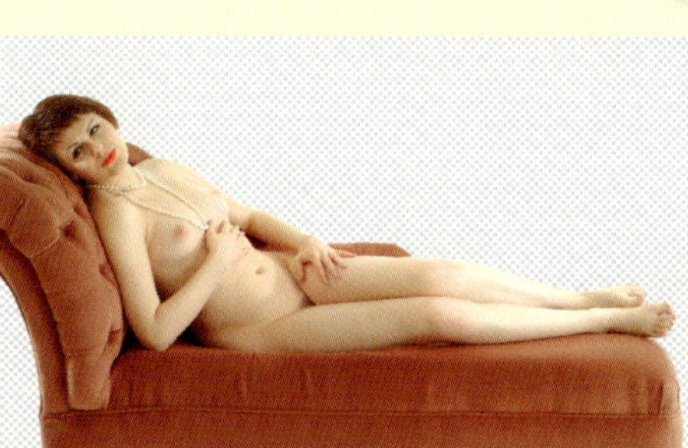

02 Go to modify again, but this time select smooth and enter a sample radius of 3 pixels. This smooths the selection out and prevents a jagged edge. Go to Select > Inverse and then Layer > New > Layer via Copy to create a new layer. Name this the Figure layer.

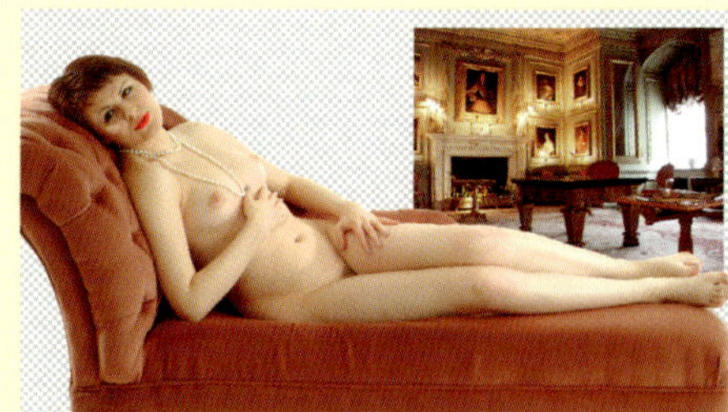

03 Load the house background picture, and drag it onto the composition. You can then close the original window. Move it between the two figure layers in the layers palette and rename it as the House layer.

BRIGHT IDEA
If you make a mistake while painting with black on a layer mask, simply switch the color to white and paint over the affected area to correct it.

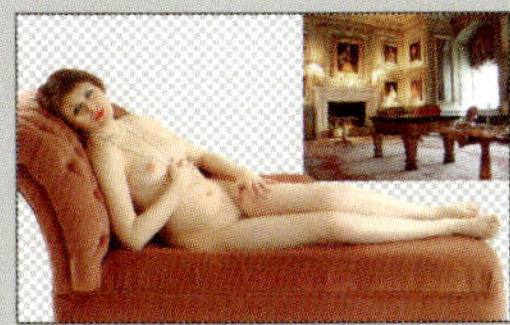

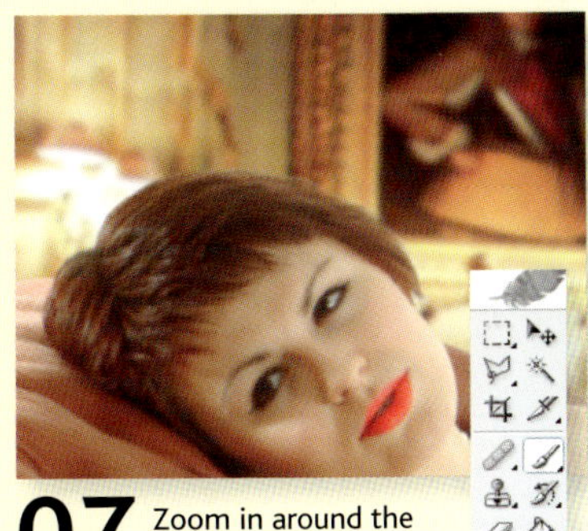

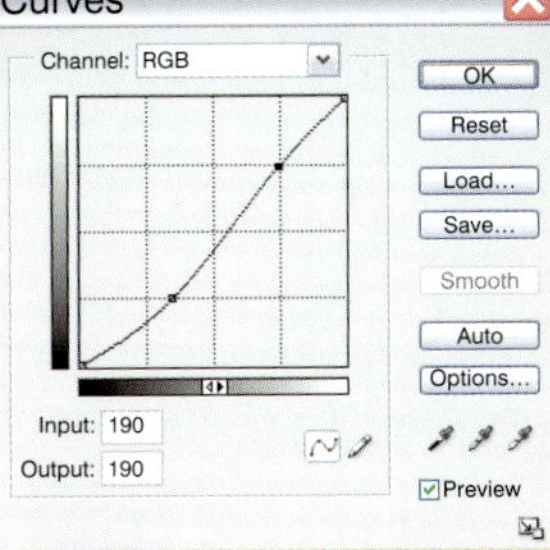

04

With the House layer selected, move the picture into the corner—it's smaller than the figure you see—and press Ctrl+A to select it. It helps if you zoom out at this point.

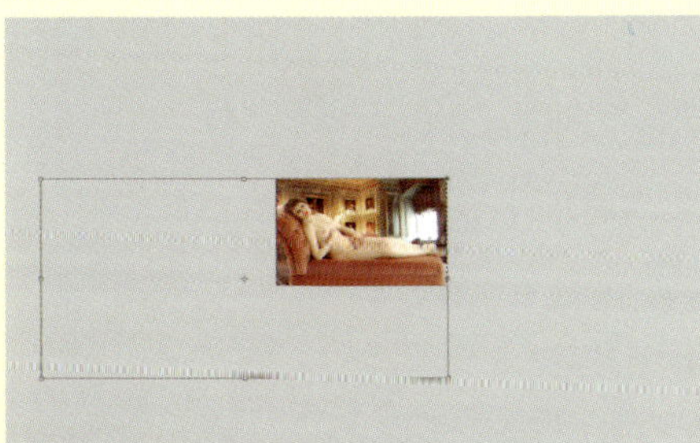

05

Go to Edit > Transform > Scale and drag one of the control handles down so that the House background is resized to fill the screen. Click on the tick symbol to confirm the transformation. Zoom back in again. Press Ctrl+D to remove the selection.

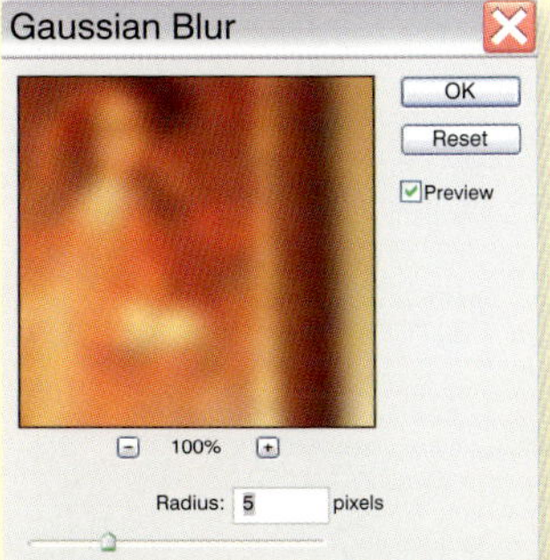

06

Use the Move tool to position the Figure layer a little further down the screen. Then, select the House layer and go to Filter > Blur > Gaussian Blur. Enter a value of 5 pixels to blur the background, which will also remove the digital noise. Select the Figure layer again and apply a 2-pixel blur to that to soften it.

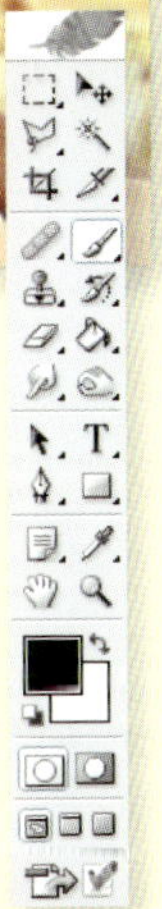

07

Zoom in around the hair area, where there are likely to be parts of the white background still showing. Select the Figure layer and then click on the add layer mask. Select the paintbrush with black paint at 24% opacity. Use this to paint on the layer mask where parts of the white background still show through. Look around the toes as well.

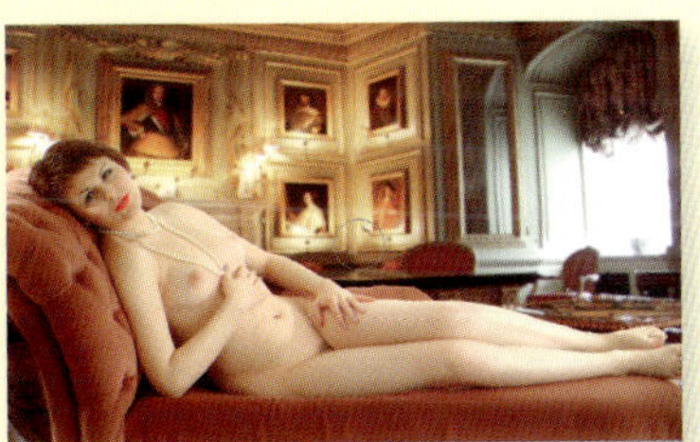

08

Go to Layers and select Flatten image. Use the Burn tool to darken the foreground of the chaise longue and the area behind the upright part. Darken the area around the toes as well.

09

Now go to Image > Adjustments > Curves. Place a control point at the 75% mark toward the top right—the values should say 190 or thereabouts. This holds the highlights. Click in the middle of the remaining line and drag down and right to darken the rest of the photos and increase the contrast and color.

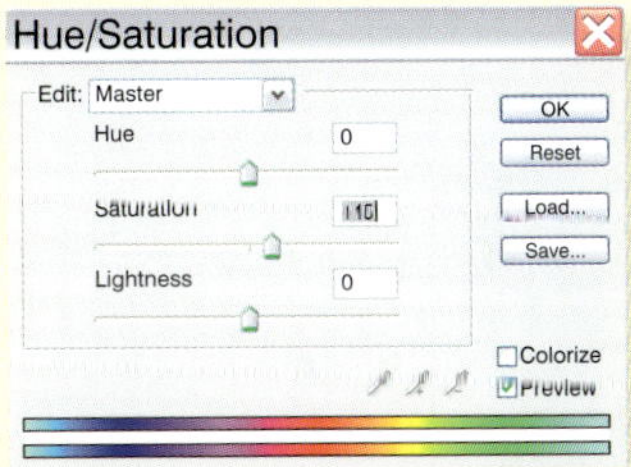

10

Go to Image > Adjustments > Hue/Saturation and increase the saturation by 15% to give it a rich, saturated look. Then apply a final crop to tidy the composition up and add a border for effect.

The completed image with a resting figure against a fine background. This has had an underpainting texture applied.

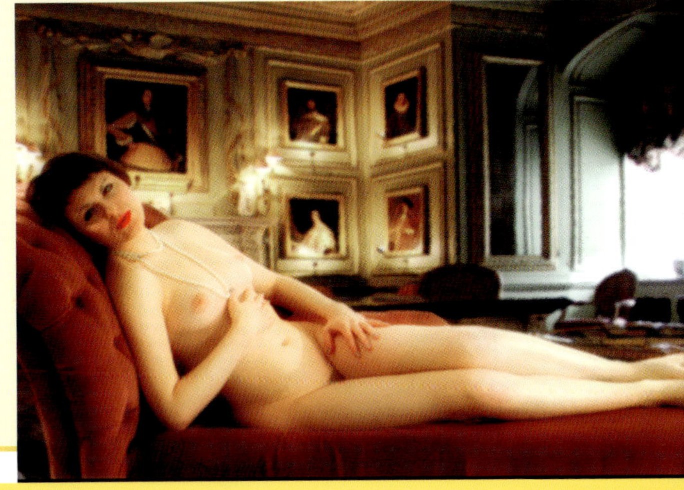

TOOLS AT A GLANCE

MAGIC WAND
MOVE TOOL
EDIT > TRANSFORM > SCALE
FILTER > BLUR > GAUSSIAN BLUR

BURN TOOL
IMAGE > ADJUSTMENTS > CURVES
IMAGE > ADJUSTMENTS > HUE/SATURATION
FILTER > ARTISTIC > UNDERPAINTING

7 STORE, PRINT, PUBLISH

From the start, you need to decide what your shot is for so you can juggle size and quality considerations against storage capacity. Hard drives are very reliable, but with ever-increasing software and operating system demands, it is in use all the time. At some point it may fail. Therefore, you need to have your photos backed up on a DVD. Then it's time to send your images out, whether in print or via the Internet and your very own Web site.

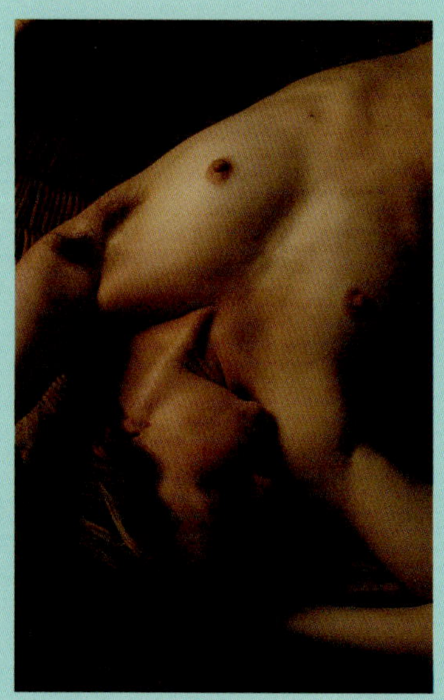
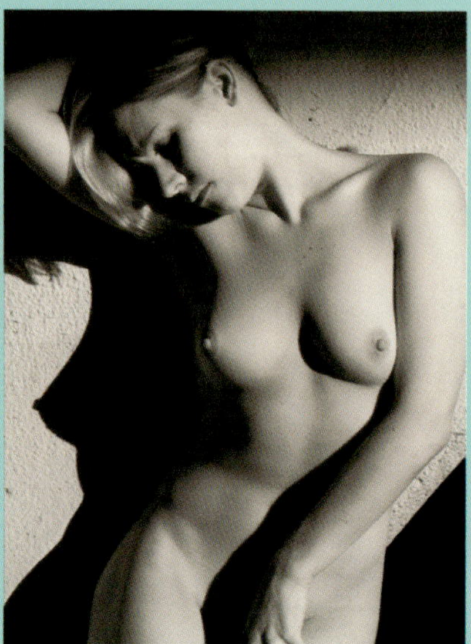
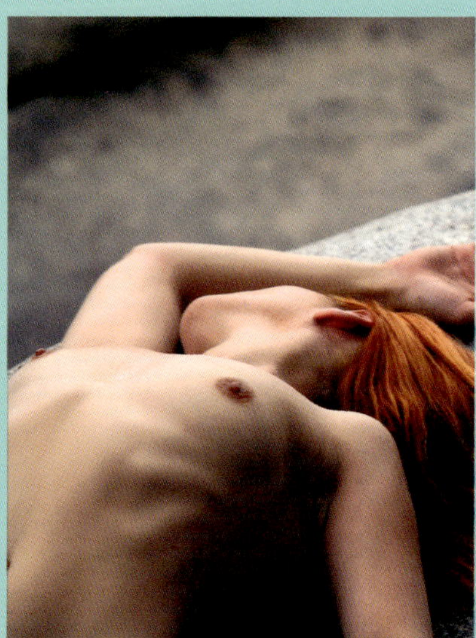

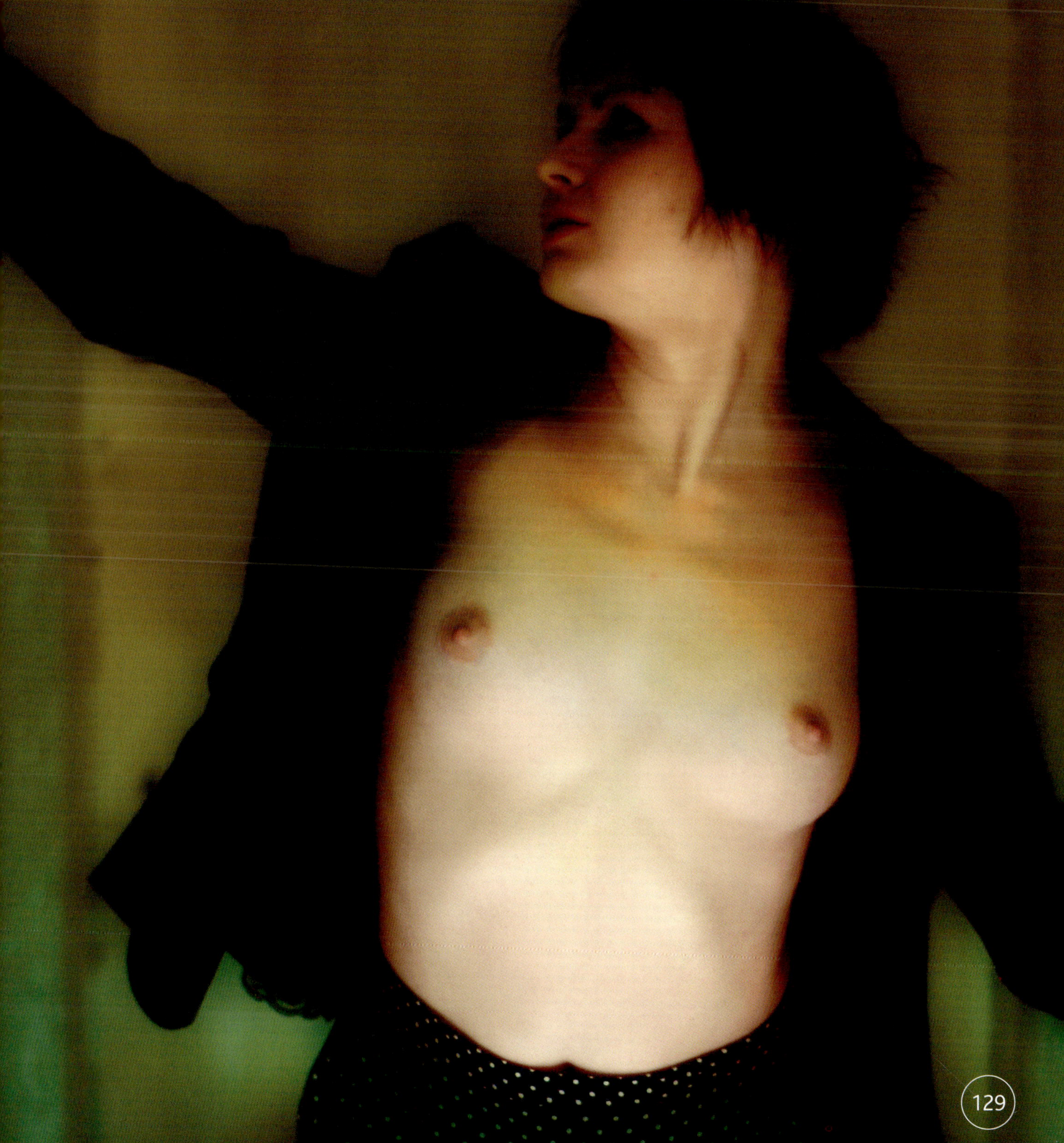

STORING YOUR IMAGES

Saving, storing, and backing up your images is a dull but essential practice in digital media management. The first decision facing you is what format to store pictures in, as this dictates how much space you will need per image. Then there is the prospect of saving files to back up media like zip disks, CDs, and DVDs, including write-once and rewriteable versions. If you are sitting there wondering about the merits of backing up images, consider this. What if your hard drive fails? All your pictures are on it, and hard drives don't last forever.

FILE FORMATS

When shooting digitally, the format of choice largely depends on the subject being shot and the capacity of the memory cards you have to hand. What is certain is that you should not use a medium-quality setting with the JPEG format, as the resulting images, though small in size, will have noticeable artefacts that detract from the image quality.

When looking at quality, such as when shooting landscapes where detail is everything, you should either shoot in TIFF or RAW format. This depends on what is available on your camera, but most SLRs support RAW. TIFFs are a standard file format that occupy a large amount of space—17Mb for a 6Mp file.

RAW is a proprietary format that belongs to each camera manufacturer and occupies less space than a TIFF file, making it more economical. The quality is just as good. The reason why you might not use it is that, unless your image-editing program has a plug-in that can read the format, you will have to convert it using a special program first. In some cases, this is no bad thing because the software supplied can alter white balance, exposure, and sharpness of the RAW image before saving it as a TIFF file.

The advantage of using JPEG files is that they are much smaller. If you set the quality to maximum, it is perfectly acceptable to shoot JPEGs for portraits and nudes for commercial use. Do not resave a JPEG file over itself, as each time it is saved it compresses the image. If the image changes at all then the compression starts again and will substantially degrade the quality. Instead, shoot JPEG, then, once edited, save as TIFF.

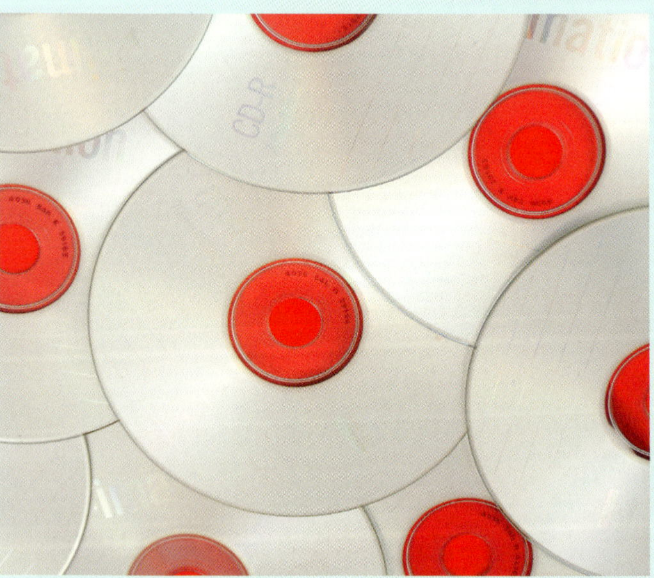

▲ You'll need around seven CDs to store what you can get on a single DVD, but they represent the cheapest option for transporting relatively small numbers of high-res files.

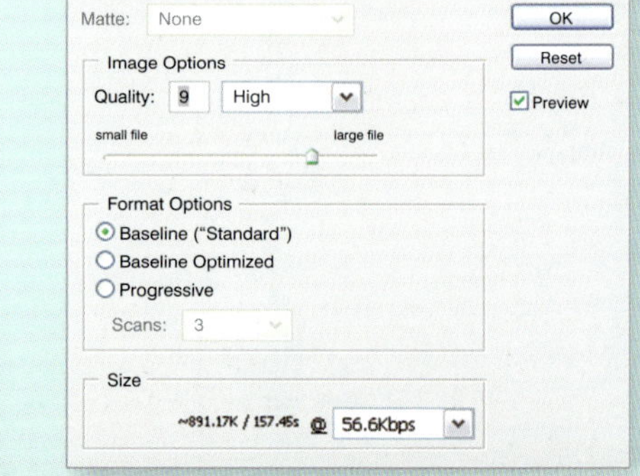

▶ When saving a file as a JPEG you can specify the level of compression to be used.

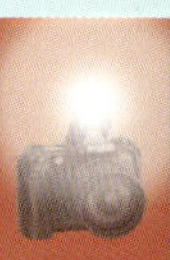

STORAGE

Initially seen as a very handy storage medium, the Zip drive and Zip disk have rather faded from general use and are now mainly used in media companies, where most machines have a Zip drive. The 100Mb Zip is impractical for today's high-resolution digital images, and while the 750Mb version does offer competition to CDs in terms of capacity, it isn't a good choice as the recipient must also have a Zip drive. Most people don't, whereas everyone has a CD drive. CDs are also very cheap.

The standard format of CDs is the CD-R, which stands for CD write once. It doesn't mean you can only write one session to a CD; it means you can only use the space on the disk once as it is being burnt on by a laser. The rewriteable format is the CD-RW, which enables the disk to be wiped and used again. The technological difference is akin to comparing records with tapes. CDs are recorded using the pit depth of the layer, whereas CD-RWs use phase change technology to magnetically encode the disc. The only point to be aware of is that CD-RWs are less, but still widely, compatible from drive to drive.

Although the 700Mb CD is good enough for dragging a pile of JPEGs around to a new computer, if you actually want to back your pictures up then the only sensible choice is the DVD. The single-sided Digital Versatile Disc can hold 4.7Gb, whereas the double-sided format can hold 9.4Gb. The standard DVD format is, like CD-Rs, a write-once format, so once it is filled, that's your lot. However, you get more than six times more space compared to a CD and the unit cost of DVDs has now dropped substantially making them very affordable.

There are two versions to the write-once format: DVD-R and DVD+R. Most DVD burners record both formats and most DVD drives read them as well. If any could be said to be the more popular, it is the DVD-R format that appears to be gaining dominance. There are two rewriteable formats as well: predictable DVD-RW and DVD+RW.

THE JPEG

JPEG stands for Joint Photographic Experts Group and is a user-configurable, compressed file format. This means that you can specify the level of compression used to balance quality against file size.

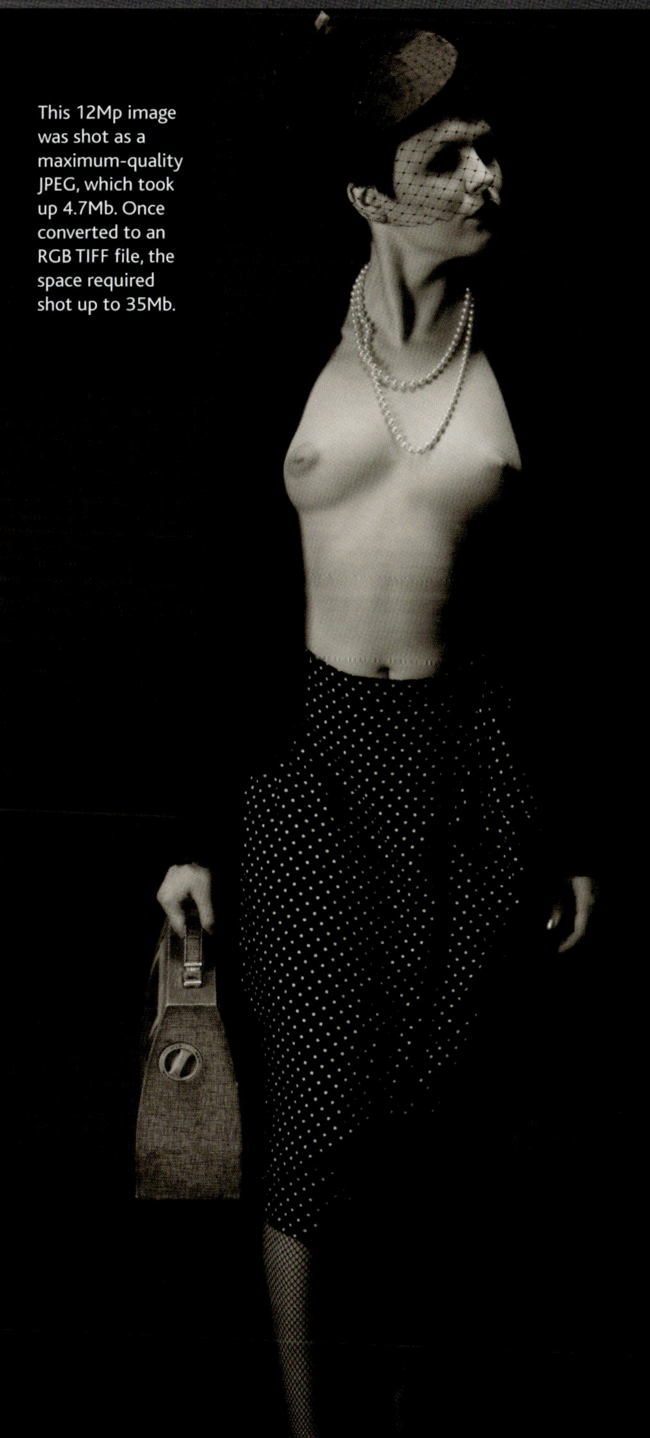

This 12Mp image was shot as a maximum-quality JPEG, which took up 4.7Mb. Once converted to an RGB TIFF file, the space required shot up to 35Mb.

BLACK AND WHITE PRINTING

Possibly more than other genres of photography, black and white suits the artistic nude. Removing color allows the viewer to concentrate on texture, lighting, tones, form, and composition. Printing it out is the natural next step, but getting consistent black and white prints can be difficult.

The first thing that can go wrong is that your black and white print can come out with a color cast—blue, brown, green; it could be any shade. This is particularly vexing for beginners because it isn't obvious why this should be the case. The reason why is that printers are CMYK devices, rather than the RGB you see on screen, and the CMYK interpretation of the picture can be different. Okay, so you're still confused—why are we talking about color in black and white prints? The reason is that the K element in CMYK is the key ink and that, in your printer, is black. However, in CMYK printing, the K is mixed with other colors to give a deeper, darker shade of black. When the printer doesn't quite mix the colors correctly, you get a color cast.

There is one quick and easy solution to this, and that is to specify in the printer driver that it should use only the black cartridge, not the color ones. However, this reduces the amount of ink used to produce the image, so it can look coarser, ruining smooth tonal graduation. Also, there are cases where certain combinations of inks and papers give color casts. While sticking to the printer manufacturer's products will avoid that particular problem, it still brings us back to the color ink problem.

The more expensive solution is to calibrate the printer. This should be done as part of an overall system calibration process, starting with the monitor. A shortcut is to acquire a printer calibration profile for your particular printer, and install that into your computer system. This should help ensure that the output is more consistent.

A practical option when fixing a color cast is to manually adjust the output from each cartridge. If the cast is cyan, reduce the output from the cyan cartridges. Do a test print and check for casts again.

SPECIALIST INKS

There are a number of replacement inks, including four shades of black and gray, and limited gamut inks, which can be installed instead of the usual color inks. These ink systems tend to come with calibration profiles for the most popular size of photo printers to give an entire ink replacement system.

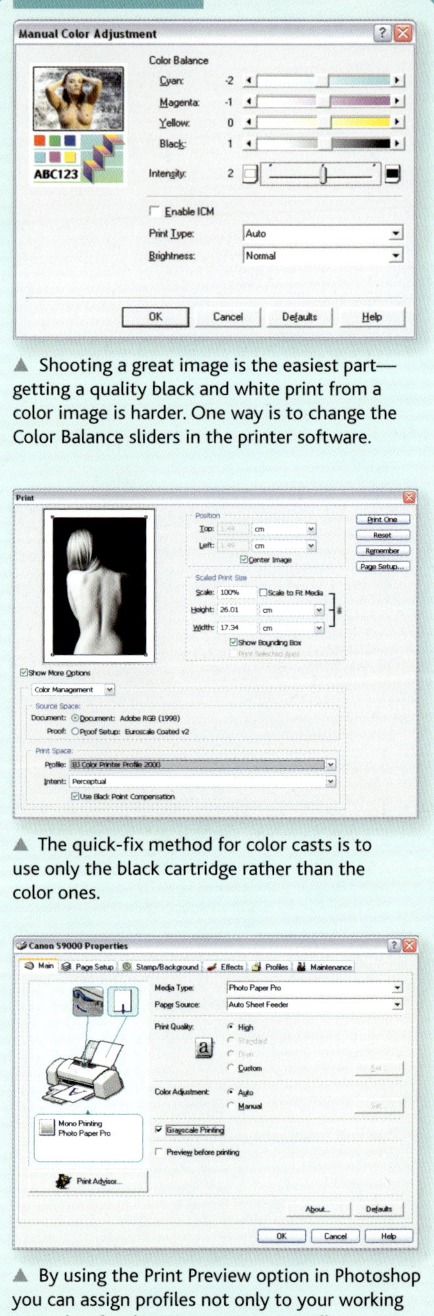

▲ Shooting a great image is the easiest part—getting a quality black and white print from a color image is harder. One way is to change the Color Balance sliders in the printer software.

▲ The quick-fix method for color casts is to use only the black cartridge rather than the color ones.

▲ By using the Print Preview option in Photoshop you can assign profiles not only to your working space, but for the printer to use as well.

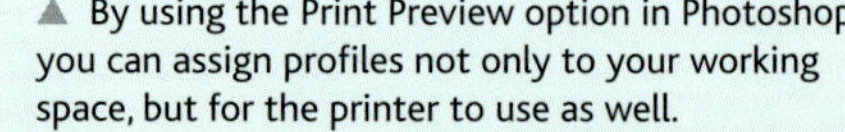

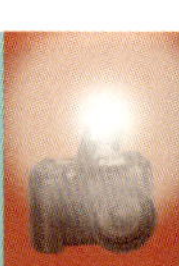

BRIGHT IDEA

If you are really serious about black and white inkjet printing, then it makes sense to have one printer dedicated to it—it avoids contamination from color printing and means it can be configured and left alone.

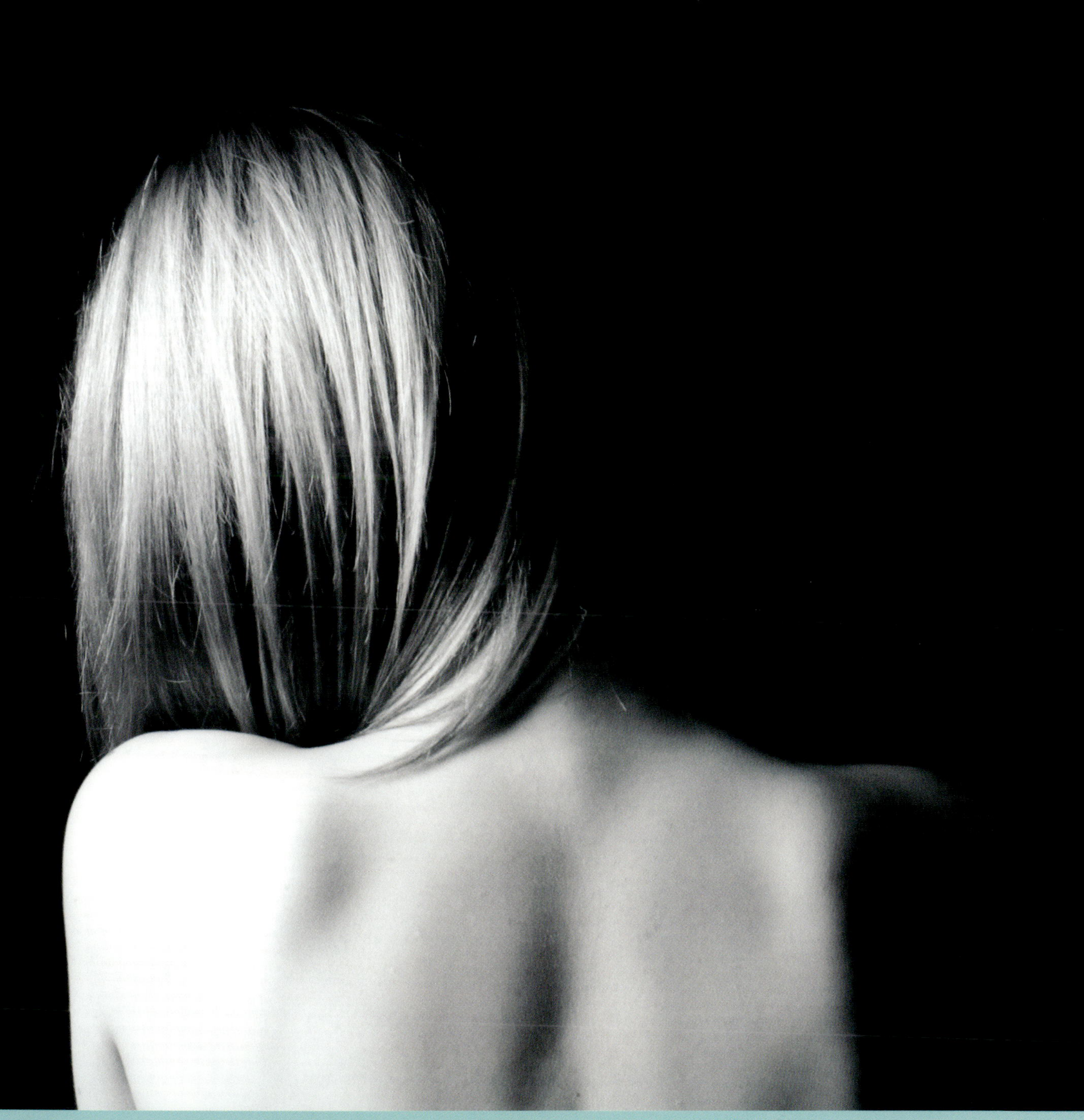

BLACK AND WHITE OPTIONS
PRINT IN GRAYSCALE
ADJUST COLOR CARTRIDGES
USE DEDICATED INKS
USE PRINTER PROFILES

PUBLISHING YOUR IMAGES

Having shot a clutch of great photos, it makes sense to show them off, whether by printing them out, or by electronic collation and dissemination. Certainly, if you are shooting for someone's portfolio, they will want to see the images being presented to them afterward. The other main area of distribution is to post images to your Web space, where everyone with Internet access can have a look. In many respects, for worldwide advertising of your skills, a Web site with your photographs is simply unbeatable in terms of distribution verses costs.

CONTACT SHEETS

A simple way of presenting a number of pictures to someone, whether they are a model and want a range to print and hand out, or a potential client who wants to pick from a selection, is to use a contact sheet. In the digital arena, this can be done in Photoshop, which comes with a handy contact-sheet generator.

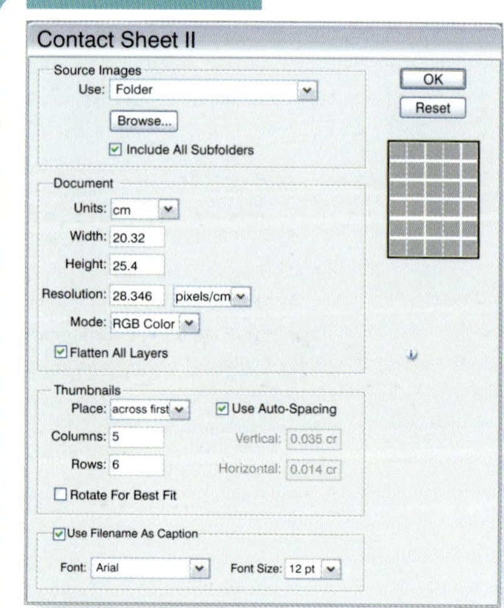

01 Go to File > Automate > Contact Sheet II and select it. This brings up the contact sheet generator screen complete with templates. You will either need to have all the images you want on the contact sheet in the same place, so that you can specify a folder, or manually select them from wherever they are on your hard drive.

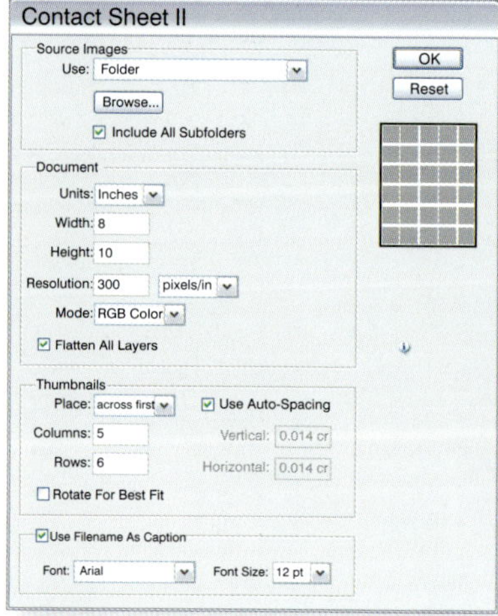

02 In the document section of contact sheet are numbers relating to width, height, and resolution. This is not the size of the images; it is the size of the final, completed document. The images will be resized to fit.

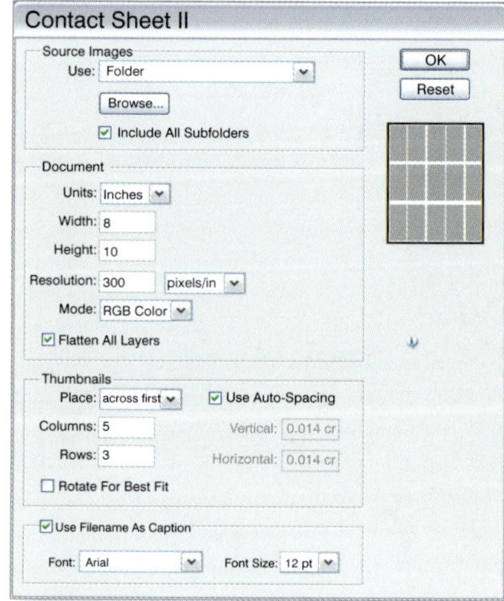

03 The thumbnails section determines how the pictures for the contact sheet are arranged. The more you have, the smaller they are. It is important to create roughly as many thumbnail spots as there are images, accepting that you may not fill all the rows and columns exactly. If you have too many spots, then half the page will be empty. It's also worth looking at whether your pictures are mainly landscape or portrait orientation before setting more columns than rows or vice versa.

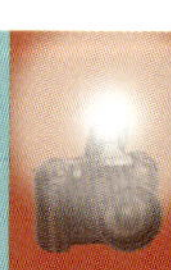

BRIGHT IDEA

Registering your own domain name costs very little, but if you can't afford to pay for Web space to host your site, use one that offers free space and use your provider's option of domain name masking and redirection to send people to it. They will think you have an expensive site with your domain name, rather than it being hosted on a free site.

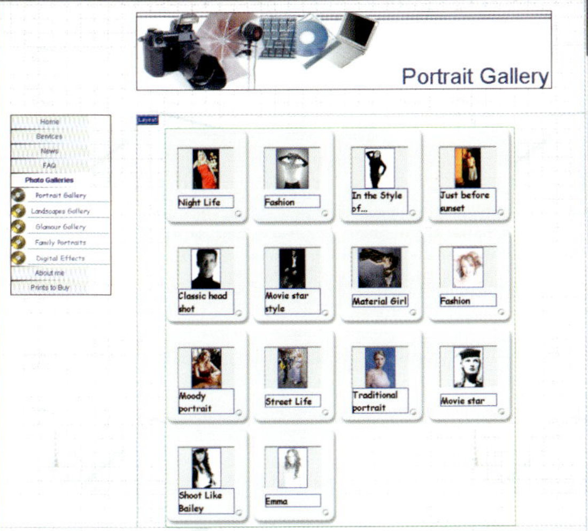

▲ This is Fusion 7, a software package that came free from my Web host.

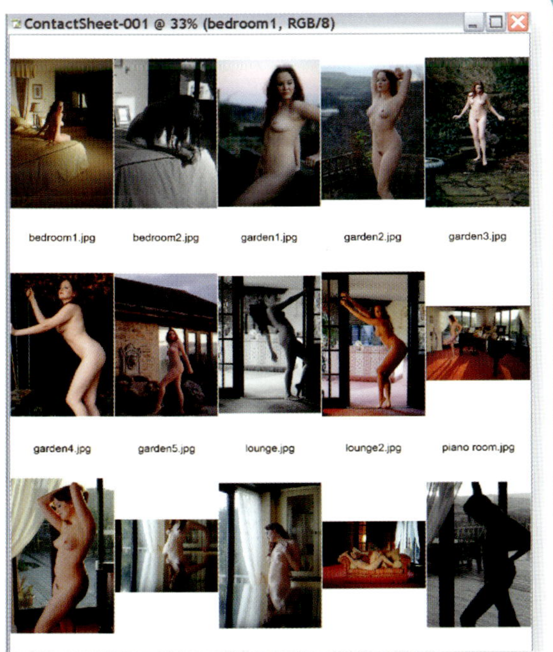

04 Finally, if you untick the Filename as Caption box, you will have to add captions afterward. Click on OK to automatically create the contact sheet.

PORTFOLIOS ON THE WEB

Most Internet Service Providers (ISPs) offer some kind of free Web space to keep your custom. It usually isn't a lot, it tends to be slow to access, and instead of your own professional-sounding domain name, it has the name of the service provider at the front. If you are trying to make a professional impression, this is the wrong way to go about it. However, if you want to showcase your photographs, then creating a site like this is a cheap way of showing off your work.

One alternative to this is to sign up for accounts with photography, model, and photographer Web sites, register your details and post some images to your account. This has the advantage that, as these sites almost always have forums for posting adverts, anyone thinking of replying can easily check out your portfolio on that site before they contact you. The disadvantage is that the format is whatever the site decides, and to get more than a handful of images uploaded, you normally need to subscribe. At that point, you might as well pay for your own Web-hosting domain name anyway.

The basics of having an online presence are that you register and own the domain name: www.duncanevans.co.uk is mine, for example. The registration fee is normally very low and lasts one or two years, then it must be re-registered, but the service provider will do that for you and just bill your credit card. The next thing to sort out is where your pictures and Web site will be physically located. While you can do this on the cheap and place it on a free site— many ISPs like AOL offer free space for their customers—if you want to put a lot of pictures up, be able to get traffic statistics, and have more than the light traffic to the site, then paying for your Web space is a better idea.

The people who sold you the domain name will also host Web space, so it makes sense to do it all in the same place. You can get Web hosting for well under $150 a year. Creating your own Web site can be a laborious task, and if you are not a wizard with HTML, Java, ActiveX, and all the other technologies, it can be mystifying. Fortunately, the same people selling you the Web space often have a complete package where a Web-creation software package is thrown in as part of the deal. This enables you to construct the site using templates for positioning, and then have automated wizards for processing the pictures and placing them within a template. You add the descriptions and the program does the hard work. It then connects to the host site server and uploads it all for you.

TOOLS AT A GLANCE
FILE > AUTOMATE > CONTACTS SHEET II

8 APPENDIX

We hope that this Digital Photography Workshop has been useful and inspirational, revealing the process and creative thinking behind some eye-catching nude photography. Now read on for a technical glossary, index, and a guide to our featured photographers.

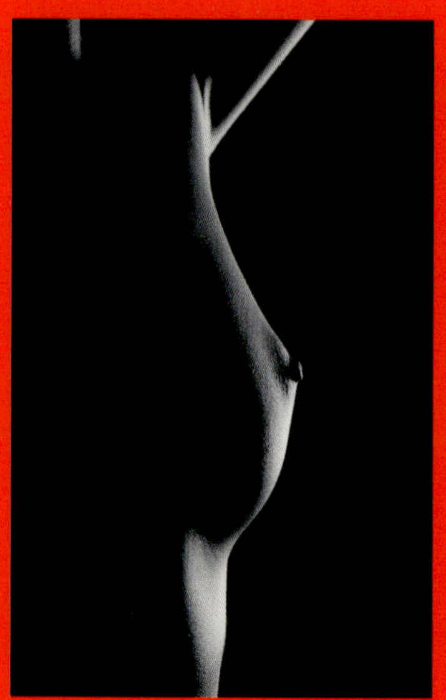

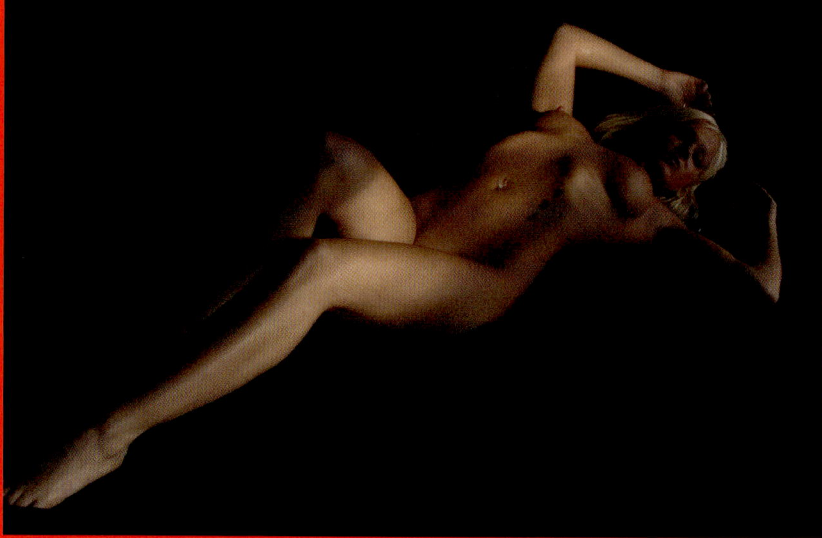

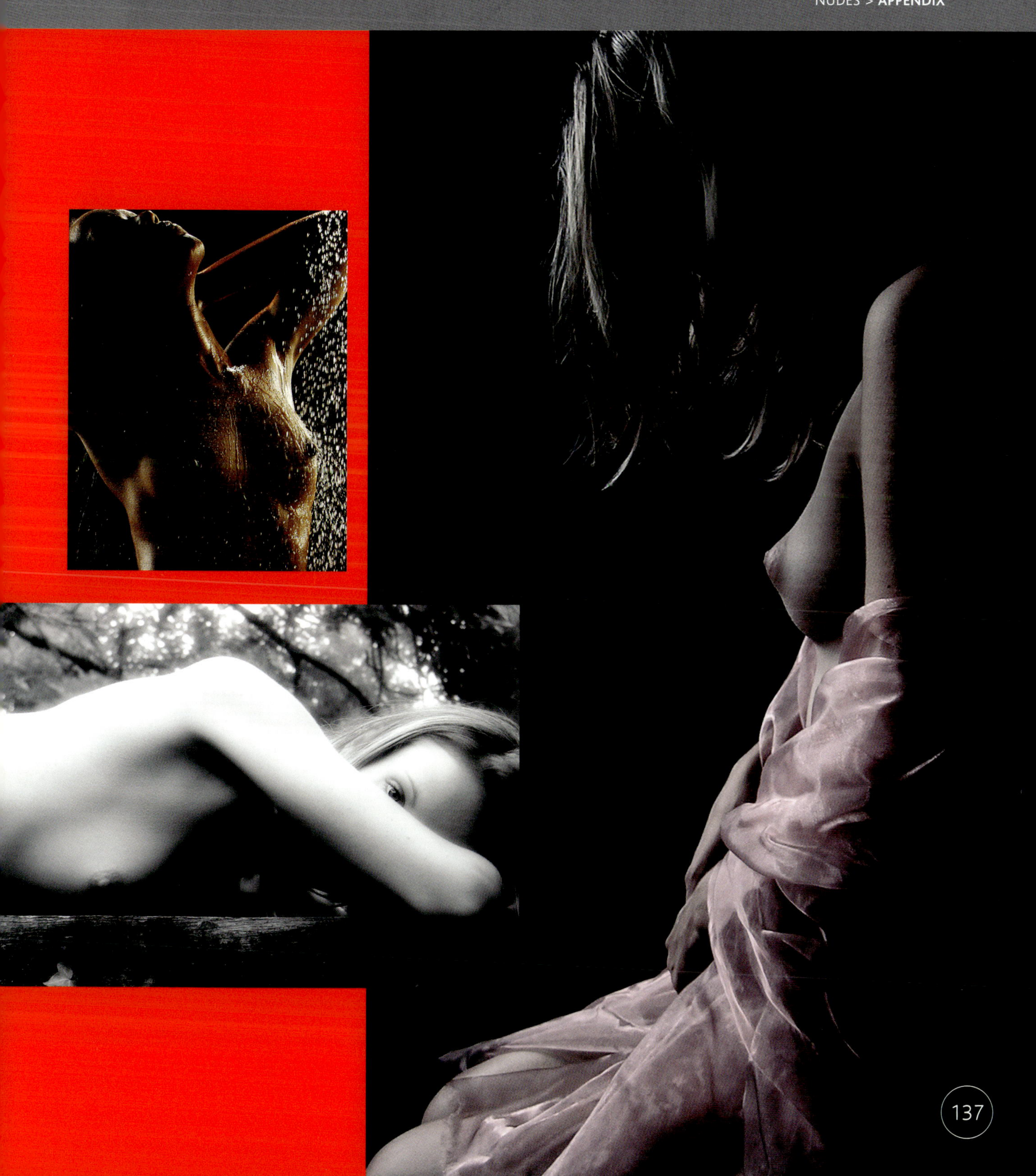

GLOSSARY

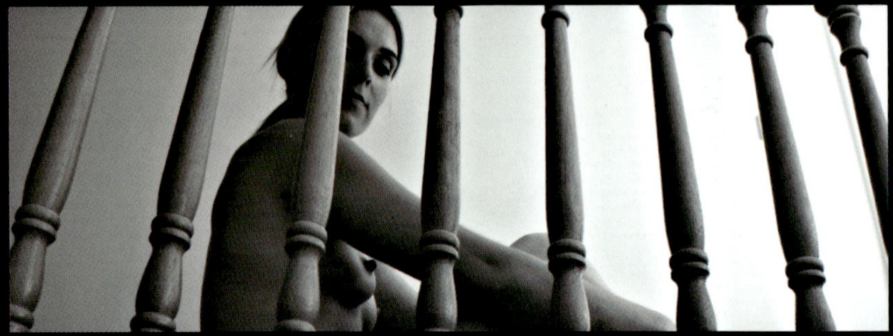

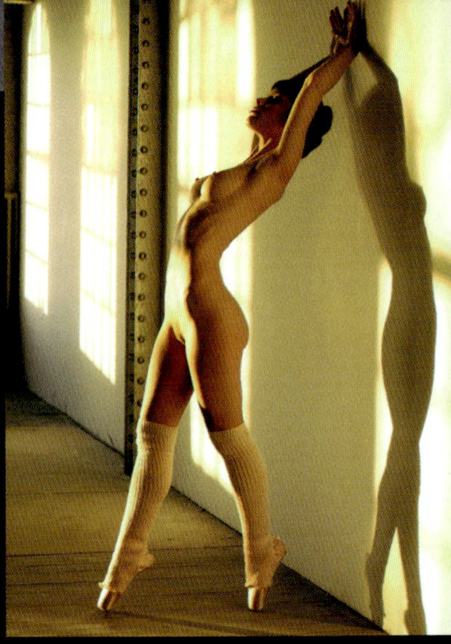

AdobeRGB 1998: color profile based on the RGB system with a wide color gamut suitable for photographic images. See sRGB.

AEL: Automatic Exposure Lock. A camera option to lock the setting of the exposure once read, so that the camera can be moved and the scene recomposed, without it being metered again, and giving a different result.

AF Illuminator: when the light isn't bright enough to allow the autofocus to detect a contrast difference, a spotting light, or infrared light, comes on to light up the target area and make it possible.

Aperture: the opening to a camera's lens that allows light into the camera to strike the CCD. See f-stop.

Aperture priority: camera shooting mode. Allows the user to set the camera's aperture (f-stop) while the camera calculates the optimum exposure time.

Artifact: minor damage or fault on a photograph, usually caused by JPEG file compression.

Automatic white balance: system within a digital camera that removes color casts in images caused by the hues of different types of light.

Bit: binary digit. Smallest unit of information used by computers.

Bitmap: digital image made of a grid of color or grayscale pixels.

Byte: a string of 8 bits. 1024 bytes make a kilobyte (KB), and 1024KB make a megabyte (MB).

CCD (charge-coupled device): electronic device that captures light waves and converts them into electrical signals.

CD-R: a compact disk that data can be written to but not erased.

CD-RW: a compact disk that can be erased and used a number of times.

Chromatic aberration: colors bordering backlit objects. Caused by the poor-quality lens systems used in many compact cameras. Can also affect high-quality optical systems, but only to a limited degree.

CMOS (Complementary Metal Oxide Semiconductor): a light-sensitive chip used in some digital cameras and scanners instead of CCDs. CMOS chips are cheaper to develop and manufacture than CCD chips, but they tend to produce softer images.

CMYK: abbreviation for cyan, magenta, yellow, and black—the secondary colors from which colors can be derived. CMYK is used to reproduce colors on the printed page and has a narrower gamut than RGB. See RGB.

CompactFlash: type of memory card with the interface built in.

Compression: process that reduces a file's size. Lossy compression systems reduce the quality of the file. Lossless compression does not damage an image. See JPEG.

Digital image: a picture made up of pixels and recorded as data.

Digital zoom: process that simulates the effect of a zoom by cropping photos and enlarging the remaining image. Reduces image size. See Interpolation and Zoom lens.

Download: process of transferring data from one source to another, typically a camera to a computer.

dpi (dots per inch): measurement of print density that defines the image size when printed, not its resolution.

DVD: Digital Versatile Disk. High-capacity storage medium like CD, but offering more than six times the space.

DVD-R: most common type of recordable DVD disk. While multisession-compatible, data cannot be erased.

DVD-RW and DVD+RW: erasable and re-recordable versions of DVD.

Dynamic range: the range of the lightest to the darkest areas in a scene that a CCD can distinguish. Also known as exposure latitude.

Electronic viewfinder: a small LCD display that replaces optical viewfinders in some digital cameras.

EXIF: Exchangeable Image File. Shooting data recorded along with the picture by a digital camera.

Exposure compensation: adjustment applied to a photograph to correct exposure, without adjusting the aperture or shutter speed.

Exposure value (EV): measurement of a photograph's brightness.

f-stop: a camera's aperture setting. A high f-stop number means the camera is using a narrow aperture.

File size: a file's size is determined by the amount of data it contains.

Image-editing software: program used to manipulate digital images. Also known as image-processing, image-manipulation, photo-editing, or imaging software.

Image resolution: number of pixels stored in a digital image.

GIF: Graphic Interchange File. Common Internet graphic format, used for banners and icons where few colors are required.

Ink-jet printer: printer that sprays fine dots of ink on to paper to produce prints.

Interpolation: a process to increase an image's resolution by adding new pixels. This can reduce image quality.

Guide Number: measurement of the range or power of a flashgun. To manually work out what camera aperture to set, divide the guide number by the distance to the object. This gives the f-stop to use. However, most flashguns also have sensors that cut the flash off when they think the exposure is correct, so the GN is more commonly used to define power.

JPEG (or JPG): file format that reduces a digital image's file size at the expense of image quality.

k/s: kilobyte per second. A measurement of data transfer rates.

Kelvin: the measurement used to classify color temperature. Daylight at midday is rated at 5,500K.

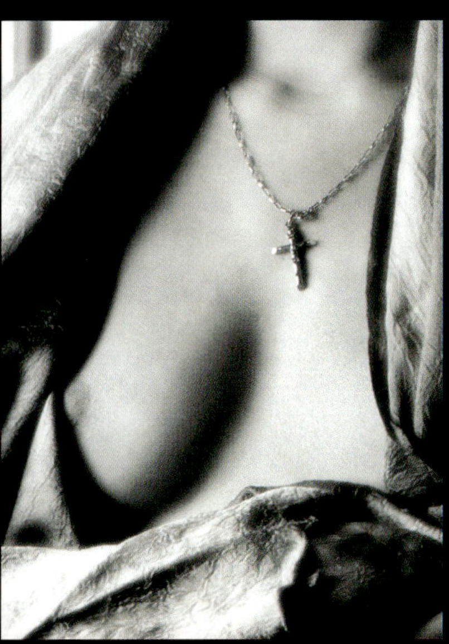

Kilobyte (k or KB): unit of computer memory. Equal to 1024 bytes.

LAB color: color mode consisting of lightness channel and two color channels, A covering green to red, and B covering blue to yellow colors.

Laser printer: printers that print documents by fusing toner or carbon powder on to paper surface.

LCD (liquid crystal display): small light display. Lit by running a current through an electrically reactive substance held between two electrodes.

LCD monitor: small color display built into most digital cameras. Allows the user to preview/review digital photos as they are taken.

Lithium-ion (or Li-ion): powerful rechargeable batteries. Not affected by the memory effect. See Ni-Cd.

MAh (milliamp hours): a unit of measure to describe a battery's power capacity.

Mb/s: Megabyte per second. A measurement of data transfer rates.

Megabyte (Mb or MB): unit of computer memory. Equal to 1024 kilobytes.

Megapixel (Mp): a million pixels. A standard term of reference for digital cameras. Multiply the maximum horizontal and vertical resolutions of the camera output and express in terms of millions of pixels. Hence a camera producing a 2400 x 1600 picture would be a 3.8Mp camera.

Memory effect: the decrease of a rechargeable battery's power capacity over time.

Memory Stick: Sony's proprietary solid-state storage media.

Microdrive: a miniature hard drive offering large storage capacities that can be used in digital cameras with a CompactFlash Type II slot.

Microsoft Windows 98/Me: home-user operating system used on PCs. Now superseded by Windows XP.

Microsoft Windows NT: the Microsoft operating system designed for businesses using more secure file handling and access. Now outdated.

Microsoft Windows 2000: a Windows NT-based system used for businesses.

Microsoft Windows XP Home: the current direction of Windows. This version is based on the NT kernal but designed for home-users.

Microsoft Windows XP Professional: version of XP for home-users, professionals, or small businesses.

MultiMedia Card: type of storage media used in digital devices.

Neutral Density filter: filter that reduces the light coming into the camera for creative purposes. A graduated ND filter progresses from gray to white, so affecting only the top or bottom of the image.

Ni-Cd or Nicad (nickel cadmium): basic type of rechargeable battery. Can last up to 1,000 charges, but can suffer from the memory effect. See Memory effect.

NiMH (nickel metal hydride): rechargeable battery. Contains twice the power of similar Ni-cd batteries. Also much less affected by the memory effect. See Memory effect.

Optical viewfinder: viewfinder that delivers the image of the scene either directly, or via mirrors, to the user, without recourse to electronics or an LCD.

Outputting: process of printing an image or configuring an image for display on the Internet.

PC card: expansion card interface, commonly used on laptop computers. A variety of PC cards offer everything from network interfaces, modems, to holders for digital camera memory cards. Some memory card readers use PC card slots (or PCMCIA cards).

PC sync: socket on a camera that allows the camera to control studio flash systems.

Pen tablet: input device that replaces a mouse. Moving a pen over a specially designed tablet controls the cursor.

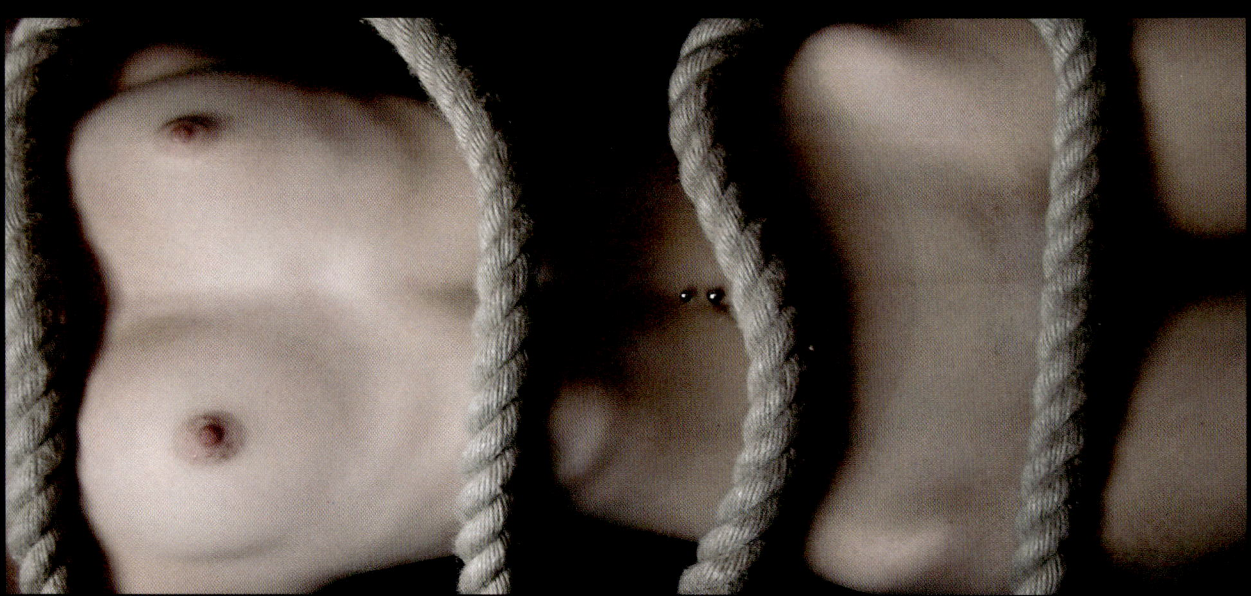

Photoshop: industry-standard image-manipulation program produced by Adobe.

Pixel: tiny square of digital data. The basis of all digital images.

Pixelation: effect when individual pixels can be seen.

Plug-in: software that integrates with a main photo-editing package to offer further functionality.

PNG: Portable Network Graphics. A file format commonly used for images used on the Internet. Can be defined in anything from 8-bit to 48-bit color.

Polarizer filter: blocks light waves at a specific orientation. Use to enhance skies and reflections or block reflections.

Printer resolution: density of the ink dots that a printer lays on paper to produce images. Usually expressed as dpi (dots per inch), but note that this is not the same thing as the dpi of an image.

RAW: this file format will record exactly what a camera's CCD/CMOS chip sees. The data will not be altered by the camera's firmware (images are not sharpened, color saturation is not increased, and noise levels will not be reduced).

RGB: additive system of color filtration. Uses the combinations of red, green, and blue to recreate colors. Standard system in digital images. See CMYK.

Secure Data (SD): a type of solid-state storage medium used in some digital cameras.

Shutter priority: camera shooting mode. The user sets the camera's shutter speed, while the camera calculates the aperture setting.

SLR: single-lens reflex camera. Has the advantage that the image it shows through the optical viewfinder is the one that the camera sees through the lens. Digital SLRs are much faster, more responsive, and more powerful than compact digital cameras.

SmartMedia: type of storage card used to store digital images. Very popular digital camera format, now replaced by x-D Picture Card format.

sRGB: common, but limited color gamut, profile of the RGB system. Most commonly used in digital cameras. See AdobeRGB.

Thumbnail: small version of an image used for identifying, displaying, and cataloguing images.

TIFF: image file format. Used to store high-quality images. Can use a lossless compression system to reduce file size, without causing a reduction in the quality of the image. Available on some digital cameras as an alternative to saving images using the JPEG format.

TTL (through-the-lens) metering: a sensor built into a camera's body that uses light coming through the lens to set the exposure.

USB 1.1 (Universal Serial Bus v1.1): external computer-to-peripheral connection that supports data transfer rates of 1.5Mb/s. One USB 1.1 port can be connected to 127 peripherals.

USB 2.0 (Hi-speed USB): a variant of USB 1.1. Supports data connection rates of up to 60Mb/s. USB 2.0 devices can be used with USB 1.1 sockets (at a much reduced speed), and USB 1.1 devices can be used in USB 2.0 sockets.

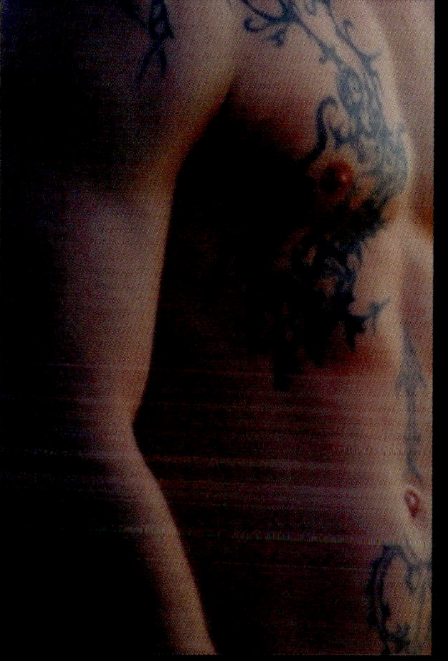

VideoCD: the forerunner to the DVD video format. Lower resolution than DVD video, but is used with standard CDs. Can be played on PCs.

WYSIWYG: acronym of "what you see is what you get." A term for a computer interface that outputs exactly what is seen on screen.

xD-Picture Card (xD Card): memory card format that has been developed by Toshiba, Fujifilm, and Olympus. Designed as a replacement for SmartMedia.

X-sync: the fastest shutter speed at which a camera can synchronize with an electronic flash.

Zoom lens (Optical zoom): a lens with a variable focal length. Offers flexibility against loss of quality and reduced aperture range.

INDEX

ACKNOWLEDGMENTS

My thanks go to the following people who submitted their images. I would also like to thank Chris Middleton at RotoVision for keeping the project on the straight and narrow. Plus, models Roxsi, Matt, Aurora, Megan, Katie, Kya, and Yasemin for great work, often in very cold conditions.

DUNCAN EVANS LRPS
E-mail: dg@duncanevans.co.uk
Web site: www.duncanevans.co.uk

ALAN COCKBURN
Alan has always loved photographing the human form, from candid shots in bus station cafés to full-blown studio setpieces. He is especially interested in the play of light and shadow on the human form.
E-mail: Porthodean@aol.com

STEPHEN HAYNES
Stephen Haynes is a fine-art photographer in Minneapolis, USA. The beauty of the nude female form is a primary focus, although he also explores stylized or geometric themes. He teaches photography workshops in Minneapolis.
E-mail: imagineer@ix.netcom.com
Web site: www.shaynes.com

DAN HOWELL
Dan Howell has been a professional magazine and advertising photographer for more than 15 years, based in the New York City area. Although the line and pose of the body is paramount in his nude work, he tries to never lose the personality of the model coming out through the face and eyes.
E-mail: photography@modelfetish.com
Web site: www.modelfetish.com

ERIC KELLERMAN
Eric is a long-term British resident of the Netherlands. He uses a digital camera, works exclusively in the studio, and virtually his only subject is the female nude.
E-mail: info@erickellermanphotography.com
Web site: www.erickellermanphotography.com

DALE LEHMER
Dale Lehmer lives in upstate New York. He started photography as a hobby many years ago, moving on to artistic nudes about five years ago. He shoots with an Olympus E-20 camera which is very good with low light. He loves to create images that express his vision of the delicate beauty of women.
E-mail: kelly@hvi.net

BRIAN MARTIN
Brian has been shooting a variety of subjects for over 20 years, most recently concentrating on the female nude. His nude work is shot digitally, but reduced to monochrome tones in an effort to emphasize the shape and form of the female body.
E-mail: martinphoto@blueyonder.co.uk
Web site: www.martinphoto.co.uk

BJÖRN OLDSEN
Björn is a resident of Germany. He aspires to create images full of light and mystery, whether it is in the studio or on location.
E-mail: bjoern@oldsen.de
Web site: www.oldsen.de

SIMON POLE
Simon's main areas of photography are landscapes and natural history. More recently he has extended his work to include working with models. Simon's photography has always been about capturing a moment in time expressing emotion, mood, expression, and subjects of interest, whether it is a landscape, flower, or person as the subject matter.
E-mail: info@simon-pole.co.uk
Web site: www.simon-pole.co.uk

MARK VARLEY
Mark produces prints for sale, primarily of landscapes, wildlife, and artistic nudes. He strives to find beauty in all things.
E-mail: markvarleyphoto@hotmail.com
Web site: www.mvp-fine-art.co.uk

SIMON YOUNG
Simon's unique and humorous teaching style incorporates ideas on how to relax clients and getting the best portrait possible.
E-mail: allinthemind@blueyonder.co.uk